Programming with JFC™

SCOTT R. WEINER

STEPHEN ASBURY

WILEY COMPUTER PUBLISHING

John Wiley & Sons, Inc.
New York • Chichester • Weinheim • Brisbane • Singapore • Toronto

For my wife Susan, who is special in too many ways to list here. Not only does she put up with my late-night working, she even likes to watch me play video games. For my daughter Emily, who has changed my life and made late-night working and video games seem less important. For my mother, who has always encouraged my talents, and my father, who always expected me to do my best. I have accomplished what I have because of them. For this reason, this book is special to me.

— Scott Weiner

For my beloved wife Cheryl, the bright light that helps me find my way, and my parents, who don't often hear how much I appreciate all of the time and energy they put into making me who I am today.

— Stephen Asbury

Publisher: Robert Ipsen
Editor: Theresa Hudson
Managing Editor: Angela Murphy
Text Design & Composition: Benchmark Productions, Inc.

This book is printed on acid-free paper. ♾

Published by John Wiley & Sons, Inc.
Published simultaneously in Canada.

Library of Congress Cataloging-in-Publication Data:

Weiner, Scott.
Programming with JFC / Scott Weiner and Stephen Asbury.
p. cm.
Includes index.
ISBN 0-471-24731-6 (pbk. / CD-ROM)
1. Java (Computer program language) 2. Java foundation classes.
I. Asbury, Stephen. II. Title.
QA76.73.J38W44 1998
005.13'3--dc21 98-14347

Printed in the United States of America.

10 9 8 7 6 5 4 3 2 1

CONTENTS

PREFACE

The first release of the Java Foundation Classes, JFC 1.1, provides a powerful set of user-interface components called Swing, as well as a framework for accessing assistive technologies. We think these libraries will revolutionize the way you write your Java programs and how users experience them. In particular, Swing provides a number of new components and defines a consistent model for interacting with these user-interface elements. By leveraging these components, you can create user-friendly Java programs, in less time and in a way that is easy to reproduce and maintain.

Swing uses the model-view-controller design pattern. Each of the components that we discuss relies on several objects to do its work. In particular, a view, or UI, object is used to define the appearance of a component. By changing these UI objects, programs can take advantage of the Swing pluggable look-and-feel architecture. With pluggable look and feels, a program can behave like a Microsoft Windows program, a Motif program, or even a platform-independent program. The model object defines data for a component. We show several examples of how you can change this object to customize the data source for your user interface.

As a whole, JFC is a powerful library for creating programs. We hope that the examples and discussions in this book motivate you to use JFC, demonstrate how easy JFC can be, and provide you with the tools to dig into JFC and customize it for your needs.

Who This Book Is For

This book was designed for Java programmers with some AWT experience who want to use JFC to create new, more powerful Java programs. We have provided background concepts for programmers who haven't used the JDK 1.1 before, but we have kept the focus on JFC rather than on details on the supporting technology. By including more than 100 example programs, this book provides numerous opportunities for programmers to see JFC in action. The level of the example programs ranges from introductory to advanced. We have also included two larger programs that show JFC in a real-world situation.

What You Need to Use This Book

The examples in this book require JDK 1.1.3 or higher and the JFC 1.1 release. Check the CD-ROM for details on installing these packages. If you already have JDK 1.1.3+ installed, then you need to install only JFC 1.1. This installation includes documentation, several examples, and the .jar files that contain the JFC .class files. JFC is pure Java so there are no binary files to unpack.

Of course, you also need an editor to write and view code. The CD-ROM includes an HTML guide that requires you to have a Web browser to view properly.

What You Will Learn

Programming with JFC primarily focuses on the Swing tool kit released with JFC 1.1. Table P.1 lists each of the chapters and a description of the information contained in that chapter.

Table P.1 Chapter Topics

Chapter	Description
Chapter 1, "Introduction"	Chapter 1 introduces the JFC 1.1 release and discusses the fundamental concepts in this tool kit.
Chapter 2, "Lightweight Components"	Lightweight components represent a step toward pure Java programming. Chapter 2 introduces lightweight components, the event model that they use to notify programs of user interaction, and the basic steps to create a JFC application.
Chapter 3, "Layout Managers, Boxes, and Borders"	Chapter 3 reviews the basic use of layout Boxes, managers, introduces several new layout managers, and discusses the Swing box component. Swing components can have visual borders; these borders are also discussed in this chapter.
Chapter 4, "Buttons, Actions, and Mouse Events"	Buttons are a common user-interface element. Chapter 4 introduces the Swing buttons and covers how to add images to them. We also cover the action events created by buttons to notify programs and the techniques for handling mouse events for a Swing component.
Chapter 5, "Combo Boxes and Lists"	Chapter 5 introduces the ComboBox and List components and discusses the techniques used to interact with and customize these components.
Chapter 6, "Sliders, Watch Events, and Scroll Panes"	Chapter 6 discusses the new Swing slider component. We also introduce the scroll pane.
Chapter 7, "Handling Simple Text Using Swing"	Swing provides several components that Using Swing manage simple text, like a text field or a text area. Chapter 7 discusses these components and the techniques used to interact with them.
Chapter 8, "Menus and Tool Bars"	Chapter 8 introduces the new, powerful Swing menu, including the techniques used to add custom graphics

Continued

Table P.1 Chapter Topics *Continued*

Chapter	Description
	to a menu. We also discuss the Swing tool bar and the Action objects that are used to organize code for tool bars and menus.
Chapter 9, "Dialogs and Option Panes"	The JOptionPane provides one-method access to flexible alert-style panels. Chapter 9 discusses the available panels and the steps used to customize them.
Chapter 10, "Timers and Progress Bars"	Chapter 10 introduces the Swing timer object that is used to send regular, time-based program notifications. We also discuss the progress bar component that displays the progress for time-intensive activities.
Chapter 11, "Trees"	Swing introduces a new, very useful tree component. Chapter 11 describes the steps used to create, customize, and provide data for these tree interface elements.
Chapter 12, "Tables"	Chapter 12 discusses the steps used to create, customize, and define data for the powerful new Swing table component.
Chapter 13, "Tabbed and Split Panes"	Many programs used tabbed and split panes to show more information in less space. Chapter 13 describes the steps used to take advantage of Swing's tabbed and split panes.
Chapter 14, "Root Panes, Layers, and Internal Frames"	Chapter 14 introduces the concept of an internal frame and the layers in which these frames exist. We also discuss the techniques used to create internal frames and customize them.
Chapter 15, "Styled Text"	Swing provides an entire framework for displaying styled text. This chapter introduces the framework and provides examples and techniques for using the components that can display styled text, HTML, and RTF.
Chapter 16, "Creating Custom JFC Components"	Chapter 16 provides a step-by-step guide for creating a custom JFC component that uses the complete Swing design model.
Chapter 17, "Other JFC Topics"	Chapter 17 includes a number of discussions and examples about other topics including the Undo framework and animated icons.
Chapter 18, "Zip and Jar Viewer Example"	Jar Viewer is a program that displays the contents of a Jar or Zip file and lets the user extract selected files.

Continued

Table P.1 Continued

Chapter	Description
	Chapter 18 steps through each of the classes used to create this application.
Chapter 19, "Search Program Example"	Chapter 19 steps through the classes used to create a program that can index, search, and display the Swing documentation as well as other HTML files.
Appendix A, "The Accessibility Framework"	JFC provides the foundation for accessing assistive technologies like braille readers and screen magnifiers. Appendix A introduces this framework.
Appendix B, "What's on the CD-ROM"	This appendix provides system requirements, installation instructions, and a summary of what's on the accompanying CD-ROM.

Using the CD-ROM

The CD-ROM included with this book includes all of the examples that we use in this book as well as others that were used to create screen shots or that didn't fit into a particular chapter. Appendix B provides more detailed information on the CD-ROM, but we want to make two points at the very beginning. First, please use the CD-ROM as you read the book. You can compile and/or run the examples, as well as copy and modify them to see what effects the various values and methods have. Second, as is common in publishing, the CD-ROM was finalized after the book. We have used this opportunity to provide any late-breaking issues and news on the CD-ROM. Open the index.html file in the root directory of the CD for a guide to the contents, as well as links to any important announcements.

Note on JFC 1.1 Versus Future Releases

This first release of JFC, JFC 1.1, is designed to run on JDK 1.1. The next release of the JDK will integrate JFC. As a result, there is an issue with the packages used for this release and the next. In this release, all of the JFC packages are contained in the com.sun.java package. This allows you, as a programmer, to include them on your Web site and have an applet download them along with your custom code. Due to security limitations, JavaSoft could not integrate JFC 1.1 into the root java package. However, in the next release of the JDK, JFC will be integrated into the java package. This may mean that you will need to change your import statements, but Sun may provide an automated mechanism for performing this update. Sun may also decide to provide the Swing libraries in both packages for portability. At this point, it's important to be aware of this issue and recognize that there may be an inconsistency when the next JDK is released.

Acknowledgments

First, we would both like to thank Alberto Ricart, Brad Green, Eric Chu, Ethan Port, Glen Sato, John Kimmell, Kerry DiGiusto, Michael Scruggs, and Shrinand Deshpande. Sometimes writing takes away from work, and we appreciate all of the work they did to hold down the fort and keep it from floating away.

And where would authors be without editors? Many thanks to Terri Hudson for taking our rough techno-babble and making it readable and useful for everyone.

We would also like to thank Adam Abramski of JavaSoft and David Moore of Netscape for helping us with the early access to JFC.

Finally, and most importantly, we would like to thank our wives. Without them we would still think that Saturday night was for staying up late—computers networked together—playing video games, eating that fifth slice of pizza, drinking the last six pack of Diet Coke, deciding whose turn it is to run to the store for more caffeine, trying to get 1000 more gold pieces to buy that cool magic bow, arguing over the right type of character to play, and stopping only to wonder why we never go on dates any more. It takes an amazing person to teach you the value of life and the importance of time. Lucky for us, there were at least two.

About the Authors

Scott Weiner and Stephen Asbury are cofounders of Paradigm Research, Inc. Paradigm Research is the premiere training company in Silicon Valley, providing instructor-led training on Java and related topics and Web-based training via their Profile distributed learning environment. More information on Paradigm Research is available at www.pri.com.

Scott Weiner is president of Paradigm Research, Inc. He has been involved in consulting with object-oriented design and programming for more than 10 years. Before founding Paradigm Research, Scott ran a mentoring program for NeXT Computers where he helped Fortune 1000 companies embrace object-oriented techniques for creating mission-critical applications. Today, Scott is leading Paradigm Research's mission to create the best training for development teams leveraging leading-edge technologies and corporate end-users using the latest productivity applications. Scott lives in Northern California with his wife Susan, his beautiful six-month-old daughter, Emily, and their two dogs, Casey and Jake.

Stephen Asbury is the VP of Engineering for Paradigm Research, Inc. When Java was first publicly announced, Stephen was in the big circus tent with thousands of his closest friends, rooting for it to succeed. Since then, Stephen has spread the word to companies like Netscape, SGI, Sun, and HP by writing and teaching courses on JDK 1.0, JDK 1.1, JDBC, IFC, as well as JavaScript and other new technologies. He is currently focused on creating a Java-based platform for delivering the best online training in the world. Stephen lives in California with his beloved wife Cheryl.

1 INTRODUCTION

Over the past few years Java has clearly made a significant impact on the development of the Web and the notion of ubiquitous computing. Anyone who has been developing with Java knows that it is powerful and provides hope for truly cross-platform, enterprise-class application development. If you have done any amount of development with Java you also recognize some of the shortcomings of a young language with few supporting tools and class libraries, a small set of components for application development, and a lack of integration with existing operating systems. At the heart of the effort to establish Java as the first choice in development languages is the JavaSoft division of Sun Microsystems. JavaSoft continues to introduce new libraries that resolve many of these shortcomings.

As part of the effort to enhance the libraries available for developing robust Java applications, JavaSoft introduced the Java Foundation Classes (JFC). These classes are designed to make the job of developing enterprise-class applications easier. JavaSoft is initially releasing JFC in two parts. JFC 1.1 is designed to run on the current JDK, Version 1.1. The full version of JFC will be available as part of the Java Development Kit (JDK), Version 1.2. The initial release of JFC 1.1 includes two key components, as shown in Table 1.1.

Table 1.1 Description of JFC 1.1 APIs

API	Description
Swing	An advanced UI library that builds on AWT. Swing provides a set of tightly integrated UI components, along with an architecture that is used to specify exactly how user interfaces are presented independent of the platform they run on.
Accessibility API	An interface designed to provide user interface "hooks" for assistive technologies such as voice recognition devices. They are designed to help people with disabilities interact and communicate more easily with computers.

JFC 1.2 will add to version 1.1 APIs by introducing a new 2D graphics library and support for drag and drop within and between JFC applications and native programs.

Swing

Swing is a powerful collection of user-interface (UI) components that include trees, buttons, tabbed panes, and styled text, to name just a few. Using these components, you can build almost any user interface without creating your own components. Certainly some commercial software may still need custom components, but corporate programmers can use Swing out of the box without adding a lot of drawing code. What you will want to do is customize the components and add event handlers to them. Figure 1.1 shows an example Swing program that we discuss in Chapter 19. This program is written using Swing components; we have customized the data and used other components as is.

Swing includes support for multiple look and feels that are changed dynamically. These look and feels define the appearance of Swing components and the way that they respond to user interactions. This means that a Swing program can look and feel like Microsoft Windows on Microsoft Windows

Figure 1.1 Example Swing program.

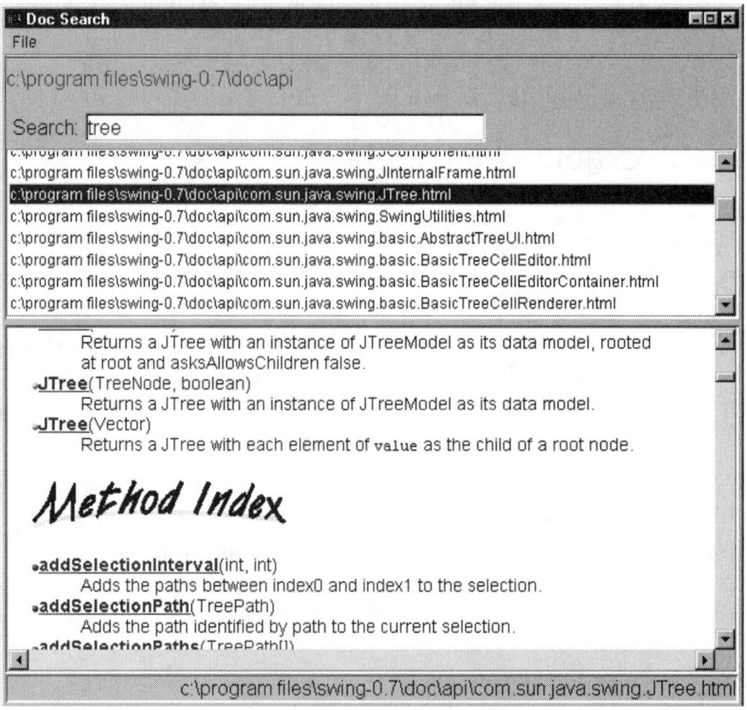

and Motif on Motif. A programmer can even have a Swing program that looks the same on all platforms.

Swing is an extension to the Lightweight UI framework that is included in the Abstract Windowing Toolkit (AWT) in the JDK Version 1.1. A group of JavaSoft engineers came up with the name "Swing" while they were developing a demo to show off the features of their new UI component set at the 1997 JavaOne conference. The demo showed the graphical capabilities of the library and made extensive use of music, featuring the sound capabilities for this UI library. They thought that relating their Java library with the type of music played by Duke Ellington, Swing, was a great tie-in with the Java mascot, Duke. The name stuck.

Swing was created as a joint effort with Netscape Communications. Netscape had been working on its own UI library for Java called the Internet Foundation Classes (IFC). Netscape decided it made more sense for JavaSoft to drive the standard so it cooperated on creating a world-class UI component library based on IFC. Of all the JFC 1.1 features, Swing will probably have the greatest impact on developers because it allows programmers to create powerful applications quickly that utilize a standard set of tools that will be supported and improved by JavaSoft.

All Swing components are 100% pure Java and adhere to the JavaBeans specification. All Swing components can interact with applications that make use of JavaBeans and, in particular, can work inside the tools that support JavaBeans. Swing components also adhere to the new Accessibility specification so that they can be accessed via assistive technologies.

Differences between AWT and Swing

The fundamental difference between AWT and Swing is in the implementation language. AWT components ultimately rely on native code in the form of peers to display themselves and respond to user input. Swing components, on the other hand, are written in pure Java. A Swing component draws itself and responds to its own events. In reality, Swing components use a partner object called a UI object to draw them and handle events, but this UI object is also written in pure Java. It is an implementation mechanism to support the pluggable look-and-feel feature that we mentioned earlier.

Because Swing components do not rely on native code, and the resulting platform-specific limitations, they are more powerful than their AWT counterparts. For example, the Swing button can display text and images, including animations. While updating these standard components, JavaSoft also added new ones that may not exist on every platform, such as trees, tables, split panes, and styled text widgets. By writing the components entirely in Java, the Swing engineers made them easier to extend, platform independent, and ultimately more dependable.

Swing also represents a redesign of some of the component inheritance hierarchies. For example, all of the Swing button classes inherit from a generic AbstractButton class that centralizes most of the button code for push buttons, toggles, check boxes, radio buttons, and even menu items. As we discuss in

Chapter 2, the Swing designers used this opportunity with a new design to create a model-view-controller style organization for each component. This design separates the data from the display, supporting the pluggable look-and-feel architecture, and makes the components easier to extend.

Technically, Swing leverages some of the AWT code to draw to the screen. This code is limited to the Applet and Window classes as well as the Graphics class. As far as possible, Swing has tried to minimize its reliance on AWT native code, but as with any programming environment, there is that thin layer where the rubber meets the road. Swing components minimize this layer in their design by making them easier for JavaSoft to support, optimize, and maintain because they have less code to port to each platform than the JDK is provided on. This relationship and dependency are pictured in Figure 1.2. Notice that Swing relies on a minimal set of classes.

Swing Packages

Swing is divided into the different packages shown in Table 1.2.

There are also individual packages for each look and feel and a package called "preview" that consists of the other components that were not ready for the 1.1 release. JavaSoft has stated explicitly that these other packages will change between JFC 1.1 and 1.2. Therefore, we have focused this book on the packages listed in Table 1.2.

Notice that the package names use the com.sun.java parent package. This approach allows them to work with the existing JDK. In the JDK 1.2 release, the Swing packages are integrated into the root java package. You can, however, either update your import statements and CLASSPATH or use a version of Swing that uses the 1.1 packages. This will be an interesting issue when JDK 1.2 is released. For now, focus on using the existing packages because they will be the most widely supported version, working with JDK 1.1 and 1.2.

Accessibility

The Accessibility framework lays the foundation for assistive technologies like magnified or braille readers. This framework defines an interface for objects to

Figure 1.2 Swing dependencies on AWT.

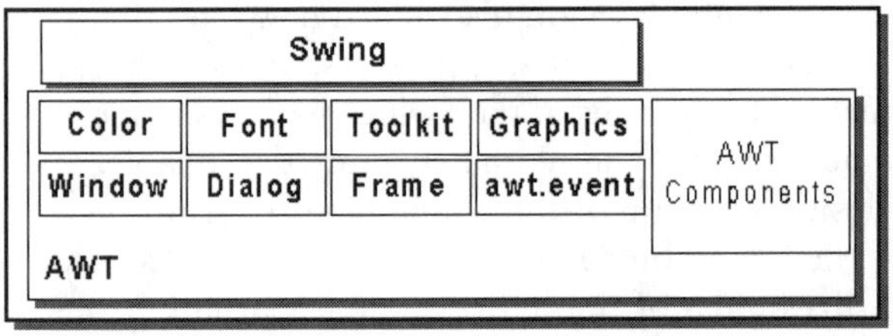

Swing
Color Font Toolkit Graphics
Window Dialog Frame awt.event
AWT Components
AWT

Table 1.2 Swing Packages

Package	Contents
com.sun.java.swing	Includes the Swing components and supporting classes
com.sun.java.swing.border	Includes the classes that define borders to adorn Swing components
com.sun.java.swing.event	Swing's event-handling specific classes, including new event and listener types
com.sun.java.swing.multi	A multiplexing look and feel used to support accessibility
com.sun.java.swing.plaf	Definitions of UI objects for the Swing components
com.sun.java.swing.table	Supporting classes for the Table component
com.sun.java.swing.text	The Swing styled text framework
com.sun.java.swing.tree	Supporting classes for the Tree component
com.sun.java.swing.undo	A basic undo framework
com.sun.java.accessibility	The accessibility API definition

get information in a component-independent manner from user-interface elements. Accessibility tools may also hook into the low-level event handling code to catch events and translate them for these assistive technologies, converting written words to spoken words or updating a customized display.

Summary

JFC 1.1 is composed of Swing and an accessibility API. Using Swing, programmers can create user interfaces with pure Java code that contain a rich collection of user-interface elements. Swing programs use a minimum of supporting native code and use flexible and powerful components. Because Swing components support JavaBeans and accessibility, they integrate well with other JavaSoft technologies and are easy to build in the new JavaBeans-oriented tools. Accessibility allows these technologies to become accessible to people requiring special assistive technologies.

2 Lightweight Components

When Java was first released, Sun provided a library for building user interfaces called the Abstract Windowing Toolkit or AWT. AWT is implemented as a set of Java classes that rely on native C code to create user-interface components. The advantage to this strategy is that implementing each component is reasonably easy. Completed Java programs looked exactly like native programs on each platform. The disadvantage to the AWT strategy is that it makes it hard, or impossible, for programmers to add their own components that look and act correctly on the various platforms to which Java is ported. Also, most Java programmers don't want to write native code that supports their latest reverse-spin widget and port that code to numerous platforms.

Companies such as Netscape Communications recognized these problems with AWT and realized that the solution to some of these problems is to write a user-interface library in pure Java. This library would work on all platforms that Java was ported to because the interfaces would be implemented entirely in Java. Because this strategy did not require any extra libraries or other baggage written in other languages such as C, these elements were considered "lightweight." This brings us to the term *lightweight component*—and the main difference between Swing and AWT. A lightweight component is a user-interface element such as a text field or a button that is written in 100% pure Java. Swing provides lightweight components while AWT uses versions of these components that are implemented as heavy or native components. This means that Swing is portable and extensible. Using Swing, developers do not have to spend as much time polishing the interface between native windowing systems and the JDK libraries. By implementing the entire Swing library in Java, JavaSoft can define its own event-handling architecture that is not directly reliant on the platform-specific libraries.

Earlier lightweight libraries suffered from a problem. To write everything in Java, the programmers had to draw the user-interface elements. But what should they look like? Should they have the look and feel of Microsoft Windows, Macintosh, Motif, or some other operating system? More importantly, do they look the same on all platforms? Before Swing, most component libraries had a Windows95 look to them, although some, like Netscape's Internet Foundation Classes (IFC), had a unique, platform-independent look. Components from these early libraries looked the same on all platforms, giving the programs that used them a different but special appearance.

When JavaSoft decided to create Swing, integrating a lightweight-component library into the Java Developer Kit (JDK), it realized that it needed to solve the platform-specific, look-and-feel problem. Two issues motivated this decision. First, many companies would not accept the platform-neutral interfaces; second, some companies wanted to design their own look and feel. After some interesting discussions, JavaSoft decided to create a library of lightweight components that support a replaceable look and feel. This means that the programmer can change the look and feel of the components to match the platform on which the program is running or design his or her own. The program can dynamically adjust its look and feel based on the platform it's running on, the user who is running the program, or on any other criteria. Imagine heart-shaped buttons on Valentine's day. This feature of Swing is called the *pluggable look and feel.* We discuss specifics of the pluggable look and feel architecture in Chapter 17. Its existence is necessary to discuss Swing components fully.

Structure of a Swing Component

To support the pluggable look and feel, the Swing designers split components into two pieces. The first piece represents the component as a whole; the second represents the component's user interface. For example, for a button, these objects are the JButton and the ButtonUI, respectively. Notice the character "J" that precedes the component type. This convention is used throughout Swing to prevent confusion between JButtons and the existing AWT Buttons.

The UI portion of a Swing component is responsible for defining its appearance. This means that the UI object must be aware of the important sizes, such as the component's defining rectangle, and define a paint method for the component. All of these UI interface objects extend the abstract class ComponentUI found in the Swing package. ComponentUI defines the basic responsibilities of a UI object using the following methods:

```
public abstract void installUI(JComponent c)
public abstract void deinstallUI(JComponent c)
public abstract void paint(Graphics g,
                                 JComponent c)
public abstract void update(Graphics g,
                                 JComponent c)
public abstract Dimension getPreferredSize(JComponent c)
public abstract Dimension getMinimumSize(JComponent c)
public abstract Dimension getMaximumSize(JComponent c)
```

We discuss the two methods used to install and un-install the UI for a component in Chapter 17.

While separating the look and feel from the component, the JavaSoft engineers realized that they could take their design a step further and increase the flexibility for configuring the Swing components. JavaSoft enabled more flexibility in the Swing component architecture by separating the data for a component from the component object and encapsulating it into something called a *model*. The role of the model is to store the state of the component. This design will be familiar to experienced object-oriented programmers as the model-view-controller architecture, as shown in Figure 2.1. In the Swing architecture, the view and controller are combined into the component and UI partnership. The model stores the data for the component.

Let's take a look at an example. When a programmer creates a JSlider, he or she actually creates a group of three objects that work together to display a working slider to the application user. The three objects are a SliderUI that paints the slider to the screen, a BoundedRangeModel object that stores the minimum and maximum values for the slider, as well as the current value, and a JSlider that provides a simple interface for the slider objects. Figure 2.2 graphically depicts this relationship. As a programmer you create a JSlider, which creates a model. The look and feel creates a UI. When the user interacts with the UI, it updates the model and its appearance. You can get information about these updates from the model directly or the JSlider.

Although Swing components are constructed as a group, programmers do not need to access each element in the group individually. For simple components like a slider, the front object, which represents the component itself, contains all the methods necessary to create and use the component. This means that the JSlider has all the methods necessary to create a slider, set its values, and retrieve the current value. For more complex objects, such as a JTable that represents a table of data elements, you may need to use the model to describe the data for the component. For example, the new tree component requires that you deal with the tree model directly, rather than handling the data for the tree. In most cases you can avoid working directly with the UI objects. These helper objects are an enabling technology for the pluggable look and feel and are not really part of the public interface for a component.

Figure 2.1 Model-view-controller architecture.

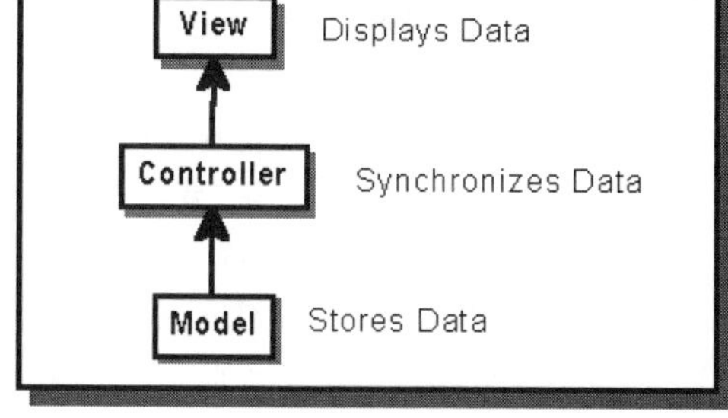

Figure 2.2 Sliders.

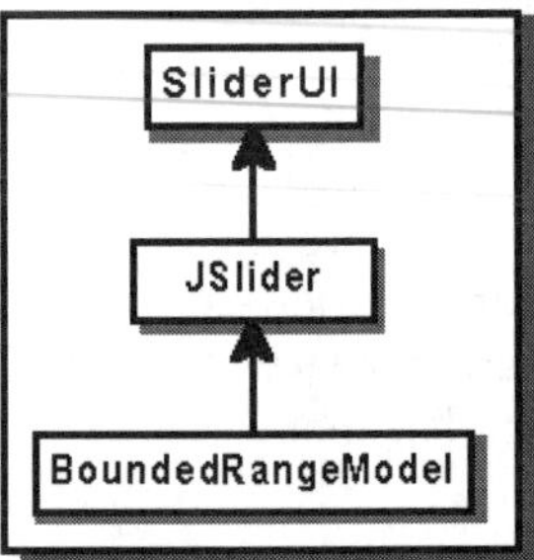

Swing components are created with constructors. Each component provides its own set of constructors based on the amount of configuration the component supports at creation. For example, a button is created with an initial icon, an initial string, or both. The JButton class creates the necessary UI and model objects when it creates a button. It's up to the programmer to change these objects if he or she does not want the default values.

JComponent

Most of the Swing components are subclasses of the Swing class JComponent. JComponent is a subclass of java.awt.Container, as pictured in Figure 2.3. This means that AWT underlies Swing. In fact, Swing leverages AWT's native code to draw to the screen. As a rule, Swing uses the minimal amount of AWT code required. This means that Swing uses AWT to create empty windows, but not necessarily the title bar, and Swing uses AWT to create a region for a button but not the button itself. Minimizing the reliance on native code makes it easier for Swing to support numerous platforms. The motivation for subclassing Container rather than Component is that it allows the Swing components to exist in a single class hierarchy whenever possible. Don't use Swing buttons as containers; that's not their purpose. They are more of an implementation detail.

JComponent defines a number of standard features for all Swing components:

- Borders
- Component-specified minimum, maximum, and preferred sizes
- Tool tips
- Slow-motion rendering that supports debugging
- Auto-scrolling
- Double buffering
- Keystroke handling
- Support for accessibility

Figure 2.3 JComponent class hierarchy.

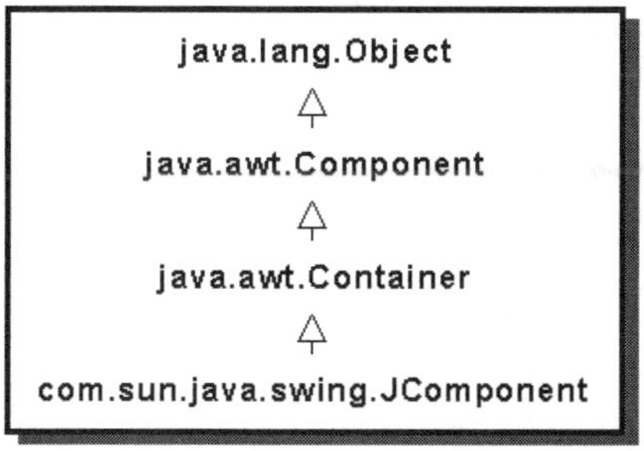

```
java.lang.Object
       ↑
java.awt.Component
       ↑
java.awt.Container
       ↑
com.sun.java.swing.JComponent
```

Swing itself defines two other features that make dealing with JComponents easier and more flexible:

1. Actions
2. Icons

Together these 10 features make Swing a powerful library for building user interfaces.

Borders

JComponent defines the concept of a border as a visual container for a component. As Figure 2.4 illustrates, a border can be a line that surrounds a button or a beveled line that surrounds a collection of items in a panel. The specifics of this visual container are defined in the com.sun.java.swing.border package with an interface called Border. The same package also defines a number of useful Border classes. These borders are discussed in detail in Chapter 3.

Because borders are represented as standard objects, you create them using *constructors*. Once the border is created, you can assign it to any JComponent using the method:

```
public void setBorder(Border aBorder);
```

This causes the component to be drawn with a border. The space between a border and the component it contains is called the *inset* and is defined as part of the border's implementation.

> **TIP**
>
> The AbstractBorder class is a complete implementation of Border; it is provided to make it easy for you to create your own border classes. In Chapter 3 we use this class to create our own border type.

Figure 2.4 Available border types.

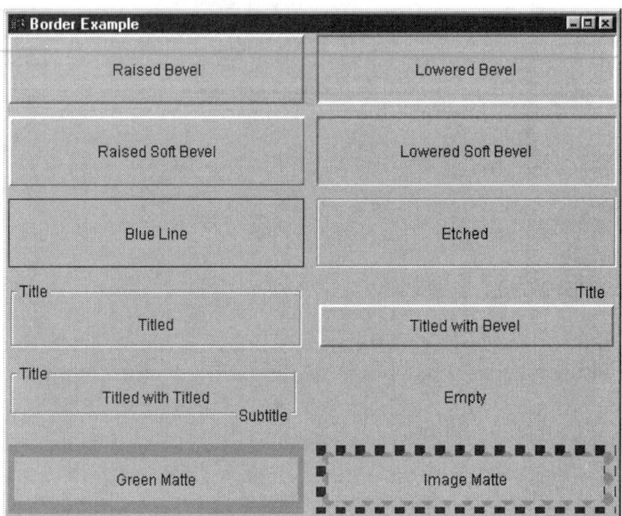

Component Sizes

JComponent has three important sizes: minimum, maximum, and preferred. The three sizes are used when the user interface that contains a component is resized. The methods that define these sizes are as follows:

```
public Dimension getMinimumSize();
public Dimension getMaximumSize();
public Dimension getPreferredSize();
```

In normal operation, a component's UI object is responsible for determining the sizes. This determination is based on the component's state. For example, a button's preferred size is based on the label and icon displayed, as well as the border. Many of our examples in this book use these methods to define the correct initial size for the example's user interface. Sometimes we return a specific size, like 100-by-100; other times we perform some calculations to determine the correct size. Our choice of implementation is based on the contents of the component and whether changing these contents changes the preferred size.

Tool Tips

All JComponents can have a tool tip assigned to them. A tool tip is a string that is displayed when the user holds the mouse over the component, as shown in Figure 2.5. The actual presentation for tool tips depends on the look and feel. Depending on which pluggable look and feel you choose, the tool tips appear differently, but they are usually displayed as a small window beside the component.

Figure 2.5 Button tool tip.

Tool tips are assigned to a component using:

```
public void setToolTipText(String txt);
```

For our example found in Figure 2.6, we use the following code in bold to assign a tool tip to a button.

```
import com.sun.java.swing.*;
import java.awt.event.*;
import java.awt.*;

public class ButtonToolTips
{
    public static void main(String s[])
    {
        JFrame frame = new JFrame("Button Tooltip Example");
        JButton b = new JButton("Hello");

        b.setToolTipText("World");

        frame.setDefaultCloseOperation(JFrame.DO_NOTHING_ON_CLOSE);
        frame.setForeground(Color.black);
        frame.setBackground(Color.lightGray);

        frame.getContentPane().add(b,"Center");

        frame.pack();
        frame.setVisible(true);
    }
}
```

The component actually creates the tool tip object that's used to display the tool tip, with this method:

```
public JToolTip createToolTip();
```

In most cases, you won't use this method. You can override createToolTip if you have a custom tool tip subclass.

The Swing libraries retrieve the contents of the tool tip using the method:

```
public String getToolTipText(MouseEvent event);
```

Normally this method simply returns the string provided in setToolTipText. You can override this method in subclasses to create custom, tool-tip zones associated with various mouse positions. For example, the following class displays the current mouse location as the tool tip.

```
import com.sun.java.swing.*;
import java.awt.event.*;

import java.awt.*;
import java.lang.*;

public class ToolTips extends JPanel
{
    public ToolTips()
    {
        setToolTipText("ToolTips");
        setBackground(Color.white);
    }

    public String getToolTipText(MouseEvent event)
    {
        return "("+event.getX()+","+event.getY()+")";
    }

    public Dimension getPreferredSize()
    {
        return new Dimension(300, 300);
    }

    public static void main(String s[])
    {
        JFrame frame = new JFrame("Tooltip Example");
        ToolTips panel = new ToolTips();

        frame.setDefaultCloseOperation(JFrame.DO_NOTHING_ON_CLOSE);
        frame.setForeground(Color.black);
        frame.setBackground(Color.lightGray);
        frame.getContentPane().add(panel,"Center");
```

```
        frame.setSize(panel.getPreferredSize());
        frame.setVisible(true);
    }
}
```

A running version of this example is shown in Figure 2.6.

Because tool tips are so easy to create they are a great way to help the user determine the functionality of the components located in a Swing interface.

Slow-Motion Rendering

Because Swing components are written in pure Java, all of the drawing commands for a component pass through a Graphics object that renders them. The Swing designers used this fact to provide a simple debugging feature for all JComponents. The debugging feature causes the component to flash as it redraws. The flashing occurs in an assignable special color so that you can see the component redraw itself. When you debug a component in this way you can try to optimize your drawing code.

To initiate this slow-motion rendering, use the class variables in Swing's DebugGraphics class to define one of three debugging options:

DebugGraphics.LOG_OPTION. Causes a text message to be printed to the console.

DebugGraphics.FLASH_OPTION. Causes the drawing of graphics to flash several times.

DebugGraphics.BUFFERED_OPTION. Creates a window that displays the operations performed on the Component's off-screen buffer.

Figure 2.6 Custom tool tips.

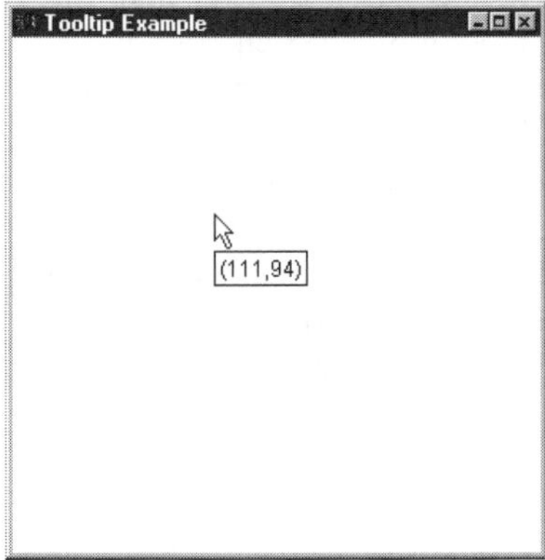

Then, assign these options to the JComponent using the setDebugGraphics-Options method. For example, to have a button flash as it redraws, you can use the code:

```
myButton.setDebugGraphicsOptions(DebugGraphics.FLASH_OPTION);
```

Auto-scrolling

JComponents know how to scroll; this ability is provided in JComponent to improve the performance and behavior of scrolling in general. Knowledge of scrolling manifests itself in two ways: auto-scrolling and scrolling a rectangular area to the visible part of the scrolling area. Auto-scrolling is used by components that live inside a scrolling area. For example, when the user drags the mouse off the auto-scrolling component, it automatically scrolls with the mouse. To activate auto-scrolling, send the message with an argument of true.

```
public void setAutoscrolls(boolean yesNo);
```

You can also use the method to tell the component to ask its parent to scroll a particular area so that it becomes visible within the clipped viewing area of the scrolling component.

```
public void scrollRectToVisible(Rectangle aRect)
```

This method works only if the parent is actually a component that scrolls.

Double Buffering

All JComponents can be told to use an off-screen buffer during drawing. An off-screen buffer is an Image that is not visible on the user's screen. Components can draw into this Image and then have the resulting bits copied onto the visible viewing area of the component. Even though this technique appears logically slower than directly drawing on the screen, the resulting image draws more smoothly and with less flicker because copying bits from the off-screen buffer is quicker than the original drawing operations, so the user does not see the drawing occurring. In practice, it may be quicker to use a buffer because rendering drawing to an image can be quicker than rendering it to the screen. When told to use a buffer, the components draw everything off-screen first, then draw the buffer to the screen, as pictured in Figure 2.7.

Swing components use buffers efficiently. If a component's parent has a buffer, the component shares the parent's buffer instead of creating its own. This means that if the top-level component in a user interface has a buffer, all of the children can share it.

Keystroke Handling

JComponents are designed to support special keystrokes. These keystrokes represent special actions that occur when the component's window is visible. For

Figure 2.7 Off-screen buffers.

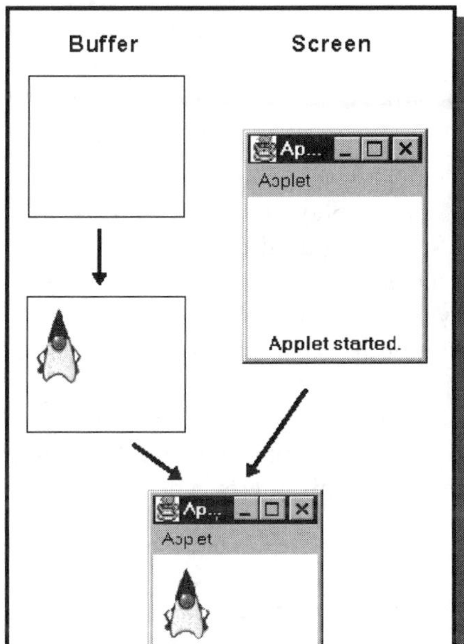

example, a button may want to associate the Alt-C keystroke with it. When the user presses Alt-c, the button is activated and cancels the window's operation. Keystrokes are represented by KeyStroke objects. These objects are registered with a component using the following method:

```
public void registerKeyboardAction(ActionListener anAction,
                                   KeyStroke aKeyStroke,
                                   int aCondition)
```

The third argument is one of the JComponent class variables:

- WHEN_FOCUSED
- WHEN_IN_FOCUSED_WINDOW
- WHEN_ANCESTOR_OF_FOCUSED_COMPONENT

Support for Accessibility

JComponent implements an interface called Accessible. This interface is the linchpin in JavaSoft's new accessibility support. Swing components are all built to fit into the accessibility framework. Developers can use this framework to provide user-interface enhancements targeted at people who require assistive technologies. For example, the accessibility framework can be used to create a viewer that enlarges the elements in a user interface so that someone with impaired vision can see them. We discuss accessibility more in Appendix A.

Icons

One of the problems with AWT is that buttons can display only text. Most people are used to buttons with images on them; JavaSoft recognized this weak point in the AWT. Because Swing components are pure Java, JavaSoft can easily support images on buttons because it did not have to rely on a platform-dependent definition for a button. Based on the same argument, Swing buttons can display any graphics that the Java platform supports.

To organize this concept of "any graphics supported by the Java Platform," Swing buttons, and other components, understand the concept of an icon. In Swing, an icon is an object that implements the Icon interface. This interface defines three methods:

```
public abstract void paintIcon(Component c,
                                  Graphics g, int x, int y);
public abstract int getIconWidth();
public abstract int getIconHeight();
```

Using these methods, a component can place an icon and have it draw itself. Swing provides an implementation of Icon that draws an image. This ImageIcon class is used to create buttons that display images. ImageIcon provides constructors that create an icon for an image by its file name, an Image object, binary data, or a URL. For example, the following code creates an ImageIcon from the file images/logo.gif.

```
ImageIcon icon = new ImageIcon("images/logo.gif");
```

The ImageIcon automatically uses MediaTracker from AWT to track the loading progress of the image data and waits until the image loads before returning the newly initialized icon.

Icons represent a generic mechanism for placing graphics of any kind on a component. Graphics allow components to convey more information to the user in less physical space. Throughout our examples we use icons to decorate menus, buttons, tool bars, and other Swing components. You can create your own Icon classes, and even animated icons. In Chapter 8, we create a custom Icon to display a color "swatch" on a menu item.

Actions

Actions encapsulate a specific function in a program. For example, an action may be used to represent the copy function in a word processor. This function may be attached to several controls, such as a tool bar and a menu item. Swing is designed to allow this type of sharing based on the event model introduced in JDK 1.1 and discussed later in this chapter.

In Swing an action is represented by an object that implements the Action interface. Often these objects are subclasses of the class AbstractAction that already implements the interface. An Action object has a set of text strings and icons associated with various labels. For example, there may be a default string and a short description string. Components that understand actions use the appropriate string for them to display. They also use the appropriate icon for them to display. This way you, the programmer, can create one action object with two components that retrieve their text and icon from the same place.

Actions also keep track of whether they are enabled. An enabled component is one that handles events generated by the user, such as a mouse click. This attribute extends to the components that use it. By tracking actions centrally, your program can enable and disable a group of related controls without having to message each one individually.

Finally, Actions implement the ActionListener interface. We discuss this interface in greater detail in Chapter 3. The ActionListener interface is used to handle notifications from components. This means that the copy action we discussed earlier would not only provide the text and icon for the copy menu, but also handle the notification that the menu was selected. This allows actions to centralize code. By encapsulating the code for handling this function in a single object, your code is more reusable.

As a programmer you probably subclass AbstractAction, use the constructor to initialize the strings and icons, and implement the method used to handle notifications. Then you can instantiate your actions and associate them with user-interface elements.

Event Handling with Swing

Swing components rely on a *delegation event model*, as shown in Figure 2.8. In this model, objects that receive user events notify registered listeners of the user activity. In most cases, the event receiver is a component, like a button, and the listener is an object written by the programmer to handle the button press. Because event receivers provide enough logic to look at a user event and notify the appropriate listeners, we call them *event processors*.

If we break the delegation event model down, we end up with three major pieces:

- Event types
- Event processors
- Event listeners

Figure 2.8 Delegation event model.

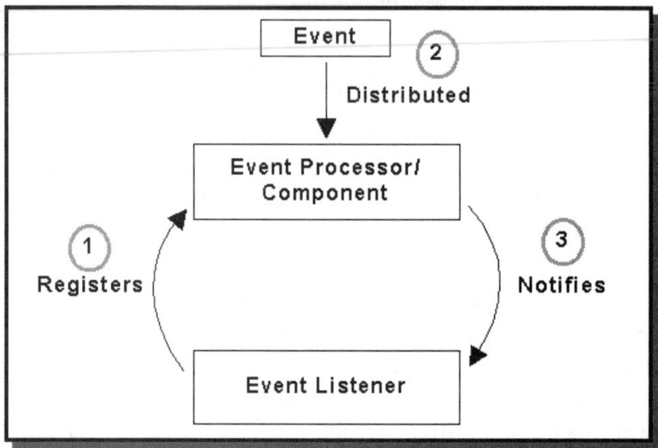

These pieces are represented with an appropriately typed object. Events are represented with objects whose class extends java.util.EventObject. A number of event types are defined in Swing, and a number of types defined in AWT are used by Swing components.

Event Types

Each event type corresponds to a different semantic meaning. For example, MouseEvents are used to represent user interaction with the mouse, whereas KeyEvents are used to represent user interactions with the keyboard. The major Swing event types and their meanings are listed in Table 2.1.

Table 2.1 Swing Event Types

Event Type	Purpose
ActionEvent	Used by components to notify the programmer of a high-level event such as a button press or the return key in a text field.
ChangeEvent	Indicates that a value has changed. It is often used by models to indicate a change in the model's data.
FocusEvent	Created when a component gains or loses keyboard focus.
InputEvent	Abstract super class for mouse and keyboard events. Input event defines methods that provide information about the current modifier keys.
ItemEvent	Used by components that support multiple, selectable items. Item events are used to indicate when the selection changes.

Table 2.1 *Continued*

Event Type	Purpose
KeyEvent	Represents a keyboard interaction—either a key press or release.
ListDataEvent	Generated when the contents of a list change.
ListSelectionEvent	Generated when the selection in a list changes.
MenuEvent	Used to indicate when a menu is selected or cancelled.
MouseEvent	Represents a user interaction with the mouse.
WindowEvent	Indicates window lifecycle events such as closing or being iconified.

Notice that not all of the event types provided by Swing are directly associated with user actions. For example, ChangeEvents are associated with changes to data, not the user interface. In other words, ChangeEvents may have no relation to user activity. On the other hand, ItemEvents may be associated with the user selecting an item in a list. This defines an indirect relationship between the user action, pressing the mouse, and a high-level event—the item selected.

Event Processors

Event processors are usually subclasses of Component. Processors receive events in the form of message arguments. For example, a button is notified of a mouse event as a processMouseEvent message with a MouseEvent object as an argument. We discuss this low-level event processing in later sections of this chapter.

Event Listeners

Event listeners are defined by an interface and provided to event processors programmatically. For example, if a programmer wants a FuzzyController object notified of a button press, he adds the FuzzyController to the button's list of action listeners. This example demonstrates three concepts.

1. The button can have more than one listener. This makes for interesting design possibilities.
2. Buttons use ActionEvents to notify listeners that they are pressed.
3. Processors need to know what message to send to the listener to notify it. These notification messages are determined ahead of time by the Swing designers in the form of interfaces. Listeners must implement the appropriate interface for the type of event they want to listen for. In our example, the FuzzyController should implement ActionListener if it wants to receive notifications of ActionEvents.

To make it easier to write complex listeners, the AWT package provides a number of adapter classes. Each adapter class implements a single-listener interface and is named by the event type and the word adapter. For example, MouseAdapter implements the MouseListener interface to process mouse events from the source component that needs to have these events handled. These adapters actually do no work in their methods. Instead, they implement all of the interface methods to do nothing. This allows a subclass to implement only the methods it wants to implement. These convenience adapters allow programmers to easily create an object that listens for mouse-down events without concern for the associated mouse-up event.

Underlying the delegation event model is a powerful concept first introduced in JDK 1.1—the *event queue*. Although this concept was present in JDK 1.1, it really comes to the forefront in Swing. Abstractly, an event queue is a list of the user events that have occurred but have not been handled yet. As shown in Figure 2.9, events are stored in the event queue until they can be processed. For example, let's say the user clicks the mouse, moves it to another area of the screen, clicks the mouse again, and then begins typing a sentence. These events may happen faster than the interface can process them. Rather than slow down or lose the events, the events are cached in an event queue and are processed in the order they occurred. This is an important concept because it means that all events are collected in one place and distributed in a single thread. All Swing events are processed through an event queue; therefore, all events are processed in the same thread. One advantage of this model is that as a programmer, you don't have to worry about multithreaded programming issues involved with events. The Swing architecture handles these issues. For example, Swing considers a paint request an event, so painting is also processed in this thread.

Figure 2.9 Event queue.

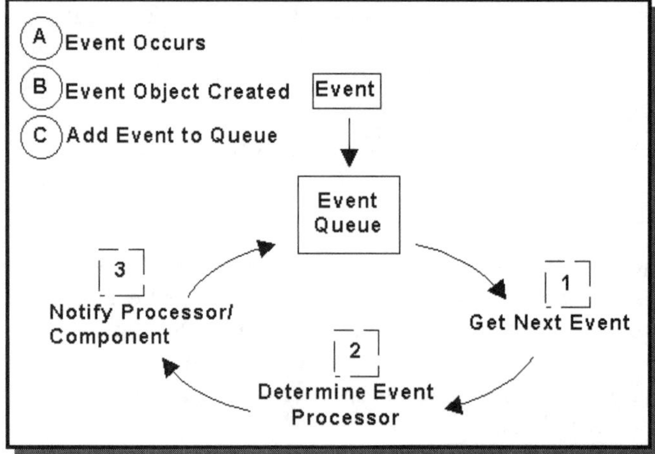

The event queue architecture allows for the creation of very flexible programs without worrying about the synchronization issues of multithreaded programming. Some of the solutions that the event queue provides are these:

- Batches paint requests to improve performance
- Batches layout validations to improve performance
- Posts events at specified intervals by using simple timer objects

The event queue is especially helpful with the timer objects. The event queue guarantees that the messages from the timer are processed in the same thread as messages from a button or a request to paint. In the past, programmers had to use thread synchronization to implement timers. This meant that the code involved in listening to the timer had to be safe from other threads, including possibly the one that would send it the cancel event.

> **NOTE**
>
> There may be situations when you need to adjust your programming to account for the single-threaded nature of events, timers, and drawing. We discuss one such situation in Chapter 10 when we integrate reading from a file with an updating progress bar.

For extensibility the EventQueue object defined for Swing supports filters that can combine, remove, and add events to the queue as appropriate. A filter can, for example, combine multiple mouse-drag events. Programmers can add events to the queue, and they can even register listeners for the queue. The listeners are notified of the events processed.

> **NOTE**
>
> If you are an experienced JDK 1.1 programmer, you will find many of the concepts in this section familiar. Please review any familiar event code but focus on the code used to create the Swing interfaces. We also point out when Swing components provide new event types that are not part of JDK 1.1.

Processing All Events

Components are notified of events via the dispatchEvent method, as pictured in Figure 2.10. This method does some event preprocessing and notifies the target by calling the processEvent method if the event is enabled. All of a component's events are filtered through this processEvent method. The processEvent method takes a single AWTEvent as an argument. The ID for the event determines what happens in the process event. For known event types, processEvent calls a secondary event-handling method. This secondary method is named after the event type. For example, mouse events are sent to the processMouseEvent method for final processing. Unknown event types are ignored by processEvent. Disabled events are ignored by dispatchEvent. For Containers, which include all subclasses of JComponent, dispatchEvent is also responsible for targeting key and mouse events appropriately.

Event enabling is accomplished two ways. First, a programmer can enable an event directly using the enableEvents and disableEvents methods in java.awt .Component. These methods take event masks defined in the java.awt.AWTEvent class (Table 2.2). Disabled events are ignored.

The second way to enable events is by adding a listener for that event type. For example, adding a MouseListener to a component automatically enables mouse events. The various listeners defined in java.awt.Component are listed in Table 2.3.

JavaSoft suggests that programmers use the listener mechanism whenever possible as this will be the preferred method for handling events in future versions of Java. If you choose to override processEvent or one of the subhandlers like processMouseEvent, be sure to call the inherited version that uses super. The versions for these methods defined in java.awt.Component include the code that notifies event listeners. If you don't call this version for the methods, you need to notify the listeners. In the case of processEvent, the Component version is also responsible for calling the subhandlers.

Figure 2.10 Event dispatching.

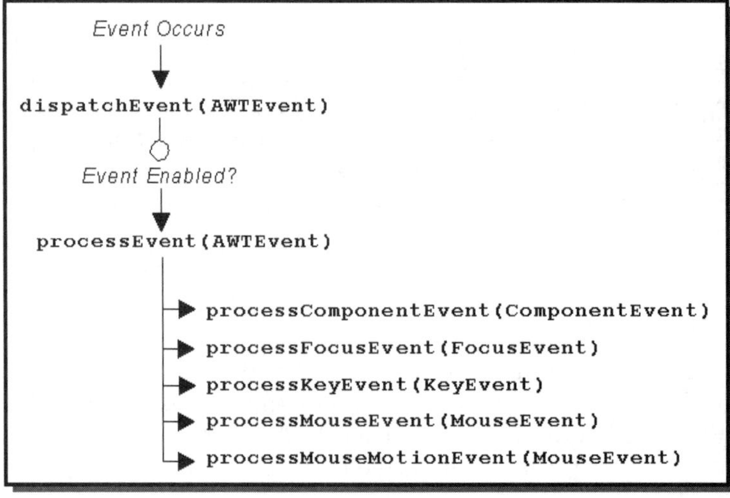

Table 2.2 AWTEvent Masks

Event Mask	The event mask for...
COMPONENT_EVENT_MASK	Selecting component events
CONTAINER_EVENT_MASK	Selecting container events
FOCUS_EVENT_MASK	Selecting focus events
KEY_EVENT_MASK	Selecting key events
MOUSE_EVENT_MASK	Selecting mouse events
MOUSE_MOTION_EVENT_MASK	Selecting mouse motion events
WINDOW_EVENT_MASK	Selecting window events
ACTION_EVENT_MASK	Selecting action events
ADJUSTMENT_EVENT_MASK	Selecting adjustment events
ITEM_EVENT_MASK	Selecting item events
TEXT_EVENT_MASK	Selecting text events

Creating a User Interface

Swing components are displayed as part of a hierarchy. This hierarchy is defined using the concept of containment. A *container* is a component that holds other components; it is similar to a page-layout program where a page may hold an image and text.

Table 2.3 Component Methods for Adding Listeners

Method	Function
addComponentListener	Adds a ComponentListener to receive component events from this component.
addFocusListener	Adds a FocusListener to receive focus events from this component.
addKeyListener	Adds a KeyListener to receive key events from this component.
addMouseListener	Adds a MouseListener to receive mouse events from this component.
addMouseMotionListener	Adds a MouseMotionListener to receive mouse motion events from this component.

The hierarchy for a Swing interface is created by instantiating components and containers and then adding the components to a container. Within a hierarchy the container that holds a component is called its parent, and the components in a container are called its children. To add the components to a container you use the add method. For example, the following code creates a JButton and a JPanel and adds the button to the panel.

```
JButton button = new JButton("Hello");
JPanel panel = new JPanel();
panel.add(button);
```

The JPanel class is used here, as well as in other programs, as a generic container. A JPanel is basically a rectangle that can hold components. You can also assign a border to a JPanel so that it creates a visual grouping of its children. JPanel, as well as the other Swing containers, supports LayoutManagers as defined in AWT. We discuss LayoutManagers and borders further in Chapter 3.

For any components, JPanel or otherwise, to be visible they must have a parent that can be displayed on the screen. Currently there are two possible top-level containers for a Swing program: windows and applets.

Both windows and applets in Swing use a master container to hold and organize all their children. This master container is called the *Root Pane* and is an instance of the RootPane class. A Root Pane provides a number of functions. First, it supports a menu bar. Second, it provides a content area for the window's or applet's children. Finally, the Root Pane provides a set of layers to use for internal frames, which are basically windows that live inside another window. We discuss them further in Chapter 14. When you want to add a component to a window or applet in Swing you actually add the component to the top-level container's Root Pane's content pane. This accounts for the menu bar and internal frames, if any.

> **NOTE**
>
> If you have used AWT, you may find the use of a Root Pane an unwanted indirection. It is necessary, though, to support the use of internal frames in a standard and consistent manner.

Swing and Windows

Swing provides two types of windows: frames and dialogs. A *frame* is a standalone window with a title bar, close box, and other features. A *dialog* is a window associated with a frame. Dialogs are used to alert users to a problem and require that they deal with the problem before interaction with the frame continues. Frames in Swing are created using the JFrame class. Dialogs are created using the JDialog class.

The following example shows how to create a frame, add a button to the frame, and then display it. Notice that the frame's content pane has a BorderLayout by default. This is equivalent to the default in AWT.

```
import com.sun.java.swing.*;
import java.awt.event.*;

import java.awt.*;
import java.lang.*;

public class Simple_Window
{
    public static void main(String s[])
    {
        JFrame frame = new JFrame("Simple Example");
        JButton button = new JButton("Hello");


frame.setDefaultCloseOperation(JFrame.DO_NOTHING_ON_CLOSE);

         frame.getContentPane().add(button,"Center");

        frame.pack();
        frame.setVisible(true);
    }
}
```

Figure 2.11 shows what the code example looks like when run. You have probably noticed that this example is very similar to the way this program would be written in AWT. Although they are similar, there are two differences: the use of the content pane and the method setDefaultCloseOperation. This method accepts one of the three arguments listed in Table 2.4.

While the close event can be handled using the operations defined in Table 2.4, Swing notifies objects of common window events like the window's close box being selected or the window being iconified using the listener model. In any case, the notifications are sent to registered listeners that implement the WindowListener interface. This interface defines a number of methods, each associated with a particular type of window event. These methods are listed in Table 2.5.

Figure 2.11 Simple JFrame.

Table 2.4 Default Window Close

DO_NOTHING_ON_CLOSE	The window performs no operation when the close box is selected.
HIDE_ON_CLOSE	The window is removed from the screen when the close box is selected. You can use the setVisible method to show the window again.
DISPOSE_ON_CLOSE	The window is removed from the screen and any underlying system resources are freed when the close box is selected. You cannot use the setVisible method to show the window again.

Table 2.5 WindowListener Methods

Method	Function
windowActivated(WindowEvent)	Invoked when a window is activated.
windowClosed(WindowEvent)	Invoked when a window has been closed.
windowClosing(WindowEvent)	Invoked when a window is in the process of being closed.
windowDeactivated(WindowEvent)	Invoked when a window is de-activated.
windowDeiconified(WindowEvent)	Invoked when a window is de-iconified.
windowIconified(WindowEvent)	Invoked when a window is iconified.
windowOpened(WindowEvent)	Invoked when a window has been opened.

The argument to all WindowListener methods is a WindowEvents object. This object provides direct access to the window associated with the event via the getWindow method. This method takes no arguments and returns the appropriate window.

We have used subclassed WindowAdapter repeatedly in our examples via the class WindowCloser. The WindowCloser class simply closes any window from which it receives a windowClosing message and then exits the program. The following code demonstrates how to do this:

```
class WindowCloser extends WindowAdapter
{
    public void windowClosing(WindowEvent e)
    {
        Window win = e.getWindow();
        win.setVisible(false);
```

```
            win.dispose();
            System.exit(0);
        }
    }
```

In the next example, shown in Figure 2.12, we display a simple JFrame object on the screen. A WindowListener method is used to print messages to the console whenever a window event occurs.

This example is implemented in the form of a subclass of Object that implements the WindowListener method. To catch the window closing and window closed events, we do not exit the program on window closing as in the previous examples; instead we exit on window closed.

```
import java.util.*;
import java.awt.*;
import java.awt.event.*;
import com.sun.java.swing.*;
import com.sun.java.swing.text.*;

public class Windows extends Object
 implements WindowListener
{
    public void windowOpened(WindowEvent e)
    {
        System.out.println("Window opened.");
    }

    public void windowClosing(WindowEvent e)
    {
        Window win = e.getWindow();

        System.out.println("Window closing.");

        win.setVisible(false);
        win.dispose();
    }

    public void windowClosed(WindowEvent e)
    {
        System.out.println("Window closed.");
        System.exit(0);
    }

    public void windowIconified(WindowEvent e)
    {
```

```
        System.out.println("Window iconified.");
    }

    public void windowDeiconified(WindowEvent e)
    {
        System.out.println("Window deiconified.");
    }

    public void windowActivated(WindowEvent e)
    {
        System.out.println("Window activated.");
    }

    public void windowDeactivated(WindowEvent e)
    {
        System.out.println("Window deactivated.");
    }

    public static void main(String s[])
    {
        JFrame frame = new JFrame("Windows");

        frame.setForeground(Color.black);
        frame.setBackground(Color.lightGray);
        frame.setDefaultCloseOperation(
                    JFrame.DO_NOTHING_ON_CLOSE);
         frame.addWindowListener(new Windows());

        frame.getContentPane().add(
                            new Label("Hello World"),"Center");

        frame.pack();
        frame.setVisible(true);
    }
}
```

Figure 2.12 Using WindowListener methods to handle events.

Because users are always asking programmers for new features and functionality, we decided to include a little present for the users in the following example. This is a fun version of the previous window-closer program that closes windows randomly. Please don't use this in the final version of a production project! This joke application displays a window that closes only when a random number is divisible by 5. It does this by extending the WindowAdapter example and implementing the WindowListener method, windowClosing. Whenever the user clicks the close box on the window, this method is invoked. If the random number is divisible by 5 then the window is closed—dispose() is called. Otherwise, nothing happens.

```
import java.awt.*;
import java.util.*;
import java.awt.event.*;
import com.sun.java.swing.*;
import com.sun.java.swing.text.*;

class MeanWindowCloser extends WindowAdapter
{
    public void windowClosing(WindowEvent e)
    {
        Window win;
        Random gen = new Random();

        if((gen.nextInt()%5) == 0)
        {
            win = e.getWindow();
            win.setVisible(false);
            win.dispose();
            System.exit(0);
        }
    }
}


public class MeanWindow extends JFrame
{
    public static void main(String[] args)
    {
        MeanWindow win;

        win = new MeanWindow();
```

```
        win.setDefaultCloseOperation(JFrame.DO_NOTHING_ON_CLOSE);
        win.addWindowListener(new MeanWindowCloser());
        win.getContentPane().add(
                                new Label("Hello World"),"Center");

        win.pack();
        win.setVisible(true);
    }
}
```

Swing and Applets

To use Swing in an applet, use the JApplet class as the parent for your applet subclass. JApplet, like JFrame, uses a Root Pane to manage its menu bar, content area, and internal frames. By using JApplet you can provide a menu with your applet and even use internal frames to organize the user interface.

Our next example, shown in Figure 2.13, defines a simple JApplet subclass with a single button on it. Notice that the content pane for the applet uses a BorderLayout by default.

```
import com.sun.java.swing.*;
import java.awt.event.*;

import java.awt.*;

public class Simple_Applet extends JApplet
{
    public void init()
    {
        JButton button = new JButton("Hello");

        setBackground(Color.lightGray);
        getContentPane().add(button,"Center");

    }
}
```

Figure 2.13 Simple JApplet.

Again, the main difference between creating a Swing applet and an AWT applet is the use of the content pane to hold all of the applet's children.

Summary

Swing provides a number of useful components that replace the components in AWT with lightweight equivalents. In creating Swing, JavaSoft has provided a number of fundamental concepts and features like Actions, tool tips, and icons to make programming easier and more consistent. In the remaining chapters we discuss the various Swing components, including buttons, styled text, trees, tabs, and split panes.

Layout Managers, Boxes, and Borders

3

If you are an experienced AWT programmer you have encountered the idea of a layout manager. If you have not used AWT, your experience with layout managers depends on the windowing systems you use. A layout manager is an object that organizes a user interface. For example, a layout manager can organize the elements of an interface into a grid or a line. As programmers, we use layout managers to set the positions of components and resize them as their parents resize.

Swing builds on the layout managers provided by AWT. Swing containers, like JFrame, JApplet, and JPanel, all use the standard AWT layout managers. Swing also provides several new layout managers that work with specific components to create new layout options.

All Swing components support borders. Borders can provide a visual separation between components or organize a group of components into a visually significant area.

In this chapter, we review the available AWT layout managers as well as the new Swing layout managers. We also discuss the borders available to Swing components and create our own border type. We also describe another type of layout object called a Box. A *Box* is a container that positions components horizontally or vertically.

Layout Managers

Layout managers are defined as classes that implement the java.awt.LayoutManager interface. This interface defines one responsibility, how to lay out the child components in a container. To perform this task, a layout manager resizes and moves the child components. One of the advantages of the layout manager mechanism is that when a container, like a window, is resized, the layout manager automatically updates the interface. For example, a layout manager for a word processor can enlarge the work area to fill the window, regardless of the window size.

To take advantage of layout managers you create a layout manager object and assign it to a container using the method:

```
public void setLayout(LayoutManager lm);
```

Once assigned, the layout manager is asked to lay out the container whenever the container is first displayed, new components are added, or it is resized. You can ask the container to recalculate its layout using the method:

```
public void validate();
```

AWT provides a number of layout managers that are used in your Swing applications. Table 3.1 lists both the existing AWT and new Swing layout managers along with their functions. The containers in Swing each have default layout managers if none are assigned to them, as shown in Table 3.2. The content pane for a JFrame or JApplet uses a BorderLayout by default; a JPanel uses a FlowLayout by default.

BorderLayout

The java.awt.BorderLayout objects organize a container into five named areas: North, South, East, West, and Center. Components can exist in one, and only one, of these areas. All areas do not have to be filled. For example, a word processor document may place a tool bar in the North area and a scroll pane in the Center, leaving the other three areas empty.

Table 3.1 Layout Managers in AWT and Swing

Layout Class	Use
BorderLayout	Lays out a container, arranging its components to fit in five regions: North, South, East, West, and Center.
BoxLayout	Places each of its managed components from left to right or from top to bottom.
CardLayout	Treats each component in the container as a card. Only one card is visible at a time, and the container acts as a stack of cards.
FlowLayout	Arranges components in a left to right flow.
GridBagLayout	Aligns components vertically and horizontally, without requiring that the components be of the same size.
GridLayout	Lays out a container's components in a rectangular grid.
OverlayLayout	Arranges components over the top of each other.
ScrollPaneLayout	Used by scrolling containers.
ViewportLayout	Makes its view the same size as the viewport; however, it will not make the view smaller than its minimum size. As the viewport grows, the view is kept bottom justified until the entire view is visible; subsequently the view is kept top justified.

Table 3.2 Default Layout Managers

Container	Default Layout
JViewport	ViewportLayout
Box	BoxLayout
JScrollPane	ScrollPaneLayout
JPanel	FlowLayout
JRootPane's Content Area	BorderLayout

The size for these areas is based on the components they contain, specifically, on the component's self-defined, preferred size. The components in the North and South positions are sized to fit the container horizontally, but they are also sized to the preferred height. The East and West components are sized to their preferred width, but they are stretched to fill the available height. The Center component is sized to fit any remaining area, ignoring its preferred size altogether.

To create a BorderLayout use one of the following constructors:

```
public BorderLayout() ;
public BorderLayout(int hGap, int vGap);
```

The first constructor creates a default border layout with no gaps between the child components. The second uses the specified vertical and horizontal gaps between components.

To add items to a container and have them appear properly in a BorderLayout you must define the area for the component when it is added to the container. Otherwise, the item is not displayed. Use the following method to make this association:

```
public void add(Component c,Object constraints);
```

Where the second argument is a string that contains one of the area names use this method:

```
North
South
East
West
Center
```

Keep in mind that these values are case sensitive. If you add a component with any other name it is ignored by the layout manger and does not appear in the container.

The following example creates a panel with a border layout and adds buttons to each of the areas. If run from the included CD-ROM, this example looks like

Figure 3.1. Notice that the components are always resized to fit their area, even when the window is resized. You may also notice in the code for this example that the custom panel we create is added to the frame's content pane in the Center area. Remember that the content area for a JFrame defaults to a BorderLayout.

```
import com.sun.java.swing.*;
import com.sun.java.swing.border.*;
import java.applet.*;
import java.awt.*;

public class BorderLayoutExample extends JPanel
{
    public BorderLayoutExample()
    {
        JButton tmp;
        Font font;

        font = new Font("Times-Roman",Font.BOLD,18);

        this.setLayout(new BorderLayout());

        tmp = new JButton("North");
        tmp.setFont(font);
        add(tmp,"North");

        tmp = new JButton("South");
        tmp.setFont(font);
        add(tmp,"South");

        tmp = new JButton("East");
        tmp.setFont(font);
        add(tmp,"East");

        tmp = new JButton("West");
        tmp.setFont(font);
        add(tmp,"West");

        tmp = new JButton("Center");
        tmp.setFont(font);
        add(tmp,"Center");
    }


    public Dimension getPreferredSize()
    {
```

```
            return new Dimension(400, 150);
        }

        public static void main(String s[])
        {
            JFrame frame = new JFrame("Border Layout Example");
            BorderLayoutExample panel = new BorderLayoutExample();

            frame.setDefaultCloseOperation(JFrame.DO_NOTHING_ON_CLOSE);
            frame.setForeground(Color.black);
            frame.setBackground(Color.lightGray);
            frame.getContentPane().add(panel,"Center");

            frame.setSize(panel.getPreferredSize());
            frame.setVisible(true);
        }
    }
```

FlowLayout

The java.awt.FlowLayout class defines a layout manager that works like a word processor. Components are displayed with their preferred size in the order in which they are added to a container. If the line of component is too wide to fit in the container, the line is wrapped, placing some components on a second line. This process is continued for as many lines as necessary to display the components. If the container is simply too small to hold all of the components, they are "displayed" invisibly below the container.

Like a word processor, a FlowLayout can have one of three alignments: left, center, or right. These are defined by class variables in the FlowLayout class and are equivalent to the text alignment options in a word processing tool.

```
FlowLayout.LEFT
FlowLayout.CENTER
FlowLayout.RIGHT
```

Figure 3.1 Organizing a container using a BorderLayout.

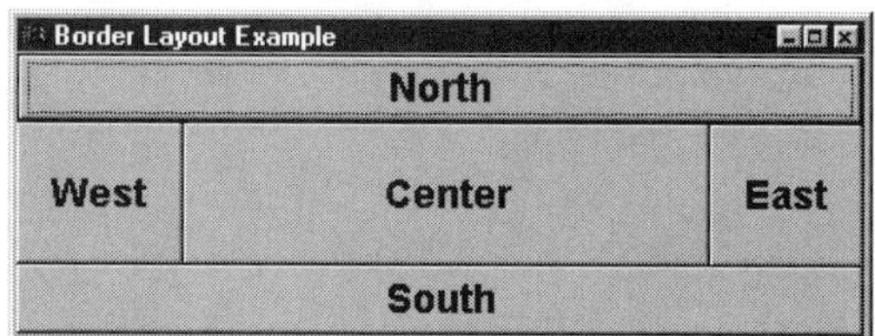

You can create a FlowLayout with one of three constructors:

```
public FlowLayout();
public FlowLayout(int align);
public FlowLayout(int align, int hgap, int vgap);
```

The default alignment is centered, and the default gap is five units for both vertical and horizontal. You add components to a container using a FlowLayout with the method:

```
public void add(Component c);
```

The order in which you want components to appear is the order in which they are added in the code.

The following example assigns a FlowLayout to JPanel and adds four buttons to the panel. This example, shown in Figure 3.2, uses a default flow layout with a centered alignment. If you run the example and resize the window, the buttons remain centered, even if they are wrapped to multiple lines. This is the behavior of a FlowLayout.

```
import com.sun.java.swing.*;
import com.sun.java.swing.border.*;
import java.applet.*;
import java.awt.*;

public class FlowLayoutExample extends JPanel
{
    public FlowLayoutExample()
    {
        JButton tmp;

        this.setLayout(new FlowLayout());

        tmp = new JButton("One");
        add(tmp);

        tmp = new JButton("Two");
        add(tmp);

        tmp = new JButton("Three");
        add(tmp);

        tmp = new JButton("Four");
        add(tmp);
    }
```

```
    public Dimension getPreferredSize()
    {
        return new Dimension(400, 100);
    }

    public static void main(String s[])
    {
        JFrame frame = new JFrame("Flow Layout Example");
        FlowLayoutExample panel = new FlowLayoutExample();

        frame.setDefaultCloseOperation(JFrame.DO_NOTHING_ON_CLOSE);
        frame.setForeground(Color.black);
        frame.setBackground(Color.lightGray);
        frame.getContentPane().add(panel,"Center");

        frame.setSize(panel.getPreferredSize());
        frame.setVisible(true);
    }
}
```

GridLayout

A java.awt.GridLayout object organizes a container into a set of equal-sized cells. This is useful for lining up UI elements like a group of radio buttons. These cells are determined based on a preset number of rows and columns. The components in a grid are resized to fit their cell. In other words, all of the components in a grid layout are the same size.

To create a GridLayout you can use one of these constructors:

```
public GridLayout();
public GridLayout(int rows, int cols);
public GridLayout(int rows, int cols, int hgap, int vgap);
```

You can use the default constructor to create a grid with one row and one column. Usually you will use the other two constructors. Both of these specify the number of rows and columns in the grid; the second also specifies a set of horizontal and vertical gaps.

Figure 3.2 FlowLayout.

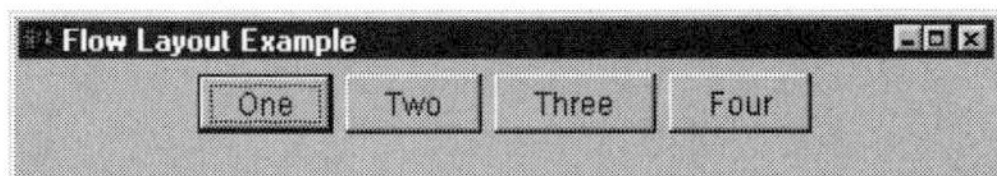

Figure 3.3 GridLayout.

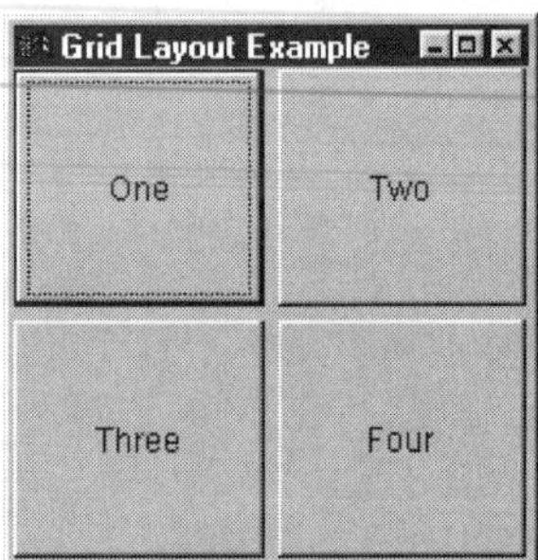

The position of a component in a grid is determined by the order in which it's added. Components are displayed from left to right and top to bottom. Columns are added to the grid if more components are added than cells exist.

The following example, shown in Figure 3.3, adds four buttons to a grid with two rows and two columns.

```
import com.sun.java.swing.*;
import com.sun.java.swing.border.*;
import java.applet.*;
import java.awt.*;

public class GridLayoutExample extends JPanel
{
    public GridLayoutExample()
    {
        JButton tmp;

        this.setLayout(new GridLayout(2,2,5,5));

        tmp = new JButton("One");
        add(tmp);

        tmp = new JButton("Two");
        add(tmp);

        tmp = new JButton("Three");
        add(tmp);

        tmp = new JButton("Four");
        add(tmp);
    }

    public Dimension getPreferredSize()
```

```
    {
        return new Dimension(200, 200);
    }

    public static void main(String s[])
    {
        JFrame frame = new JFrame("Grid Layout Example");
        GridLayoutExample panel = new GridLayoutExample();

        frame.setDefaultCloseOperation(JFrame.DO_NOTHING_ON_CLOSE);
        frame.setForeground(Color.black);
        frame.setBackground(Color.lightGray);
        frame.getContentPane().add(panel,"Center");

        frame.setSize(panel.getPreferredSize());
        frame.setVisible(true);
    }
}
```

ViewportLayout

A JViewportLayout is used with a container called a JViewPort. The layout makes its view the same size as the viewport; however, it will not make the view smaller than its minimum size. As the viewport grows the view is kept bottom justified until the entire view is visible; subsequently, the view is kept top justified.

For example, a JScrollPane is a JComponent that uses a JViewport to hold the scrolled component. You can use a viewport without a scroll pane. The viewport positions its one component in the upper left corner and resizes it to its preferred size. This behavior is handled with a layout manager called ViewportLayout in the Swing library.

Our next example—pictured in Figure 3.4—displays two custom components in two viewports. Notice that the one component is small so it is displayed fully and that the other component is too big and is clipped. If the window is resized, this component becomes fully visible.

```
import com.sun.java.swing.*;
import com.sun.java.swing.border.*;
import java.applet.*;
import java.awt.*;

public class VPortLayoutExample extends JPanel
{
    public VPortLayoutExample()
    {
        IconComp ic;
```

```
        JViewport subPanel;

        this.setLayout(new GridLayout(1,2,10,10));

        ic = new IconComp(new ImageIcon("images/shapes.gif"));
        subPanel = new JViewport();
        subPanel.setView(ic);
        add(subPanel);

        ic = new IconComp(new ImageIcon("images/logo.gif"));
        subPanel = new JViewport();
        subPanel.setView(ic);
        add(subPanel);
    }

    public Dimension getPreferredSize()
    {
        return new Dimension(400, 150);
    }

    public static void main(String s[])
    {
        JFrame frame = new JFrame("View Port Layout Example");
        VPortLayoutExample panel = new VPortLayoutExample();

        frame.setDefaultCloseOperation(JFrame.DO_NOTHING_ON_CLOSE);
        frame.setForeground(Color.black);
        frame.setBackground(Color.lightGray);
        frame.getContentPane().add(panel,"Center");

        frame.setSize(panel.getPreferredSize());
        frame.setVisible(true);
    }
}
```

Figure 3.4 Viewports.

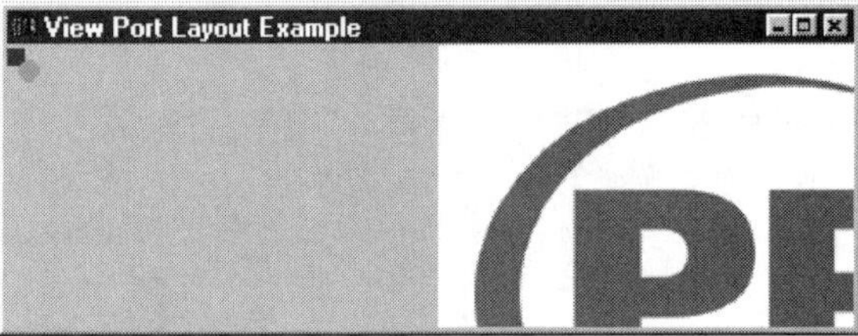

The custom components in this next example—called IconComp—display an icon, then retrieve their preferred size from that icon. You may find this class useful in other programs that need to display an Icon by itself.

```
class IconComp extends JComponent
{
    Icon icon;

    public IconComp(Icon i)
    {
        icon = i;
    }

    public Dimension getPreferredSize()
    {
        return new Dimension(icon.getIconWidth(),icon.getIconHeight());
    }

    public Dimension getMinimumSize()
    {
        return getPreferredSize();
    }

    public void paint(Graphics g)
    {
        icon.paintIcon(this,g,0,0);
    }
}
```

Working without a Layout Manager

You may decide that you want to control the position and size of the components in your Swing interface. In this case, you can set a container's layout manager to null. You are responsible, however, for any resizing that occurs when the container resizes.

To position the components in a null layout, use the methods:

```
public void setLocation(int x, int y);
public void setLocation(Point p);
```

Use the following methods to set the size of your components:

```
public void setSize(int width, int height);
public void setSize(Dimension d);
```

Or, use this method to resize and position a component in one step:

```
public void setBounds(int x, int y, int width, int height);
public void setBounds(Rectangle r);
```

The following example, shown in Figure 3.5, adds four buttons to a JPanel with no layout manager. The buttons are positioned in a 2 5 2 grid with each button 100 units wide and 100 units tall. Notice that there is extra space below and to the right of the components. If you resize the window this space will grow and shrink. In fact, if you make the window too small, some or all of the buttons will be clipped from view.

```
import com.sun.java.swing.*;
import java.awt.*;
import java.applet.*;

public class NoLayout extends JPanel
{
    public NoLayout()
    {
        Button tmp;

        setLayout(null);

        tmp = new Button("North West");
        tmp.setBounds(0,0,100,100);
        add(tmp);

        tmp = new Button("North East");
        tmp.setBounds(100,0,100,100);
        add(tmp);

        tmp = new Button("South West");
        tmp.setBounds(0,100,100,100);
        add(tmp);

        tmp = new Button("South East");
        tmp.setBounds(100,100,100,100);
        add(tmp);
    }

    public Dimension getPreferredSize()
    {
        return new Dimension(250, 250);
    }
```

```
    public static void main(String s[])
    {
        JFrame frame = new JFrame("No Layout Example");
        NoLayout panel = new NoLayout();

        frame.setDefaultCloseOperation(JFrame.DO_NOTHING_ON_CLOSE);
        frame.setForeground(Color.black);
        frame.setBackground(Color.lightGray);
        frame.getContentPane().add(panel,"Center");

        frame.setSize(panel.getPreferredSize());
        frame.setVisible(true);
    }
}
```

Combining Layout Managers

In a large program, a single layout manager is probably not sufficient to define an interface. In this case, you can use JPanels to organize interface areas. Build the interface by creating components, add them to a panel, and then add the panel to another panel or container. This technique builds a tree of containers, each with its own layout manager. For example, the word processor—pictured in Figure 3.6—has a scroll pane that uses a viewport to hold the main document. The scroll pane itself uses a ScrollPaneLayout to organize its scrollers and the viewport. This scroll pane is placed in the center of a border layout on the content pane. A tool bar is placed in the North area of the same content pane.

Fortunately, in this case, most of the layout creation is handled by the scroll pane, making the layout easy to manage. In your applications, however, you may end up building more complex combinations of layouts and containers. Swing provides containers that work with layout managers to help you with sophisticated layout designs. One container that can help with this process is the Box container provided by Swing.

Figure 3.5 No layout manager.

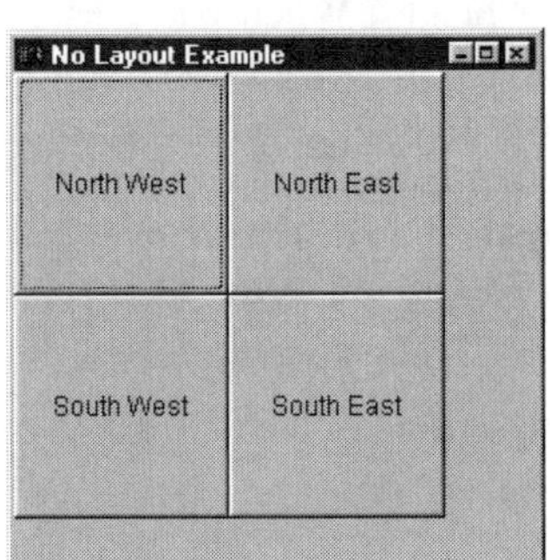

Figure 3.6 Combining layouts.

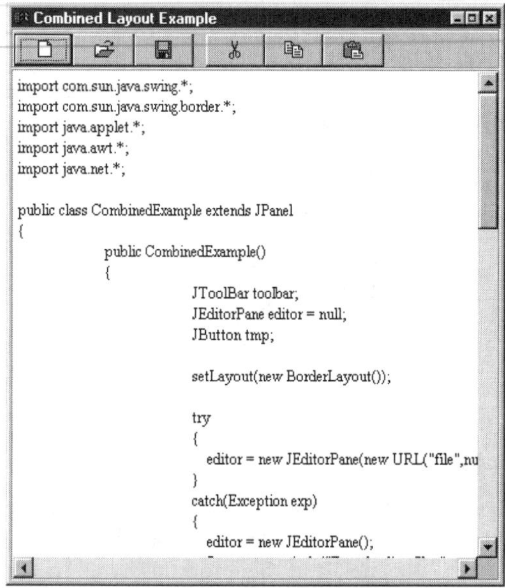

Boxes

A *Box* is a container that positions components horizontally or vertically. The Swing Box class uses a BoxLayout as a layout manager. Box also provides a number of useful filler components that can be used to force the box to a particular size or to affect the repositioning of components during resizing.

To create a box, use one of the following Box static methods:

```
public static Box createHorizontalBox();
public static Box createVerticalBox();
```

A horizontal box, like the one in Figure 3.7, and a vertical box, like the one in Figure 3.8, appear.

Struts are components that have a particular width or height. When you create a user interface with a box, you can use struts to force space between two components. You can also use a strut to specify a size for the component by creating a strut with a particular dimension. For example, if you want to make sure that two text fields are spaced five pixels apart, you could create a strut that is five pixels in length in between the two included text fields. You create struts with the Box static methods:

```
public static Component createHorizontalStrut(int width);
public static Component createVerticalStrut(int height);
```

Figure 3.7 Horizontal box example.

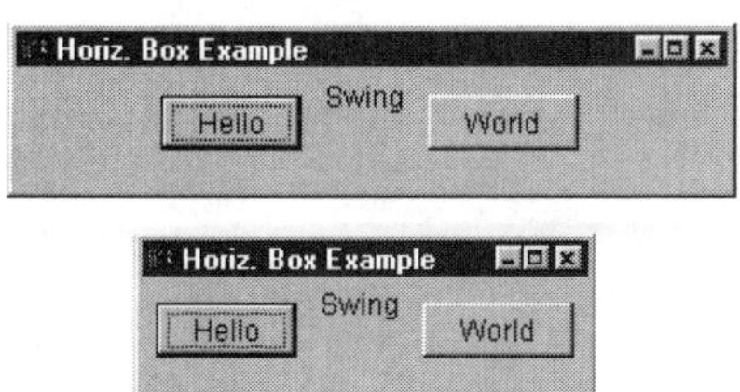

Horizontal struts either force space between components in a horizontal box or provide a minimum width for a vertical box. Vertical struts either force space between components in a vertical box or provide a minimum height for a horizontal box.

Glue is a component that grows to fill needed space. You can use glue to create flexible regions between components or between a component and the side of the box. For example, if you have a group of components that you would like to keep close together, such as a label, a noneditable text element that displays a string, and a text field, you could use glue to "attach" these components so that even when the container resizes, the components stay together and maintain their distance from each other. Glue is created using the Box static methods:

```
public static Component createHorizontalGlue();
public static Component createVerticalGlue();
```

To demonstrate boxes we have created two examples. The first example shows how to create a horizontal box. Notice that when the box is resized, the glue on either side of the components fills up the extra space, keeping the components in the center (see Figure 3.7).

The code for this example is as follows:

```
import com.sun.java.swing.*;
import java.awt.event.*;
import java.awt.*;

public class HBoxExample extends JPanel
{
    public HBoxExample()
    {
        Box hBox;
        JButton button1,button2;
        JLabel label;
        Component glue,strut;

        hBox = Box.createHorizontalBox();
```

```
        setLayout(new BorderLayout());
        add(hBox,"Center");

        button1 = new JButton("Hello");
        button2 = new JButton("World");

        label = new JLabel("Swing");

        glue = Box.createHorizontalGlue();

        hBox.add(glue);

        hBox.add(button1);

        strut = Box.createHorizontalStrut(10);

        hBox.add(strut);

        hBox.add(label);

        strut = Box.createHorizontalStrut(10);

        hBox.add(strut);

        hBox.add(button2);

        glue = Box.createHorizontalGlue();

        hBox.add(glue);
    }

    public Dimension getPreferredSize()
    {
        return new Dimension(200, 70);
    }

    public static void main(String s[])
    {
        JFrame frame = new JFrame("Horiz. Box Example");
        HBoxExample panel = new HBoxExample();

        frame.setDefaultCloseOperation(JFrame.DO_NOTHING_ON_CLOSE);
        frame.setForeground(Color.black);
        frame.setBackground(Color.lightGray);
```

```
            frame.getContentPane().add(panel,"Center");

            frame.setSize(panel.getPreferredSize());
            frame.setVisible(true);
        }
    }
```

Similarly, the next example—pictured in Figure 3.8—creates a vertical box and adds the same set of buttons, glue, and struts.

The code for this example is as follows:

```
import com.sun.java.swing.*;
import java.awt.event.*;
import java.awt.*;

public class VBoxExample extends JPanel
{
    public VBoxExample()
    {
        Box vBox;
        JButton button1,button2;
        JLabel label;
        Component glue,strut;

        vBox = Box.createVerticalBox();

        setLayout(new BorderLayout());
        add(vBox,"Center");

        button1 = new JButton("Hello");
        button2 = new JButton("World");

        label = new JLabel("Swing");

        glue = Box.createVerticalGlue();

        vBox.add(glue);

        vBox.add(button1);

        strut = Box.createVerticalStrut(10);

        vBox.add(strut);

        vBox.add(label);
```

```
        strut = Box.createVerticalStrut(10);

        vBox.add(strut);

        vBox.add(button2);

        glue = Box.createVerticalGlue();

        vBox.add(glue);
    }

    public Dimension getPreferredSize()
    {
        return new Dimension(60, 200);
    }

    public static void main(String s[])
    {
        JFrame frame = new JFrame("Vert. Box Example");
        VBoxExample panel = new VBoxExample();

        frame.setDefaultCloseOperation(JFrame.DO_NOTHING_ON_CLOSE);
        frame.setForeground(Color.black);
        frame.setBackground(Color.lightGray);
        frame.getContentPane().add(panel,"Center");

        frame.setSize(panel.getPreferredSize());
        frame.setVisible(true);
    }
}
```

Figure 3.8 Vertical box example.

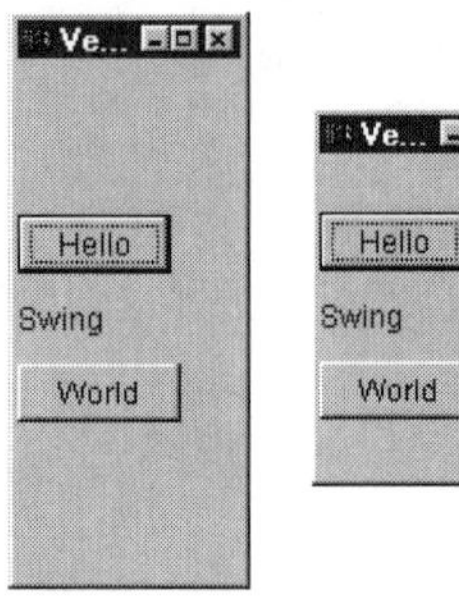

The Box class can also create a component with a fixed, rigid size. This component will take up space in your UI and act as an invisible filler, allowing you to put a fixed amount of distance between elements of your UI. Use the following method to create one of these components.

```
public static Component createRigidArea(Dimension d);
```

Borders

All JComponents can have a border assigned to them. This border, defined by the com.sun.java.swing.border.Border interface, draws itself around the component based on a set of insets, which define the size of the border at the left, right, top, and bottom. Borders are assigned to components using the method:

```
public void setBorder(Border b);
```

By default, a JComponent does not have a border. You can use borders on panels or other containers as well as on labels. By assigning borders to containers, you can create a user interface that organizes itself visually so that the user can see controls for similar functionality grouped together.

As well as defining the concept of a border, the Swing border package includes a number of useful border classes. These borders, pictured in Figure 3.9, provide a wide range of possibilities for user interface design.

The Swing borders and their functions are shown in Table 3.3. You can also create your own borders by subclassing AbstractBorder and implementing the

Figure 3.9 Swing borders.

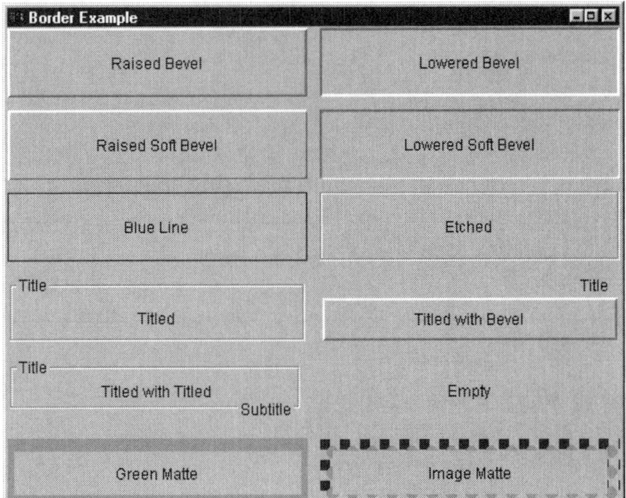

Table 3.3 Swing Borders and Their Use

Border Type	Use
BevelBorder	A simple two-line bevel border
SoftBevelBorder	A raised or lowered bevel with softened corners
LineBorder	A line border of arbitrary thickness and of a single color
EtchBorder	A simple etched border
EmptyBorder	An empty, transparent border that takes up space but does no drawing
MatteBorder	A matte-like border of either a solid color or a tiled icon
CompoundBorder	A composite border used to compose two Border objects into a single border by nesting an inside Border object within the insets of an outside Border object
TitledBorder	An arbitrary border with the addition of a String title in a specified position and justification

appropriate methods, as discussed at the end of this section. Before we dive into creating our own border class, let's look at the available borders and how to use them.

Bevel Borders

Swing provides two types of beveled borders: BevelBorder and SoftBevelBorder. A beveled border is a set of colors used to draw a frame around a rectangular area. When the colors are picked correctly, the bevel provides the appearance of a raised or lowered area, as shown in Figure 3.10.

As a result, there are two types of beveled borders, indicated by a value stored in the two BevelBorder class variables:

```
BevelBorder.RAISED
BevelBorder.LOWERED
```

When you create a bevel border you can assign the types using these values. The difference between a BevelBorder and a SoftBevelBorder border is the width of the bevel. SoftBevelBorder is actually a subclass of BevelBorder.

Figure 3.10 Bevel border example.

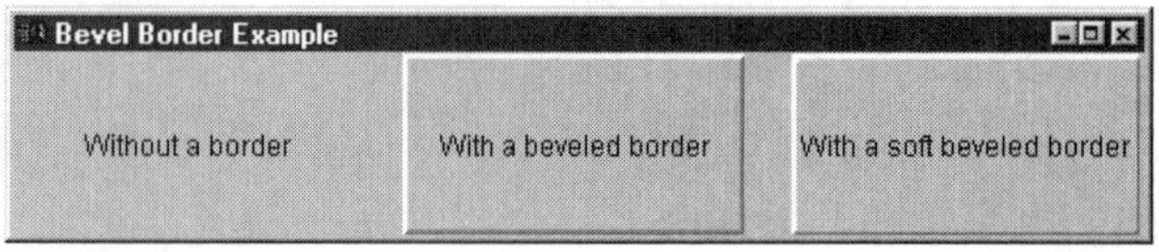

Bevel Border Example

Without a border | With a beveled border | With a soft beveled border

You should use three constructors for a BevelBorder. The first one allows you to define a border that is either raised or lowered. The bevel color is defined with the container. The second and third constructor allow you to create a border with specific colors for the various components of the bevel.

```
public BevelBorder(int bevelType);
public BevelBorder(int bevelType, Color highlight, Color shadow);
public BevelBorder(int bevelType,
                    Color highlightOuter, Color highlightInner,
                    Color shadowOuter, Color shadowInner);
```

To create a SoftBevelBorder, use these constructors that work similarly to the BevelBorder constructors:

```
public SoftBevelBorder(int bevelType);
public SoftBevelBorder(int bevelType, Color highlight, Color shadow);
public SoftBevelBorder(int bevelType,
                    Color highlightOuter, Color highlightInner,
                    Color shadowOuter, Color shadowInner);
```

Both of these classes provide a mechanism for setting the shadow and highlight of colors. By default, the colors for a bevel border are derived from the component to which the border is assigned.

Here is an example that shows a label with no border, a bevel border, and a soft-bevel border.

```
import com.sun.java.swing.*;
import com.sun.java.swing.border.*;
import java.awt.event.*;
import java.awt.*;

public class SBorderExample extends JPanel
{
    public SBorderExample()
    {
        BevelBorder border;
        SoftBevelBorder sborder;
        JLabel label;

        setLayout(new GridLayout(1,3,20,20));

        label = new JLabel("Without a border",JLabel.CENTER);
        add(label);

        label = new JLabel("With a beveled border",JLabel.CENTER);
        border = new BevelBorder(BevelBorder.RAISED);
```

```
        label.setBorder(border);
        add(label);

        label = new JLabel("With a soft beveled border",JLabel.CENTER);
        sborder = new SoftBevelBorder(BevelBorder.RAISED);
        label.setBorder(sborder);
        add(label);
    }

    public Dimension getPreferredSize()
    {
        return new Dimension(500, 100);
    }

    public static void main(String s[])
    {
        JFrame frame = new JFrame("Bevel Border Example");
        SBorderExample panel = new SBorderExample();

        frame.setDefaultCloseOperation(JFrame.DO_NOTHING_ON_CLOSE);
        frame.setForeground(Color.black);
        frame.setBackground(Color.lightGray);
        frame.getContentPane().add(panel,"Center");

        frame.setSize(panel.getPreferredSize());
        frame.setVisible(true);
    }
}
```

Line Borders

A LineBorder is basically the outline of a rectangle. You specify the line width and color for this outline when you create the border using the following constructors:

```
public LineBorder(Color color);
public LineBorder(Color color, int thickness);
```

You can also create the most common colored line borders using static methods:

```
public static Border createBlackLineBorder();
public static Border createGrayLineBorder();
```

Etched Borders

An EtchedBorder uses a pair of colors to draw a rectangular outline that looks as if it was etched out of the background, as shown in Figure 3.11.

Figure 3.11 Etched border example.

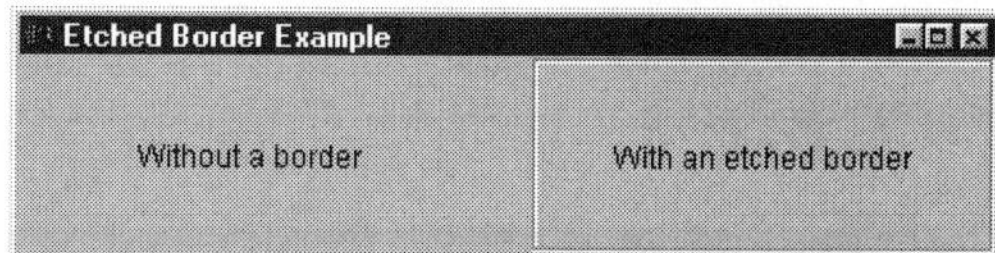

To create an EtchedBorder use one of the constructors:

```
public EtchedBorder();
public EtchedBorder(Color highlight, Color shadow);
```

By default, etch will be drawn using the component's foreground and background colors.

The screen shot for Figure 3.11 was created using the following example. This program displays two labels in a grid. One label has no border; the other has an etched border.

```
import com.sun.java.swing.*;
import com.sun.java.swing.border.*;
import java.awt.event.*;
import java.awt.*;

public class EBorderExample extends JPanel
{
    public EBorderExample()
    {
        EtchedBorder border;
        JLabel label;

        setLayout(new GridLayout(1,2,20,20));

        label = new JLabel("Without a border",JLabel.CENTER);
        add(label);

        label = new JLabel("With an etched border",JLabel.CENTER);
        border = new EtchedBorder();
        label.setBorder(border);
        add(label);
    }

    public Dimension getPreferredSize()
    {
        return new Dimension(400, 100);
    }
```

```
    public static void main(String s[])
    {
        JFrame frame = new JFrame("Etched Border Example");
        EBorderExample panel = new EBorderExample();

        frame.setDefaultCloseOperation(JFrame.DO_NOTHING_ON_CLOSE);
        frame.setForeground(Color.black);
        frame.setBackground(Color.lightGray);
        frame.getContentPane().add(panel,"Center");

        frame.setSize(panel.getPreferredSize());
        frame.setVisible(true);
    }
}
```

Empty Borders

An EmptyBorder is really just a set of insets that take up space. The empty border does not draw anything, but it separates the component it borders from its surroundings. You create an empty border with the insets that you want it to have using either of these constructors:

```
public EmptyBorder(int top, int left,
                        int bottom, int right);
public EmptyBorder(Insets insets);
```

Matte Borders

A MatteBorder is like an empty border in that you assign it a set of insets. The matte border either fills its assigned space with a color or tiles an icon over the space. Tiling an icon creates a repeated pattern that covers the entire area with an icon. The type of matte used is assigned during creation, as defined by the following constructors:

```
public MatteBorder(int top, int left,
                        int bottom, int right, Color color);
public MatteBorder(int top, int left,
                        int bottom, int right, Icon tileIcon);
```

Compound Borders

A CompoundBorder is a border inside another border. In general, compound borders are used to create titles on other border styles. You can create a compound border from any two borders by using this method:

```
public CompoundBorder(Border outsideBorder,
                      Border insideBorder);
```

Titled Borders

TitledBorders are perhaps the most complex border type. A titled border draws a string of text based on a specified location and justification. The border can have an assigned font and text color, and it can be built to surround another border. A number of constructors are provided for creating these borders (Table 3.4).

The positions for the string title are specified using values stored in the following TitledBorder class variables:

```
ABOVE_BOTTOM
ABOVE_TOP
BELOW_BOTTOM
BELOW_TOP
BOTTOM
TOP
```

The justifications for the string are also specified with static variables:

```
CENTER
LEFT
RIGHT
```

Table 3.4 TitledBorder Constructors

Constructor	Description
TitledBorder(Border)	Creates a TitledBorder instance with the specified border and no title.
TitledBorder(Border, String)	Creates a TitledBorder instance with the specified border and title.
TitledBorder(Border, String, int, int)	Creates a TitledBorder instance with the specified border, title, title-justification, and title-position.
TitledBorder(Border, String, int, int, Font)	Creates a TitledBorder instance with the specified border, title, title-justification, title-position, and title-font.
TitledBorder(Border, String, int, int, Font, Color)	Creates a TitledBorder instance with the specified border, title, title-justification, title-position, title-font, and title-color.
TitledBorder(String)	Creates a TitledBorder instance that uses an etched border.

Figure 3.12 Titled borders.

To give you an idea of the various title positions possible, we have created an example that displays a titled border with each variable setting listed above. This example, shown in Figure 3.12, adds a titled border to a label. Eighteen of these bordered labels are created and placed in a grid layout.

The code for this example is as follows:

```
import com.sun.java.swing.*;
import com.sun.java.swing.border.*;
import java.awt.event.*;
import java.awt.*;

public class TBorderExample extends JPanel
{
    public TBorderExample()
    {
        TitledBorder border;
        JLabel label;

        setLayout(new GridLayout(6,3,5,5));

        //AboveTop left
```

```
label = new JLabel("Above Top, Left",JLabel.CENTER);
border = new TitledBorder("Title");
border.setTitlePosition(TitledBorder.ABOVE_TOP);
border.setTitleJustification(TitledBorder.LEFT);
label.setBorder(border);
add(label);

//AboveTop center

label = new JLabel("Above Top, Center",JLabel.CENTER);
border = new TitledBorder("Title");
border.setTitlePosition(TitledBorder.ABOVE_TOP);
border.setTitleJustification(TitledBorder.CENTER);
label.setBorder(border);
add(label);

//AboveTop right

label = new JLabel("Above Top, Right",JLabel.CENTER);
border = new TitledBorder("Title");
border.setTitlePosition(TitledBorder.ABOVE_TOP);
border.setTitleJustification(TitledBorder.RIGHT);
label.setBorder(border);
add(label);

//Top left

label = new JLabel("Top, Left",JLabel.CENTER);
border = new TitledBorder("Title");
border.setTitlePosition(TitledBorder.TOP);
border.setTitleJustification(TitledBorder.LEFT);
label.setBorder(border);
add(label);

//Top center

label = new JLabel("Top, Center",JLabel.CENTER);
border = new TitledBorder("Title");
border.setTitlePosition(TitledBorder.TOP);
border.setTitleJustification(TitledBorder.CENTER);
label.setBorder(border);
add(label);

//Top right
```

```
label = new JLabel("Top, Right",JLabel.CENTER);
border = new TitledBorder("Title");
border.setTitlePosition(TitledBorder.TOP);
border.setTitleJustification(TitledBorder.RIGHT);
label.setBorder(border);
add(label);

//BelowTop left

label = new JLabel("Below Top, Left",JLabel.CENTER);
border = new TitledBorder("Title");
border.setTitlePosition(TitledBorder.BELOW_TOP);
border.setTitleJustification(TitledBorder.LEFT);
label.setBorder(border);
add(label);

//BelowTop center

label = new JLabel("Below Top, Center",JLabel.CENTER);
border = new TitledBorder("Title");
border.setTitlePosition(TitledBorder.BELOW_TOP);
border.setTitleJustification(TitledBorder.CENTER);
label.setBorder(border);
add(label);

//BelowTop right

label = new JLabel("Below Top, Right",JLabel.CENTER);
border = new TitledBorder("Title");
border.setTitlePosition(TitledBorder.BELOW_TOP);
border.setTitleJustification(TitledBorder.RIGHT);
label.setBorder(border);
add(label);

//AboveBottom left

label = new JLabel("Above Bottom, Left",JLabel.CENTER);
border = new TitledBorder("Title");
border.setTitlePosition(TitledBorder.ABOVE_BOTTOM);
border.setTitleJustification(TitledBorder.LEFT);
label.setBorder(border);
add(label);

//AboveBottom center
```

```
label = new JLabel("Above Bottom, Center",JLabel.CENTER);
border = new TitledBorder("Title");
border.setTitlePosition(TitledBorder.ABOVE_BOTTOM);
border.setTitleJustification(TitledBorder.CENTER);
label.setBorder(border);
add(label);

//AboveBottom right

label = new JLabel("Above Bottom, Right",JLabel.CENTER);
border = new TitledBorder("Title");
border.setTitlePosition(TitledBorder.ABOVE_BOTTOM);
border.setTitleJustification(TitledBorder.RIGHT);
label.setBorder(border);
add(label);

//Bottom left

label = new JLabel("Bottom, Left",JLabel.CENTER);
border = new TitledBorder("Title");
border.setTitlePosition(TitledBorder.BOTTOM);
border.setTitleJustification(TitledBorder.LEFT);
label.setBorder(border);
add(label);

//Bottom center

label = new JLabel("Bottom, Center",JLabel.CENTER);
border = new TitledBorder("Title");
border.setTitlePosition(TitledBorder.BOTTOM);
border.setTitleJustification(TitledBorder.CENTER);
label.setBorder(border);
add(label);

//Bottom right

label = new JLabel("Bottom, Right",JLabel.CENTER);
border = new TitledBorder("Title");
border.setTitlePosition(TitledBorder.BOTTOM);
border.setTitleJustification(TitledBorder.RIGHT);
label.setBorder(border);
add(label);

//BelowBottom left
```

```
        label = new JLabel("Below Bottom, Left",JLabel.CENTER);
        border = new TitledBorder("Title");
        border.setTitlePosition(TitledBorder.BELOW_BOTTOM);
        border.setTitleJustification(TitledBorder.LEFT);
        label.setBorder(border);
        add(label);

        //BelowBottom center

        label = new JLabel("Below Bottom, Center",JLabel.CENTER);
        border = new TitledBorder("Title");
        border.setTitlePosition(TitledBorder.BELOW_BOTTOM);
        border.setTitleJustification(TitledBorder.CENTER);
        label.setBorder(border);
        add(label);

        //BelowBottom right

        label = new JLabel("Below Bottom, Right",JLabel.CENTER);
        border = new TitledBorder("Title");
        border.setTitlePosition(TitledBorder.BELOW_BOTTOM);
        border.setTitleJustification(TitledBorder.RIGHT);
        label.setBorder(border);
        add(label);
    }

    public Dimension getPreferredSize()
    {
        return new Dimension(450, 500);
    }

    public static void main(String s[])
    {
        JFrame frame = new JFrame("Titled Border Example");
        TBorderExample panel = new TBorderExample();

        frame.setDefaultCloseOperation(JFrame.DO_NOTHING_ON_CLOSE);
        frame.setForeground(Color.black);
        frame.setBackground(Color.lightGray);
        frame.getContentPane().add(panel,"Center");

        frame.setSize(panel.getPreferredSize());
        frame.setVisible(true);
    }
}
```

Notice that TitledBorder provides methods to assign the title, position, justification, font, color, and subborder for a titled border.

Border Example

To create the example in Figure 3.9, we used most of the borders discussed in this chapter. We actually used a titled border to show what a compound border looks like because this is probably the most common use of a border combination. This example is slightly repetitive because there are so many border types, but we have highlighted key techniques for creating each border type and for assigning its attributes.

```
import com.sun.java.swing.*;
import com.sun.java.swing.border.*;
import java.awt.event.*;
import java.awt.*;

public class BorderExample extends JPanel
{
    public BorderExample()
    {
        Border border;
        JLabel label;
        ImageIcon icon = new ImageIcon("images/shapes.gif");

        setLayout(new GridLayout(6,2,10,10));

        //Raised bevel border

        label = new JLabel("Raised Bevel",JLabel.CENTER);
        border = new BevelBorder(BevelBorder.RAISED);
        label.setBorder(border);
        add(label);

        //Lowered bevel border

        label = new JLabel("Lowered Bevel",JLabel.CENTER);
        border = new BevelBorder(BevelBorder.LOWERED);
        label.setBorder(border);
        add(label);

        //Raised soft bevel border

        label = new JLabel("Raised Soft Bevel",JLabel.CENTER);
        border = new SoftBevelBorder(BevelBorder.RAISED);
        label.setBorder(border);
```

```
add(label);

//Lowered soft bevel border

label = new JLabel("Lowered Soft Bevel",JLabel.CENTER);
border = new SoftBevelBorder(BevelBorder.LOWERED);
label.setBorder(border);
add(label);

//line border

label = new JLabel("Blue Line",JLabel.CENTER);
border = new LineBorder(Color.blue);
label.setBorder(border);
add(label);

//etched border

label = new JLabel("Etched",JLabel.CENTER);
border = new EtchedBorder();
label.setBorder(border);
add(label);

//titled border

label = new JLabel("Titled",JLabel.CENTER);
border = new TitledBorder("Title");
label.setBorder(border);
add(label);

//title with bevel

label = new JLabel("Titled with Bevel",JLabel.CENTER);
border = new TitledBorder(new BevelBorder(BevelBorder.RAISED)
                          ,"Title");
((TitledBorder)border).setTitlePosition(TitledBorder.ABOVE_TOP);
((TitledBorder)border).setTitleJustification(TitledBorder.RIGHT);
label.setBorder(border);
add(label);
```

```
        //title with title

        label = new JLabel("Titled with Titled",JLabel.CENTER);
        border = new TitledBorder(new TitledBorder("Title"),"Subtitle");
        ((TitledBorder)border).setTitlePosition(TitledBorder.BOTTOM);
        ((TitledBorder)border).setTitleJustification(TitledBorder.RIGHT);
        label.setBorder(border);
        add(label);

        //empty border

        label = new JLabel("Empty",JLabel.CENTER);
        border = new EmptyBorder(10,10,10,10);
        label.setBorder(border);
        add(label);

        //matte border with color

        label = new JLabel("Green Matte",JLabel.CENTER);
        border = new MatteBorder(10,5,10,5,Color.green);
        label.setBorder(border);
        add(label);

        //matte border with image

        label = new JLabel("Image Matte",JLabel.CENTER);
        border = new MatteBorder(10,10,10,10,icon);
        label.setBorder(border);
        add(label);
    }

    public Dimension getPreferredSize()
    {
        return new Dimension(500, 400);
    }

    public static void main(String s[])
    {
        JFrame frame = new JFrame("Border Example");
```

```
        BorderExample panel = new BorderExample();

        frame.setDefaultCloseOperation(JFrame.DO_NOTHING_ON_CLOSE);
        frame.setForeground(Color.black);
        frame.setBackground(Color.lightGray);
        frame.getContentPane().add(panel,"Center");

        frame.setSize(panel.getPreferredSize());
        frame.setVisible(true);
    }
}
```

Custom Borders

You can create your own border types by implementing the Border interface. This interface defines three methods:

```
public abstract void paintBorder(Component c,
                                 Graphics g,
                                 int x,
                                 int y,
                                 int width,
                                 int height)
```

This method paints the border for the specified component with the specified position and size.

C—the component for which this border is being painted

g—the graphics to paint

x—the x position of the border

y—the y position of the border

width—the width of the border

height—the height of the border

```
public abstract Insets getBorderInsets(Component c)
```

This method returns the insets of the border where “c” is the component for which this border insets value applies.

```
public abstract boolean isBorderOpaque()
```

This method returns whether the border is opaque. If the border is opaque, it is responsible for filling in its own background when painting.

To make implementing borders easier, Swing provides the AbstractBorder class. This class implements Border and provides a few convenience methods. To implement your border, you can subclass AbstractBorder, return the correct set of insets, and implement the paintBorder methods.

As an example of a custom border we have created a subclass of AbstractBorder that is created with a set of insets and draws triangles to fill these insets. The code for this custom border is as follows:

```
import com.sun.java.swing.*;
import com.sun.java.swing.border.*;
import java.awt.event.*;
import java.awt.*;

public class TriBorder extends AbstractBorder
{
    Insets ins;

    private TriBorder()
    {
    }

    public TriBorder(int top,int left,int bottom,int right)
    {
        ins = new Insets(top,left,bottom,right);
    }

    public TriBorder(Insets i)
    {
        ins=i;
    }

    public Insets getBorderInsets(Component c)
    {
        return ins;
    }

    public void paintBorder(Component c, Graphics g,
                            int x, int y, int width, int height)
    {
        int triW,triH;
        int i,max;
        int xp[],yp[];

        xp = new int[4];
        yp = new int[4];
```

```
g.setColor(Color.black);

//Draw the triangles on the top

triW = ins.left;
triH = ins.top;
max = triW + x + width;

for(i=x;i<max;i+=triW)
{
    xp[0] = i;
    xp[1] = i+(triW/2);
    xp[2] = i+triW;
    xp[3] = i;

    yp[0] = y+triH;
    yp[1] = y;
    yp[2] = y+triH;
    yp[3] = y+triH;

    g.fillPolygon(xp,yp,4);
}

//Draw the triangles on the bottom

triW = ins.left;
triH = ins.bottom;
max = triW + x + width;

for(i=x;i<max;i+=triW)
{
    xp[0] = i;
    xp[1] = i+(triW/2);
    xp[2] = i+triW;
    xp[3] = i;

    yp[0] = y+height;
    yp[1] = y+height-triH;
    yp[2] = y+height;
    yp[3] = y+height;

    g.fillPolygon(xp,yp,4);
}
```

```
            //Draw the triangles on the left

            triW = ins.left;
            triH = ins.top;
            max = y + height - triH;

            for(i=y+triH;i<max;i+=triH)
            {
                xp[0] = x;
                xp[1] = x+(triW/2);
                xp[2] = x+triW;
                xp[3] = x;

                yp[0] = i+triH;
                yp[1] = i;
                yp[2] = i+triH;
                yp[3] = i+triH;

                g.fillPolygon(xp,yp,4);
            }

            //Draw the triangles on the left

            triW = ins.right;
            triH = ins.top;
            max = y + height - triH;

            for(i=y+triH;i<max;i+=triH)
            {
                xp[0] = x+width-triW;
                xp[1] = x+width-(triW/2);
                xp[2] = x+width;
                xp[3] = x+width-triW;

                yp[0] = i+triH;
                yp[1] = i;
                yp[2] = i+triH;
                yp[3] = i+triH;

                g.fillPolygon(xp,yp,4);
            }
        }
    }
```

Figure 3.13 Custom border example.

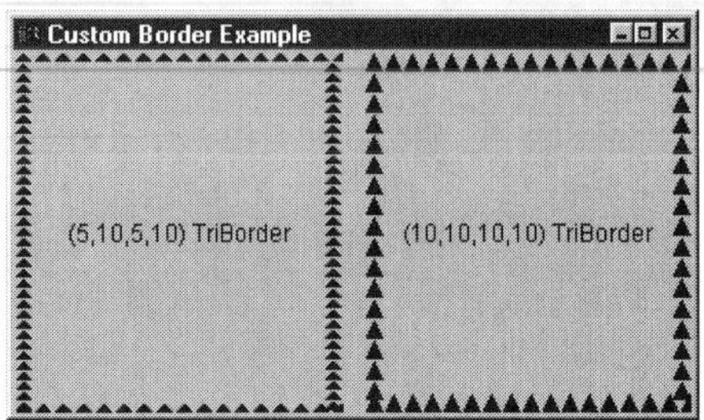

We have also created a small example program, pictured in Figure 3.13, that creates two TriBorders and assigns them to labels.

```
import com.sun.java.swing.*;
import com.sun.java.swing.border.*;
import java.awt.event.*;
import java.awt.*;

public class CBorderExample extends JPanel
{
    public CBorderExample()
    {
        Border border;
        JLabel label;

        setLayout(new GridLayout(1,2,10,10));

        border = new TriBorder(5,10,5,10);
        label = new JLabel("(5,10,5,10) TriBorder",JLabel.CENTER);
        label.setBorder(border);
        add(label);

        border = new TriBorder(10,10,10,10);
        label = new JLabel("(10,10,10,10) TriBorder",JLabel.CENTER);
        label.setBorder(border);
        add(label);
    }

    public Dimension getPreferredSize()
    {
        return new Dimension(350, 200);
```

```
    }

    public static void main(String s[])
    {
        JFrame frame = new JFrame("Custom Border Example");
        CBorderExample panel = new CBorderExample();

        frame.setDefaultCloseOperation(JFrame.DO_NOTHING_ON_CLOSE);
        frame.setForeground(Color.black);
        frame.setBackground(Color.lightGray);
        frame.getContentPane().add(panel,"Center");

        frame.setSize(panel.getPreferredSize());
        frame.setVisible(true);
    }
}
```

Border Factory

Finally, Swing provides a class called BorderFactory that provides static methods for creating borders. The interesting feature for these methods is that they try to use shared-border objects rather than creating new ones. If you use a lot of the same type of border, with the same attributes, you may want to take advantage of the BorderFactory class to reduce memory usage and object creation overhead.

Style Guidelines

The decision to use layout managers or to position components manually depends on whether your user interface can be resized. For an applet, the interface is usually fixed in size, so positioning each element by hand may be acceptable. If the applet creates an external window, you are writing an application, or you use internal frames, however, using a layout manager is probably easier. Without a layout manager you duplicate existing code to support resizing. Even though each layout manager is fairly limited in its capability, you can combine them to create practically any user interface layout that you need.

In general, you should use horizontal and vertical gaps to separate components inside a layout-managed area. This is also true when you combine layout managers. Provide space between the containers that are used to organize the user interface. Pick a gap size, like 5, 10, or 12, and use it consistently. This technique adds a professional polish to your user interface because all of the elements are spaced similarly.

When possible, and when aesthetically pleasing, use borders to visually organize your interface. One great place to use a border is around a set of check boxes or radio buttons that control a specific function in the program. You might also use them to set various forms apart from each other. Be careful to avoid using too many borders as you may fragment the interface and make it hard for users to find what they are looking for. Moderation is definitely one of the watchwords of layout management and user-interface design in Swing.

Keep in mind that users may need to move the mouse between elements or follow the cursor as they press the Tab key. Use this knowledge to organize your interface in a way that makes it easy for users to see what they are doing. Help them to move to the next task quickly and efficiently.

Buttons, Actions, and Mouse Events

4

Buttons are probably the most common and simple component in user-interface design. The concept of a button shows up on dialog boxes, in tool bars, and in menus. Swing provides a number of useful button types: the common press-release button, a toggle button, a check box, and a radio button. Later we will see that menu items are also a special kind of button.

Visually a button is a component that has a text label and an image, either of which is optional. When a button is pressed and released, an ActionEvent is sent to all registered ActionListeners. Programmers can also handle the mouse events for a button or any other Swing component directly by using the delegation event model discussed in Chapter 2. In this chapter, we discuss buttons, the actions they create, and the mechanisms used to notify the button of the mouse events that trigger an action.

Buttons

Even though the concept of a button is general, there are several specific kinds. The Swing designers decided to create a separate class for each button type. To maximize code reuse and to reduce learning time, all buttons share a common superclass. All buttons are descendants of an abstract class called AbstractButton. This abstract class defines most of the methods for a button. You don't create instances of AbstractButton; you create instances of its subclasses. The subclasses are JButton, JToggleButton, JCheckBox, and JRadioButton. The relationship between AbstractButton and its subclasses is shown in Figure 4.1.

By providing the AbstractButton class, the Swing designers were able to minimize the code required to implement each of the standard button classes. This approach improves performance and provides a single location for most of the functionality and learning time associated with buttons.

Buttons display two types of information: graphic images and text. Both of these items are optional. You can have a button with only text or only graphics. Also, the text and graphics can change based on user interaction. For instance, a button image may change to acknowledge the click visually when the user presses the button. A button's text conveys an action that the user can expect the button

Figure 4.1 The button class hierarchy.

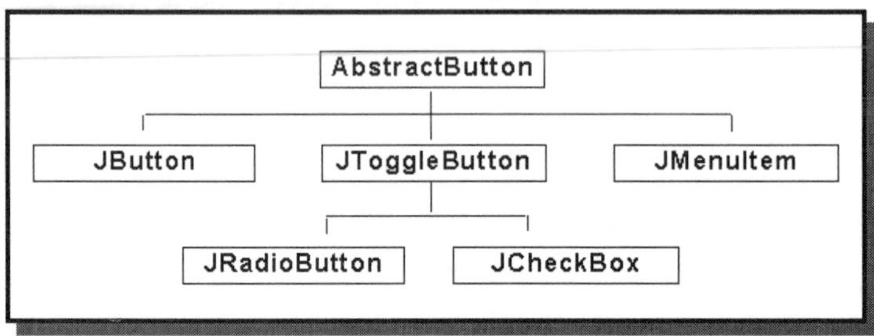

to cause when it is activated. AbstractButton provides an interface that positions the text in the button relative to the image and borders of the button. This positioning allows you to control whether the text is left of the graphic, on top of it, below it, or to the right of it. It allows you to choose if the text and graphic are aligned toward each side or centered.

The position of the text and icon relative to the button's border is specified using the methods:

```
public void setHorizontalAlignment(int align);
public void setVerticalAlignment(int align);
```

The argument "align" is one of the static variables: TOP, BOTTOM, CENTER, LEFT, or RIGHT. These variables are defined in the interface SwingConstants, as implemented by AbstractButton. The default value for both directions is CENTER. This alignment affects both a button's label and its icon. An example displaying all nine text and label alignments is pictured in Figure 4.2.

Figure 4.2 Button text labels.

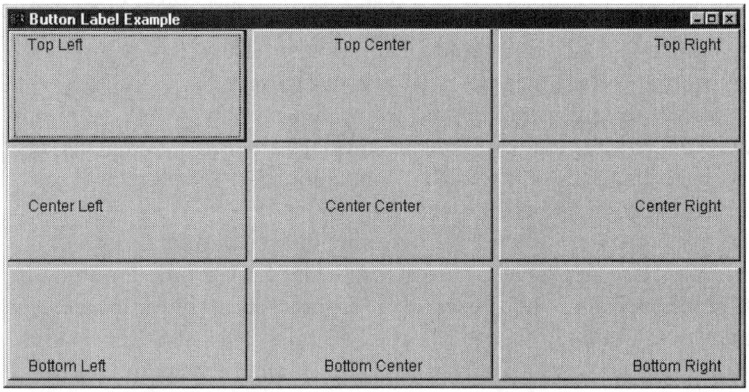

The relationship between the label and icon is assigned using the methods:

```
public void setHorizontalTextPosition(int textPosition);
public void setVerticalTextPosition(int textPosition);
```

An example of the nine possible combinations for these text positions is pictured in Figure 4.3.

Buttons can have seven icons associated with them. They are:

Default. This icon is displayed when the button is drawn on the screen, not pressed, and does not have the mouse over it.

Selected. This icon is used by toggle-style buttons and is displayed when the button is selected.

Pressed. This icon is used when a button is pressed before it is released.

Disabled. This icon is displayed when the button is disabled.

Disabled selected. This icon is displayed when a selected button is disabled.

Rollover. This icon is displayed when the mouse is moved over a button before it is pressed. If the mouse is moved off the button, the default icon is redisplayed.

Rollover selected. This icon is displayed when the mouse is moved over a selected button.

To set the icon for a button, use one of the following methods:

```
public void setIcon(Icon i);
public void setDisabledIcon(Icon i);
public void setDisabledSelectedIcon(Icon i);
public void setPressedIcon(Icon i);
public void setRolloverIcon(Icon i);
public void setRolloverSelectedIcon(Icon i);
public void setSelectedIcon(Icon i);
```

Figure 4.3 Button text positions.

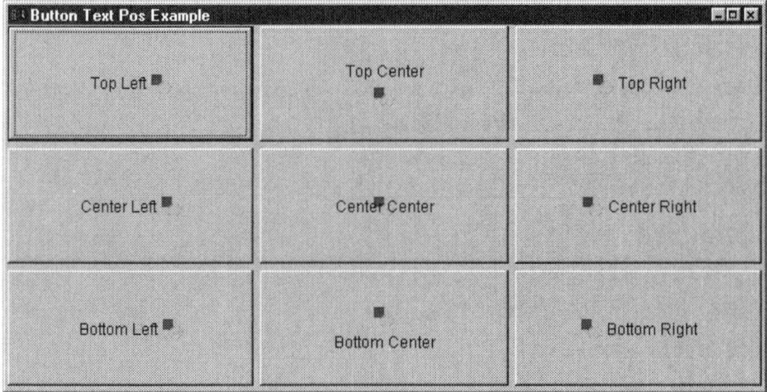

The following example creates a panel that displays several buttons. The example program uses most of the icon types previously listed. There are three buttons. The first button displays an image that changes when the user moves (or rolls) the cursor over the button and changes to another image when the button is pressed. A rollover Icon is often used to highlight the button so the user knows the button is selectable. The second button has an image displayed when the button is disabled. If this button is enabled, this image is replaced with the default button image. The third button is a toggle button. When pressed, a toggle button remains in either the on or off state, similar to a light switch.

```
import com.sun.java.swing.*;
import java.awt.event.*;
import java.awt.*;

public class ButtonExample extends JPanel
{
    public ButtonExample()
    {
        ImageIcon buttonImage=new ImageIcon("images/b.gif");
        ImageIcon pressImage=new ImageIcon("images/p.gif");
        ImageIcon selImage=new ImageIcon("images/p.gif");
        ImageIcon disabledImage=new ImageIcon("images/d.gif");
        ImageIcon rolloverImage=new ImageIcon("images/r.gif");
        ImageIcon selrolloverImage=new ImageIcon("images/l.gif");
        AbstractButton button;
        Font font;

        //Make the default font bigger, and buffer the example
        font = new Font("Serif",Font.PLAIN,16);
        setFont(font);
        setDoubleBuffered(true);

        setLayout(new GridLayout(1,3,5,5));

        button = new JButton();
        button.setIcon(buttonImage);
        button.setPressedIcon(pressImage);
        button.setRolloverIcon(rolloverImage);
        add(button);

        button = new JButton();
        button.setIcon(buttonImage);
        button.setDisabledIcon(disabledImage);
        button.setEnabled(false);
```

```
        add(button);


        button = new JToggleButton();
        button.setIcon(buttonImage);
        button.setSelectedIcon(selImage);
        button.setRolloverIcon(rolloverImage);
        button.setRolloverSelectedIcon(selrolloverImage);
        add(button);
    }

    public Dimension getPreferredSize()
    {
        return new Dimension(200, 70);
    }

    public static void main(String s[])
    {
        JFrame frame = new JFrame("Button Example");
        ButtonExample panel = new ButtonExample();

        frame.setDefaultCloseOperation(JFrame.DO_NOTHING_ON_CLOSE);
        frame.setForeground(Color.black);
        frame.setBackground(Color.lightGray);
        frame.getContentPane().add(panel,"Center");

        frame.setSize(panel.getPreferredSize());
        frame.setVisible(true);
    }
}
```

Figure 4.4 shows the button icons we created.

Because you can control the placement and style of the graphic and text of a button, the appearance of a button is limited only by your imagination. Keep in mind that the Button's UI object defines the current look and feel. Not all looks and feels will use all of the icon styles.

Figure 4.4 Button icons.

JButton

JButton is the Swing replacement for the AWT Button class. JButtons are basic push buttons. The user presses the button; the button provides some visual feedback and then notifies the program of the user's action. We have already used JButtons in our previous examples in this chapter.

JButton extends AbstractButton and has constructors that allow you to create a button with a text label, a graphic, or both. The constructors are shown in Table 4.1.

JButton uses an object that implements the ButtonUI interface to define its look and feel. ButtonUI extends the ComponentUI interface and adds the method:

```
public abstract Insets getDefaultMargin(AbstractButton b)
```

The default margin is used to create the button's initial insets if none is provided. The default margin is defined by the current look and feel. These insets are then used to position the label inside the button. JButton uses an object that implements the ButtonModel interface to store its state. A button's state is pretty simple. Basically, it stores that a button is on or off.

JToggleButton

JToggleButton also extends AbtractButton. Items of this type retain their state. Unlike JButton, when a JToggleButton is pressed it stays in that state—pressed—until it is pressed again.

The creation methods for a JToggleButton are shown in Table 4.2.

The JToggleButton class uses a ToggleButtonUI to paint itself. The ToggleButtonUI inherits from ButtonUI and adds no new methods. Like the JButton, JToggleButton uses a ButtonModel to store its state.

JCheckBox

JCheckBox extends JToggleButton. A CheckBox uses a look-and-feel specific icon to indicate that it is on or off. The JCheckBox class is similar to the CheckBox class in AWT 1.1. In AWT 1.1, however, CheckBoxes were used both for check boxes and radio buttons. Also in version 1.1, a CheckBox could belong

Table 4.1 Button Constructors

Method	Function
JButton()	Creates a button with no set text or icon.
JButton(Icon)	Creates a button with an icon.
JButton(String)	Creates a button with text.
JButton(String, Icon)	Creates a button with text and an icon.

Table 4.2 JToggleButton Constructors

Method	Function
JToggleButton()	Creates a toggle button with no set text.
JToggleButton(Icon)	Creates a toggle button with an icon.
JToggleButton(Glyph, boolean)	Creates a toggle button with an icon that uses the Boolean to specify if the button is selected.
JToggleButton(String)	Creates a toggle button with text.
JToggleButton(String, boolean)	Creates a toggle button that uses the Boolean to specify if the button is selected.
JToggleButton(String, Icon)	Creates a toggle button.
JToggleButton(String, Icon, boolean)	Creates a toggle button that uses the Boolean to specify if the button is selected.

to a group in which only one check box was selected at a time. In Swing, this capability is not supported. A new class, JRadioButton, has been added to perform this task. Check boxes are simply on/off buttons that exist individually. Radio buttons belong to a group. This approach is a logical separation of UI elements, especially because the two types of components appear differently to the user. In the case of a JCheckBox, the user interface usually involves a check box of some kind, although you can set the button up to use images, or some other icon to indicate selection.

The constructors for a JCheckBox are shown in Table 4.3.

Table 4.3 JCheckBox Constructors

Method	Function
JCheckBox()	Creates a check box with no set text or image.
JCheckBox(Icon)	Creates a check box with an icon.
JCheckBox(Icon, boolean)	Creates a check box with an icon. Setting the Boolean to true turns the check box on, false turns it off.
JCheckBox(String)	Creates a check box with text.
JCheckBox(String, boolean)	Creates a check box with text. Setting the Boolean to true turns the check box on, false turns it off.
JCheckBox(String, Icon)	Creates a check box with a text label and an icon.
JCheckBox(String, Icon, boolean)	Creates a check box with a text label and an icon. Setting the Boolean to true turns the check box on, false turns it off.

A JCheckBox uses a CheckBoxUI object to paint itself. CheckBoxUI extends ToggleButtonUI and adds no new methods. JCheckBox relies on a ButtonModel to retain its state.

Our next example creates two check boxes. The first is a standard check box with a text label containing the string "Save." The other check box uses icons to represent the checked (w_check.gif) and unchecked (no_check.gif) appearance.

```
import com.sun.java.swing.*;
import java.awt.event.*;
import java.awt.*;

public class CheckboxExample extends JPanel
{
    public CheckboxExample()
    {
        ImageIcon buttonImage=new ImageIcon("images/no_check.gif");
        ImageIcon selImage=new ImageIcon("images/w_check.gif");
        AbstractButton button;
        Font font;

        //Make the default font bigger, and buffer the example
        font = new Font("Serif",Font.PLAIN,16);
        setFont(font);
        setDoubleBuffered(true);

        setLayout(new GridLayout(1,2,5,5));

        button = new JCheckBox("Save");
        add(button);

        button = new JCheckBox(buttonImage);
        button.setSelectedIcon(selImage);
        add(button);
    }

    public Dimension getPreferredSize()
    {
        return new Dimension(200, 70);
    }

    public static void main(String s[])
    {
        JFrame frame = new JFrame("Checkbox Example");
```

```
        CheckboxExample panel = new CheckboxExample();

        frame.setDefaultCloseOperation(JFrame.DO_NOTHING_ON_CLOSE);
        frame.setForeground(Color.black);
        frame.setBackground(Color.lightGray);
        frame.getContentPane().add(panel,"Center");

        frame.setSize(panel.getPreferredSize());
        frame.setVisible(true);
    }
}
```

Figure 4.5 shows the two check boxes that we created.

JRadioButton

JRadioButton extends JToggleButton. In Swing, a JRadioButton object is a component that displays both a radio-style icon and a text label. Radio buttons are usually displayed in groups. Only one radio button in a group is selected at a time. This technique is useful for giving a user a set of options that are always visible where only one choice is valid at a time. To put radio buttons in a group use the ButtonGroup class. Button groups form a contract between several buttons. When a button is selected it tells the group, which in turn notifies the other buttons in the group. Only one button in the group can be selected at a time, and the currently selected button is automatically deselected if the user chooses a different button in the group. The following code shows how to create a ButtonGroup and add a button to it:

```
ButtonGroup bg = new ButtonGroup();
bg.add(new JRadioButton("I vote for Bill"));
bg.add(new JRadioButton("I vote For Jane"));
```

The constructors for a JRadioButton are shown in Table 4.4.

JRadioButton uses a RadioButtonUI object to paint itself. The RadioButtonUI extends ButtonUI and adds no new methods. JRadioButton also uses a ButtonModel to retain its state.

The following example creates two sets of radio buttons. The first is a standard set of radio buttons, each with a text label. The other set uses icons to define

Figure 4.5 JCheckBoxes.

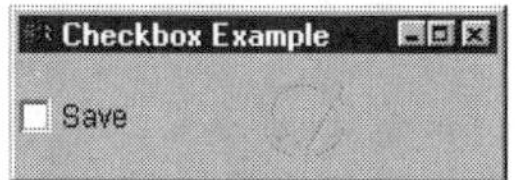

Table 4.4 JRadioButton Constructors

Method	Function
JRadioButton()	Creates a radio button with no set text or image.
JRadioButton(Icon)	Creates a radio button with an icon.
JRadioButton(Icon, boolean)	Creates a radio button with an icon. Setting the Boolean to true turns the radio button on, false turns it off.
JRadioButton(String)	Creates a radio button with text.
JRadioButton(String, boolean)	Creates a radio button with text. Setting the Boolean to true turns the radio button on, false turns it off.
JRadioButton(String, Icon)	Creates a radio button with a text label and an icon.
JRadioButton(String, Icon, boolean)	Creates a radio button with a text label and an icon. Setting the Boolean to true turns the radio button on, false turns it off.

the selected and normal appearance of the radio buttons. Note that by default no button is selected to begin with. If you want to have a default radio button selected, you must do this yourself.

```
import com.sun.java.swing.*;
import java.awt.event.*;
import java.awt.*;

public class RadioExample extends JPanel
{
    public RadioExample()
    {
        ImageIcon buttonImage=new ImageIcon("images/ex.gif");
        ImageIcon selImage=new ImageIcon("images/check.gif");
        AbstractButton button;
        ButtonGroup group;
        Font font;

        //Make the default font bigger, and buffer the example
        font = new Font("Serif",Font.PLAIN,16);
        setFont(font);
        setDoubleBuffered(true);

        setLayout(new GridLayout(2,2,5,5));
```

```
        group = new ButtonGroup();

        button = new JRadioButton("Save");
        group.add(button);
        add(button);

        button = new JRadioButton("Delete");
        group.add(button);
        add(button);

        group = new ButtonGroup();

        button = new JRadioButton(buttonImage);
        button.setSelectedIcon(selImage);
        group.add(button);
        add(button);

        button = new JRadioButton(buttonImage);
        button.setSelectedIcon(selImage);
        group.add(button);
        add(button);
    }

    public Dimension getPreferredSize()
    {
        return new Dimension(250, 100);
    }

    public static void main(String s[])
    {
        JFrame frame = new JFrame("RadioButton Example");
        RadioExample panel = new RadioExample();

        frame.setDefaultCloseOperation(JFrame.DO_NOTHING_ON_CLOSE);
        frame.setForeground(Color.black);
        frame.setBackground(Color.lightGray);
        frame.getContentPane().add(panel,"Center");

        frame.setSize(panel.getPreferredSize());
        frame.setVisible(true);
    }
}
```

Figure 4.6 shows the two radio buttons that we created.

Figure 4.6 JRadioButtons.

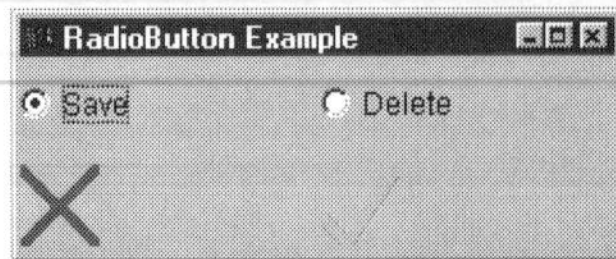

Action Events

We have looked at creating a button and displaying it. Now we will look at the mechanism and objects used to handle the process of responding to a user activating a button. When a user clicks a button or presses a keyboard equivalent for that button, the button activates by sending an action event to a handler.

Action events are used to represent high-level user activity like pressing a button or pressing the Return key in a text field. Components can use action events to hide the low-level mechanics of dealing with user events from a programmer, allowing them to focus on the user's intent. In the Swing package several classes use actions. These actions are listed in Table 4.5 along with the user activity that triggers the action.

One important consideration when using actions is that the component, not the programmer, defines when the action is triggered. The programmer's job is to read the documentation of a component to determine the action trigger and then program the code accordingly. Components that define action semantics use the ActionListener interface to notify other objects that an action has occurred. The ActionListener defines a single method called actionPerformed. The complete signature for actionPerformed is as follows:

```
public void actionPerformed(ActionEvent e);
```

The argument for actionPerformed is an ActionEvent object. ActionEvent is a subclass of java.awt.AWTEvent, which extends java.util.EventObject. Like all events, ActionEvents have a source. In the case of an action, the source is the object that triggered the action. In other words, the source for a button-press

Table 4.5 Swing Action Events

Action Event	User Activity
JButton	The user presses the button.
JCheckBox	The user selects the check box.
JMenuItem	The user selects the item.
JTextField	The user presses the Return key, while the text field is accepting text.

action is the button. Listeners can retrieve this source from the event object using the method getSource, which takes no arguments, as shown here:

```
public Object getSource();
```

To register for action event notifications, a programmer adds a listener to the interesting components' list of action listeners. The method for adding action listeners is addActionListener and takes a single argument—the listener, as shown here:

```
public void addActionListener(ActionListener al);
```

Most components that maintain action listeners also keep track of a string called an action command. This string is used in the creation of the components' ActionEvent objects and can be used by a programmer to identify the object that created the event. Use the ActionEvent method getActionCommand to determine the command for a particular event.

```
public String getActionCommand();
```

The following example, pictured in Figure 4.7, uses action events to print messages to the console when a radio button is pressed, a button is pressed, or a text field has the Return key pressed in it.

This example is implemented as a subclass of JPanel. A main class method creates a Frame for the panel and displays it. A helper class called WindowCloser is used to close the window when the close box is selected. Notice that Actions implements the ActionListener interface and is assigned as an ActionListener for each user-interface element. Actions implements the method actionPerformed, which gets called by the UI elements that have Actions registered as an ActionListener.

```
import java.util.*;
import java.awt.*;
import java.awt.event.*;
import com.sun.java.swing.*;
import com.sun.java.swing.text.*;

public class Actions extends JPanel
implements ActionListener
{
    public Actions()
```

Figure 4.7 Using actions to handle events.

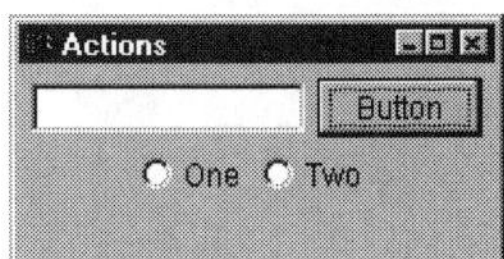

```
{
    JTextField field;
    JButton button;
    JRadioButton radioButton;
    ButtonGroup grp;

    setBackground(Color.lightGray);
    /*
     * Turn on buffering to reduce flicker.
     */
    setDoubleBuffered(true);

    field = new JTextField(10);
    field.addActionListener(this);
    field.setActionCommand("Text Field Activated");
    add(field);

    button = new JButton("Button");
    button.addActionListener(this);
    button.setActionCommand("Button Activated");
    add(button);

    grp = new ButtonGroup();

    radioButton =  new JRadioButton("One");
    radioButton.addActionListener(this);
    radioButton.setActionCommand("One Activated");
    grp.add(radioButton);
    add(radioButton);

    radioButton =  new JRadioButton("Two");
    radioButton.addActionListener(this);
    radioButton.setActionCommand("Two Activated");
    grp.add(radioButton);
    add(radioButton);
}

public void actionPerformed(ActionEvent e)
{
    String cmd;
    Object source;

    source = e.getSource();
```

```
            cmd = e.getActionCommand();

            System.out.println("Action: "
                                +cmd
                                +"\n\tperformed by: "+source);
            System.out.println();
        }

        public Dimension getPreferredSize()
        {
            return new Dimension(200, 100);
        }

        public static void main(String s[])
        {
            JFrame frame = new JFrame("Actions");
            Actions panel = new Actions();

            frame.setForeground(Color.black);
            frame.setBackground(Color.lightGray);
            frame.addWindowListener(new WindowCloser());
            frame.getContentPane().add(panel,"Center");

            frame.setSize(panel.getPreferredSize());
            frame.setVisible(true);
        }
    }

    class WindowCloser extends WindowAdapter
    {
        public void windowClosing(WindowEvent e)
        {
            Window win = e.getWindow();
            win.setVisible(false);
            win.dispose();
            System.exit(0);
        }
    }
```

We have highlighted some of the key portions of this example in bold to draw your attention to them. Although this is a simple example, it demonstrates how to define an ActionListener, add it to a component, and respond to notification of action events. In future examples, we use these techniques extensively to implement the user-interface portions of our programs.

In Chapter 2, we discussed the concept of an Action object. The Action interface extends ActionListener to include methods for managing text and icons. You can use Action objects as ActionListeners for buttons and text fields in the same way that you can use them in a menu.

MouseEvents

A mouse event is generated when the user interacts with the mouse. Mouse events include mouse movements and clicking and releasing mouse buttons. Each mouse-event type includes information about the event such as the screen coordinate where a mouse was located when the user clicked the right mouse button.

Swing provides two mechanisms for handling mouse events. First, a low-level event processing architecture allows a component to see and react to all mouse events. The second mechanism for handling mouse events is the delegation model that uses listeners. In both techniques, mouse events have been separated into two categories: mouse motion events and everything else. Mouse motion events include the mouse moving over a component and the mouse being dragged with the button pressed on a component. Other mouse events include a button press or release and the mouse entering or exiting a component's borders. Although both of these mechanisms are provided, JavaSoft suggests that programmers rely on the standard delegation model whenever possible. This model allows programmers to customize a component's behavior without subclassing.

Mouse events are initially processed by a method called processEvent. All of a component's events are filtered through this fundamental method. The processEvent method separates mouse events from mouse motion events and forwards their care to a pair of helper methods called processMouseEvent and processMouseMotionEvent. Custom components that want to handle these events should override the appropriate method. In your subclass implementation of any event-processing method, however, you should call the inherited version via super. The Component classes version of these processing methods notifies listeners of the events. If you don't use the inherited version, then you are responsible for notifying the listeners.

To improve performance, Swing is designed to ignore events in which no object is interested. In the case of mouse events, this means that the Component class's processEvent method ignores mouse events if not told to do otherwise. Events are enabled and disabled using the methods enableEvents and disableEvents.

```
public void enableEvents(long mask);
public void disableEvents(long mask);
```

These methods take as arguments a mask defined from class variables in the class AWTEvent.

```
AWTEvent.MOUSE_EVENT_MASK
AWTEvent.MOUSE_MOTION_EVENT_MASK
```

The technique for enabling and disabling mouse events, as well as processing mouse events, is demonstrated in the following subclass of JCanvas called NoMouseCanvas. This class defines a canvas that draws itself and prints a message when it processes a mouse event. NoMouseCanvas provides two public methods for turning on and off mouse-event processing. These methods are used by a later example.

```
class NoMouseCanvas extends JComponent
{
    public NoMouseCanvas()
    {
        enableMouse();
    }

    public void paint(Graphics g)
    {
        Rectangle bounds = getBounds();
        g.setColor(Color.blue);
        g.fillRect(0,0,bounds.width,bounds.height);
    }

    public void processMouseEvent(MouseEvent evt)
    {
        System.out.println("Got mouse event");
        System.out.println("\tx="+evt.getX());
        System.out.println("\ty="+evt.getY());
        System.out.println("\tclicks="+evt.getClickCount());
        super.processMouseEvent(evt);
    }

    public void processMouseMotionEvent(MouseEvent evt)
    {
        System.out.println("Got mouse motion event");
        System.out.println("\tx="+evt.getX());
        System.out.println("\ty="+evt.getY());
        super.processMouseEvent(evt);
    }

    public void enableMouse()
    {
        System.out.println("\t*** Enabling Mouse ***");
        enableEvents(AWTEvent.MOUSE_EVENT_MASK);
        enableEvents(AWTEvent.MOUSE_MOTION_EVENT_MASK);
    }
```

```
    public void disableMouse()
    {
        System.out.println("\t*** Disabling Mouse ***");
        disableEvents(AWTEvent.MOUSE_EVENT_MASK);
        disableEvents(AWTEvent.MOUSE_MOTION_EVENT_MASK);
    }
}
```

Although mouse events can be processed directly, JavaSoft suggests that programmers use the standard delegation model for all events, including mouse events. To handle all mouse events via listeners, you need to implement two interfaces, MouseListener and MouseMotionListener, found in java.awt.event package. You can implement these listeners in one class or two. By separating mouse actions and mouse motion events, your components do not have to process all of the move and drag events associated with a component if they do not want to process them.

As we said, listeners are added to a component using the methods addMouseListener and addMouseMotionListener, respectively. An object implementing the MouseListener or MouseMotionListener interface can be used to handle mouse events. The methods used to assign a mouse listener are listed below.

```
public void addMouseListener(MouseListener ml);
public void addMouseMotionListener(MouseMotionListener ml);
```

Adding a listener automatically enables the associated events. In other words, when you add a MouseListener, the component automatically has the AWTEvent.MOUSE_EVENT_MASK enabled if it is not already enabled.

TIP

Always call the inherited version of processMouseEvent or processMouseMotionEvent to notify listeners. Use listeners instead of raw mouse-event processing whenever possible. Otherwise, the Component may not behave properly.

The next example shows a subclass of JCanvas called NoMouseListenerCanvas. This special canvas is similar to the previous example called NoMouseCanvas. In this case, the canvas acts as a listener for its own mouse events and prints messages based on the events that occur. Two public methods are provided to turn mouse-event processing on and off by adding and removing the listeners.

```
class NoMouseListenerCanvas extends JComponent
implements MouseListener, MouseMotionListener
{
    public NoMouseListenerCanvas()
```

```
    {
        enableMouse();
    }

    public void paint(Graphics g)
    {
        Rectangle bounds = getBounds();
        g.setColor(Color.red);
        g.fillRect(0,0,bounds.width,bounds.height);
    }

    public void mouseClicked(MouseEvent evt)
    {
        System.out.println("\tMouse clicked");
    }

    public void mouseEntered(MouseEvent evt)
    {
        System.out.println("\tMouse entered");
    }

    public void mouseExited(MouseEvent evt)
    {
        System.out.println("\tMouse exited");
    }

    public void mousePressed(MouseEvent evt)
    {
        System.out.println("\tMouse pressed");
    }

    public void mouseReleased(MouseEvent evt)
    {
        System.out.println("\tMouse released");
    }

    public void mouseDragged(MouseEvent evt)
    {
        System.out.println("\tMouse dragged");
    }

    public void mouseMoved(MouseEvent evt)
    {
        System.out.println("\tMouse moved");
```

```
    }

    public void enableMouse()
    {
        System.out.println("\t*** Enabling Mouse"
                              +" Listener***");
        addMouseListener(this);
        addMouseMotionListener(this);
    }

    public void disableMouse()
    {
        System.out.println("\t*** Disabling Mouse"
                              +" Listener***");
        removeMouseListener(this);
        removeMouseMotionListener(this);
    }
}
```

To test the NoMouseCanvas and NoMouseListenerCanvas classes, we have written a small subclass of JPanel that creates one of each canvas type and then displays them. A check box is included to enable and disable mouse processing. Some template code also puts the panel in a window and displays it. This example is pictured in Figure 4.8.

```
public class NoMice extends JPanel
implements ItemListener
{
    NoMouseCanvas target;
    NoMouseListenerCanvas target2;

    public NoMice()
    {
        JPanel tmpPanel = new JPanel();
        JCheckBox onOff = new JCheckBox("Enabled",true);

        target = new NoMouseCanvas();
        target2 = new NoMouseListenerCanvas();

        onOff.addItemListener(this);

        tmpPanel.add(onOff);

        setLayout(new BorderLayout());
```

```
        add(tmpPanel,"South");

        tmpPanel = new JPanel();
        tmpPanel.setLayout(new GridLayout(1,2));
        tmpPanel.add(target);
        tmpPanel.add(target2);
        add(tmpPanel,"Center");
    }

    public void itemStateChanged(ItemEvent e)
    {
        if(e.getStateChange() == ItemEvent.SELECTED)
        {
            target.enableMouse();
            target2.enableMouse();
        }
        else
        {
            target.disableMouse();
            target2.disableMouse();
        }
    }


    public Dimension getPreferredSize()
    {
        return new Dimension(200, 100);
    }

    public static void main(String s[])
    {
        JFrame frame = new JFrame("Mouse Events");
        NoMice panel = new NoMice();

        frame.setForeground(Color.black);
        frame.setBackground(Color.lightGray);
        frame.addWindowListener(new WindowCloser());
        frame.getContentPane().add(panel,"Center");

        frame.setSize(panel.getPreferredSize());
        frame.setVisible(true);
    }
}
```

Figure 4.8 Handling mouse events in the NoMouseCanvas and NoMouseListenerCanvas.

```
class WindowCloser extends WindowAdapter
{
    public void windowClosing(WindowEvent e)
    {
        Window win = e.getWindow();
        win.setVisible(false);
        win.dispose();
        System.exit(0);
    }
}
```

In general, you should use the mouse listener interfaces to customize your components. Save direct event processing for situations that cannot be managed using the listener mechanism.

In our final mouse-event example, shown in Figure 4.9, we process both mouse and key events. This example displays a single character wherever the mouse is pressed. The character is changed when the user types on the keyboard. The MouseEvent object is used to determine the location of the character.

```
import java.util.*;
import java.awt.*;
import java.awt.event.*;
import com.sun.java.swing.*;
import com.sun.java.swing.text.*;

class KeyCatcher extends KeyAdapter
{
    Target target;

    public KeyCatcher(Target tp)
    {
        target = tp;
    }

    public void keyTyped(KeyEvent e)
    {
        target.setChar(e.getKeyChar());
```

```
    }
}

class MouseCatcher extends MouseAdapter
{
    Target target;

    public MouseCatcher(Target tp)
    {
        target = tp;
    }

    public void mouseClicked(MouseEvent e)
    {
        target.setLoc(e.getPoint());
        target.requestFocus();
    }
}

class Target extends JComponent
{
    char curChar[];
    Point curLoc;

    public Target()
    {
        curChar = new char[1];
        curChar[0] = 'x';

        addKeyListener(new KeyCatcher(this));
        addMouseListener(new MouseCatcher(this));
    }

    public void setLoc(Point p)
    {
        curLoc = p;
        repaint();
    }

    public void setChar(char c)
    {
        curChar[0] = c;
    }

    public char curChar()
```

```
    {
        return curChar[0];
    }

    public void paint(Graphics g)
    {
        Rectangle bounds = getBounds();
        Font bigFont = new Font("Times-Roman",Font.PLAIN,24);

        g.setFont(bigFont);

        g.setColor(Color.white);
        g.fillRect(0,0,bounds.width,bounds.height);

        if(curLoc != null)
        {
            g.setColor(Color.black);
            g.drawChars(curChar,0,1,curLoc.x,curLoc.y);
        }
    }
}

public class TargetPractice extends JPanel
{
    public TargetPractice()
    {
        Target target = new Target();

        setLayout(new BorderLayout());
        add("Center",target);
    }

    public Dimension getPreferredSize()
    {
        return new Dimension(200, 200);
    }

    public static void main(String s[])
    {
        JFrame frame = new JFrame("TargetPractice");
        TargetPractice panel = new TargetPractice();

        frame.setForeground(Color.black);
        frame.setBackground(Color.lightGray);
        frame.addWindowListener(new WindowCloser());
```

Figure 4.9 Target practice.

```
        frame.getContentPane().add(panel,"Center");

        frame.setSize(panel.getPreferredSize());
        frame.setVisible(true);
    }
}

class WindowCloser extends WindowAdapter
{
    public void windowClosing(WindowEvent e)
    {
        Window win = e.getWindow();
        win.setVisible(false);
        win.dispose();
        System.exit(0);
    }
}
```

Notice that we used different objects to handle the mouse and key events. Moreover, the listeners are defined as subclasses of adapter classes to minimize the amount of code we need to write.

> **TIP**
>
> mouseUp and mouseDrag events are sent to the component that received the mouseDown event, even if the mouse is no longer over it.

Style Guidelines

When using buttons, organize related items together on the user interface. If you decide to use images with your buttons, keep in mind that bright colors attract attention; you probably don't want to use a red button for a rarely used option and a gray button for a frequently used option.

Another common issue when using images is that check boxes and radio buttons should still look like buttons. If you use an image that does not represent itself as a switch or check box of some sort, the user may not recognize these controls for what they are.

Radio buttons that share a button group should be placed together logically. Although the button group does not require the buttons to be in the same location, or even on the same window, users can be confused if the buttons are not visually grouped in some way. In Chapter 3, when we discussed borders, you saw how you could place a border around a group to organize the group's elements logically.

Actions are one of the main mechanisms for receiving user input. It's important to organize your code so that the actions do not overwhelm a single listener. In particular, you should use multiple listeners for all but the simplest interfaces. One easy way to do this is to use Action objects. Create a subclass of AbstractAction for each functional unit in your program. Implement the actionPerformed method for each action class to perform the necessary code, possibly messaging a more central controller-type object. Use instances of these action classes as listeners for buttons, tool bar items, and menus. This allows the same listener to participate in event handling for multiple controls but still separates your code functionally. An example of this technique appears in Chapter 8.

Finally, when processing mouse events, use listeners whenever possible. Although primitive, mouse-event handling is powerful and rarely necessary. Listeners can perform the same functionality in most cases. Listeners can also be used to implement mouse-event handling for a control that you did not write. For example, you can use a mouse listener to receive notifications of a mouse event on a button even before you receive the ActionEvent from that button. When we discuss keyboard events in Chapter 7, we will see that KeyListeners can also be used to listen for events on Swing controls. This is like listening for the Delete key on a list component.

Combo Boxes and Lists

5

A common UI requirement is to present users with a set of choices from which they can choose. The AWT, for instance, provides list and choice objects that let users select from a list of commands. Swing adds two key components for providing users with a set of choices. JComboBox provides a pop-up set of choices from which the user can choose one item. For example, in an airline reservation system you could use a JComboBox to allow the user to select from a list of source and destination cities. A JList provides a set of choices, which may be a scrolling list, from which the user can select one or more items. Both of these components rely on rendering objects to actually draw the interface for each item. These objects can be customized, and they can support icons or other adornments. The combo box also supports editors that allow users to add choices to the existing set.

JComboBox

JComboBox is similar to the Choice component in AWT 1.1, but it is more flexible. When the user clicks on a combo box it expands to reveal all the choices within it. The user can select an item from this list of possible choices, and the choice list closes with the newly selected item now displayed in the combo box. The default JComboBox, shown in Figure 5.1, displays text and is not editable. These features are configurable.

Use the default constructor JComboBox() to create a combo box. Once the combo box is created, add items using the addItem method to add an object to the end of the list or use the insertItemAt method to place an object at a certain location in the list.

```
public void addItem(Object anObject);
public void insertItemAt(Object anObject, int index);
```

Notice that the items are added as objects. JComboBox uses an object that implements the ListCellRenderer interface to display its list of possible values and the selected value. The default renderer uses the method toString to convert each object into a string before that string is displayed.

Figure 5.1 JComboBox.

You can remove objects from a combo box using the three methods shown in Table 5.1.

Once your combo box is created, you can manage the selected index by invoking setSelectIndex to specify which item should be selected in the combo box, or you can use getSelectedIndex to get the index of the currently selected item in the combo box, as shown here:

```
public void setSelectedIndex(int anIndex);
public int getSelectedIndex();
```

If you would rather use the actual object to set the selection, you can use the method setSelectedItem, passing in the object as a parameter. You can also use getSelectedItem to return the object currently selected. You can choose to use methods or the index methods, based on your implementation preference:

```
public void setSelectedItem(Object anObject);
public Object getSelectedItem();
```

An index of 0 indicates the first possible item. The index of the last possible item is determined by retrieving the total number of items and subtracting 1, using the following method:

```
public int getItemCount();
```

The combo box supports the use of arrow keys by default and provides a mechanism for jumping to an item based on the first letter in its string representation. This jumping mechanism is handled by default in the Windows look and feel, and it can be triggered programmatically using the following method:

```
public boolean selectWithKeyChar(char keyChar);
```

When you call this method, the combo box selects the first item that starts with the provided letter and returns true. If no item starts with that letter, the box does nothing and returns false.

The combo box displays items in a window that pops up when you press the combo box with your mouse. You can control the number of visible items in this list using the following method:

```
public void setMaximumRowCount(int count);
```

Table 5.1 JComboBox Removing Methods

Method	Function
public void removeItem(Object anObject);	Removes a specific object from the list.
public void removeItemAt(int anIndex);	Removes an object located at the anIndex.
public void removeAllItems();	Removes all objects from the list.

If more than the maximum number of items is possible, use a scroll bar to provide access to them.

We created the screenshot in Figure 5.1 using the following simple example of a combo box. In this example, we create a combo box using the default constructor and add three string objects to it: Gold, Silver, and Bronze.

```
import com.sun.java.swing.*;
import java.awt.event.*;
import java.awt.*;

public class SimpleComboExample extends JPanel
{
    public SimpleComboExample()
    {
        JComboBox comboBox;
        Font f;

        f = new Font("SanSerif",Font.PLAIN,24);
        setFont(f);
        setLayout(new BorderLayout());

        comboBox = new JComboBox();
        comboBox.setFont(f);

        comboBox.addItem("Gold");
        comboBox.addItem("Silver");
        comboBox.addItem("Bronze");

        add(comboBox,"Center");
    }

    public Dimension getPreferredSize()
    {
        return new Dimension(100, 60);
    }
```

```
    public static void main(String s[])
    {
        JFrame frame = new JFrame("SimpleComboBox Example");
        SimpleComboExample panel = new SimpleComboExample();

        frame.setDefaultCloseOperation(JFrame.DO_NOTHING_ON_CLOSE);
        frame.setForeground(Color.black);
        frame.setBackground(Color.lightGray);
        frame.getContentPane().add(panel,"Center");

        frame.setSize(panel.getPreferredSize());
        frame.setVisible(true);
    }
}
```

The default model for the JComboBox is ComboBoxDataModel, which extends the ListDataModel. The advantage of this model is that either object can be used to display the list of choices. The ComboBoxDataModel adds two methods to ListDataModel:

```
void setSelectedValue(Object anObject)
Object getSelectedValue()
```

The selected value is the value that has been selected among the possible values. This method is added in the data model because an editable JComboBox can have a current value that is not part of the possible values.

ComboBox Renderers

JComboBox's UI is a subclass of ComponentUI. The ComboBoxUI object uses ListCellRenderer objects to help it do its work. A ListCellRenderer is an object that displays the information in the JComboBox. The renderer must implement the following method from the ListCellRenderer interface:

```
public abstract Component getListCellRendererComponent(JList list,
                                                      Object value,
                                                      int index,
                                                      boolean isSelected,
                                                      boolean cellHasFocus)
```

This method returns a component that, when told to paint displays the appropriate representation of this object, for this list. In the following example, shown in Figure 5.2, a JComboBox is created and a custom render is created that draws a graphic to the left of the value. This example requires two classes: the custom renderer called MyRenderer and the code that creates the combo box and

Figure 5.2 JComboBox with a custom renderer.

assigns a renderer to it. The main example code is contained in the class ComboExample.

The code for the custom renderer is quite simple because we use a JLabel to do most of the drawing work. When the combo box requests the component to draw an item, the renderer sets the font for its label to the list's font. Next, it assigns an Icon and foreground color depending on whether the item is selected. Finally, the item is converted to a string, and that string is assigned to the label before it is returned.

```
import java.lang.*;
import com.sun.java.swing.*;
import java.awt.*;

public class MyRenderer extends Object
implements ListCellRenderer
{
    ImageIcon checkIcon;
    ImageIcon unCheckIcon;
    JLabel theLabel;

    public MyRenderer()
    {
        checkIcon = new ImageIcon("images/check.gif");
        unCheckIcon = new ImageIcon("images/ex.gif");
        theLabel = new JLabel();
    }

    public Component getListCellRendererComponent(JList list,
                                Object value,
                                int index,
                                boolean isSelected,
                                boolean cellHasFocus)
```

```
    {
        theLabel.setFont(list.getFont());

        if(isSelected)
        {
            theLabel.setForeground(Color.blue);
            theLabel.setIcon(checkIcon);
        }
        else
        {
            theLabel.setForeground(Color.black);
            theLabel.setIcon(unCheckIcon);
        }

        theLabel.setText(value.toString());

        return theLabel;
    }
}
```

To test this renderer we created a simple example that creates a combo box and then displays it. Notice that we set the combo box's font to 18 points so that the custom renderers' actions are more pronounced. We do this for demonstration purposes only.

```
import com.sun.java.swing.*;
import java.awt.event.*;
import java.awt.*;

public class ComboExample extends JPanel
{
    public ComboExample()
    {
        JComboBox glyphComboBox;
        Font f;

        f = new Font("Serif",Font.PLAIN,18);
        setFont(f);
        setLayout(new BorderLayout());

        glyphComboBox = new JComboBox();
        glyphComboBox.setFont(f);
```

```
        glyphComboBox.setRenderer(new MyRenderer());

        glyphComboBox.addItem("Gold");
        glyphComboBox.addItem("Silver");
        glyphComboBox.addItem("Bronze");

        add(glyphComboBox,"Center");
    }

    public Dimension getPreferredSize()
    {
        return new Dimension(140, 60);
    }

    public static void main(String s[])
    {
        JFrame frame = new JFrame("ComboBox Example");
        ComboExample panel = new ComboExample();

        frame.setDefaultCloseOperation(JFrame.DO_NOTHING_ON_CLOSE);
        frame.setForeground(Color.black);
        frame.setBackground(Color.lightGray);
        frame.getContentPane().add(panel,"Center");

        frame.setSize(panel.getPreferredSize());
        frame.setVisible(true);
    }
}
```

ComboBox Editors

Combo boxes use custom editors that support editing. The ComboBoxEditor is an interface for the object that is used to edit the value in the JComboBox. The methods that a ComboBoxEditor must implement are shown in Table 5.2.

The default ComboBoxEditor is a simple text editor that behaves like a text field.

To make a combo box editable you must call setEditable, as shown here:

```
combBoxInstance.setEditable(true);
```

This method installs the current editor. To assign a new editor to the combo box, use the method:

```
public void setEditor(ComboBoxEditor e);
```

Table 5.2 ComboBoxEditor Methods

Method	Function
AddActionListener(ActionListener)	Adds an ActionListener to the Editor. Use this method to ensure that objects are notified when the JComboBox value changes. This method is useful only if the JComboBox is set editable.
GetEditorComponent()	Returns the component used for editing.
GetItem()	Returns the edited item.
RemoveActionListener(ActionListener)	Removes an ActionListener for this editor.
selectAll()	Selects the entire item edited and starts editing.
setItem(Object)	Sets the item to be edited.

The editor publishes action events when the user is finished editing. In the case of a text field-like editor these notifications usually occur when the user presses the Return key. To add the new values to the JComboBox you need to implement an ActionListener that handles the adding behavior.

The next example, pictured in Figure 5.3, implements a ComboBoxEditor that adds ActionListeners to an editor field. When the action key—carriage return by default—is pressed, the ActionListener is notified and then requests that the JComboBox add the current value of the editor to the list. We retain a pointer to the editor so that you can access its value. This example is implemented in two classes. The first class, AddFieldEditor, is the ComboBoxEditor class. The second class, AddExample, provides a main method that creates a combo box and assigns the editor to it.

The editor for this example, AddFieldEditor, uses a Swing implementation of a text field, JTextField, to handle most of the work. Basically, the current item is treated as a string. The text field is supplied with this string; when the text field is activated, it's up to the action listeners to handle the notification.

Figure 5.3 Custom ComboBox editor.

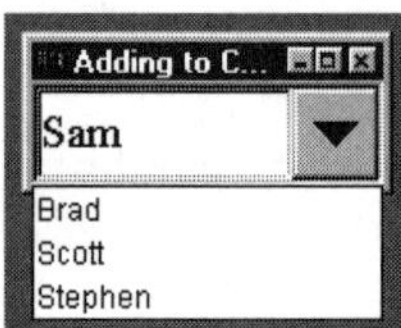

```
import com.sun.java.swing.*;
import java.awt.*;
import java.awt.event.*;

public class AddFieldEditor extends Object
implements ComboBoxEditor
{
    JTextField theField;
    Object curItem;

    public AddFieldEditor()
    {
        theField = new JTextField();
    }

    public  void setItem(Object anObject)
    {
        curItem = anObject;

        if(curItem != null)
        {
            String str;

            str= curItem.toString();
            theField.setText(str);
        }
        else
        {
            theField.setText("");
        }
    }

    public Component getEditorComponent()
    {
        return theField;
    }

    public  Object getItem()
    {
        Object retVal;

        if((curItem == null)||(curItem instanceof String))
        {
```

```
            retVal = theField.getText();
        }
        else
        {
            retVal = curItem;
        }

        return curItem;
    }

    public  void selectAll()
    {
        theField.selectAll();
    }

    // Pass the ActionListener on to the field
    public void addActionListener(ActionListener l)
    {
        theField.addActionListener(l);
    }

    public  void removeActionListener(ActionListener l)
    {
        theField.removeActionListener(l);
    }
}
```

The remainder of this example is implemented in the form of a subclass of JPanel. The panel contains a single combo box with our custom editor assigned to it. When the editor is created, our custom panel adds itself to the editor as an ActionListener. The actionPerformed method adds a new string item to the combo box with the editor's current value. When run, this example looks like the program in Figure 5.3.

```
import com.sun.java.swing.*;
import java.awt.event.*;
import java.awt.*;

public class AddExample extends JPanel
implements ActionListener
{
    JComboBox addBox;
    AddFieldEditor addEditor;
```

```
    public AddExample()
    {
        Font f;

        f = new Font("Serif",Font.PLAIN,18);
        setFont(f);
        setLayout(new BorderLayout());

        addBox = new JComboBox();
        addBox.setFont(f);

        // Sets the maximum row count.
        // If there are more than ten rows
        // then the JComboBox will add a scroll bar.
        addBox.setMaximumRowCount(10);

        //Create the new editor
        addEditor = new AddFieldEditor();
        addEditor.getEditorComponent().setFont(f);

        // Set the combo box as an ActionListener for the editor
        addEditor.addActionListener(this);

        addBox.setEditor(addEditor);
        addBox.setEditable(true);

        addBox.addItem("Brad");
        addBox.addItem("Scott");
        addBox.addItem("Stephen");

        add(addBox,"Center");
    }


    public void actionPerformed(ActionEvent e)
    {
        String value;
        JTextField editorComp;

        editorComp = ((JTextField)addEditor.getEditorComponent());
        value = editorComp.getText();
        addBox.addItem(value);
```

```
    }

    public Dimension getPreferredSize()
    {
        return new Dimension(100,60);
    }

    public static void main(String s[])
    {
        JFrame frame = new JFrame("Adding to ComboBox Example");
        AddExample panel = new AddExample();

        frame.setDefaultCloseOperation(JFrame.DO_NOTHING_ON_CLOSE);
        frame.setForeground(Color.black);
        frame.setBackground(Color.lightGray);
        frame.getContentPane().add(panel,"Center");

        frame.setSize(panel.getPreferredSize());
        frame.setVisible(true);
    }
}
```

Complete ComboBox Example

To tie our discussion of JComboBox together, we created an example that uses a custom renderer and a custom editor. The renderer merely displays items in a label with the correct font. This is actually a useful item because the default renderer does not perform this operation. The custom editor provides two key functions. First, it jumps to an item in the combo box when the user types in it. For example, if there is an item called "bear" in the list of choices and the user types "be" in the editor, the editor will fill in the "ar" and select it so the user can type over it if he or she chooses. Second, the editor automatically adds items to the list when an ActionEvent occurs. The editor, however, checks to make sure the new item is not in the list of available choices.

The code for our renderer is as follows:

```
import java.lang.*;
import com.sun.java.swing.*;
import java.awt.*;

public class SimpleRenderer extends Object
implements ListCellRenderer
{
    ImageIcon checkIcon;
```

```
        ImageIcon unCheckIcon;
        JLabel theLabel;

        public SimpleRenderer()
        {
            theLabel = new JLabel();
        }

        public Component getListCellRendererComponent(JList list,
                                Object value,
                                int index,
                                boolean isSelected,
                                boolean cellHasFocus)

        {
            theLabel.setFont(list.getFont());

            if(isSelected)
            {
                theLabel.setForeground(Color.blue);
            }
            else
            {
                theLabel.setForeground(Color.black);
            }

            theLabel.setText(value.toString());

            return theLabel;
        }
    }
```

The key aspect of this renderer is that it uses the list's font to display the current item as a string. It also changes the current color based on whether the current item is selected.

Our custom editor is more complex. First, the editor supplies a JTextField used for editing. Second, the editor acts as a KeyListener for the text field. This is an interesting technique that is available only because of the delegation event model that AWT and Swing use. The editor listens for key-release events and uses these events to update the text field. If a special key such as the Delete key or an arrow key is pressed, the editor ignores them. If a letter is pressed, the editor uses a simple linear search to look for an item that starts with the existing string in the text field and fills in the text field's data to match this item. Then the editor selects the text it added to allow the user to continue typing over the possible match.

Finally, the editor is an ActionListener for the text field, and it adds items to its combo box when an action occurs. Before adding the item, however, the editor makes sure that the new item is not the currently selected item. This should prevent duplicates from being added to the list, although it's not necessarily a foolproof method.

```
import com.sun.java.swing.*;
import java.awt.*;
import java.awt.event.*;

public class JumptoFieldEditor extends KeyAdapter
implements ComboBoxEditor, ActionListener
{
    JTextField theField;
    Object curItem;
    JComboBox box;

    public JumptoFieldEditor(JComboBox c)
    {
        box = c;
        theField = new JTextField();
        theField.addKeyListener(this);
        theField.addActionListener(this);
    }

    public  void setItem(Object anObject)
    {
        curItem = anObject;

        if(curItem != null)
        {
            String str;

            str= curItem.toString();
            theField.setText(str);
        }
        else
        {
            theField.setText("");
        }
    }

    public Component getEditorComponent()
    {
        return theField;
```

```
    }

    public  Object getItem()
    {
        Object retVal;

        if((curItem == null)||(curItem instanceof String))
        {
            retVal = theField.getText();
        }
        else
        {
            retVal = curItem;
        }

        return curItem;
    }

    public  void selectAll()
    {
        theField.selectAll();
    }

    // Pass the ActionListener on to the field
    public void addActionListener(ActionListener l)
    {
        theField.addActionListener(l);
    }

    public  void removeActionListener(ActionListener l)
    {
        theField.removeActionListener(l);
    }

    public void keyReleased(KeyEvent evt)
    {
        int curLen;
        String curVal;


        curVal = theField.getText();

        if(curVal != null) curLen = curVal.length();
        else curLen = 0;
```

```
        //ignore arrow keys, delete,
        //and the shift key
        if((evt.getKeyCode() == KeyEvent.VK_UP)
            ||(evt.getKeyCode() == KeyEvent.VK_DOWN)
            ||(evt.getKeyCode() == KeyEvent.VK_LEFT)
            ||(evt.getKeyCode() == KeyEvent.VK_RIGHT)
            ||(evt.getKeyCode() == KeyEvent.VK_SHIFT)
            ||(evt.getKeyCode() == KeyEvent.VK_DELETE)
            ||(evt.getKeyCode() == KeyEvent.VK_BACK_SPACE))
        {
            return;
        }

        if(curLen > 0)
        {
            int i,max;
            String item;

            max = box.getItemCount();

            for(i=0;i<max;i++)
            {
                item = box.getItemAt(i).toString();

                if(item.startsWith(curVal))
                {
                    box.setSelectedIndex(i);
                    setItem(box.getSelectedItem());
                    theField.select(curLen,item.length());
                    break;
                }
            }
        }
    }

    public void actionPerformed(ActionEvent e)
    {
        String value;

        value = theField.getText();

        if(!value.equals(box.getSelectedItem()))
        {
```

```
                box.addItem(value);
            }
        }
    }
```

You may find this editor useful in your own programs because it provides a function common to editable combo boxes in Windows applications.

We created a simple example, shown in Figure 5.4, that uses our editor and renderer. This example is similar to the previous one in that it creates a single combo box, initializes it, and assigns a new editor and renderer.

```
import com.sun.java.swing.*;
import java.awt.event.*;
import java.awt.*;

public class JumptoExample extends JPanel
{
    JComboBox addBox;
    JumptoFieldEditor addEditor;

    public JumptoExample()
    {
        Font f;

        f = new Font("Serif",Font.PLAIN,18);
        setFont(f);
        setLayout(new BorderLayout());

        addBox = new JComboBox();
        addBox.setFont(f);

        // Sets the maximum row count.
        // If there are more than ten rows
        // then the JComboBox will add a scroll bar.
        addBox.setMaximumRowCount(10);

        addBox.setRenderer(new SimpleRenderer());

        //Create the new editor
        addEditor = new JumptoFieldEditor(addBox);
        addEditor.getEditorComponent().setFont(f);

        addBox.setEditor(addEditor);
        addBox.setEditable(true);
```

```
        addBox.addItem("Brad");
        addBox.addItem("Scott");
        addBox.addItem("Stephen");

        addBox.setSelectedIndex(0);
        add(addBox,"Center");
    }

    public Dimension getPreferredSize()
    {
        return new Dimension(150,60);
    }

    public static void main(String s[])
    {
        JFrame frame = new JFrame("Jumping ComboBox Example");
        JumptoExample panel = new JumptoExample();

        frame.setDefaultCloseOperation(JFrame.DO_NOTHING_ON_CLOSE);
        frame.setForeground(Color.black);
        frame.setBackground(Color.lightGray);
        frame.getContentPane().add(panel,"Center");

        frame.setSize(panel.getPreferredSize());
        frame.setVisible(true);
    }
}
```

One of the techniques we used in this example is setting the selected index to 0 after we created the combo box. This is a common technique, one that is used if no other selection is preferred. If you don't initialize the selected item, there may or may not be one, depending on the editor.

Item Events

JDK 1.1 introduced the concept of an item event. An *item event* is a system event that is generated based on some selection change in a UI element that supports this mechanism. In Swing, the JComboBox class relies on these events to notify a listener that a choice was made. Item events are distributed to item listeners. *Item*

Figure 5.4 Combo box using a custom editor and renderer.

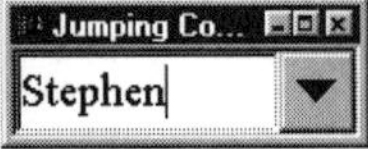

listeners are objects that implement the ItemListener interface and respond to item events. The ItemListener interface defines a single method:

```
public void itemStateChanged(ItemEvent evt)
```

The argument to itemStateChanged is an ItemEvent. ItemEvent is a subclass of java.awt.AwtEvent and defines the method getItemSelectable to return the item that was selected and a method getItem that returns the component used to select the item.

```
public ItemSelectable getItemSelectable()
public Object getItem()
```

The component that distributes item events must implement the ItemSelectable interface from the java.awt package. ItemSelectable defines the methods used to register listeners and retrieves the selected items. In general, you may find it more useful to use a Component's own methods to determine the selected items, rather than the generic mechanism defined in this interface. The methods defined in the ItemSelectable interface include getSelectedObject to return the selected object and addItemListener and removeItemListener for adding and removing an ItemListener from the object:

```
public abstract Object[] getSelectedObjects()
public abstract void addItemListener(ItemListener l)
public abstract void removeItemListener(ItemListener l)
```

In the following example, shown in Figure 5.5, we display a JComboBox and a JTextField. An ItemListener is used to update the text field when the combo box's value is changed. The object Choice implements the ItemListener interface and, therefore, implements the method itemStateChanged. By adding our object (this) to the item listener list for the combo box, the Choice object is notified when the combo box changes its selection. We take this opportunity to set the value of the text field to the value of the selected item in the combo box.

This example is implemented in the form of a subclass of JPanel. A main class method creates a Frame for the panel and displays it. A helper class called WindowCloser is used to close the window when the close box is selected.

```
import java.util.*;
import java.awt.*;
import java.awt.event.*;
import com.sun.java.swing.*;
import com.sun.java.swing.text.*;

public class Choices extends JPanel
implements ItemListener
{
    JComboBox myChoice;
```

```
JTextField field;

public Choices()
{
    setBackground(Color.lightGray);
    /*
     * Turn on buffering to reduce flicker.
     */
    setDoubleBuffered(true);

    field = new JTextField(10);
    add(field);

    myChoice = new JComboBox();
    myChoice.addItem("Primary");
    myChoice.addItem("Secondary");
    myChoice.addItem("Tertiary");
    myChoice.addItemListener(this);
    add(myChoice);
}

public void itemStateChanged(ItemEvent evt)
{
    Object value;

    if(evt.getSource() == myChoice)
    {
        value = myChoice.getSelectedItem();
        field.setText(value.toString());
    }
}

public Dimension getPreferredSize()
{
    return new Dimension(200, 100);
}

public static void main(String s[])
{
    JFrame frame = new JFrame("Choices");
    Choices panel = new Choices();

    frame.setForeground(Color.black);
```

```
        frame.setBackground(Color.lightGray);
        frame.addWindowListener(new WindowCloser());
        frame.getContentPane().add(panel,"Center");

        frame.setSize(panel.getPreferredSize());
        frame.setVisible(true);
    }
}

class WindowCloser extends WindowAdapter
{
    public void windowClosing(WindowEvent e)
    {
        Window win = e.getWindow();
        win.setVisible(false);
        win.dispose();
        System.exit(0);
    }
}
```

JComboBox also supports ActionListeners and notifies the listeners when a selection is made via an ActionEvent.

JList

A JList is a vertical set of cells that display a list of items to the user. This list could be used in a file dialog to allow the selection of one or more files. Normally, this list is placed in a JScrollPane so that it doesn't have to be large enough to display all its items simultaneously.

Jlist provides a default constructor and three other constructors that make it very convenient to display a collection of items in the list. You can pass to a JList constructor an object implementing the ListModel interface, an array of objects, or a vector of objects. The ListModel is discussed later in this section. You can create a JList with any one of these four constructors:

Figure 5.5 Using an item listener to update a text field from a combo box.

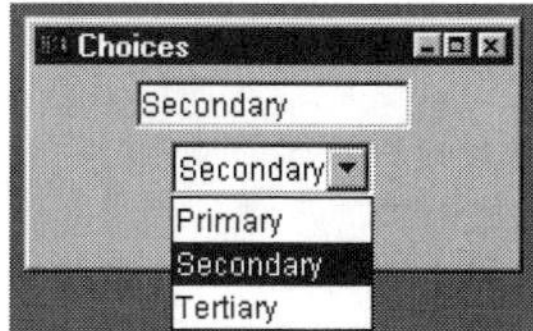

```
public JList();
public JList(ListModel dataModel);
public JList(Object listData[]);
public JList(Vector listData);
```

As with a JComboBox, the data for a JList is specified as a set of objects. It is up to a ListCellRenderer to provide a visual representation of these objects. Normally, this representation is simply the results of the object's toString method. The data in a JList is managed with a ListModel. You can assign data to a list in the form of a *vector* or an *object array* using the methods:

```
public void setListData(Object listData[]);
public void setListData(Vector listData);
```

The following example, pictured in Figure 5.6, displays a simple list. The data from this list is assigned using a vector with three strings in it.

```
import com.sun.java.swing.*;

import java.awt.event.*;
import java.awt.*;
import java.util.*;

public class SimpleListExample extends JPanel
{
    public SimpleListExample()
    {
        JList list;
        Vector data;
        Font f;

        f = new Font("SanSerif",Font.PLAIN,24);
        setFont(f);
        setLayout(new BorderLayout());

        list = new JList();
        list.setFont(f);

        data = new Vector();
        data.addElement("Gold");
        data.addElement("Silver");
        data.addElement("Bronze");
        data.addElement("Copper");
        data.addElement("Iron");
        data.addElement("Platinum");
```

```
        data.addElement("Titanium");



        list.setListData(data);

        add(new JScrollPane(list),"Center");
    }

    public Dimension getPreferredSize()
    {
        return new Dimension(100, 100);
    }

    public static void main(String s[])
    {
        JFrame frame = new JFrame("Simple List Example");
        SimpleListExample panel = new SimpleListExample();

        frame.setDefaultCloseOperation(JFrame.DO_NOTHING_ON_CLOSE);
        frame.setForeground(Color.black);
        frame.setBackground(Color.lightGray);
        frame.getContentPane().add(panel,"Center");

        frame.setSize(panel.getPreferredSize());
        frame.setVisible(true);
    }
}
```

ListModel

Once your list has data, you can interact with it through the model. A list's model must implement the ListModel interface that defines two methods for accessing its

Figure 5.6 Displaying a set of objects in a JList.

data. The method getSize returns the length of the list, and the method getElementAt returns the object located at a specified location in the list:

```
public int getSize();
public Object getElementAt(int index);
```

The DefaultListModel class provides methods for adding data as well as for accessing the model. This model provides an interface similar to the java.util.Vector. The methods of DefaultListModel are found in Table 5.3.

List Selections

A JList has a more complex selection mechanism than a JComboBox. In particular, a list can allow single selections, multiple selections, or multiple-disjoint selections. As a result, there are several ways to interact with the list when requesting its selection. The first way to interact with a list's selection is by index. If the list has only one item selected it stores a single selected index. If several items are selected, an array of indices is used. An index of 0 indicates the first possible item. The methods shown in Table 5.4 are provided to set and retrieve either a single index or an array.

Table 5.3 Methods of DefaultListModel

Method	Function
public int getSize();	Returns the length of the list.
public Object getElementAt (int index);	Returns the object at the index in the model.
public int size();	Returns the number of elements in the list.
public Object elementAt (int index);	Returns the element at the specified index.
public void setElementAt (Object obj, int index);	Places an object at the index position in the list.
public void removeElementAt (int index);	Removes the object at the index location in the list.
public void insertElementAt (Object obj, int index);	Inserts the specified object at the specified index.
public void addElement (Object obj);	Adds an object to the end of the list.
public boolean removeElement (Object obj);	Removes the specific object from the list.
public void removeAllElements();	Removes all objects from the list.

Table 5.4 Methods for Retrieving Indices from a JList

Method	Function
public void setSelectedIndices (int indices[]);	Selects a set of cells at locations in the indices array.
public int getSelectedIndex();	Returns the index of the first selected item in the list.
public int[] getSelectedIndices();	Returns an array of all selected items in the list.

If you request the selected index and more than one item is selected, the first selected index is returned. You can also get to this first item by asking for the minimum selection index. This minimum and the associated maximum are accessed using two methods:

```
public int getMinSelectionIndex();
public int getMaxSelectionIndex();
```

These indices, however, do not account for disjoint selections, and all of the items between the minimum and maximum selection indexes are not selected.

Because a list can support disjoint selections, there are methods to manage selection intervals. These methods create a selection with a start and an end index. The selection includes all of the list elements between these two indices and the elements at each end point. The set method replaces the current selection with the given interval; the add method creates a union of the existing selected items and the new selection interval.

```
public void setSelectionInterval(int start, int end);
public void addSelectionInterval(int start, int end);
```

You can also select items in the list using the item itself. In this case you use the method:

```
public void setSelectedValue(Object anObject,
                             boolean shouldScroll);
```

This method takes the item to select and a Boolean that indicates whether the list should scroll to make the item visible. In general it's important to scroll the current selection to visible, and this value is true.

You can access the selected value or values using two methods:

```
public Object getSelectedValue();
public Object[] getSelectedValues();
```

As we mentioned before, a list can support several selection modes. The current mode can be assigned using static variables from the ListSelectionModel interface:

SINGLE_SELECTION. Allows only one item to be selected at a time.

SINGLE_INTERVAL_SELECTION. Allows multiple items to be selected, but only if they are contiguous. This selection is often made when the Shift key is held down during the selection process.

MULTIPLE_INTERVAL_SELECTION. Allows the user to select multiple-disjoint items. Usually, these selections are made while the user holds down the Control key.

Pass these variables to the JList method setSelectionMode to set the selection mode, as shown here:

```
public void setSelectionMode(int selectionMode);
```

The following example displays a list that supports disjoint selections, as shown in Figure 5.7. The code for setting the selection mode and initializing the current selection is in bold.

```
import com.sun.java.swing.*;

import java.awt.event.*;
import java.awt.*;
import java.util.*;

public class MSelListExample extends JPanel
{
    public MSelListExample()
    {
        JList list;
        Vector data;
        Font f;

        f = new Font("SanSerif",Font.PLAIN,24);
        setFont(f);
        setLayout(new BorderLayout());

        list = new JList();
        list.setFont(f);

        data = new Vector();
        data.addElement("Gold");
        data.addElement("Silver");
        data.addElement("Bronze");
        data.addElement("Copper");
        data.addElement("Nickel");
        data.addElement("Iron");

        list.setListData(data);
```

```
        list.setSelectedIndex(1);

        int mode = ListSelectionModel.MULTIPLE_INTERVAL_SELECTION;
        list.setSelectionMode(mode);

        add(new JScrollPane(list),"Center");
    }

    public Dimension getPreferredSize()
    {
        return new Dimension(120, 120);
    }

    public static void main(String s[])
    {
        JFrame frame = new JFrame("List Selection Example");
        MSelListExample panel = new MSelListExample();

        frame.setDefaultCloseOperation(JFrame.DO_NOTHING_ON_CLOSE);
        frame.setForeground(Color.black);
        frame.setBackground(Color.lightGray);
        frame.getContentPane().add(panel,"Center");

        frame.setSize(panel.getPreferredSize());
        frame.setVisible(true);
    }
}
```

List Renderers

Like JComboBox, JList supports custom ListCellRenderers. A list cell renderer is an object that implements the ListCellRenderer interface. Its job is to draw the individual cells of the JList. These renderers are created in an identical fashion to the renderer for a combo box, and you can, in fact, use the same renderers for both components. The renderer for a list is assigned using the following method:

Figure 5.7 JList handling disjoint selections.

```
public void setCellRenderer(ListCellRenderer cellRenderer);
```

This renderer can display strings, icons, and other graphics for each item in the list.

In our next example, we create a reusable list renderer that relies on a particular type of object added to the list. This example uses three classes: one to hold the data, one to render the data, and one to create a list with data. We have defined the ListItem class to hold items in the list. You may want to extend this class for your own applications by having it hold other objects.

```
import com.sun.java.swing.*;

import java.awt.event.*;
import java.awt.*;

class ListItem
{
    protected Icon icon;
    protected String title;

    public ListItem(String t,Icon i)
    {
        icon = i;
        title = t;
    }

    public Icon getIcon()
    {
        return icon;
    }

    public String getTitle()
    {
        return title;
    }
}
```

As you can see, a ListItem stores a string title and an icon. Our custom renderer uses these two values to display the item in the list. Like the combo box renderer examples, this renderer uses a JLabel to draw the cell. The label is initialized to the current list items: icon and title. The label is also set to the correct font, and its color is set to indicate a selection. We get the selection color from the list itself using the methods that the list provides to assign and access a selection foreground and background color.

```
import java.lang.*;
import com.sun.java.swing.*;
import java.awt.*;
```

```
public class ListItemRenderer extends Object
implements ListCellRenderer
{
    JLabel theLabel;

    public ListItemRenderer()
    {
        theLabel = new JLabel();
        theLabel.setOpaque(true);
    }

    public Component getListCellRendererComponent(JList list,
                                Object value,
                                int index,
                                boolean isSelected,
                                boolean cellHasFocus)

    {
        ListItem li=null;

        if(value instanceof ListItem) li = (ListItem) value;

        theLabel.setFont(list.getFont());

        if(isSelected)
        {
            theLabel.setBackground(list.getSelectionBackground());
            theLabel.setForeground(list.getSelectionForeground());
        }
        else
        {
            theLabel.setBackground(list.getBackground());
            theLabel.setForeground(list.getForeground());
        }

        if(li != null)
        {
            theLabel.setText(li.getTitle());
            theLabel.setIcon(li.getIcon());
        }
        else
        {
            theLabel.setText(value.toString());
```

```
        }

        return theLabel;
    }
}
```

You may notice that we made the label opaque so that it would fill its background with the assigned color. This is necessary because the label is transparent by default and draws only its icon and title. Our example program is pictured in Figure 5.8. Notice that the items are the correct font and that the selected item is highlighted with blue. This example creates a Vector of ListItem objects with various icons and assigns them to the list as its data.

```
import com.sun.java.swing.*;

import java.awt.event.*;
import java.awt.*;
import java.util.*;

public class ListExample extends JPanel
{
    public ListExample()
    {
        JList list;
        Font f;
        Icon icon;
        Vector data;

        f = new Font("Serif",Font.PLAIN,18);
        setFont(f);
        setLayout(new BorderLayout());

        list = new JList();
        list.setFont(f);

        list.setCellRenderer(new ListItemRenderer());

        data = new Vector();

        icon = new ImageIcon("images/check.gif");
        data.addElement(new ListItem("Check",icon));

        icon = new ImageIcon("images/ex.gif");
        data.addElement(new ListItem("Ex",icon));
```

```
        icon = new ImageIcon("images/shapes.gif");
        data.addElement(new ListItem("Shapes",icon));

        list.setListData(data);
        list.setSelectedIndex(1);

        add(new JScrollPane(list),"Center");
    }

    public Dimension getPreferredSize()
    {
        return new Dimension(140, 100);
    }

    public static void main(String s[])
    {
        JFrame frame = new JFrame("List Example");
        ListExample panel = new ListExample();

        frame.setDefaultCloseOperation(JFrame.DO_NOTHING_ON_CLOSE);
        frame.setForeground(Color.black);
        frame.setBackground(Color.lightGray);
        frame.getContentPane().add(panel,"Center");

        frame.setSize(panel.getPreferredSize());
        frame.setVisible(true);
    }
}
```

List Selection Events

Events generated by selections in a list are handled indirectly through a model. JLists have relationships with two models. The first model stores the list's data and implements the ListModel interface. The second model keeps track of the list's selection information and implements the ListSelectionModel interface.

Figure 5.8 Custom list renderers.

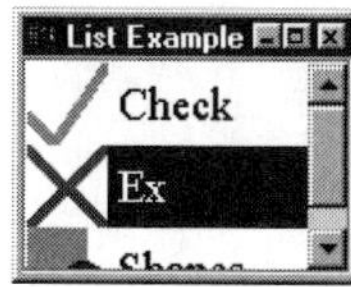

Changes to the list's selection are tracked with the selection model, and notifications are sent from the selection model to registered list selection listeners.

List selection listeners implement the ListSelectionListener interface. ListSelectionListener defines a single method that is called when the selection's value changes:

```
public abstract void valueChanged(ListSelectionEvent e)
```

The argument to valueChanged is a ListSelectionEvent object. ListSelectionEvent is a subclass of java.util.EventObject and defines two new methods that return the first and last rows whose selection value may have changed:

```
public int getFirstIndex()
public int getLastIndex()
```

The indices in the selection event represent the items that may have changed state. They are not necessarily the items that were selected. You need to go back to the list's selection model to determine the actual selected items.

In the following example, we register an object as a ListSelectionListener and update a text field when the list's selected value changes. Our listener actually displays the selection using three mechanisms. First, the items between the ListSelectionEvent's first and last index are displayed in a text field. Next, the items between the minimum and maximum selection indices are displayed. Finally, the actual selected values are displayed. In all cases, the "selected" items are displayed as a single string made by concatenating the items together, separating them with a space.

This example is implemented in the form of a subclass of JPanel. A main class method creates a Frame for the panel and displays it. A helper class called WindowCloser is used to close the window when the close box is selected. This example also shows how to create a list using an array of objects, rather than a Vector.

```
import java.applet.*;
import java.util.*;
import java.awt.*;
import java.awt.event.*;
import com.sun.java.swing.*;
import com.sun.java.swing.event.*;

public class Selections extends JPanel
implements ListSelectionListener
{
    JTextField indField;
    JTextField selIndField;
    JTextField actField;
    JList list;
```

```
public Selections()
{
    String items[] = {"one","two","three","four"
                      ,"five","six","seven"};
    JPanel footer,tmp;

    setLayout(new BorderLayout());
    setBackground(Color.lightGray);
    /*
     * Turn on buffering to reduce flicker.
     */
    setDoubleBuffered(true);

    list = new JList(items);
    list.addListSelectionListener(this);
    add(new JScrollPane(list),"Center");

    footer = new JPanel();
    footer.setLayout(new GridLayout(3,1,5,5));

    tmp = new JPanel();
    tmp.add(new JLabel("Evt index:"));
    indField = new JTextField(20);
    tmp.add(indField);

    footer.add(tmp);

    tmp = new JPanel();
    tmp.add(new JLabel("Min/max index:"));
    selIndField = new JTextField(20);
    tmp.add(selIndField);

    footer.add(tmp);

    tmp = new JPanel();
    tmp.add(new JLabel("Sel values:"));
    actField = new JTextField(20);
    tmp.add(actField);

    footer.add(tmp);

    add(footer,"South");
}
```

```
public void valueChanged(ListSelectionEvent e)
{
    int first,last;
    int i;
    String newVal = "";
    ListModel listData = list.getModel();
    Object selValues[];

    /*
     * Display the information from the event.
     */
    first = e.getFirstIndex();
    last = e.getLastIndex();

    for(i=first;i<=last;i++)
    {
        if(i!=first) newVal+=" ";
        newVal += listData.getElementAt(i);
    }

    indField.setText(newVal);

    /*
     * Display the every thing in sel indexes
     * first and last will be -1
     * if there is no selection.
     */
     newVal = "";

    first = list.getMinSelectionIndex();
    last = list.getMaxSelectionIndex();

    for(i=first;i<=last;i++)
    {
        if(i!=first) newVal+=" ";
        newVal += listData.getElementAt(i);
    }

    selIndField.setText(newVal);

    //Display the actual selected values

    selValues = list.getSelectedValues();
```

```
            last = selValues.length;

            newVal = "";

            for(i=0;i<last;i++)
            {
                if(i!=0) newVal+=" ";
                newVal += selValues[i].toString();
            }

            actField.setText(newVal);
        }

        public Dimension getPreferredSize()
        {
            return new Dimension(350, 350);
        }

        public static void main(String s[])
        {
            JFrame frame = new JFrame("Selections");
            Selections panel = new Selections();

            frame.setForeground(Color.black);
            frame.setBackground(Color.lightGray);
            frame.addWindowListener(new WindowCloser());
            frame.getContentPane().add(panel,"Center");

            frame.setSize(panel.getPreferredSize());
            frame.setVisible(true);
        }
    }

    class WindowCloser extends WindowAdapter
    {
        public void windowClosing(WindowEvent e)
        {
            Window win = e.getWindow();
            win.setVisible(false);
            win.dispose();
            System.exit(0);
        }
    }
```

Figure 5.9 List selections.

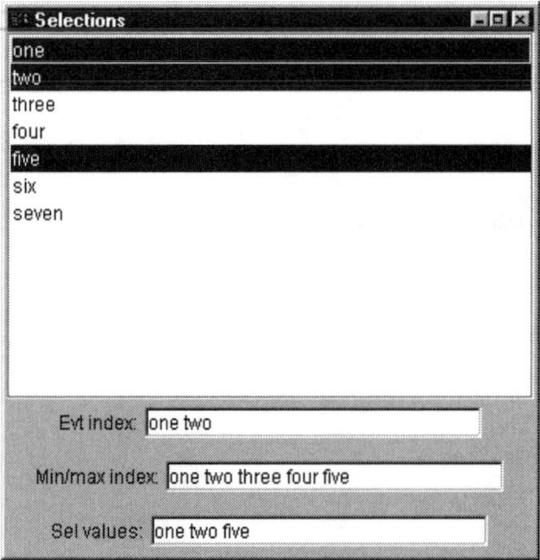

Figure 5.9 shows the list selections that we created.

Handling Mouse Clicks

In some applications, users perform special actions on list items by double-clicking on them. To support this functionality you need to use MouseListeners. The following example uses a listener to check for double-clicks and then prints a message to the console if one of these clicks occurs.

The listener for this example extends MouseAdapter. When a mouse click occurs, the listener asks the list to convert the location of the mouse click to an item index. Next, the listener retrieves the list's model and acquires the item at the specified index. Finally, the listener ensures that the item is visible using the following method:

```
public void ensureIndexIsVisible(int index);
```

This method scrolls the list as necessary to display the item. Finally, a message is printed to the console with the item's string value.

```
class DoubleClicker extends MouseAdapter
{
    protected JList list;

    public DoubleClicker(JList l)
    {
        list = l;
    }
```

```
    public void mouseClicked(MouseEvent e)
    {
        if(e.getClickCount() == 2)
        {
            ListModel model;
            int index = list.locationToIndex(e.getPoint());
            Object item;

            model = list.getModel();
            item = model.getElementAt(index);

            list.ensureIndexIsVisible(index);

            System.out.println("Double clicked on " + item);
        }
    }
}
```

The remaining code for this example creates a list, assigns it some data, and adds a DoubleClicker to the list as a MouseListener. Again, we see the power of the delegation event model. You don't have to subclass JList to add this type of functionality. You can add it with listeners instead.

```
import com.sun.java.swing.*;

import java.awt.event.*;
import java.awt.*;
import java.util.*;

public class DoubleClickExample extends JPanel
{
    public DoubleClickExample()
    {
        JList list;
        Vector data;
        Font f;

        f = new Font("SanSerif",Font.PLAIN,24);
        setFont(f);
        setLayout(new BorderLayout());

        list = new JList();
```

```
        list.setFont(f);

        data = new Vector();
        data.addElement("Gold");
        data.addElement("Silver");
        data.addElement("Bronze");

        list.setListData(data);
        list.setSelectedIndex(1);

        list.addMouseListener(new DoubleClicker(list));

        add(new JScrollPane(list),"Center");
    }

    public Dimension getPreferredSize()
    {
        return new Dimension(100, 100);
    }

    public static void main(String s[])
    {
        JFrame frame = new JFrame("Double Click Example");
        DoubleClickExample panel = new DoubleClickExample();

        frame.setDefaultCloseOperation(JFrame.DO_NOTHING_ON_CLOSE);
        frame.setForeground(Color.black);
        frame.setBackground(Color.lightGray);
        frame.getContentPane().add(panel,"Center");

        frame.setSize(panel.getPreferredSize());
        frame.setVisible(true);
    }
}
```

Figure 5.10 shows what the code looks like when run.

Figure 5.10 Mouse clicks.

Style Guidelines

In general, you should use a JList to provide a large set of choices or when multiple selections are available. Use a JComboBox when there is a small set of choices or if you want to allow the user to edit the list. The combo box takes up less space, making it useful in a cramped interface; the list usually requires a scroll pane to make it usable. Whichever component you use, make sure to initialize the selection. If possible, select the most common choice, so that the user doesn't have to change the selection in as many cases as possible.

Think about using custom renderers and editors like the ones in the examples. These can make lists and combo boxes more visually appealing and more usable. The JumptoEditor pictured in Figure 5.4 gives power users, or at least keyboard-centric users, the ability to select items quickly without "resorting" to the mouse.

Sliders, Watch Events, and Scroll Panes

6

With the release of Swing, JavaSoft provides the first real slider component in the JDK standard libraries. This slider is used for graphically displaying bounded, numerical user entry. A slider is similar to a scroller except that it is specifically used for data entry, rather than for moving objects in a view. In previous JDK releases, programmers had to rely on scroll bars to perform the same functionality. Swing has separated these two component types into JSliders and JScrollPanes. JSliders are used for numerical entry; JScrollPanes use scroll bars to handle user operations.

Swing also provides a generic mechanism for notifying objects of changes to the value of a slider. This mechanism uses ChangeEvents to notify listeners of a change to some value. Sliders and many of the models used by Swing components rely on change events to notify their interested listeners.

Sliders

Swing provides a true slider component called JSlider to replace the scroll bar in situations where the user simply selects a numerical value. Sliders have seven values that describe their look and feel:

Minimum value. The lowest possible value of the slider.

Maximum value. The highest possible value of the slider.

Current value. The current value of the slider.

Extent of the knob. The width of the knob in units.

Position of major tick marks. Spacing between large ticks or markings that display the discrete values on the slider.

Position of minor tick marks. Spacing for small ticks on the slider.

The slider's orientation. The position of the slider, either horizontal or vertical.

All of the slider's values are used with a SliderUI object to draw the slider appropriately. They also update the slider's BoundedRangeModel when the user moves the knob.

Table 6.1 JSlider Constructors

Constructor	Function
JSlider()	Creates a slider with all default values.
JSlider(int,int,int,int)	Creates a slider with the specified orientation, minimum, maximum, and current values.

JSliders are created using one of the constructors shown in Table 6.1.

To set the values for a slider, you can use the following methods:

```
public void setExtent(int i);
public void setMajorTickSpacing(int i);
public void setMaximum(int i);
public void setMinimum(int i);
public void setMinorTickSpacing(int i);
public void setOrientation(int i);
public void setValue(int i);
```

This equivalent set of methods can retrieve the slider's values:

```
public int getExtent();
public int getMajorTickSpacing();
public int getMaximum();
public int getMinimum();
public int getMinorTickSpacing();
public int getOrientation();
public int getValue();
```

The slider must be told whether to display the ticks and tick labels. Use the setPaintTicks method to have the slider draw the tick marks on the slider itself. Use the setPaintLabels method to enable drawing of value labels along the slider:

```
public void setPaintTicks(boolean b);
public void setPaintLabels(boolean b);
```

You can also configure the slider to snap to the tick values using the method:

```
public void setSnapToTicks(boolean b);
```

In the following example, shown in Figure 6.1, we display five sliders in both the horizontal and vertical orientation. This allows us to show a variety of effects caused by different slider values.

This example is implemented as a subclass of JPanel. We have highlighted some of the key aspects of the code. As in some of our other examples, we have also used tool tips to indicate the slider's properties while the program is running.

Figure 6.1 Slider example.

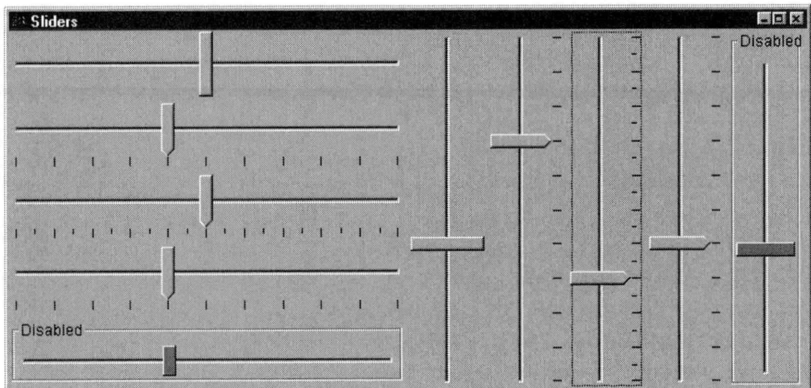

You can run this example from the included CD-ROM and hold the mouse over a slider to see the tool-tip message.

```
import java.util.*;
import java.awt.*;
import java.awt.event.*;
import com.sun.java.swing.*;
import com.sun.java.swing.border.*;

public class Sliders extends JPanel
{
    public Sliders()
    {
        JPanel left, right;
        JSlider slider;

        setBackground(Color.lightGray);
        setLayout(new GridLayout(1,2,5,5));
        /*
         * Turn on buffering to reduce flicker.
         */
        setDoubleBuffered(true);

        left = new JPanel();
        left.setLayout(new GridLayout(5,1,5,5));

        //Plain slider
        slider = new JSlider(JSlider.HORIZONTAL, 0, 100, 40);
```

```
slider.setToolTipText("0-100");
left.add(slider);

//Slider with major ticks
slider = new JSlider(JSlider.HORIZONTAL, 0, 100, 40);
slider.setToolTipText("Major ticks");
slider.setMajorTickSpacing(10);
slider.setPaintTicks(true);
left.add(slider);

//Slider with major and minor ticks
slider = new JSlider(JSlider.HORIZONTAL, 0, 100, 40);
slider.setToolTipText("Major & minor ticks");
slider.setMajorTickSpacing(10);
slider.setMinorTickSpacing(5);
slider.setPaintTicks(true);
left.add(slider);

//Slider with big extent
slider = new JSlider(JSlider.HORIZONTAL, 0, 100, 40);
slider.setToolTipText("0-100, extent = 20, snaps");
slider.setMajorTickSpacing(10);
slider.setExtent(20);
slider.setPaintTicks(true);
slider.setSnapToTicks(true);
left.add(slider);

//Disabled,bordered slider
slider = new JSlider(JSlider.HORIZONTAL, 0, 100, 40);
slider.setToolTipText("Disabled, bordered");
slider.setEnabled(false);
slider.setBorder(new TitledBorder("Disabled"));
left.add(slider);

add(left);

right = new JPanel();
right.setLayout(new GridLayout(1,5,5,5));

//Plain slider
slider = new JSlider(JSlider.VERTICAL, 0, 100, 40);
slider.setToolTipText("0-100");
right.add(slider);

//Slider with major ticks
```

```
        slider = new JSlider(JSlider.VERTICAL, 0, 100, 40);
        slider.setToolTipText("Major ticks");
        slider.setMajorTickSpacing(10);
        slider.setPaintTicks(true);
        right.add(slider);

        //Slider with major and minor ticks
        slider = new JSlider(JSlider.VERTICAL, 0, 100, 40);
        slider.setToolTipText("Major & minor ticks");
        slider.setMajorTickSpacing(10);
        slider.setMinorTickSpacing(5);
        slider.setPaintTicks(true);
        right.add(slider);

        //Slider with big extent
        slider = new JSlider(JSlider.VERTICAL, 0, 100, 40);
        slider.setToolTipText("0-100, extent = 20, snaps");
        slider.setMajorTickSpacing(10);
        slider.setExtent(20);
        slider.setPaintTicks(true);
        slider.setSnapToTicks(true);
        right.add(slider);

        //Disabled,bordered slider
        slider = new JSlider(JSlider.VERTICAL, 0, 100, 40);
        slider.setToolTipText("Disabled, bordered");
        slider.setEnabled(false);
        slider.setBorder(new TitledBorder("Disabled"));
        right.add(slider);

        add(right);
    }

    public Dimension getPreferredSize()
    {
        return new Dimension(650, 300);
    }

    public static void main(String s[])
    {
        JFrame frame = new JFrame("Sliders");
        Sliders panel = new Sliders();

        frame.setDefaultCloseOperation(JFrame.DO_NOTHING_ON_CLOSE);
        frame.setForeground(Color.black);
```

```
        frame.setBackground(Color.lightGray);
        frame.getContentPane().add(panel,"Center");

        frame.setSize(panel.getPreferredSize());
        frame.setVisible(true);
    }
}
```

Change Events

Many of the components and other objects in Swing allow the user to change a value. The meaning of this value can range dramatically based on the component. Regardless of the value type, these components use ChangeEvents to notify ChangeListeners when the value changes. For example, JSliders use change events to notify an object that their value has changed. A slider can be used to set the zoom level on a picture. As the user moves the slider, the associated image can scale from 1 to 100 percent. Changes are even used by noncomponents. For example, button models use change listeners to notify the button of changes, such as button presses, to the model's attributes.

ChangeListener is the interface that defines the relationship between the changer and the listener. ChangeListener defines a single method:

```
public void stateChanged(ChangeEvent e)
```

ChangeListeners normally register with the component they want to listen to using the method:

```
public void addChangeListener(ChangeListener l)
```

Some objects, however, provide other methods for registering the change listener. As we discuss the various components in Swing we indicate the proper methods for registering a change listener. You may also want to use the JDK and Swing documentation to identify the correct syntax for registering with a particular component or object.

The argument to stateChanged is a ChangeEvent object. ChangeEvent is a subclass of java.util.EventObject. Unlike ActionEvents, ChangeEvents do not contain extra information beyond the EventObject's source instance variable. In the case of a change event, the source is the object whose value is changing. To retrieve this object, use the method:

```
Object getSource()
```

Given the source, you can typecast it to the correct class and use methods of that class to learn about the change. The following example uses change events to update a text field when a slider is moved.

This example is implemented in the form of a subclass of JPanel. A main class method creates a Frame for the panel and then displays it. A helper class called WindowCloser is used to close the window when the close box is selected.

```
import java.applet.*;
import java.util.*;
import java.awt.*;
import java.awt.event.*;
import com.sun.java.swing.*;
import com.sun.java.swing.event.*;

public class Changes extends JPanel
implements ChangeListener
{
    JTextField field;

    public Changes()
    {
        JSlider slider;

        setBackground(Color.lightGray);
        setLayout(new GridLayout(1,2,10,10));
        /*
         * Turn on buffering to reduce flicker.
         */
        setDoubleBuffered(true);

        field = new JTextField("50",3);
        add(field);

        /*
         * Create a slider that is 5 wide and goes from 0 to 100.
         * The actual maximum is 105 to account for the sliders
         * extent/width.
         */
        slider = new JSlider(JSlider.HORIZONTAL,0,105,50);
        slider.setExtent(5);
        slider.addChangeListener(this);
        add(slider);
    }

    public void stateChanged(ChangeEvent e)
    {
        Object src;
```

```
        src = e.getSource();

        if(src instanceof JSlider)
        {
            JSlider slide = (JSlider) src;
            field.setText(Integer.toString(slide.getValue()));
        }
    }

    public Dimension getPreferredSize()
    {
        return new Dimension(200, 50);
    }

    public Dimension getMinimumSize()
    {
        return new Dimension(25, 25);
    }

    public Dimension getMaximumSize()
    {
        return getPreferredSize();
    }

    public static void main(String s[])
    {
        JFrame frame = new JFrame("Changes");
        Changes panel = new Changes();

        frame.setForeground(Color.black);
        frame.setBackground(Color.lightGray);
        frame.addWindowListener(new WindowCloser());
        frame.getContentPane().add(panel,"Center");

        frame.setSize(panel.getPreferredSize());
        frame.setVisible(true);
    }
}

class WindowCloser extends WindowAdapter
{
    public void windowClosing(WindowEvent e)
    {
        Window win = e.getWindow();
```

```
            win.setVisible(false);
            win.dispose();
            System.exit(0);
        }
    }
```

Figure 6.2 shows the updated text field when the slider is moved.

We have highlighted some of the key portions of this example using bold text to draw your attention to them. Although this is a simple example, it demonstrates how to define a ChangeListener, add it to a component, and respond to notification of change events. In future examples, we use these techniques to implement the user interface portions of our programs.

In our second example for this chapter we see how a ChangeListener is used to listen for changes to a button model's state. This example actually uses both actions and changes to keep a set of check boxes in sync with a button model. As in the first code listing, this example is implemented in the form of a subclass of JPanel. A main class method creates a Frame for the panel and displays it. A helper class called WindowCloser is used to close the window when the close box is selected.

```
import java.util.*;
import java.awt.*;
import java.awt.event.*;
import com.sun.java.swing.*;
import com.sun.java.swing.event.*;

public class ButtonModels extends JPanel
implements ActionListener, ChangeListener
{
    ButtonModel theModel;
    JCheckBox disableSwitch;
    JCheckBox armedSwitch;
    JCheckBox selectedSwitch;
    JCheckBox pressedSwitch;
    JButton exampleButton;

    public ButtonModels()
    {
        JPanel tmpPanel = new JPanel();
        GridLayout grid = new GridLayout(4,1,10,5);
```

Figure 6.2 Using ChangeListeners to handle slider updates.

```
        setLayout(new BorderLayout());
        /*
         * Turn on buffering to reduce flicker.
         */
        setDoubleBuffered(true);

        tmpPanel.setLayout(grid);

        armedSwitch = new JCheckBox("Armed");
        armedSwitch.addActionListener(this);
        tmpPanel.add(armedSwitch);

        disableSwitch = new JCheckBox("Disabled");
        disableSwitch.addActionListener(this);
        tmpPanel.add(disableSwitch);

        selectedSwitch = new JCheckBox("Selected");
        selectedSwitch.addActionListener(this);
        tmpPanel.add(selectedSwitch);

        pressedSwitch = new JCheckBox("Pressed");
        pressedSwitch.addActionListener(this);
        tmpPanel.add(pressedSwitch);

        add(tmpPanel,"West");

        tmpPanel = new JPanel();

        exampleButton = new JButton("Example");
        theModel = exampleButton.getModel();
        theModel.addChangeListener(this);
        tmpPanel.add(exampleButton);

        tmpPanel.add(new JButton("PlaceHolder"));

        add(tmpPanel,"Center");
    }

    //Handle model changes
    public void stateChanged(ChangeEvent e)
    {
        disableSwitch.setSelected(!theModel.isEnabled());
        armedSwitch.setSelected(theModel.isArmed());
        selectedSwitch.setSelected(theModel.isSelected());
```

```
        pressedSwitch.setSelected(theModel.isPressed());
    }

    //Handle changes to a checkbox
    public void actionPerformed(ActionEvent e)
    {
        theModel.setEnabled(!disableSwitch.isSelected());
        theModel.setArmed(armedSwitch.isSelected());
        theModel.setSelected(selectedSwitch.isSelected());
        theModel.setPressed(pressedSwitch.isSelected());
    }

    public Dimension getPreferredSize()
    {
        return new Dimension(200, 120);
    }

    public Dimension getMinimumSize()
    {
        return new Dimension(25, 25);
    }

    public Dimension getMaximumSize()
    {
        return getPreferredSize();
    }

    public static void main(String s[])
    {
        JFrame frame = new JFrame("Button Models");
        ButtonModels panel = new ButtonModels();

        frame.setForeground(Color.black);
        frame.setBackground(Color.lightGray);
        frame.addWindowListener(new WindowCloser());
        frame.getContentPane().add(panel,"Center");

        frame.setSize(panel.getPreferredSize());
        frame.setVisible(true);
    }
}

class WindowCloser extends WindowAdapter
{
```

Figure 6.3 Examining the changes in the button model.

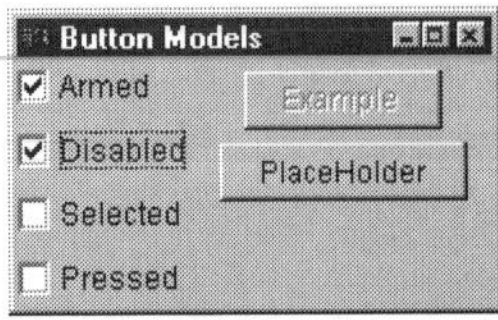


```
    public void windowClosing(WindowEvent e)
    {
        Window win = e.getWindow();
        win.setVisible(false);
        win.dispose();
        System.exit(0);
    }
}
```

Figure 6.3 shows the changes to the button model's state.

In general, you use models for more complex components like lists, trees, and tables. We used the button model in this example, both to explore the meanings behind its values and for simplicity.

Scroll Panes

Swing provides a generic component for scrolling other components in the form of JScrollPane. A scroll pane is actually a collection of several objects. First, there is the component to scroll. Next, there is a JViewPort that holds the scrolling component and clips it to fit inside the Scroll pane. The viewport is also responsible for moving the component around. Next, JScrollBars are used to tell the viewport where to position the component. Finally, a row and column header is used to display tick marks, rulers, or some other measure during scrolling. Figure 6.4 shows how these elements are combined in a word processor. In this case, the column header is used to display a ruler that scrolls with document horizontally.

The easiest way to use a scroll pane is to create one using the constructor:

```
public JScrollPane(Component c);
```

This creates a scroll pane with the specified component inside it. The scroll pane has both horizontal and vertical scrollbars—if necessary—and omits one or both scroll bars if they are not necessary.

You can also use the constructor where "hsp" and "vsp" are the horizontal and vertical scroll bar policies:

```
public JScrollPane(Component c, int hsp, int vsp);
```

Figure 6.4 ScrollPane elements.

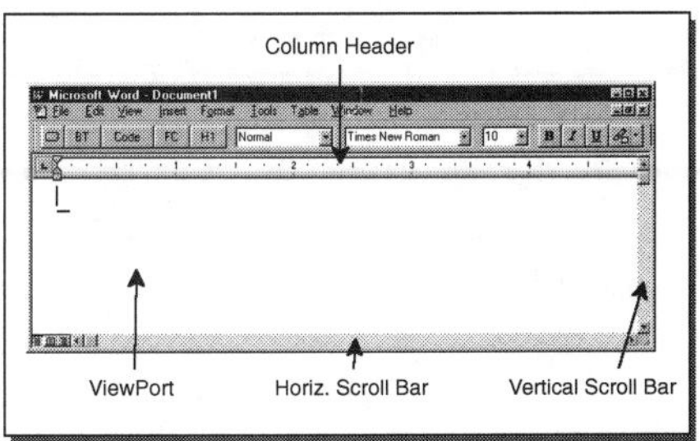

Table 6.2 shows the values that are set using the class variables of ScrollPaneConstants as implemented by JScrollPane.

As well as providing these policies during construction, you can set them using the scroll pane methods where the parameter x is one of the values in Table 6.2:

```
public void setHorizontalScrollBarPolicy(int x);
public void setVerticalScrollBarPolicy(int x);
```

The following example creates a subclass of JComponent that displays an image. One of these components is created and added to a JScrollPane before the scroll pane is added to a window. Notice that the component uses the method

Table 6.2 ScrollPane Constants for Setting Scroller Behavior

Variable	**Meaning**
HORIZONTAL_SCROLLBAR_ALWAYS	Sets a visible horizontal scroll bar on the pane regardless of the content's size.
HORIZONTAL_SCROLLBAR_AS_NEEDED	Sets the horizontal scroll bar to display only if the content of the pane is larger than the visible area.
HORIZONTAL_SCROLLBAR_NEVER	Turns off the horizontal scroll bar regardless of the size of the content area.
VERTICAL_SCROLLBAR_ALWAYS	Sets a visible vertical scroll bar on the pane regardless of the content's size.
VERTICAL_SCROLLBAR_AS_NEEDED	Sets the vertical scroll bar to display only if the content of the pane is larger than the visible area.
VERTICAL_SCROLLBAR_NEVER	Turns off the vertical scroll bar regardless of the size of the content area.

scrollRectToVisible to tell the scroll pane what to display. The scroll pane also works with the component to implement an auto-scrolling feature.

```
import com.sun.java.swing.*;
import java.awt.event.*;
import java.awt.*;

public class AutoScrollExample extends JComponent
{
    Image img;

    public void paint(Graphics g)
    {
        if(img == null)
        {
            img = getToolkit().getImage("logo.gif");
        }

        g.drawImage(img,0,0,600,600,this);
    }

    public Dimension getPreferredSize()
    {
        return new Dimension(600, 600);
    }

    public static void main(String s[])
    {
        JFrame frame = new JFrame("AutoScroll Example");
        AutoScrollExample comp = new AutoScrollExample();

        frame.setDefaultCloseOperation(JFrame.DO_NOTHING_ON_CLOSE);
        frame.setForeground(Color.black);
        frame.setBackground(Color.lightGray);
        frame.getContentPane().add(new JScrollPane(comp),"Center");

        frame.setSize(new Dimension(300,300));
        frame.setVisible(true);

        comp.setAutoscrolls(true);

        comp.scrollRectToVisible(new Rectangle(150,150,300,300));
    }
}
```

Figure 6.5 Scrolling an image using auto-scroll.

Figure 6.5 shows the ScrollPane scrolling an image.

Style Guidelines

Use sliders only when the user has a clear range of values from which to choose. It's also useful to provide a text field with the slider that allows the user to type in a specific value, rather than trying to find that value using the mouse. Many users find the process of carefully dragging the mouse time-consuming and tedious. They prefer to enter a number using the keyboard. Sliders, however, can be the best interface choice when the user wants to change a value dynamically, observing the changes in real time. For instance, it is more effective to adjust your longitude or latitude on a visual map using a slider than typing in each coordinate, then moving and typing it in another one. In this case, the text field can be used for the final value, but the slider is used to identify the preferred range.

Often an interface can exceed a reasonable window size. For example, a spreadsheet is often larger than the screen. In cases like this you need to use a scroll pane. Luckily, the Swing scroll pane, JScrollPane, is easy to use and provides the scrolling behavior you require with little or no additional coding. You might say that you get scrolling for your component for "free." Make sure to put all of your tables, lists, trees, and text areas in a scroll pane unless you are positive that their data will not exceed the available space. That said, it's not generally a good idea to place a panel or collection of interface elements in a scrolling area. Users expect the UI elements, such as buttons, sliders, and text fields, to remain fairly stationary in the user interface. An exception to this rule is a form on a Web page. Web pages often scroll, and the form elements scroll off the screen. Because users find this confusing, you should avoid scrolling in your Web form design. Use scrolling for large monolithic components, not forms.

HANDLING SIMPLE TEXT USING SWING

7

A great deal of emphasis is placed on text handling in the user interface of applications. That's because text is the most significant form of input and output in most applications. Swing provides a number of components that handle text in the UI. These components include a label that displays read-only text, a text field that enters a single line of text, and a text area that enters multiple lines of text. Each of these components deals with a single string with one set of font styles applied. In Chapter 15 we also see that Swing provides components for managing multiple lines of styled text, including bold, italic, and even HTML styles.

These text components simplify the processing of user input and application output in the user interface. To take advantage of these components you should understand the underlying event mechanism for handling key events as well as the higher-level mechanisms for managing the text those key events create. Key events are slightly more complex to handle than mouse events because they have no location associated with them. When a key is pressed, how does your application know where to display the character associated with that key? The answer is that both Swing and AWT keep track of the currently selected component. The component is said to have *focus*. Swing also provides support for the use of Tab keys to navigate the interface by changing the currently focused component. In this chapter we discuss not only how to receive notification of focus changes, but also how to create a component that can receive the keyboard's focus.

Labels

A label in Swing is like a button that can't be pressed. For instance, a data entry form usually contains a set of text labels that denote the information input into the associated text field such as name, city, state, zip, and so on. The JLabel class is a Swing label that defines a simple, rectangular component that draws a text message and an icon.

JLabel has constructors that allow you to create a label with a text string, a graphic, or both. The constructors are shown in Table 7.1.

Table 7.1 JLabel Constructors

Method	Function
JLabel()	Creates a label with no set text or icon.
JLabel(Icon)	Creates a label with an icon.
JLabel(String)	Creates a label with text.
JLabel(String, Icon)	Creates a label with text and an icon.
JLabel(Icon,int)	Creates a label with an icon, using the specified horizontal alignment.
JLabel(String,int)	Creates a label with text, using the specified horizontal alignment.
JLabel(String, Icon,int)	Creates a label with text and an icon, using the specified horizontal alignment.

The position of the text and icon relative to the label's border is specified using the following methods for horizontal and vertical alignment:

```
public void setHorizontalAlignment(int align);
public void setVerticalAlignment(int align);
```

The argument "align" is one of the static variables:

```
TOP
BOTTOM
CENTER
LEFT
RIGHT
```

These variables are defined in the interface SwingConstants as implemented by JLabel. The default value for both directions is CENTER. This alignment affects both a label's text and its icon. The nine possible combinations of the horizontal and vertical alignment are pictured in Figure 7.1.

The relationship between the text and icon is assigned using the following methods:

```
public void setHorizontalTextPosition(int textPosition);
public void setVerticalTextPosition(int textPosition);
```

Figure 7.2 shows the possible combinations of text positions relative to an icon. Because JLabel is a rather simple object compared to the others we have discussed, let's look at an example without further discussion. This example is pictured in Figure 7.3.

Figure 7.1 Possible alignments of text and icons on a label.

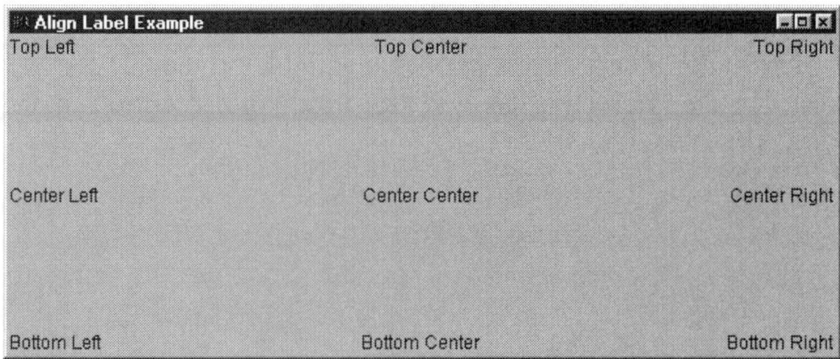

Figure 7.2 Possible text positions for labels.

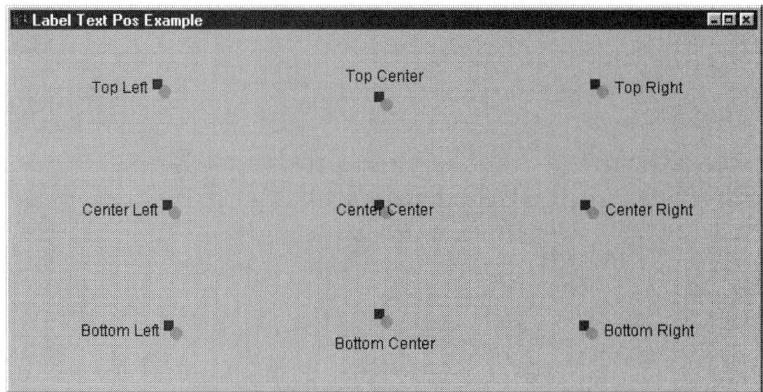

Figure 7.3 Examples of JLabel.

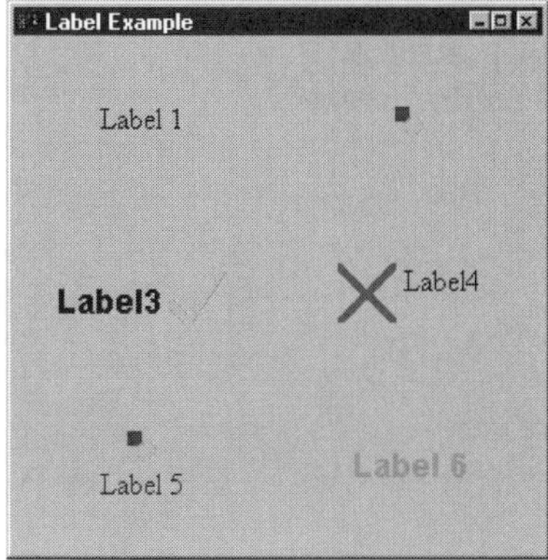

This example is implemented as a subclass of JPanel. Six JLabels are displayed in a grid. Each label has a different attributes set. These attributes are provided in the label's tool tip, which appears when you hold the mouse over the label. The code for this example, as with the others in this book, is available on the CD-ROM. We have highlighted some of the interesting methods to draw your attention to the major functionality in the label.

```
import com.sun.java.swing.*;
import java.awt.event.*;
import java.awt.*;

public class LabelExample extends JPanel
{

    public LabelExample()
    {
        ImageIcon img;
        JLabel label;
        Font font,bold;

        //Make the default font bigger, and buffer the example
        font = new Font("Serif",Font.PLAIN,16);
        bold = new Font("SanSerif",Font.BOLD,18);
        setFont(font);
        setDoubleBuffered(true);

        setLayout(new GridLayout(3,2,5,5));

        label = new JLabel("Label 1");
        label.setFont(font);
        label.setToolTipText("Just Text");
        label.setHorizontalAlignment(label.CENTER);
        label.setVerticalTextPosition(label.BOTTOM);
        label.setHorizontalTextPosition(label.CENTER);
        add(label);

        img = new ImageIcon("images/shapes.gif");

        label = new JLabel();
        label.setFont(font);
        label.setIcon(img);
        label.setToolTipText("Just Image");
```

```
label.setHorizontalAlignment(label.CENTER);

add(label);

img = new ImageIcon("images/check.gif");

label = new JLabel("Label3");
label.setFont(font);
label.setIcon(img);
label.setToolTipText("Text and Image, bold font."
                        +" Text at bottom left");
label.setVerticalTextPosition(label.BOTTOM);
label.setHorizontalAlignment(label.CENTER);
label.setHorizontalTextPosition(label.LEFT);
label.setFont(bold);
add(label);


img = new ImageIcon("images/ex.gif");

label = new JLabel("Label4");
label.setFont(font);
label.setIcon(img);
label.setToolTipText("Text and Image. Text at top-right");
label.setVerticalTextPosition(label.TOP);
label.setHorizontalAlignment(label.CENTER);
label.setHorizontalTextPosition(label.RIGHT);
add(label);

img = new ImageIcon("images/shapes.gif");

label = new JLabel("Label 5");
label.setFont(font);
label.setIcon(img);
label.setToolTipText("Text and Image, blue foreground");
label.setVerticalTextPosition(label.BOTTOM);
label.setHorizontalAlignment(label.CENTER);
label.setHorizontalTextPosition(label.CENTER);
label.setForeground(Color.blue);
add(label);

label = new JLabel("Label 6");
```

```
        label.setToolTipText("Text, Green and Bold");
        label.setVerticalTextPosition(label.BOTTOM);
        label.setHorizontalAlignment(label.CENTER);
        label.setHorizontalTextPosition(label.CENTER);
        label.setFont(bold);
        label.setForeground(Color.green);
        add(label);
    }

    public Dimension getPreferredSize()
    {
        return new Dimension(300, 300);
    }

    public static void main(String s[])
    {
        JFrame frame = new JFrame("Label Example");
        LabelExample panel = new LabelExample();

        frame.setDefaultCloseOperation(JFrame.DO_NOTHING_ON_CLOSE);
        frame.setForeground(Color.black);
        frame.setBackground(Color.lightGray);
        frame.getContentPane().add(panel,"Center");

        frame.setSize(panel.getPreferredSize());
        frame.setVisible(true);
    }
}
```

Figure 7.3 shows examples of JLabel features.

Text Components

JavaSoft increased code reuse and decreased the size of the Swing library by creating a semi-abstract, superclass for the available text components. This defining superclass is called JTextComponent and is defined in the package com.sun.java.swing.text. JTextComponent defines the architecture for a text component and implements the methods that manipulate a textual content. Table 7.2 shows these methods.

JTextComponent provides a sophisticated mechanism for handling text processing. Swing provides two subclasses of JTextComponent that simplify common text-handling behaviors. These subclasses, JTextField and JtextArea, are equivalent to the AWT TextField and TextArea classes. The majority of the methods used to interact with text fields and text areas are inherited from JTextComponent and are listed in Table 7.3.

Table 7.2 JTextComponent Methods and Their Functions

Method	Function
public void setText(String text)	Sets the text for this text component.
public String getText()	Returns the string contained in the text component.
public synchronized void selectAll()	Selects all the text in the text component.
public void select(int selection Start,int selectionEnd)	Selects a range of text in the text component.
public String getSelectedText()	Returns a string containing the portion of the text component's text that is currently selected.
public void replaceSelection (String content)	Replaces the text currently selected in text component with the content string.

Table 7.3 Text-Handling Methods of JTextComponent

Method	Function
Public Color getCaretColor()	Returns the current color used to draw the caret or cursor.
Public void setCaretColor(Color c)	Sets the current color used to render the caret.
Public Color getSelectionColor()	Returns the current color used to render the selection.
Public void setSelectionColor(Color c)	Sets the current color used to render the selection.
Public Color getSelectedTextColor()	Returns the current color used to render the selected text.
Public void setSelectedTextColor (Color c)	Sets the current color used to render the selected text.
Public Color getDisabledTextColor()	Returns the current color used to render the disabled text.
Public void setDisabledTextColor (Color c)	Sets the current color used to render the disabled text.
Public void replaceSelection (String content)	Replaces the currently selected text in the text component with the content string. If there is no selection this is equivalent to an insert operation. If the content string is null, then this operation is equivalent to a deletion of the current selection.

Continued

Table 7.3 Text-Handling Methods of JTextComponent (*Continued*)

Method	Function
Public String getText (int offs,int len)	Returns a portion of the text represented by the text component. Throws BadLocationException if the offset or length are invalid.
Public void cut()	Moves the currently selected range to the system clipboard, where it can be shared with other applications. The current selection for this text component is reset.
Public void copy()	Copies the currently selected range of text to the system clipboard. The current selection remains intact.
Public void paste()	Copies the contents of the system clipboard into the text component. If there is already a selection in the component, it is replaced with the contents of the clipboard. If there is no selection, the clipboard contents are inserted in front of the current insert position in the text component.
Public void moveCaretPosition (int pos)	Moves the caret to a new position, leaving behind a mark defined by the last time CaretPosition was called. This is how a selection is created.
Public void setFocusAccelerator (char aKey)	Sets the key accelerator, a keyboard character that has been associated with this component, that will cause the receiving text component to get the focus.
Public char getFocusAccelerator()	Returns the key accelerator that will cause the receiving text component to get the focus. Returns \0 if no focus accelerator has been set.
Public void setCaretPosition (int position)	Sets the position of the text insertion caret for the text component. Throws: IllegalArgument-Exception if position is less than 0 or greater than the length of the associated text.
Public int getCaretPosition()	Returns the position of the text insertion caret for the text component.
Public void setText(String t)	Sets the text of this text component to the specified string.
Public String getText()	Returns the text contained in this text component.

Table 7.3 Continued

Method	Function
Public String getSelectedText()	Returns the selected text contained in this text component. Throws: IllegalArgumentException if the selection isn't valid for some reason.
Public boolean isEditable()	Returns the Boolean indicating whether this text component is editable.
Public synchronized void setEditable(boolean b)	Sets the specified Boolean to indicate whether this text component should be editable.
Public synchronized int getSelectionStart()	Returns the selected text's starting position.
Public synchronized void setSelectionStart(int selectionStart)	Sets the selection start to the specified position. The new starting point is constrained to be before or at the current selection end.
Public synchronized int getSelectionEnd()	Returns the selected text's ending position.
Public synchronized void setSelectionEnd(int selectionEnd)	Sets the selection end to the specified position. The new end point is constrained to be at or after the current selection start.
Public void select(int selectionStart, int selectionEnd)	Selects the text found between the specified start and end locations. This call is provided for backward compatibility. The preferred way to manage selection is by calling setCaretPosition followed by moveCaretPostion.
Public synchronized void selectAll()	Selects all the text in the Text component.

Text Fields

JTextField defines a component that contains a single string of unstyled text. The size of a field is defined with the number of columns that it's told to display. By default a JTextField is 0 columns wide. If it's created with a default value, the field is as wide as the string in the current font. Aside from the constructors that allow you to create different default values for the columns and content, JTextField defines only one main feature not inherited from JTextComponent: the use of action events. Action events notify a program when the user presses the Return key. We discussed ActionEvents in Chapter 4. Because JTextFields are simple objects, we provide a small example that demonstrates the various constructors and includes code for setting a field's font. The running version of this example is pictured in Figure 7.4. At first glance, the user interface for this example is odd. We intended it to be that way to highlight the behavior of each constructor.

This example is implemented in the form of a subclass of JPanel. A main class method creates a Frame for the panel and then displays it. When this window appears you see four text fields, each created with a different constructor. Notice that the default constructor creates a very short field. You must resize this field or rely on the layout manager to resize it before it is useful. In general, the best way to create a text field is to provide the number of columns and, possibly, an initial value to ensure that the field is sized correctly.

```
import java.util.*;
import java.awt.*;
import java.awt.event.*;
import com.sun.java.swing.*;
import com.sun.java.swing.text.*;

public class Fields extends JPanel
{
    public Fields()
    {
        JTextField field;
        JPanel tmpPanel;
        Font font;

        /*
         * Use a grid layout, and turn on buffering to reduce flicker.
         */
        setLayout(new GridLayout(4,1,10,10));
        setBackground(Color.lightGray);
        setDoubleBuffered(true);

        /*
         * Create a field with 10 columns.
         * Set the font to 16pt. plain serif.
         */
        field = new JTextField(10);
        font = new Font("Serif",Font.PLAIN,16);
        field.setFont(font);

        /* Add the field to a panel first, to prevent
         * unwanted resizing.
         */
        tmpPanel = new JPanel();
        tmpPanel.setLayout(new FlowLayout(FlowLayout.CENTER));
```

```
tmpPanel.add(field);
add(tmpPanel);


/*
 * Create a field with the initial string "hello".
 * Set the font to 18pt. Bold sanserif.
 * Make the field non-editable.
 */
field = new JTextField("Hello");
field.setEditable(false);
font = new Font("Sanserif",Font.BOLD,18);
field.setFont(font);

/* Add the field to a panel first, to prevent
 * unwanted resizing.
 */
tmpPanel = new JPanel();
tmpPanel.setLayout(new FlowLayout(FlowLayout.CENTER));
tmpPanel.add(field);
add(tmpPanel);

/*
 * Create a field with the initial string "World", and 15
 * columns.
 * Set the font to 14pt. Italic sanserif.
 */
field = new JTextField("World",15);
font = new Font("Sanserif",Font.ITALIC,14);
field.setFont(font);

/* Add the field to a panel first, to prevent
 * unwanted resizing.
 */
tmpPanel = new JPanel();
tmpPanel.setLayout(new FlowLayout(FlowLayout.CENTER));
tmpPanel.add(field);
add(tmpPanel);

/*
 * Create a default field.
 * Set the font to 20pt. plain serif.
 */
field = new JTextField();
font = new Font("Serif",Font.PLAIN,20);
```

```
        field.setFont(font);

        /* Add the field to a panel first, to prevent
         * unwanted resizing.
         */
        tmpPanel = new JPanel();
        tmpPanel.setLayout(new FlowLayout(FlowLayout.CENTER));
        tmpPanel.add(field);
        add(tmpPanel);


    }

    public Dimension getPreferredSize()
    {
        return new Dimension(200, 200);
    }

    public static void main(String s[])
    {
        JFrame frame = new JFrame("Fields");
        Fields panel = new Fields();

        frame.setDefaultCloseOperation(JFrame.DO_NOTHING_ON_CLOSE);
        frame.setForeground(Color.black);
        frame.setBackground(Color.lightGray);
        frame.getContentPane().add(panel,"Center");

        frame.setSize(panel.getPreferredSize());
        frame.setVisible(true);
    }
}
```

Figure 7.4 shows examples of JTextFields.

Password Fields

When creating applications that require the user to enter confidential information, such as login passwords, it's customary to blank out the text field so that as the user types a password he or she does not have to worry about people seeing it. You have probably noticed that automatic teller machines behave this way when you enter your personal identification number (PIN). Swing provides a subclass of JTextField called JPasswordField that performs this function. You create a JPasswordField using the constructors in Table 7.4.

Figure 7.4 Examples of JTextFields.

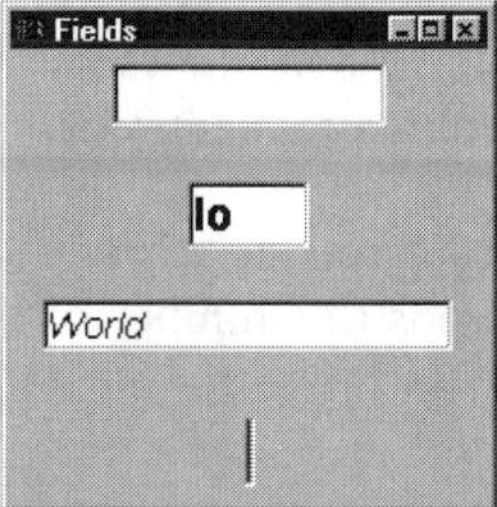

A JPasswordField is a text field that uses an echo character to hide the user's actual entry. For instance, when a user types in the password "HeLLO&Dolly", all that's visible in the password field, with an echo character of asterisk, is "***********". The echo character is set using the following method:

```
public void setEchoChar(char c);
```

You can test if an echo character is set using the following method:

```
public boolean echoCharIsSet();
```

If no echo character is set, the password field may or may not display the content based on the current look and feel. In fact, the field may ignore the echo character altogether, depending on the installed look and feel. Other than the echo character behavior, the JPasswordField behaves like a JTextField.

Table 7.4 Constructors for a JPasswordField

Method	Function
JPasswordField()	Constructs a new JPasswordField.
JPasswordField(Document, String, int)	Constructs a new JPasswordField that uses the given text storage model, given text string, and the given number of columns.
JPasswordField(int)	Constructs a new empty JPasswordField with the specified number of columns.
JPasswordField(String)	Constructs a new JPasswordField initialized with the specified text string.
JPasswordField(String, int)	Constructs a new JPasswordField initialized with the specified text string and number of columns.

Text Areas

JTextAreas are similar to JTextFields except they contain multiple rows. As with JTextFields, the assigned number of rows and columns for an area determines its preferred size. Because a text area can be used to provide unlimited text entry, it is often added to scroll panes before displayed.

JTextAreas support the Tab key. The number of spaces to associate with this key is configured using the setTabSize method, where size is the number of characters to which a tab is equivalent.

```
public void setTabSize(int size);
```

Because JTextAreas are simple subclasses of JTextFields, we provide a small example that demonstrates the various constructors, and includes code for setting a field's font. The running version of this example is pictured in Figure 7.5.

This example is implemented in the form of a subclass of JPanel.

```
import java.util.*;
import java.awt.*;
import java.awt.event.*;
import com.sun.java.swing.*;
import com.sun.java.swing.text.*;

public class Areas extends JPanel
{
    public Areas()
    {
        JTextArea area;
        JPanel tmpPanel;
        Font font;

        /*
         * Use a grid layout, and turn on buffering to reduce flicker.
         */
        setLayout(new GridLayout(4,1,10,10));
        setBackground(Color.lightGray);
        setDoubleBuffered(true);

        /*
         * Create a area with 10 rows and columns.
         * Set the font to 16pt. plain serif.
         */
        area = new JTextArea(10,10);
        font = new Font("Serif",Font.PLAIN,16);
        area.setFont(font);
```

```
        add(area);


        /*
         * Create a area with the initial string "hello".
         * Set the font to 18pt. Bold sanserif.
         * Make the area non-editable.
         */
        area = new JTextArea("Hello");
        area.setEditable(false);
        font = new Font("Sanserif",Font.BOLD,18);
        area.setFont(font);

        add(new JScrollPane(area));

        /*
         * Create a area with the initial string "World", and 10
         * rows,15 columns.
         * only allow vertical scrollbars
         * Set the font to 14pt. Italic sanserif.
         */
        area = new JTextArea("World",10,15);
        font = new Font("Sanserif",Font.ITALIC,14);
        area.setFont(font);

        add(new JScrollPane(area));

        /*
         * Create a default area.
         * Set the font to 20pt. plain serif.
         */
        area = new JTextArea();
        font = new Font("Serif",Font.PLAIN,20);
        area.setFont(font);

        add(new JScrollPane(area));
    }

    public Dimension getPreferredSize()
    {
        return new Dimension(300, 500);
    }
```

```
    public static void main(String s[])
    {
        JFrame frame = new JFrame("Areas");
        Areas panel = new Areas();

        frame.setDefaultCloseOperation(JFrame.DO_NOTHING_ON_CLOSE);
        frame.setForeground(Color.black);
        frame.setBackground(Color.lightGray);
        frame.getContentPane().add(panel,"Center");

        frame.setSize(panel.getPreferredSize());
        frame.setVisible(true);
    }
}
```

Figure 7.5 shows examples of JTextAreas.

Handling Text-Related Events with Swing

To manage text components you need to know two things:

1. How to create the various text components described in the previous sections of this chapter
2. How to handle and respond to the events generated by these objects

The events that are of special concern for text handling are *focus events* and *key events.* Focus events are generated with the object that currently has the keyboard focus. This means that it's currently receiving keyboard input. Key events are related to keyboard activities such as key presses or key releases.

Focus Events

Mouseless operation was originally introduced into the JDK in version 1.1. It consists of two techniques: focus traversal and menu shortcuts. *Focus traversal* is a programmer-defined system that allows the user to move keyboard focus using the keyboard instead of the mouse. Often the Tab key is used to change focus. *Menu shortcuts* are programmer-defined keys that the user can press to activate a drop-down menu. Notice that both of these techniques keep the user's hands on the keyboard. This makes them useful to power users, who probably touch type and find using the mouse inefficient at times. Mouseless operations can also improve accessibility because the keyboard is operated with Boolean operations such as press/release, rather than the highly sensitive dragging required for mouse use. Your interaction with mouseless operations is relatively easy to implement, but it can add a lot to the final program. We discuss focus traversal here because it relates to key events specifically. Menu shortcuts are discussed in Chapter 8, as part of our discussion of menus.

Figure 7.5 Creating JTextAreas.

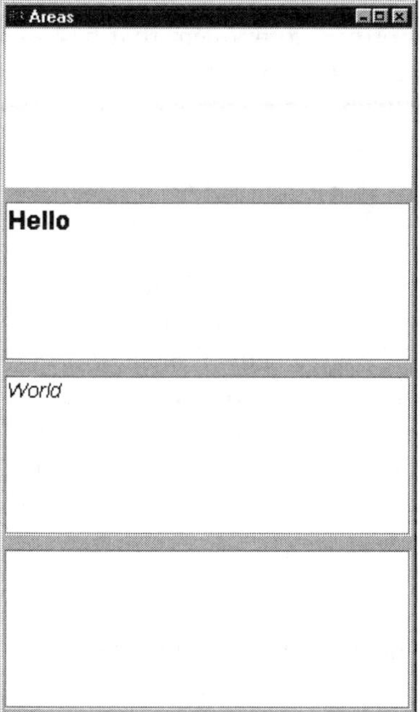

Focus Traversal Technique

The focus traversal system is designed to give users the ability to tab between components. The Tab key moves forward through the traversal path, and the Shift-Tab combination moves backward through the traversal path. The default order of traversal is the order in which items are added to their container. This system is hierarchical, so that the ultimate order is created with flattening the hierarchy.

Using focus traversal with provided components is automatic. Simply add them to the user interface and they participate in the focus traversal system appropriately, based on the current look and feel. If you want to create your own components and have them participate in focus traversal, follow these four steps.

1. Override the isFocusTraversable method inherited from JComponent and return "true."
2. Handle mouse-down events by implementing the MouseListener interface and setting your object as a mouse listener for your component.
3. When this object receives a mouse-down event, request focus by calling the component's method setFocus.

4. Implement a paint method to provide some form of visual feedback when the component has focus.

These steps rely on the use of FocusEvents to notify a component that has keyboard focus. The 1.1 version of the JDK introduced the concept of *focus events*. An item is focused when it is the target for keyboard events. Logically there can only be one focused component at a time, making the change of focus an important occurrence. An example occurs when the user tabs from the name field in a form to the address field. In this case, the name field loses focus and the address field gains focus.

All Swing components can notify listeners about focus events. To register as a listener, an object must implement the FocusListener interface. This interface defines two methods: focusGained and focusLost. The focusGained method is invoked when the object receives focus. This means it can now receive keyboard events. The focusLost method is invoked when the object loses focus. This means it's no longer the object that receives keyboard events. The syntax for these methods is as follows:

```
public void focusGained(FocusEvent e)
public void focusLost(FocusEvent e)
```

Use the addFocusListener method to add a focus listener to a component:

```
public void addFocusListener(FocusListener fl);
```

In our next example we display several JTextFields. A FocusListener is used to print a message when the focus changes for any field.

This example is implemented in the form of a subclass of JPanel. A main class method creates a Frame for the panel and then displays it. A helper class called WindowCloser is used to close the window when the close box is selected.

Figure 7.6 shows how focus events are intercepted.

Figure 7.6 Focus traversal example.

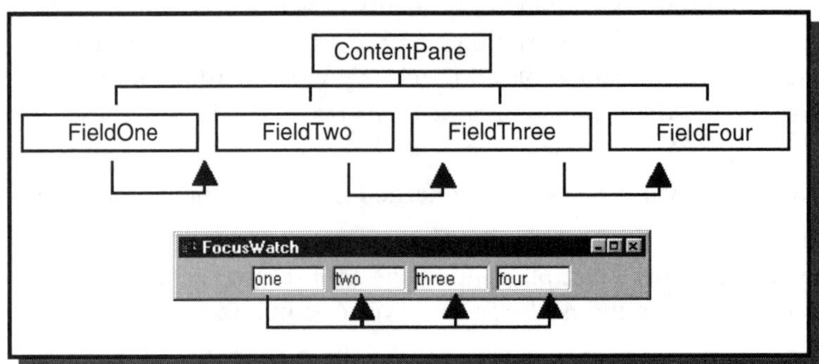

```
import java.applet.*;
import java.util.*;
import java.awt.*;
import java.awt.event.*;
import com.sun.java.swing.*;
import com.sun.java.swing.text.*;

public class FocusWatch extends JPanel
implements FocusListener
{
    public FocusWatch()
    {
        JTextField field;
        /*
         * Turn on buffering to reduce flicker.
         */
        setDoubleBuffered(true);

        field = new JTextField("one",5);
        field.addFocusListener(this);
        add(field);

        field = new JTextField("two",5);
        field.addFocusListener(this);
        add(field);

        field = new JTextField("three",5);
        field.addFocusListener(this);
        add(field);

        field = new JTextField("four",5);
        field.addFocusListener(this);
        add(field);
    }

    public void focusGained(FocusEvent e)
    {
        JTextField field = (JTextField) e.getSource();
        String text = field.getText();
        System.out.println("Focus gained by: "+text);
    }

    public void focusLost(FocusEvent e)
```

```
    {
        JTextField field = (JTextField) e.getSource();
        String text = field.getText();
        System.out.println("Focus lost by: "+text);
    }

    public Dimension getPreferredSize()
    {
        return new Dimension(350, 50);
    }

    public static void main(String s[])
    {
        JFrame frame = new JFrame("FocusWatch");
        FocusWatch panel = new FocusWatch();

        frame.setForeground(Color.black);
        frame.setBackground(Color.lightGray);
        frame.addWindowListener(new WindowCloser());
        frame.getContentPane().add(panel,"Center");

        frame.setSize(panel.getPreferredSize());
        frame.setVisible(true);
    }
}

class WindowCloser extends WindowAdapter
{
    public void windowClosing(WindowEvent e)
    {
        Window win = e.getWindow();
        win.setVisible(false);
        win.dispose();
        System.exit(0);
    }
}
```

We have highlighted some of the key portions of this example using bold text to draw your attention to them. Although this is a simple example, it demonstrates how to define a FocusListener, add it to a component, and respond to notification of item events. Notice that we add the same focus listener to each text field and then read the value in the event to determine which field has gained or lost focus.

The following example demonstrates how you can implement custom components that handle focus traversal. This example is implemented as a simple subclass of JComponent that is focus traversal and highlights itself when it has focus.

When run, the example program looks like Figure 7.7. Be sure to try using the Tab and Shift-Tab operations to change focus in the running program. Note that pressing these keys "jumps" your focus to the next or previous field. We have implemented this example in one file for simplicity. The first part of our example defines a class called Lense that accepts focus.

```
import java.applet.*;
import java.util.*;
import java.awt.*;
import java.awt.event.*;
import com.sun.java.swing.*;
import com.sun.java.swing.border.*;


class Lense extends JComponent
implements MouseListener, FocusListener
{
    boolean hasFocus;

    public Lense()
    {
        addMouseListener(this);
        addFocusListener(this);
    }

    public void paint(Graphics g)
    {
        Rectangle bounds = getBounds();
        g.setColor(Color.gray);
        g.fillRect(0,0,bounds.width,bounds.height);

        if(hasFocus)
        {
            g.setColor(Color.green);
            g.drawRect(0,0,bounds.width-1,bounds.height-1);
        }
```

Figure 7.7 Handling focus events.

```
        else
        {
            g.setColor(Color.black);
            g.drawRect(0,0,bounds.width-1,bounds.height-1);
        }
    }

    public Dimension getPreferredSize()
    {
        return new Dimension(16,16);
    }

    public Dimension getMinimumSize()
    {
        return new Dimension(16,16);
    }

    public boolean isFocusTraversable()
    {
        return true;
    }

    public void focusGained(FocusEvent e)
    {
        hasFocus = true;
        repaint();
    }

    public void focusLost(FocusEvent e)
    {
        hasFocus = false;
        repaint();
    }

    public void mouseClicked(MouseEvent evt)
    {
        requestFocus();
    }

    public void mouseEntered(MouseEvent evt)
    {
    }

    public void mouseExited(MouseEvent evt)
```

```
        {
        }

        public void mousePressed(MouseEvent evt)
        {
        }

        public void mouseReleased(MouseEvent evt)
        {
        }
    }
```

The remainder of this example creates several Lenses objects and displays them.

```
    public class Lenses extends JPanel
    {
        public Lenses()
        {
            setBackground(Color.lightGray);

            setLayout(new GridLayout(1,4,5,5));
            add(new Lense());
            add(new Lense());
            add(new Lense());
            add(new Lense());
        }
        public Dimension getPreferredSize()
        {
            return new Dimension(300, 200);
        }

        public static void main(String s[])
        {
            JFrame frame = new JFrame("Focus Example");
            Lenses panel = new Lenses();

            frame.setForeground(Color.black);
            frame.setBackground(Color.lightGray);
            frame.addWindowListener(new WindowCloser());
            frame.getContentPane().add(panel,"Center");

            frame.setSize(panel.getPreferredSize());
            frame.setVisible(true);
        }
    }
```

```
class WindowCloser extends WindowAdapter
{
    public void windowClosing(WindowEvent e)
    {
        Window win = e.getWindow();
        win.setVisible(false);
        win.dispose();
        System.exit(0);
    }
}
```

Figure 7.8 shows a set of components that use focus traversal.

You can manage the focus traversal of your interface by creating a custom FocusManager. Subclass FocusManager, and use this static method to make your focus manager the current one:

```
public static void setCurrentManager(FocusManager fm);
```

Keyboard Events

Swing provides two mechanisms for handling key events. First, there is a low-level, event-processing architecture. This design allows a component to see and react to all key events. The second mechanism for handling key events is the delegation model using listeners, as described in Chapter 2. Although both of these mechanisms are provided, JavaSoft suggests that programmers rely on the standard delegation model whenever possible. This model allows programmers to customize a component's behavior without subclassing.

Key events are separated into three types:

Key press. Sent when the user presses keyboard key.

Key release. Sent when the user releases a key on the keyboard key.

Key typed. Platform-independent version of the previous two event types.

Figure 7.8 Custom components that support focus traversal.

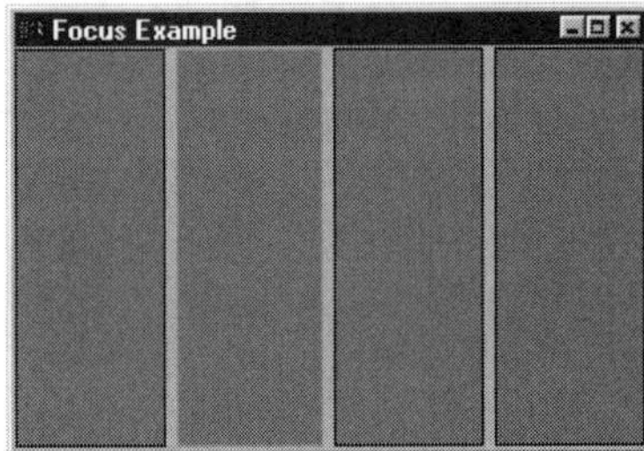

The key-typed event is provided as a platform-independent notification when a key is typed, regardless of how the Swing library discovered the typing. In Swing this distinction is of less value than in AWT, where the components rely on native code for notification of events.

Raw key events are initially processed by a method called processEvent. In fact, all of a component's events are filtered through this fundamental method. The processEvent method separates key events from other event types and forwards them to the processKeyEvent method. Custom components that want to handle these raw events override processKeyEvent. In your subclass's implementation for any event-processing method, call the inherited version via super. The Component classes version for these processing methods notifies listeners of the events. If you don't use the inherited version then you are responsible for notifying listeners.

TIP

Always call the inherited version of the processKeyEvent method to notify listeners. To ensure that listeners are notified correctly, use listeners instead of raw, key-event processing when possible.

To improve performance, Swing is designed to ignore events that no object is watching for. For instance, if your application isn't interested in the user releasing the mouse button that was previously pressed, then your application can ignore this event type, saving valuable processing time. In the case of key events, this means that the Component's processEvent method ignores key events if not told to do otherwise. Events are enabled and disabled using the methods enableEvents and disableEvents.

```
public void enableEvents(long mask);
public void disableEvents(long mask);
```

These methods take as arguments a mask defined from class variables in the class AWTEvent.

```
AWTEvent.KEY_EVENT_MASK
```

To handle key events via listeners, you need to implement the KeyListener interface. This interface defines three methods:

```
public abstract void keyTyped(KeyEvent e)
public abstract void keyPressed(KeyEvent e)
public abstract void keyReleased(KeyEvent e)
```

Listeners are added to a component using the addKeyListener method. Adding a listener automatically enables the associated events. In other words, when you add a KeyListener, the component automatically enables AWTEvent .KEY_EVENT_MASK if it's not already enabled. Upon notification, the listener

Table 7.5 KeyEvent Methods and Their Functions

Method	Function
Public int getKeyCode()	Returns the integer key-code associated with the key in this event. For KEY_TYPED events, keyCode is VK_UNDEFINED.
Public char getKeyChar()	Returns the character associated with the key in this event. If no valid Unicode character exists for this key event, keyChar is CHAR_UNDEFINED.
Public static String getKeyText (int keyCode)	Returns a String describing the keyCode, such as "HOME," "F1," or "A."
Public static String getKeyModifiersText(int modifiers)	Returns a String describing the modifier key(s), such as "Shift" or "Ctrl+Shift."
Public boolean isActionKey()	Returns whether the key in this event is an action key, as defined in Event.java.

receives a KeyEvent object. KeyEvent is a subclass of java.awt.event.InputEvent and provides a number of useful methods, as shown in Table 7.5.

These methods provide information about the key that was pressed as well as the character represented by that key. Some are inherited from the InputEvent class so that they can be used with mouse events as well.

The KeyEvent class also provides constants, via class variables, that define the key codes for events in the Swing library. Some of these key codes are listed in Table 7.6.

Table 7.6 Key Codes for Key Event Handling

Key Code	Notes
CHAR_UNDEFINED	KEY_PRESSED and KEY_RELEASED events that do not map to a valid Unicode character do not have a defined keyChar.
VK_0 - VK_9	VK_0 - VK_9 are the same as ASCII 0 thru 9.
VK_A - VK_Z	VK_A - VK_Z are the same as ASCII A thru Z.
VK_ALT	The Alt key.
VK_BACK_QUOTE	The backquote `.
VK_BACK_SLASH	The backslash \.
VK_BACK_SPACE	The backspace key.
VK_CONTROL	The Control key.
VK_DELETE	The Delete key.

Table 7.6 Continued

Key Code	Notes
VK_DOWN	The down arrow.
VK_END	The end key.
VK_ENTER	The enter key.
VK_ESCAPE	The Escape key.
VK_F1	The F1 key.
VK_F2	The F2 key.
VK_F3	The F3 key.
VK_F4	The F4 key.
VK_F5	The F5 key.
VK_F6	The F6 key.
VK_F7	The F7 key.
VK_F8	The F8 key.
VK_F9	The F9 key.
VK_F10	The F10 key.
VK_F11	The F11 key.
VK_F12	The F12 key.
VK_INSERT	The Insert key.
VK_KANA	For Japanese keyboards.
VK_KANJI	For Japanese keyboards.
VK_LEFT	The left arrow key.
VK_PAGE_DOWN	The Page Down key.
VK_PAGE_UP	The Page Ip key.
VK_RIGHT	The right arrow key.
VK_SHIFT	The Shift key.
VK_SLASH	The slash key /.
VK_SPACE	The space key.
VK_TAB	The Tab key.
VK_UP	The up arrow key.

In the following example we have connected a custom object to a JTextField as a KeyListener. This demonstrates the power of the delegation event model to extend existing classes without subclassing. Our listener prints information about each key event. In particular, the key code, character, modifiers, and full key text are printed for key-press and key-release events. Key-typed events don't provide valid key code information so it is not included in the message. Because Swing is platform independent, you will find that typing a key results in three messages: first a key press, followed with a key type, and finally a key release.

This example is implemented in the form of a subclass of JPanel. A main class method creates a Frame for the panel and displays it. A helper class called WindowCloser is used to close the window when the close box is selected.

```
import java.util.*;
import java.awt.*;
import java.awt.event.*;
import com.sun.java.swing.*;
import com.sun.java.swing.text.*;

public class Echo extends JPanel
implements KeyListener
{
    public Echo()
    {
        JTextField field;

        setBackground(Color.lightGray);

        field = new JTextField(25);
        field.addKeyListener(this);
        add(field);
    }

    public void keyPressed(KeyEvent e)
    {
        char character;
        int mods;
        String modText;

        character = e.getKeyChar();

        System.out.print(character+" - ");
        System.out.print(KeyEvent.getKeyText(e.getKeyCode()));
        System.out.print(" ");

        mods = e.getModifiers();

        if(mods != 0)
```

```
        {
            modText = KeyEvent.getKeyModifiersText(mods);
            System.out.print(modText);
            System.out.print(" ");
        }

        System.out.println("pressed.");
    }

    public void keyReleased(KeyEvent e)
    {
        char character;
        int mods;
        String modText;

        character = e.getKeyChar();

        System.out.print(character+" - ");
        System.out.print(KeyEvent.getKeyText(e.getKeyCode()));
        System.out.print(" ");

        mods = e.getModifiers();

        if(mods != 0)
        {
            modText = KeyEvent.getKeyModifiersText(mods);
            System.out.print(modText);
            System.out.print(" ");
        }

        System.out.println("released.");
    }

    public void keyTyped(KeyEvent e)
    {
        char character;
        int mods;
        String modText;

        character = e.getKeyChar();

        System.out.print(character+" - ");

        mods = e.getModifiers();

        if(mods != 0)
        {
            modText = KeyEvent.getKeyModifiersText(mods);
```

```
            System.out.print(modText);
            System.out.print(" ");
        }

        System.out.println("typed.");
    }

    public Dimension getPreferredSize()
    {
        return new Dimension(300, 50);
    }

    public Dimension getMinimumSize()
    {
        return new Dimension(25, 25);
    }

    public Dimension getMaximumSize()
    {
        return getPreferredSize();
    }

    public static void main(String s[])
    {
        JFrame frame = new JFrame("Echo");
        Echo panel = new Echo();

        frame.setForeground(Color.black);
        frame.setBackground(Color.lightGray);
        frame.addWindowListener(new WindowCloser());
        frame.getContentPane().add(panel,"Center");

        frame.setSize(panel.getPreferredSize());
        frame.setVisible(true);
    }
}

class WindowCloser extends WindowAdapter
{
    public void windowClosing(WindowEvent e)
    {
        Window win = e.getWindow();
        win.setVisible(false);
        win.dispose();
        System.exit(0);
    }
}
```

Figure 7.9 Handling key events.

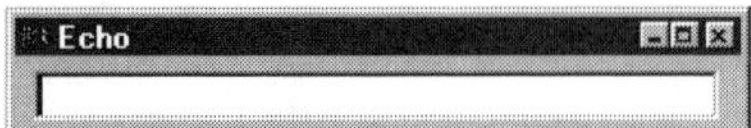

Figure 7.9 shows the handling and processing of key events.

We have highlighted some of the key portions of this example using bold text to draw your attention to them. Notice that we create a key listener that is sent key events from the text field. We then request the key and modifier codes from the event and display the results. Although this is a simple example, it demonstrates how to define a KeyListener, add it to a component, and respond to notification of key events.

> **TIP**
>
> The java.awt.KeyAdapter class implements all of the KeyListener methods. The default implementation is empty, but you can define a subclass that overrides only those methods in which you are interested. This allows you to implement a KeyListener without having to implement each method.

Style Guidelines

Many of the applications created by corporate programmers are centered on the concept of form entry. With labels and text fields, you can create these form entry applications in a user-friendly manner. Accompany all text fields with an associated label, as shown in Figure 7.10; for example, a hotel reservation system that has a screen that contains guests' check-in information. Next to each data entry field such as guest's name, address, room number, and so on, there could be a label that describes the associated field.

When possible use image labels to draw attention to important form elements. For example, if the customer must provide a credit card number when registering, you can create a label with a picture of a credit card next to the appropriate field.

Figure 7.10 Example of a form application.

Forms

Name:

Address:

State: Zip:

Phone:

Figure 7.11 Examples of weak form design.

You can post a yellow flag next to fields that must be filled in, such as the work phone number.

When building form-based interfaces try to keep the text fields approximately the same size, possibly adjusting the size of a field to match the expected data. Also, match the labels for each form element to the other members of that form. If you place one image label with two text labels, the image stands out, but the overall interface suffers from inconsistency. Instead use all images or all text labels to create a well-balanced form. Figure 7.11 shows a weak form-based interface.

As with mouse events, use KeyListeners whenever possible rather than raw event processing. By using listeners you can receive notification of key events on existing Swing controls, like text fields or lists. This listener mechanism is an easy way to provide keyboard navigation for your interface. In the same way that the tab key allows the power user to move between components, key listeners enable power users to activate and make selections. One example of this technique is to use a key listener with a list and have the key listener move the selection based on the arrow keys, or even insert an item into the list if the Insert key is pressed.

Finally, when your application is first started, select one of the components or text fields. Especially in a form interface this technique enables your program to be more user friendly by allowing the user to start working immediately.

MENUS AND TOOL BARS

8

In most user interfaces, such as Microsoft Windows, the majority of a program's functionality is accessed via menus and tool bars. Menus provide a primarily text-based list of operations that the user can choose to perform. Tool bars, as pictured in Figure 8.1, are usually a set of buttons or other components that graphically, or with single words, provide quick access to important program functions.

By providing access to functionality in menus and tool bars, programs make it easy for users to do their work. Swing provides a pure Java implementation of the Menu and tool bar components. Swing also provides a pop-up menu item to provide context-sensitive access to menu-based functionality.

Power users are often identified by their desire to work more quickly. Power users usually prefer to access functionality without removing their hands from the keyboard. Both menus and tool bars require mouse-based access, thus making them less than optimal for a user who is typing. To aid power users, Swing menus provide shortcuts or key accelerators. These shortcuts allow the user to access a menu item with the keyboard, as mentioned in Chapter 7.

Tool bars and menus often provide access to the same program functionality. In other words, the user can often perform the same tasks by either selecting a menu item or pressing a button on a tool bar. Swing helps programmers organize this code redundancy by providing the concept of an action. We mentioned actions in Chapter 2. In this chapter we use actions to create menu items and to link the functionality of a menu item and a button.

Figure 8.1 Tool bars.

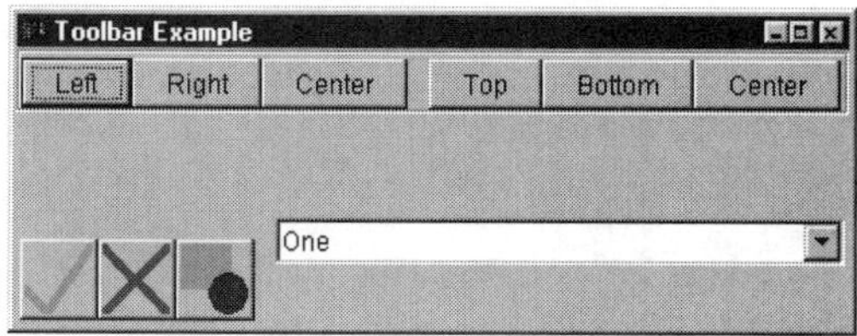

Figure 8.2 Swing menu objects.

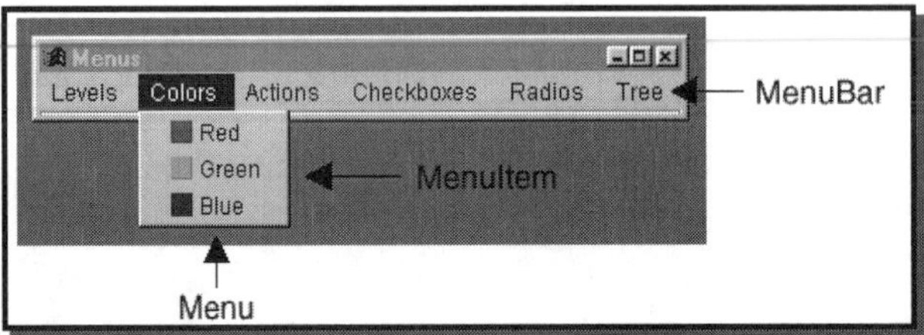

Menus

Three types of objects are used to define a Swing menu: menu bar, menu items, and menus. The *menu bar* is a singular object that acts as the root for all menus and items. *Menu items* are any items on a menu. *Menus* are a special kind of menu item that stores a list of menu items and then display them when the menu item is selected. This relationship between menu bar, menu item, and menu is pictured in Figure 8.2. The appearance for all three menu components is defined by an associated UI object. This allows the current look and feel to define the way menus look and behave.

In previous releases of the JDK, menus were available via native menu components. Swing menus provide several advantages over the native menus. First, JMenuItems can display both text and icons, shown in Figure 8.3, that give the programmer more flexibility. Second, JMenuBar is just a subclass of JComponent, so menus are placed anywhere that they make sense to the programmer. The menu bar can be part of an applet, for instance. Finally, menu items can be different sizes depending on their contents, again making them more flexible. In all cases, menus are rooted at the menu bar and form a hierarchy under this look-and-feel-dependent menu bar.

The power of menu items is increased by an elegant implementation and design choice. JMenuItem is a subclass of AbstractButton. This means that menu items have all of the methods and functionality of these buttons, including alignment methods for the icon and text. Swing also provides two special types of menu items called JCheckBoxMenuItem and JRadioButtonMenuItem. JCheckBoxMenuItems behave like check box buttons; they are checked on or off regardless of the state

Figure 8.3 Menus with icons.

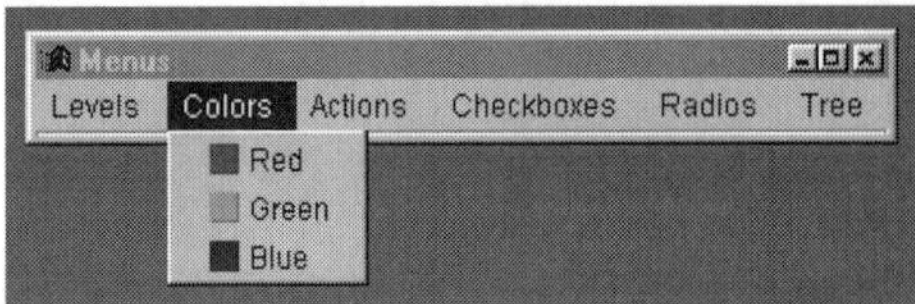

Figure 8.4 Check box menu items.

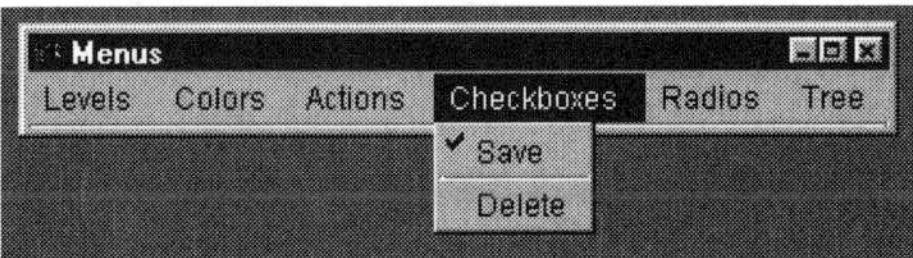

of any other menu items. You use JCheckBoxMenuItems for tasks such as allowing the user to set application options on or off. Examples of the check box menu items are pictured in Figure 8.4.

JRadioButtonMenuItems behave like radio buttons. They allow you to create menu item groups where only one item in the group is selected at a time. As with JRadioButtons, you can assign a JRadioButtonMenuItem to a ButtonGroup. This creates groups of menu items that automatically update and allow only one item to be selected at a time.

Creating a Menu

To create a menu bar, you typically begin by creating the JMenuBar object. This object is created with the default constructor:

```
public JMenuBar();
```

Next create Menus using one of the constructors found in Table 8.1.

Add the menus to the bar using the following JMenuBar method:

```
public void add(Menu m);
```

Menus are displayed from left to right in the order that they are added to a menu bar based on the installed look and feel. Some look and feels may display menus differently.

Once a menu is created, you can add items to it. JMenu provides four methods for adding items, as shown in Table 8.2.

Table 8.1 Menu Constructors

Method	**Function**
Public JMenu()	Creates a default menu.
Public JMenu(String)	Creates a menu and sets the title of the menu to the string.
Public JMenu(String, boolean)	Creates a menu and sets the title of the menu to the string. The Boolean argument may be used by some look and feels to support tear-off menus.

Table 8.2 Menu Methods for Adding Items

Method	Function
Public void add(Action a)	Adds a menu item to the menu and associates it with the action. The menu item takes its title from the Action. The Action is notified when the menu item is selected.
Public void add(Component c)	Adds components as a menu item to the menu. Components added to menus create flexible and arbitrary user interfaces. For example, Figure 8.5 shows a Tree component in a menu.
Public void add(JMenuItem c)	Adds a simple menu item to the menu.
Public void add(String s)	Adds a menu item to the menu with the string as its title.

By providing all of these methods you can decide whether to create the items first and configure them before adding them to the menu.

You can also insert items into a menu using the methods found in Table 8.3.

Separators are used to separate items visually in a menu. Use the following method to add a separator to a menu.

```
public void addSeparator();
```

This separator appears in the order that it's added, or you can insert a separator at a specified index, as shown here:

```
public void insertSeparator(int index);
```

Menu items are removed from the menu using the methods shown in Table 8.4.

Table 8.3 More Methods for Adding Items to a Menu

Method	Function
Public void insert(Action a, int i)	Inserts a menu item based on the action at the index position identified by the integer.
Public void insert(JMenuItem i, int index)	Inserts a menu at the index position identified by the integer.
Public void insert(String s, int index)	Inserts a menu item with the string as its tile at the index position identified by the integer.

Figure 8.5 A menu with a tree item.

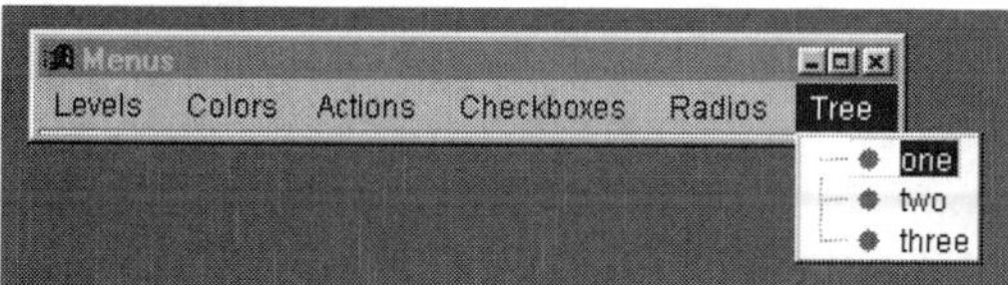

When your menu bar is completed you can add it to a frame or applet's root pane using the following method:

```
public void setMenuBar(JMenuBar bar);
```

Because the AWT Frame class already defines setMenuBar, JFrame provides a convenient method for assigning the frame. It looks like this:

```
public void setJMenuBar(JMenuBar bar);
```

To demonstrate the creation of a menu, we have included a simple example. This example, pictured in Figure 8.6, provides a number of interesting features:

- There is a custom class that implements an Icon called Swatch that's used to draw colored squares for several menu items.
- Images are displayed in menu items.
- The menu items resize as needed to draw the icons and text.
- Menu items are disabled.
- Check box and radio button-style menus are supported.
- Menus can hold arbitrary components.

Most of these features are highlighted in the code to draw your attention to them. This example includes a main method that creates a frame and a menu and assigns the menu to the frame. To get the most from this example, run it from the accompanying CD-ROM. A screen shot cannot provide a reasonable view of the menu.

Table 8.4 Methods for Removing an Item from a Menu

Method	Function
Public void remove(Action a)	Removes the menu item associated with the specified action from the menu.
Public void remove(int index)	Removes the menu item at the index position specified by the integer.
Public void remove(JMenuItem i)	Removes the specified menu item from the menu.
Public void removeAll()	Removes all menu items from the menu.

```
import java.util.*;
import java.awt.*;
import java.awt.event.*;
import com.sun.java.swing.*;
import com.sun.java.swing.text.*;

public class Menus
{
    public static void main(String s[])
    {
        JFrame frame = new JFrame("Menus");
        JMenuBar bar = new JMenuBar();
        JMenu menu = new JMenu("Levels");
        JMenuItem tmp;
        Icon anIcon;

        tmp = new JMenuItem("Primary");
        menu.add(tmp);

        tmp = new JMenuItem("Secondary");
        menu.add(tmp);

        tmp = new JMenuItem("Tertiary");
        menu.add(tmp);

        bar.add(menu);

        menu = new JMenu("Colors");

        tmp = new JMenuItem("Red");
        anIcon = new Swatch(Color.red);
        tmp.setIcon(anIcon);
        tmp.setHorizontalTextPosition(tmp.RIGHT);
        menu.add(tmp);

        tmp = new JMenuItem("Green");
        anIcon = new Swatch(Color.green);
        tmp.setIcon(anIcon);
        tmp.setHorizontalTextPosition(tmp.RIGHT);
        menu.add(tmp);

        tmp = new JMenuItem("Blue");
        anIcon = new Swatch(Color.blue);
        tmp.setIcon(anIcon);
```

```
tmp.setHorizontalTextPosition(tmp.RIGHT);
menu.add(tmp);

bar.add(menu);

menu = new JMenu("Actions");

tmp = new JMenuItem("Shapes");
anIcon = new ImageIcon("images/shapes.gif");
tmp.setIcon(anIcon);
menu.add(tmp);

tmp = new JMenuItem("X");
anIcon = new ImageIcon("images/ex.gif");
tmp.setIcon(anIcon);
menu.add(tmp);

tmp = new JMenuItem("Check");
anIcon = new ImageIcon("images/check.gif");
tmp.setEnabled(false);
menu.add(tmp);

bar.add(menu);

menu = new JMenu("Checkboxes");

tmp = new JCheckBoxMenuItem("Save");
menu.add(tmp);

menu.addSeparator();

tmp = new JCheckBoxMenuItem("Delete");
menu.add(tmp);

bar.add(menu);

menu = new JMenu("Radios");

ButtonGroup grp = new ButtonGroup();

tmp = new JRadioButtonMenuItem("Yes");
grp.add(tmp);
menu.add(tmp);
```

```
        tmp = new JRadioButtonMenuItem("No");
        grp.add(tmp);
        menu.add(tmp);

        bar.add(menu);

        //Create a menu with a tree component in it
        menu = new JMenu("Tree");

        Vector data = new Vector();
        data.addElement("one");
        data.addElement("two");
        data.addElement("three");

        menu.add(new JTree(data));
        bar.add(menu);

        frame.setJMenuBar(bar);

        frame.setDefaultCloseOperation(JFrame.DO_NOTHING_ON_CLOSE);
        frame.setForeground(Color.black);
        frame.setBackground(Color.lightGray);
        frame.pack();
        frame.setVisible(true);
    }
}
```

Figure 8.6 shows an example of various menus and menu items.

As part of this example, we created a custom Icon that displays a colored square. We called this icon class Swatch. You can see in the following code that creating Swatch is quite simple. It requires only three methods, indicating how easy it is to extend the appearance of a Swing application by creating custom Icon types.

```
import com.sun.java.swing.*;
import java.awt.*;
//Simple icon that displays a colored square
class Swatch implements Icon
{
    Color color;
```

Figure 8.6 Menu example.

```
    public Swatch(Color c)
    {
        this.color = c;
    }

    public void paintIcon(Component c,Graphics g, int x, int y)
    {
        //Save the current color, don't stomp on it
        Color oldColor = g.getColor();
        g.setColor(color);
        g.fill3DRect(x,y,getIconWidth(), getIconHeight(), true);
        g.setColor(oldColor);
    }

    public int getIconWidth()
    {
        return 12;
    }

    public int getIconHeight()
    {
        return 12;
    }
}
```

Handling Menu Events

When a user interacts with your menus by selecting an item in them, your application can handle the events generated in a number of ways. The application can use menu events that are produced by menus. It can use action listeners to monitor the menu items themselves or through the use of menu listeners. A MenuEvent is defined as a subclass of EventObject from java.util. It's generated with menus when a menu item is posted, selected, or canceled. Menu items can have action listeners and action commands just like buttons. This means that the menu-item action listener can receive notification of menu selections using the same ActionListener interface that we discussed in Chapter 4. Menus also notify menu listeners of menu usage. These menu listeners are notified using the methods in the MenuListener interface when a menu is activated or deactivated. The MenuListener interface defines the following methods:

```
public void menuSelected(MenuEvent e);
public void menuDeselected(MenuEvent e);
public void menuCancelled(MenuEvent e);
```

As a programmer, you can use these notifications to enable and disable menu items that are displayed.

The following example, pictured in Figure 8.7, demonstrates a menu that uses action commands and menu events.

This example is implemented in the form of a subclass of JPanel. A main class method creates a Frame for the panel and displays it. A helper class called WindowCloser is used to close the window when the close box is selected. Try running this example from the CD-ROM to see exactly how these events are distributed to the menu and action listeners. Notice that the menu items have action commands associated with them. These actions are sent as part of the event when the menu item is selected. The ActionListener uses these action commands to determine which menu is selected.

If the user chooses the "Quit" menu item, the program exits.

```
import java.util.*;
import java.awt.*;
import java.awt.event.*;
import com.sun.java.swing.*;
import com.sun.java.swing.event.*;

public class Menus extends JPanel
implements ActionListener, MenuListener
{
    JTextField field;

    public Menus(JFrame frm)
    {
        JMenuBar bar = new JMenuBar();
        JMenu menu = new JMenu("Levels");
        JMenuItem tmp;

        setBackground(Color.lightGray);
        setLayout(new BorderLayout());
        /*
         * Turn on buffering to reduce flicker.
         */
        setDoubleBuffered(true);

        menu.addMenuListener(this);

        tmp = new JMenuItem("Primary");
        tmp.addActionListener(this);
        tmp.setActionCommand("Primary");
```

```
        menu.add(tmp);

        tmp = new JMenuItem("Secondary");
        tmp.addActionListener(this);
        tmp.setActionCommand("Secondary");
        menu.add(tmp);

        tmp = new JMenuItem("Tertiary");
        tmp.addActionListener(this);
        tmp.setActionCommand("Tertiary");
        menu.add(tmp);

        tmp = new JMenuItem("Quit");
        tmp.addActionListener(this);
        tmp.setActionCommand("Quit");
        menu.add(tmp);

        bar.add(menu);

        frm.setJMenuBar(bar);

        field = new JTextField(10);
        field.addActionListener(this);
        field.setActionCommand("Text Field Activated");
        add(field,"South");

    }

    public void actionPerformed(ActionEvent e)
    {
        String cmd;
        cmd = e.getActionCommand();

        field.setText("Action: "+cmd);

        if(cmd.equals("Quit"))
        {
            System.exit(0);
        }
    }

    public void menuSelected(MenuEvent e)
    {
```

```
            field.setText("Menu selected");
        }

        public void menuDeselected(MenuEvent e)
        {
            field.setText("Menu deselected");
        }

        public void menuCancelled(MenuEvent e)
        {
            field.setText("Menu cancelled");
        }

        public Dimension getPreferredSize()
        {
            return new Dimension(200, 100);
        }

        public static void main(String s[])
        {
            JFrame frame = new JFrame("Menus");
            Menus panel = new Menus(frame);

            frame.setForeground(Color.black);
            frame.setBackground(Color.lightGray);
            frame.addWindowListener(new WindowCloser());
            frame.getContentPane().add(panel,"Center");

            frame.setSize(panel.getPreferredSize());
            frame.setVisible(true);
        }
    }

    class WindowCloser extends WindowAdapter
    {
        public void windowClosing(WindowEvent e)
        {
            Window win = e.getWindow();
            win.setVisible(false);
            win.dispose();
            System.exit(0);
        }
    }
```

Figure 8.7 shows menu events and the commands handled.

Figure 8.7 Menu events.

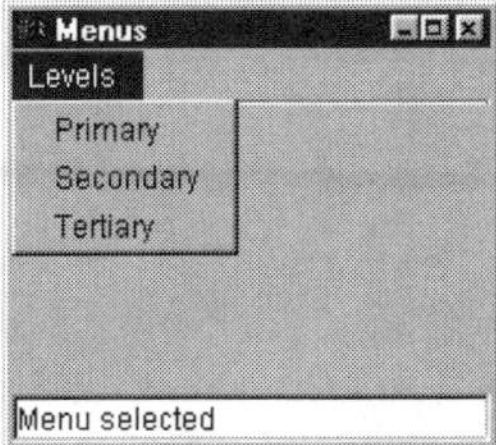

Menus and Actions

You may recall from Chapter 2 that Swing defines an Action as an ActionListener with a set of strings and icons associated with it. Actions also keep track of whether they are enabled. When we discussed menu creation, we mentioned that a menu has an Action added to it. With menu, the menu actually has a menu item added to it. The menu item is initialized to use the Action's default text string as its label and assigns the Action object as one of its ActionListeners. In other words, when the item is selected, the Action is notified. The menu item also registers with the Action for notification if the Action's state changes. In particular, if the Action is disabled, the menu item is automatically disabled.

Figure 8.8 shows an example that adds two Actions to a menu. The actions are *custom objects*. Specifically they are instances of the BuddyAction class. BuddyAction is a subclass of AbstractAction, which implements the entire Action interface except for the actionPerformed method inherited from the ActionListener interface. Our BuddyAction initializes its icon and text. A BuddyAction also defines an instance variable to hold another BuddyAction. When a BuddyAction receives notification of an action it disables itself and enables its buddy. In the following code example, this behavior manifests itself as the two menu items turn each other on and off. When one menu item is selected it notifies its action. That action disables itself and enables its buddy. When the action is disabled or enabled, the associated menu item is notified and enables or disables itself appropriately. The example itself consists of a single frame with a menu and two buttons. The menu contains two menu items created using a pair of BuddyActions.

We have also included an action called QuitAction that causes the program to exit.

```
import com.sun.java.swing.*;
import java.awt.*;
import java.awt.event.*;
class BuddyAction extends AbstractAction
{
    Action buddy;

    public BuddyAction(String name)
```

```
    {
        Icon img = new ImageIcon("images/shapes.gif");
        setIcon(Action.SMALL_ICON,img);
        setIcon(Action.DEFAULT,img);
        setText(Action.DEFAULT,name);
    }

    public void setBuddy(Action a)
    {
        buddy = a;
    }

    public void actionPerformed(ActionEvent evt)
    {
        if(buddy != null)
        {
            buddy.setEnabled(true);
            setEnabled(false);
        }
    }
}
```

The code for the QuitAction is also a subclass of AbstractAction. In this case, the action takes a frame as part of its constructor; when activated, it closes the frame before exiting the program.

```
import java.awt.*;
import com.sun.java.swing.*;
import com.sun.java.swing.event.*;
import java.awt.event.*;

public class QuitAction extends AbstractAction
{
    JFrame frame;

    public QuitAction(JFrame f)
    {
        frame = f;
        setText(Action.DEFAULT,"Quit");
    }

    public void actionPerformed(ActionEvent evt)
    {
        frame.setVisible(false);
        frame.dispose();
```

```
            System.exit(0);
        }
    }
```

The core example code builds a menu with the three actions and displays them in a window.

```
import java.util.*;
import java.awt.*;
import java.awt.event.*;
import com.sun.java.swing.*;
import com.sun.java.swing.event.*;

public class MenusActions extends JFrame
{
    public MenusActions()
    {
        JMenuBar bar = new JMenuBar();
        JMenu menu = new JMenu("Buddies");
        BuddyAction dee,dum;
        Button button;

        setTitle("Menus and Actions");
        getContentPane().setBackground(Color.lightGray);
        getContentPane().setLayout(new FlowLayout());

        dee = new BuddyAction("TweedleDee");
        dum = new BuddyAction("TweedleDum");

        dee.setBuddy(dum);
        dum.setBuddy(dee);

        button = new Button("TweedleDee");
        button.addActionListener(dee);
        getContentPane().add(button);

        button = new Button("TweedleDum");
        button.addActionListener(dum);
        getContentPane().add(button);

        menu.add(dee);
        menu.add(dum);

        menu.addSeparator();
        menu.add(new QuitAction(this));
```

```
        bar.add(menu);

        setJMenuBar(bar);

    }

    public Dimension getPreferredSize()
    {
        return new Dimension(200, 100);
    }

    public static void main(String s[])
    {
        JFrame frame = new MenusActions();

        frame.setForeground(Color.black);
        frame.setBackground(Color.lightGray);
        frame.addWindowListener(new WindowCloser());

        frame.setSize(frame.getPreferredSize());
        frame.setVisible(true);
    }
}
```

Figure 8.8 shows the BuddyAction handled.

Notice that the Action objects are not only used to create menu items but are also used as ActionListeners for the buttons. These Actions are used to represent core application functionality, like saving. They encapsulate the code for saving, the name to associate with this action "Save," and the icon to display that represents the function.

Menu Shortcuts

In Chapter 7, we introduced the concept of mouseless operation. This feature of Swing provides two technologies: menu shortcuts and focus traversal. We discussed focus traversal in the context of keyboard-oriented components. In this chapter, we discuss how menu shortcuts are processed with menus. Menu shortcuts allow the

Figure 8.8 Menus with actions.

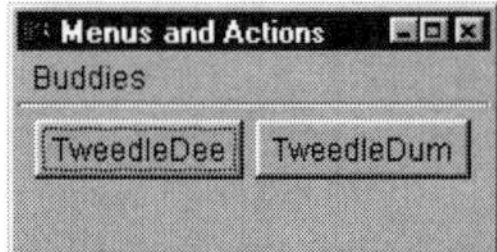

user to use the keyboard to select a menu item instead of using the mouse. The MenuShortcut class was introduced in JDK 1.1 to represent these keyboard shortcuts. A MenuShortcut object holds a key code and a Boolean flag that indicates if the Shift key is required to activate the shortcut. Once created, a MenuShortcut can be added to a JMenuItem either as an argument to the constructor or in the setShortcut method, as shown here.

```
public void setShortcut(MenuShortcut ms);
```

Remember that with MenuShortcuts, the way they are activated is platform dependent. For example, Microsoft Windows uses the Control key. In this case, the Control key is considered a key accelerator. That means that the Control key must be pressed in conjunction with the shortcut key to invoke the shortcut. For example, pressing Control and the C key (Control-C) invokes the edit menu's copy command for most Microsoft Windows applications. The default Toolkit object for your program can provide the key code for the accelerator key via the getMenuShortcutKeyMask method. The menu-shortcut accelerator is sometimes referred to as a *modifier key*.

Swing menu items can use MenuShortcuts to assign key accelerators to the menu items. The concept of a key accelerator is defined in the AbstractButton class. Remember that JMenuItem inherits from AbstractButton, so the code for button shortcuts is leveraged to support menu shortcuts. You can assign these key accelerators directly or with a MenuShortcut. To assign an accelerator directly, use the following method:

```
public void setKeyAccelerator(int keyAccelerator);
```

Our next example, pictured in Figure 8.9, demonstrates several menu key accelerators. Depending on the current look and feel, these accelerators are activated differently. You can, for example, use the Alt key and an accelerator to bring up a menu, then select an item via its accelerator. Note that the Control key may not be the accelerator key on your platform. For instance, on a Macintosh computer the Command key is typically the default accelerator. Run the example program on the CD-ROM and activate the shortcuts. This should change the text message displayed. Activating the "q" shortcut quits the program.

This example also uses the Action events from menus for notification. The menu shortcuts for the first three items are assigned as key accelerators; the last item is assigned using a MenuShortcut object. Both techniques may result in the same functionality, depending on the current look and feel.

```
import java.applet.*;
import java.util.*;
import java.awt.*;
import java.awt.event.*;
import com.sun.java.swing.*;
import com.sun.java.swing.border.*;
```

```
public class MenuShort extends JPanel
implements ActionListener
{
    JTextField status;

    public MenuShort(JFrame frm)
    {
        JMenuBar bar = new JMenuBar();
        JMenu menu = new JMenu("Levels");
        JMenuItem item;

        menu.setKeyAccelerator('l');

        item = new JMenuItem("Primary");
        item.setKeyAccelerator('p');
        item.addActionListener(this);
        item.setActionCommand("Primary");
        menu.add(item);

        item = new JMenuItem("Secondary");
        item.setKeyAccelerator('s');
        item.addActionListener(this);
        item.setActionCommand("Secondary");
        menu.add(item);

        item = new JMenuItem("Tertiary");
        item.setKeyAccelerator('t');
        item.addActionListener(this);
        item.setActionCommand("Tertiary");
        menu.add(item);

        item = new JMenuItem("Quit");
        item.setShortcut(new MenuShortcut('q'));
        item.addActionListener(this);
        item.setActionCommand("Quit");
        menu.add(item);

        bar.add(menu);

        frm.setJMenuBar(bar);

        status = new JTextField(20);
        status.requestFocus();
        add(status);
```

```
        setStatus("Hello World");
    }

    public void actionPerformed(ActionEvent evt)
    {
        setStatus(evt.getActionCommand());

        if(evt.getActionCommand().equals("Quit"))
        {
            System.exit(0);
        }
    }

    public void setStatus(String str)
    {
        status.setText(str);
    }

    public Dimension getPreferredSize()
    {
        return new Dimension(300, 200);
    }

    public static void main(String s[])
    {
        JFrame frame = new JFrame("Shortcut Example");
        MenuShort panel = new MenuShort(frame);

        frame.setForeground(Color.black);
        frame.setBackground(Color.lightGray);
        frame.addWindowListener(new WindowCloser());
        frame.getContentPane().add(panel,"Center");

        frame.setSize(panel.getPreferredSize());
        frame.setVisible(true);
    }
}

import java.awt.*;
import java.awt.event.*;
class WindowCloser extends WindowAdapter
{
    public void windowClosing(WindowEvent e)
    {
```

```
        Window win = e.getWindow();
        win.setVisible(false);
        win.dispose();
        System.exit(0);
    }
}
```

Figure 8.9 shows a menu bar that accepts keyboard shortcuts.

Pop-up Menus

In JDK 1.1, JavaSoft started to provide support for pop-up menus. These are context-sensitive menus that the user can access with the mouse by clicking on a component, as shown in Figure 8.10. Netscape Navigator uses these menus to provide several choices when selecting a link, such as opening it in a new window or frame. MS Word also uses these menus to allow cut/copy/paste or spelling corrections. In Microsoft Windows, the right mouse button is used to access these pop-up menus. Other systems may use different activation schemes.

Swing supports pop-up menus via the JPopupMenu class. Once created, a JPopupMenu holds JMenuItems like a normal menu.

The interesting aspect of adding pop-up menus to your applications is not so much the menu itself, which is created like a normal menu and handled via normal action events, but the activation mechanism. Components that handle mouse events can check with the MouseEvent object to determine if a pop-up menu should be activated. MouseEvents respond to the isPopupTrigger method with a Boolean that indicates if the system-dependent mechanism for activating a pop-up menu was selected.

```
public boolean isPopupTrigger();
```

Components that want to provide pop-up menus either implement the processMouseEvent method and enable their mouse event mask or use a MouseListener. When a mouse event occurs, processMouseEvent or the mouse

Figure 8.9 Menu shortcuts.

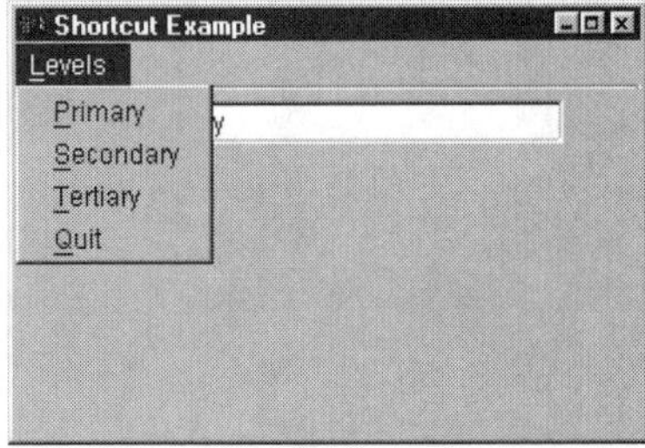

Figure 8.10 Pop-up menu.

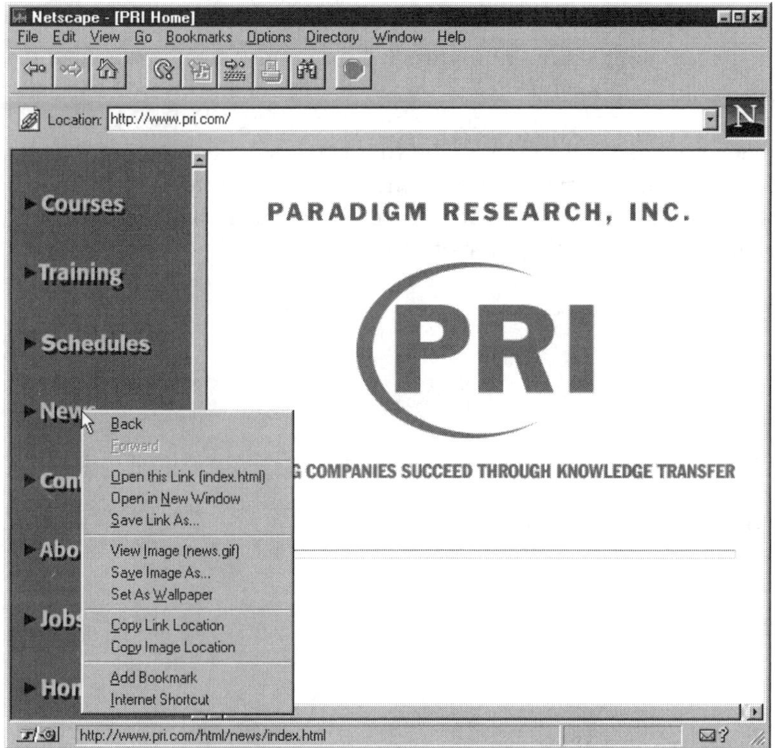

listener sees if the event is a pop-up trigger and, if so, shows the pop-up menu. Of course, JavaSoft suggests that the MouseListener approach is the more approved mechanism. You will also find that by using a MouseListener, you can associate pop-up menus with components that you did not write.

To display a JPopupMenu, use the following method where "invoker" is the component that the pop-up is displayed for and x and y are the pop-up menu's location. In general, you should get the x and y location for a pop-up menu from the MouseEvent that activated it.

```
public void show(Component invoker,  int x, int y);
```

JPopupMenu supports PopopMenuListeners. These listeners implement the following methods:

```
public void popupMenuWillBecomeVisible(PopupMenuEvent e);
public void popupMenuWillBecomeInvisible(PopupMenuEvent e);
public void popupMenuCanceled(PopupMenuEvent e);
```

Basically, a PopupMenuListener is notified when the menu is displayed and when it's removed from the screen. Actual notification of a selection in the menu is handled using ActionEvents.

The following example, pictured in Figure 8.11, demonstrates how a custom component activates pop-up menus. Selections in the menu are printed to the console when you run this program from the accompanying CD-ROM. This example is implemented as three classes. The first class is a custom component that supports a pop-up menu, acts as an ActionListener for the items in the pop-up menu, and then implements PopupMenuListener. All of these classes are implemented in the same file, so they rely on the same set of import statements.

```
import java.applet.*;
import java.util.*;
import java.awt.*;
import java.awt.event.*;
import com.sun.java.swing.*;
import com.sun.java.swing.event.*;

public class Popup extends JComponent
implements ActionListener,PopupMenuListener
{
    JPopupMenu popup;

    public Popup()
    {
        JMenuItem mi;

        popup = new JPopupMenu();

        mi = new JMenuItem("This");
        mi.addActionListener(this);
        mi.setActionCommand("This");
        popup.add(mi);

        mi = new JMenuItem("That");
        mi.addActionListener(this);
        mi.setActionCommand("That");
        popup.add(mi);

        mi = new JMenuItem("The Other");
        mi.addActionListener(this);
        mi.setActionCommand("The Other");
```

```
        popup.add(mi);

        popup.addPopupMenuListener(this);
        popup.setOpaque(true);
        popup.setLightWeightPopupEnabled(true);

        addMouseListener(new PopupMouser(popup));
    }

    public void paint(Graphics g)
    {
        Dimension size = getSize();
        g.setColor(Color.darkGray);
        g.fillRect(0,0,size.width,size.height);
    }

    public void actionPerformed(ActionEvent e)
    {
        String command = e.getActionCommand();

        System.out.println(command);
    }

    /* Popup Listener Methods*/
    public void popupMenuWillBecomeVisible(PopupMenuEvent e)
    {
        System.out.println("Popup will become visible.");
    }

    public void popupMenuWillBecomeInvisible(PopupMenuEvent e)
    {
        System.out.println("Popup will become invisible.");
    }

    public void popupMenuCanceled(PopupMenuEvent e)
    {
        System.out.println("Popup cancelled.");
    }

    public Dimension getPreferredSize()
    {
        return new Dimension(300, 300);
```

```
    }

    public static void main(String s[])
    {
        JFrame frame = new JFrame("Popup Example");
        Popup pup = new Popup();

        frame.setForeground(Color.black);
        frame.setBackground(Color.lightGray);
        frame.addWindowListener(new WindowCloser());
        frame.getContentPane().add(pup,"Center");

        frame.setSize(pup.getPreferredSize());
        frame.setVisible(true);
    }
}
```

The second class is a subclass of MouseAdapter that implements MouseListener. When the pop-up trigger occurs, the PopupMouser displays the pop-up menu for the component on which the mouse event occurred at the x and y location of the mouse event.

```
class PopupMouser extends MouseAdapter
{
    JPopupMenu popup;

    public PopupMouser(JPopupMenu p)
    {
        popup = p;
    }

    public void mouseReleased(MouseEvent e)
    {
        if (e.isPopupTrigger())
        {
            popup.show(e.getComponent(), e.getX(), e.getY());
        }
    }

    public void mousePressed(MouseEvent e)
    {
        if (e.isPopupTrigger())
        {
            popup.show(e.getComponent(), e.getX(), e.getY());
```

```
        }
    }
}
```

The third class is a subclass of WindowAdapter that closes the window for the application when the user selects the close box.

```
class WindowCloser extends WindowAdapter
{
    public void windowClosing(WindowEvent e)
    {
        Window win = e.getWindow();
        win.setVisible(false);
        win.dispose();
        System.exit(0);
    }
}
```

Figure 8.11 shows an example of using pop-up menus.

You may have noticed the following method sent to the JPopupMenu after it was created in the constructor for the Popup class:

```
public void setLightWeightPopupEnabled(boolean aFlag);
```

When this flag is true, the code for JPopupMenu tries to use a lightweight component to display the menu. If a lightweight component can't be used, then an actual window is created to display the pop-up menu. The decision of whether to use a lightweight component is based on the location of the pop-up menu and its size. Basically, if the menu is displayed completely on top of an existing Swing window, then a lightweight menu can be used; otherwise, a window is required to account for the overlap.

Figure 8.11 Custom component that activates pop-up menus.

Figure 8.12 Tool bar.

Tool Bars

A tool bar, as defined by the JToolBar class, is a bordered row of components with optional separators, as shown in Figure 8.12.

The appearance of a border is controlled using the method:

```
public void setBorderPainted(boolean b);
```

The distance between the border and the contents is assigned using the following method:

```
public void setMargin(Insets m);
```

Components are added to a tool bar using one of two methods:

```
public void add(Component c);
public void add(Action a);
```

When an Action is used to add a component, a JButton is created that uses the Icon from the Action. The Action is also associated with the button as an ActionListener. If you add components directly, you are responsible for assigning event listeners to them. The order that items are added to the tool bar is the order in which they appear, depending on the current look and feel.

To create a tool bar:

Create an instance of JToolBar with:

```
JToolBar bar = new JToolBar()
```

Add components to the tool bar with:

```
bar.add(aComponent);
JButton b = bar.add(anAction);
```

Add separators to the tool bar as necessary using the addSeparator() method, as shown here:

```
bar. addSeparator();
```

Once you have created a tool bar, add it to another container. Tool bars are often added to the "north" side, or top, of a border layout.

Depending on the look and feel, your tool bar may support dragging. This means that the user can grab the tool bar and drag it off the existing component

Figure 8.13 Floating tool bar.

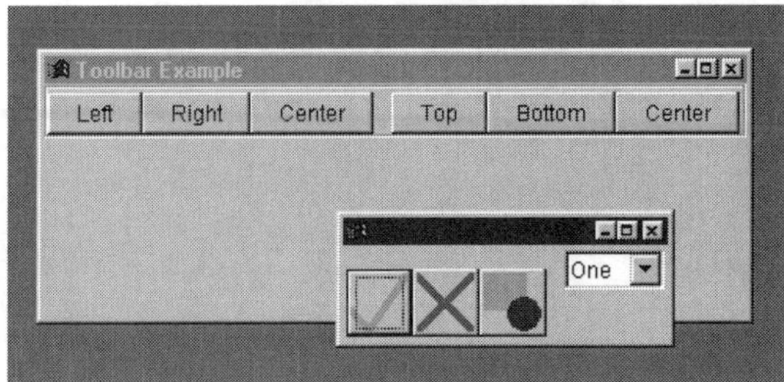

into its own window. Figure 8.13 shows the same example as Figure 8.14 with the bottom tool bar dragged off into its own window.

Our example, pictured in Figure 8.14, creates two tool bars. The tool bars are added to the north and south sides of a border layout. We have tried to minimize our code for simplicity. In doing so we have avoided temporary variables and used inline construction instead. The first tool bar is created using JButtons and a separator. The second tool bar is created using three custom Action classes and a combo box. All of the classes for this example are implemented in the same file, so they share the import statements.

```
import java.awt.*;
import java.awt.event.*;
import com.sun.java.swing.*;
import com.sun.java.swing.border.*;

public class Toolbars extends JPanel
{
    public Toolbars()
    {
        JToolBar bar;
        JComboBox combo;

        setBackground(Color.lightGray);
        setLayout(new BorderLayout());

        bar = new JToolBar();

        bar.add(new JButton("Left"));
        bar.add(new JButton("Right"));
        bar.add(new JButton("Center"));
        bar.addSeparator();
```

```
        bar.add(new JButton("Top"));
        bar.add(new JButton("Bottom"));
        bar.add(new JButton("Center"));

        add(bar,"North");

        bar = new JToolBar();
        bar.setBorderPainted(false);

        bar.add(new CheckAction());
        bar.add(new ExAction());
        bar.add(new ShapesAction());

        bar.addSeparator();

        combo = new JComboBox();
        combo.addItem("One");
        combo.addItem("Two");
        combo.addItem("Three");

        bar.add(combo);

        add(bar,"South");
    }

    public Dimension getPreferredSize()
    {
        return new Dimension(400, 150);
    }

    public static void main(String s[])
    {
        JFrame frame = new JFrame("Toolbar Example");
        Toolbars panel = new Toolbars();

        frame.setForeground(Color.black);
        frame.setBackground(Color.lightGray);
        frame.addWindowListener(new WindowCloser());
        frame.getContentPane().add(panel,"Center");

        frame.setSize(panel.getPreferredSize());
        frame.setVisible(true);
```

```
    }
}
```

The custom Actions in this example initialize their icons and provide a simple actionPerformed method. Keep in mind that in a larger program, these Actions may be used to create tool bar items and menu items, thus centralizing your code.

```
class CheckAction extends AbstractAction
{
    public CheckAction()
    {
        Icon img = new ImageIcon("images/check.gif");
        setIcon(Action.SMALL_ICON,img);
        setIcon(Action.DEFAULT,img);
        setText(Action.DEFAULT,"Check");
    }


    public void actionPerformed(ActionEvent evt)
    {
        System.out.println("Check");
    }
}


class ExAction extends AbstractAction
{
    public ExAction()
    {
        Icon img = new ImageIcon("images/ex.gif");
        setIcon(Action.SMALL_ICON,img);
        setIcon(Action.DEFAULT,img);
        setText(Action.DEFAULT,"Ex");
    }


    public void actionPerformed(ActionEvent evt)
    {
        System.out.println("Ex");
    }
}

class ShapesAction extends AbstractAction
```

```
{
    public ShapesAction()
    {
        Icon img = new ImageIcon("images/shapes.gif");
        setIcon(Action.SMALL_ICON,img);
        setIcon(Action.DEFAULT,img);
        setText(Action.DEFAULT,"Shapes");
    }


    public void actionPerformed(ActionEvent evt)
    {
        System.out.println("Shapes");
    }
}
```

This example uses the same WindowCloser class that we have seen before to handle the window's Close box.

```
class WindowCloser extends WindowAdapter
{
    public void windowClosing(WindowEvent e)
    {
        Window win = e.getWindow();
        win.setVisible(false);
        win.dispose();
        System.exit(0);
    }
}
```

Figure 8.14 shows our example with the tool bars on the window.

Notice that the current UI for JToolBar is rather simple. It's possible for other look and feels to provide expandable/contractable tool bars if this is appropriate.

Figure 8.14 Tool bars on the north and south sides of a border layout.

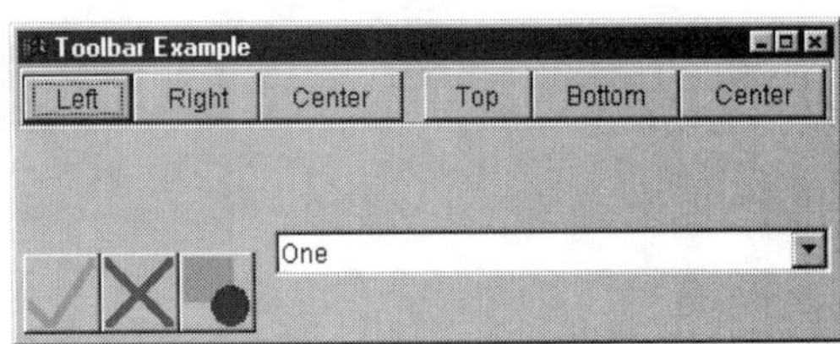

The ability to design your own UI object for the JFC components allows JavaSoft to provide this simple encapsulation of the toolbar concept without implementing every program's idea of a tool bar, while still allowing other programmers to build on top of JavaSoft's work.

Style Guidelines

Most users prefer as many mechanisms as possible for accessing a program's functionality, as long as these mechanisms are consistent. With tool bars and menus, you can easily give users two mechanisms that provide easy access to program code. Use tool bars for major program functionality and menus for access to all program features.

Tool bars are generally displayed at the top of a window and should be added to the north side of a BorderLayout to make it easy for the dragging mechanism to place a tool bar back on its parent if the user chooses to "dock" a floating tool bar.

Use menu shortcuts to assist power users. Try to use standard shortcuts when possible, like "f" for the File menu and "s" for Save. This minimizes the learning curve for your applications and makes power users happy. Pop-up menus also help advanced users access important functionality in a context-sensitive manner.

As you write more and more Swing programs, you will probably want to make a collection of useful Icon types, like the Swatch class in our menu example. These Icons can be highly reusable and definitely spruce up your interface.

DIALOGS AND OPTION PANES

9

User interfaces often use special windows called *dialogs* to provide information to the user. These dialogs are also used to retrieve information from the user. For example, an alert dialog may display an error message, and another dialog may request the user's name. Swing provides a parent class for all dialogs called JDialog as well as a powerful class called JOptionPane that can create dialogs. With an option pane you can create almost any dialog for providing information or for requesting confirmation or other input from a user. For example, the alert dialog in Figure 9.1 was created with a JOptionPane using a single line of code.

JavaSoft is also planning to provide other dialogs for file and color. These items, however, are not available in the initial release of JFC.

JDialog

JDialog is a subclass of java.awt.Dialog. As such, a JDialog adds two key features to a normal window. First, a JDialog can have a parent frame. Second, it can be modal. A modal dialog prevents events from passing to any component in its parent frame. When a JDialog is modal, it also blocks in its show method—when you put the dialog on screen by sending it show, this method won't return until the dialog is removed from the screen. By taking advantage of a blocking show, you can write your code logically, without having to rely on events from the dialog to continue an action that was started before you displayed the dialog.

You can create a generic JDialog using the constructors listed in Table 9.1.

Figure 9.1 Alert dialog created with JOptionPane.

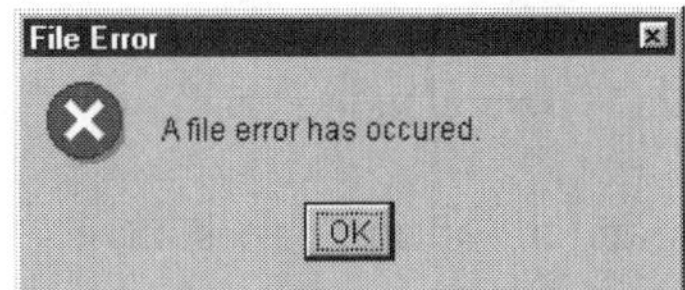

Table 9.1 JDialog Constructors

Constructor	Function
Public JDialog(Frame parent)	Creates a nonmodal dialog with the specified parent.
Public JDialog(Frame parent, boolean modal)	Creates a dialog with the specified parent and modality.
Public JDialog(Frame parent, String title)	Creates a nonmodal dialog with the specified parent and title.
Public JDialog(Frame parent, String title, boolean modal)	Creates a nonmodal dialog with the specified parent, title, and modality.

In general, you will use the JOptionPane for common dialog use, and you will subclass JDialog to create your own dialog types. Once you create a dialog you can add items to it. Like JFrame and JApplet, however, JDialog uses a root pane to manage its contents. If you want to add an item to the dialog, you need to add it to the content pane or whichever pane is appropriate.

You can control a dialog's modality using the setModal method shown here:

```
public void setModal(boolean tf);
```

Finally, a dialog can be positioned relative to another component, possibly one on the parent window, using the setLocationRelativeTo method:

```
public void setLocationRelativeTo(Component c);
```

If the specified component is not visible, or if no component is provided, the dialog is centered on the screen.

JOptionPane

Many of the common dialog style operations are handled using a JOptionPane. The JOptionPane class defines four styles of dialogs, as shown in Table 9.2. Each style is configurable, and you can also create your own style.

Each of these styles is accessible via class methods in JOptionPane. In the following sections we discuss each style individually and list the associated class methods there. All the methods we discuss have an equivalent method for creating an option pane as an internal frame. For example, showMessageDialog creates and shows a message style dialog in a Jdialog; showInternalMessageDialog displays the same option pane in an internal frame.

Regardless of the style of option pane that you create, all option panes have the same basic layout, as pictured in Figure 9.2. Basically, the option pane has a set of buttons for the user to press, an area for input, a message area, and an

Table 9.2 Option Pane Styles

Style	Purpose
Confirm	A dialog that requests confirmation from the user.
Input	A dialog that requests information from the user.
Message	A dialog that displays a message and is configured to show different icons based on the message.
Option	A general-option dialog that you configure.

icon. Not all of these areas necessarily contain components and take up space. For example, if you display a message pane, the input area is empty.

The current look and feel can override this layout.

Option Attributes

JOptionPane defines several attributes that are used to configure the pane before it is displayed. We have listed these attributes in Table 9.3, including a description of the attribute's use. Keep in mind that not all of the attributes are relevant for every type of option pane.

The message for an option pane is defined as an instance of Object. This means that it can be a string, component, or even an array. Depending on the type of message provided, the option pane displays it differently. Table 9.4 lists how each message type is treated.

By supporting arrays of message elements, the JOptionPane displays multiline messages or even forms. Although you normally assign an option pane's message as part of its construction, you can also assign the message using the following method:

```
public void setMessage(Object newMessage);
```

An option pane can have a message type. This message type is used to define the default icon for the pane. If you provide your own icon, this message type is ignored by the current look and feel. The look and feel may also change other

Figure 9.2 Option pane layout.

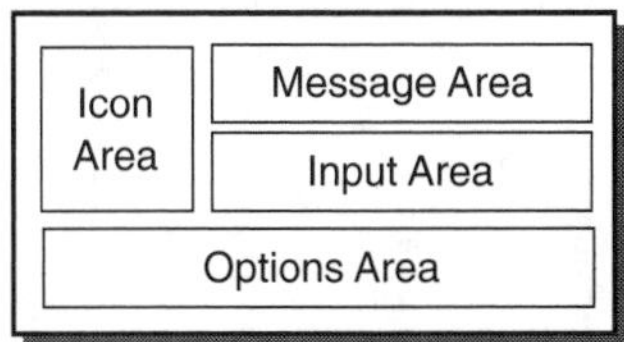

Table 9.3 Option Pane Attributes

Attribute	Use
parent	The parent component for the option pane. This component does not have to be a frame; the option pane finds the appropriate frame to act as a parent for the JDialog.
title	The title to display on the option pane's dialog or internal frame.
message	The message to display.
message type	The type of message displayed. The value of this attribute sets the option pane's default icon.
selection values	Choices available to the user.
Option type	The buttons to display to the user.
Options	User-defined buttons to display to the user.
Icon	The icon to display on the option pane.

aspects of the option pane's appearance based on the message type. Each type is defined as a class variable of JOptionPane. A list of the available types is provided in Table 9.5.

Although you normally assign an option pane's message type as part of its construction, you can also assign it using the method:

```
public void setMessageType(int newType);
```

The option type for an option pane is used to determine the buttons to display in the option button's area. There are four default settings for this value. You can also create your own button combinations if you use a generic option pane. Each default value is defined as a class variable for JOptionPane, as shown in Table 9.6.

Table 9.4 Option Pane Message Treatment

Object Type	Treatment
Array of objects	Each object is displayed as a message. The objects are handled from first to last and top to bottom. Therefore, the first element of the array appears at the top of the message area.
Component	Add the component to the message area as is.
Icon	Wrapped in a JLabel and displayed.
All other objects	Converted to a string and displayed in a JLabel.

Table 9.5 Message Types

Type	Purpose
ERROR_MESSAGE	A message that indicates an error has occurred in the program.
INFORMATION_MESSAGE	A message that provides information to the user.
WARNING_MESSAGE	A message that provides a warning to the user. This type can be used in conjunction with a confirmation pane.
QUESTION_MESSAGE	A message that asks a question; this type is usually reserved for confirmation or input style option panes.
PLAIN_MESSAGE	A plain text message with no specific type. The look and feel may decide not to provide an icon for this type.

Although you will normally assign an option pane's option type as part of its construction, you can also assign it using the following method:

```
public void setOptionType(int newType);
```

You will normally assign an option pane's icon as part of its construction or rely on the default icon, but you can also assign it using the setIcon method, as shown here:

```
public void setIcon(Icon newIcon);
```

We discuss the selection values and options in our discussions on input panes and general option panes, respectively.

Message Panes

Perhaps the easiest option pane to create is a message pane. This pane displays a message to the user with an icon based on the message type. In general, a single "OK" button is provided to remove the pane from the screen. This style of pane

Table 9.6 Option Types

Type	Purpose
DEFAULT_OPTION	Use the default options as defined by the option pane.
YES_NO_OPTION	Provide a yes and no option.
YES_NO_CANCEL_OPTION	Provide a yes, no, and cancel option.
OK_CANCEL_OPTION	Provide an OK and a cancel option.

Table 9.7 Methods for Showing a Message Pane

Method	Function
Public static void showMessageDialog (Component parentComponent, Object message)	Displays a dialog using the specified parent and message. The title is "Message" and the message type is INFORMATION_MESSAGE.
Public static void showMessageDialog (Component parentComponent, Object message, String title, int messageType)	Displays a dialog using the specified parent, message, title, and message type.
public static void showMessageDialog (Component parentComponent, Object message, String title, int messageType, Icon icon)	Displays a dialog using the specified parent, message, title, message type, and icon.

is not intended to retrieve user input, and the methods that display it don't return any values.

To show a message pane, you can use the methods listed in Table 9.7.

All of these methods are class methods for JOptionPane. They attempt to reuse components when possible, making this a memory-efficient mechanism for creating dialogs. Remember that there are equivalent methods to create a message pane for an internal frame.

We created several examples to show you what the dialogs created by these methods look like. We have not included the entire code of the example here, only the code for displaying the option pane. The entire example is found on the CD-ROM. The context for all of these examples is a JPanel so "this" refers to the panel itself.

The following code was used to create the information pane in Figure 9.3.

```
JOptionPane.showMessageDialog(this
                             ,"Something Important Has Happened."
                             ,"Important"
                             ,JOptionPane.INFORMATION_MESSAGE);
```

The following code was used to create the warning pane in Figure 9.4.

Figure 9.3 Informational message pane.

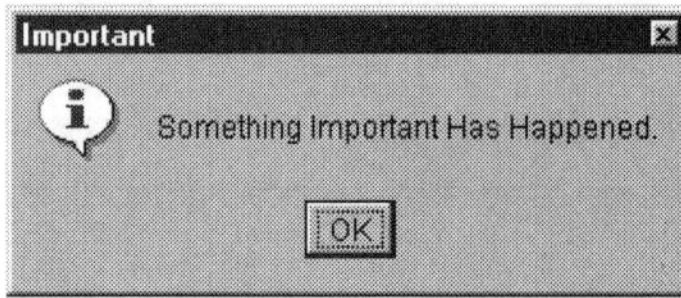

Figure 9.4 Warning message pane.

```
JOptionPane.showMessageDialog(this
                              ,"Watch Out, Don't Go There."
                              ,"Warning"
                              ,JOptionPane.WARNING_MESSAGE);
```

The following code was used to create the error pane in Figure 9.5.

```
JOptionPane.showMessageDialog(this
                              ,"A file error has occurred."
                              ,"File Error"
                              ,JOptionPane.ERROR_MESSAGE);
```

Although the question message type is usually reserved for confirmation-style dialogs, we have applied it to a message pane. The following code was used to create the question pane in Figure 9.6.

```
JOptionPane.showMessageDialog(this
                              ,"A Question For You."
                              ,"?????"
                              ,JOptionPane.QUESTION_MESSAGE);
```

The following code was used to create the plain message pane in Figure 9.7.

```
JOptionPane.showMessageDialog(this
                              ,"Something plain has occurred."
                              ,"Plain Stuff"
                              ,JOptionPane.PLAIN_MESSAGE);
```

You can assign your own icon to a message pane. The following code was used to create the pane in Figure 9.8.

```
ImageIcon icon;
icon = new ImageIcon("images/shapes.gif");

JOptionPane.showMessageDialog(this
                              ,"Check out the cool icon."
                              ,"Icon"
                              ,JOptionPane.PLAIN_MESSAGE
                              ,icon);
```

Figure 9.5 Error message pane.

Figure 9.6 Question message pane.

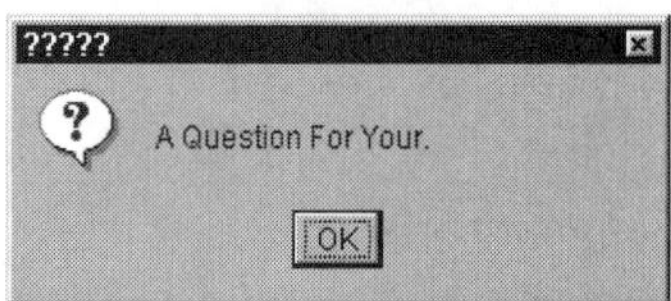

Figure 9.7 Plain message pane.

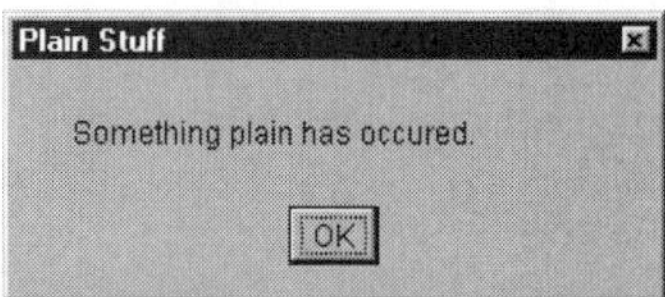

Figure 9.8 Custom icon for a message pane.

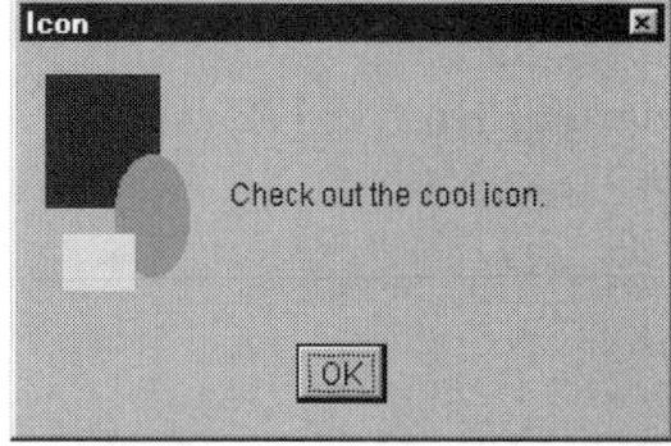

Figure 9.9 Message pane with an array message.

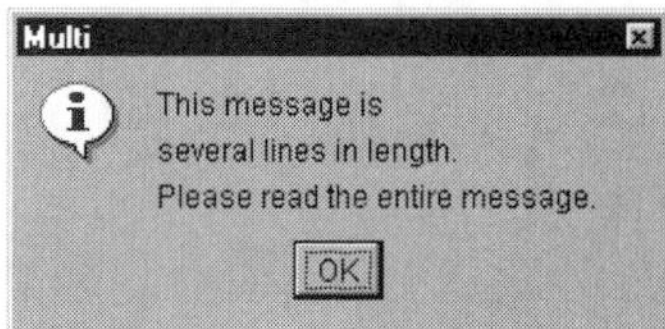

Table 9.8 Methods That Show a Confirm Dialog

Method	Function
public static int showConfirmDialog (Component parentComponent, Object message)	Creates a confirm style option pane with the specified parent and message. The message type is QUESTION_MESSAGE; the title is "Select an Option"; the option type is YES_NO_CANCEL_OPTION.
public static int showConfirmDialog (Component parentComponent, Object message, String title, int optionType)	Creates a confirm style option pane with the specified parent, message, title, and option type. The message type is QUESTION_MESSAGE.
public static int showConfirmDialog (Component parentComponent, Object message, String title, int optionType, int messageType)	Creates a confirm style option pane with the specified parent, message, title, option type, and message type.

Our final message pane example relies on the fact that a message is an array of objects. In this example, pictured in Figure 9.9, an array of strings is used to create a multiline message for the user.

```
String[] msg = {"This message is "
               ,"several lines in length."
               ,"Please read the entire message."};

JOptionPane.showMessageDialog(this
                             ,msg
                             ,"Multi"
                             ,JOptionPane.INFORMATION_MESSAGE);
```

Confirm Panes

Slightly different from the message-style option pane is a confirm-style option pane. This type of pane is used to request a decision from the user. For instance, you may want a confirmation panel display that asks the user if he or she wants to save the work before the application quits. Based on the option type, the decision can be yes/no or yes/no/cancel. The methods for showing a confirm-style option pane are listed in Table 9.8. All of these methods return an "int" to indicate the user's choice.

These methods are class methods for JOptionPane. They attempt to reuse components when possible, making this a memory-efficient mechanism for creating dialogs. There are equivalent methods to create a message pane for an internal frame.

Table 9.9 Confirm Dialog Return Values

Return Value	Cause
YES_OPTION	The user pressed the Yes button.
NO_OPTION	The user pressed the No button.
OK_OPTION	The user pressed the OK button.
CANCEL_OPTION	The user pressed the Cancel button.
CLOSE_OPTION	The user closed the dialog with the close box.

The methods that show a confirm dialog each return an integer with code that represents the user's action on that dialog. This integer has one of six values, depending on the user's action. These values are defined as class variables on JOptionPane and listed in Table 9.9. Some values are not valid for all confirm dialogs. For example, the default dialog has no cancel buttons, so you can't get the CANCEL_OPTION.

The following example, pictured in Figure 9.10, creates a confirm dialog when the user presses a button. The results from the confirmation are printed to the console.

```
import com.sun.java.swing.*;
import java.awt.event.*;

import java.awt.*;
import java.lang.*;

public class ConfirmExample extends JPanel
implements ActionListener
{
    public ConfirmExample()
    {
        JButton go = new JButton("Go");
        go.addActionListener(this);
        add(go);
    }

    public void actionPerformed(ActionEvent e)
    {
        int result;

        result = JOptionPane.showConfirmDialog(this
                                        ,"Continue Processing.");
```

```
            if(result == JOptionPane.YES_OPTION)
            {
                System.out.println("Got Yes!");
            }
            else if(result == JOptionPane.NO_OPTION)
            {
                System.out.println("Got No.");
            }
            else if(result == JOptionPane.CANCEL_OPTION)
            {
                System.out.println("Got Cancel :-(");
            }
            else if(result == JOptionPane.CLOSED_OPTION)
            {
                System.out.println("Dialog Closed");
            }
        }

        public Dimension getPreferredSize()
        {
            return new Dimension(100, 60);
        }

        public static void main(String s[])
        {
            JFrame frame = new JFrame("Confirm");
            ConfirmExample panel = new ConfirmExample();

            frame.setForeground(Color.black);
            frame.setBackground(Color.lightGray);
            frame.addWindowListener(new WindowCloser());
            frame.getContentPane().add(panel,"Center");

            frame.setSize(panel.getPreferredSize());
            frame.setVisible(true);
        }
    }
```

We have also included the WindowCloser class in this example to handle the window close box. This class is included in the same file and inherits the import statements.

```
import java.awt.*;
import java.awt.event.*;
class WindowCloser extends WindowAdapter
```

Figure 9.10 Confirm dialog.

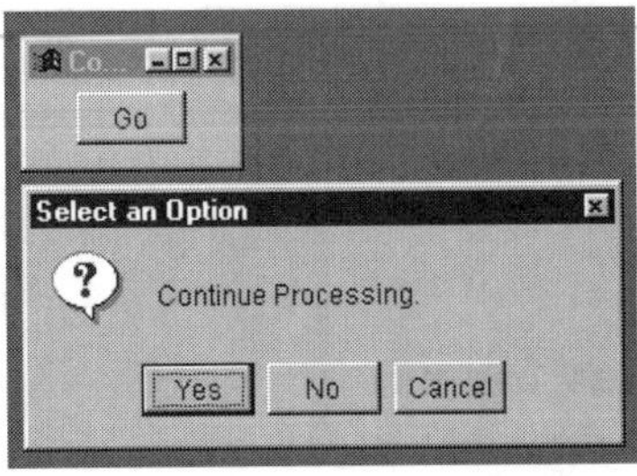


```
{
     public void windowClosing(WindowEvent e)
     {
          Window win = e.getWindow();
          win.setVisible(false);
          win.dispose();
          System.exit(0);
     }
}
```

Figure 9.10 shows a confirm dialog.

We also created a similar example that provides only yes and no options. The code for creating the panel pictured in Figure 9.11 is as follows:

```
result = JOptionPane.showConfirmDialog(this
                                        ,"Continue Processing."
                                        ,"Query"
                                        ,JOptionPane.YES_NO_OPTION);
```

Input Panes

Often option panes are used to request information from the user. For example, you may use an option pane to request a user's password. There are three methods for displaying this type of option pane, as shown in Table 9.10. The first two methods display a pane with a single text field for entry. The third method provides a combo box or list for the user to choose from.

Figure 9.11 Confirm dialog with YES_NO_OPTION.

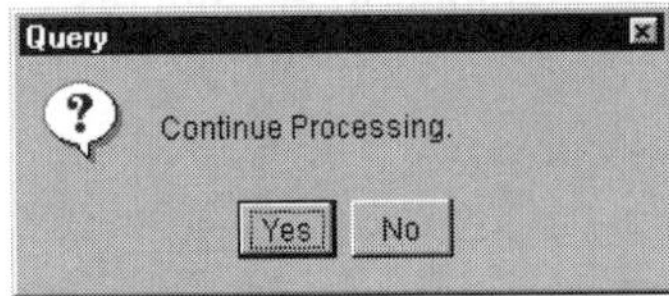

Table 9.10 Methods to Display an Input Pane

Method	Function
public static String showInputDialog (Component parentComponent, Object message)	Displays an input pane with the specified parent and message. A single text field is available for user input. The title is "Input," the message type is QUESTION_MESSAGE, and the option type is OK_CANCEL_OPTION.
public static String showInputDialog (Component parentComponent, Object message, String title, int messageType)	Displays an input pane with the specified parent, message, title, and message type. The option type is OK_CANCEL_OPTION. A single text field is available for user input.
public static Object showInputDialog (Component parentComponent, Object message, String title, int messageType, Icon icon, Object selectionValues[], Object initialSelectionValue)	Displays an input pane with the specified parent, message, title, message type, and icon. The option type is OK_CANCEL_OPTION. A JComboBox or JList is created to display the selectionValues, and the initialSelectionValue is selected if it's not null. The decision of what component to display is up to the current look and feel.

All these methods are class methods for JOptionPane. They attempt to reuse components when possible, making this a memory-efficient mechanism for creating dialogs. Remember that there are equivalent methods to create a message pane for an internal frame.

For the methods that display a text field, the return value is a string that contains the text in the text field. For the method that displays a combo box or list, the return value is the currently selected object. The return value is null if the user cancels or closes the dialog. You may also want to determine if a string return value's length is 0 to make sure that the user did not just click the OK button without typing in a value.

The following example displays an input dialog when a button is pressed. A message is printed to the console based on the value of the user's input. We have included our WindowCloser class in this file to handle the window's close box.

```
import com.sun.java.swing.*;
import java.awt.event.*;

import java.awt.*;
import java.lang.*;
```

```
public class InputExample extends JPanel
implements ActionListener
{
    public InputExample()
    {
        JButton go = new JButton("Go");
        go.addActionListener(this);
        add(go);
    }

    public void actionPerformed(ActionEvent e)
    {
        String result;

        result = JOptionPane.showInputDialog(this
                                    ,"What is your name?");

        if((result == null)
            || (result.length() == 0))
        {
            System.out.println("Shy are we ;-)");
        }
        else
        {
            System.out.println("Hello "+result);
        }
    }

    public Dimension getPreferredSize()
    {
        return new Dimension(100, 60);
    }

    public static void main(String s[])
    {
        JFrame frame = new JFrame("Input");
        InputExample panel = new InputExample();

        frame.setForeground(Color.black);
        frame.setBackground(Color.lightGray);
        frame.addWindowListener(new WindowCloser());
        frame.getContentPane().add(panel,"Center");
```

```
        frame.setSize(panel.getPreferredSize());
        frame.setVisible(true);
    }
}
```

We have also included the WindowCloser class in this example to handle the window close box. This class is included in the same file, and inherits the import statements.

```
class WindowCloser extends WindowAdapter
{
    public void windowClosing(WindowEvent e)
    {
        Window win = e.getWindow();
        win.setVisible(false);
        win.dispose();
        System.exit(0);
    }
}
```

When the code is run it produces an input dialog shown in Figure 9.12.

We also created an example that provides a list of choices. This example is pictured in Figure 9.13. The code for the complete example is similar to the previous one. The main exception is the code used to display the dialog. This looks like the following:

```
Object result;
String[] selValues = {"Java"
                      ,"C"
                      ,"C++"
                      ,"Perl"
                      ,"JavaScript"
                      ,"COBOL"
                      ,"Visual Basic"};

String initSel = "Java";

result = JOptionPane.showInputDialog(this
                        ,"What is your favorite prog. language?"
                        ,"Pick a language"
                        ,JOptionPane.QUESTION_MESSAGE
                        ,null
                        ,selValues
                        ,initSel);
```

Figure 9.12 Input dialog.

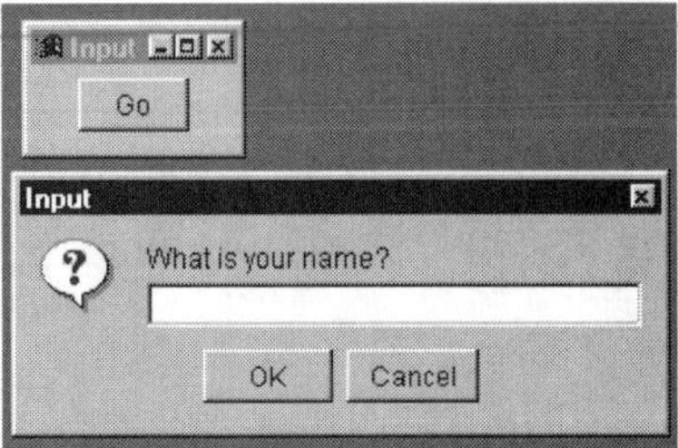

In this case, the result is an object that indicates the selected value. This value is not necessarily a string; it's whatever object you used to define the selected values.

General Option Panes

The final method for displaying an option dialog is the most flexible. This method allows you to configure the options available to the user, as well as the message and other attributes:

```
public static int showOptionDialog(Component parentComponent,
                                   Object message,
                                   String title,
                                   int optionType,
                                   int messageType,
                                   Icon icon,
                                   Object options[],
                                   Object initialValue)
```

This method brings up a modal dialog with a specified icon, where the initial choice is determined by the initialValue parameter and the number of choices is determined by the optionType parameter.

The return value for this method is an integer that indicates the index of the selected option.

The options for a general option dialog are treated as one of three options, as shown in Table 9.11. All of the options are displayed in order from left to right in the options area.

Figure 9.13 Input dialog with selection values.

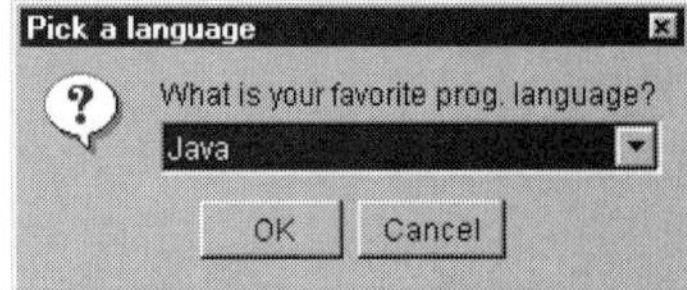

Table 9.11 Treatment of Options

Option Type	Treatment
Component	Displayed in the options area.
String	Used to create a JButton and added to the options area.
Other Object	Converted to a string, used to create a Jbutton, and added to the options area.

The initialValue is either null or one of the options that was passed in. This option is "selected" initially. Most likely this selection takes the form of the element with focus.

The following example, pictured in Figure 9.14, creates a general option pane with a JProgressBar as one of its message items. A single string is used as an option to allow the user to "cancel" the current activity. For simplicity, our example just counts to 100 using a timer. This technique is almost the same as the one used by the ProgressMonitor discussed in Chapter 10 to display a progress panel.

```
import com.sun.java.swing.*;
import java.awt.event.*;

import java.awt.*;
import java.lang.*;

public class ProgExample extends JPanel
implements ActionListener
{
    JProgressBar bar;
    JButton go;
    Timer ticker;

    public ProgExample()
    {
        go = new JButton("Go");
        go.addActionListener(this);
        add(go);

        bar = new JProgressBar();
        bar.setMinimum(0);
        bar.setMaximum(100);
        bar.setValue(0);

        ticker = new Timer(20,this);
        ticker.setRepeats(true);
```

```
        ticker.stop();
    }

    public void actionPerformed(ActionEvent e)
    {
        if(e.getSource() == go)
        {
            int result;
            Object msg[];
            Object options[];

            msg = new Object[2];

            msg[0] = "Current Load Progress";
            msg[1] = bar;

            options = new Object[1];

            options[0] = "Cancel Load";

            bar.setValue(0);
            ticker.start();

            result = JOptionPane.showOptionDialog(this
                                        ,msg
                                        ,"Progress"
                                        ,JOptionPane.OK_CANCEL_OPTION
                                        ,JOptionPane. PLAIN_MESSAGE
                                        ,null
                                        ,options
                                        ,options[0]);

            ticker.stop();
        }
        else if(e.getSource() == ticker)
        {
            int curProg = bar.getValue();

            if(curProg >= 99)
            {
                bar.setValue(100);
                ticker.stop();
                getToolkit().beep();
```

```
                }
                else
                {
                    bar.setValue(curProg+1);
                }
            }
        }

    public Dimension getPreferredSize()
    {
        return new Dimension(100, 60);
    }

    public static void main(String s[])
    {
        JFrame frame = new JFrame("Progress");
        ProgExample panel = new ProgExample();

        frame.setForeground(Color.black);
        frame.setBackground(Color.lightGray);
        frame.addWindowListener(new WindowCloser());
        frame.getContentPane().add(panel,"Center");

        frame.setSize(panel.getPreferredSize());
        frame.setVisible(true);
    }
}
```

We have also included the WindowCloser class in this example to handle the window close box. This class is included in the same file and inherits the import statements.

```
class WindowCloser extends WindowAdapter
{
    public void windowClosing(WindowEvent e)
    {
        Window win = e.getWindow();
        win.setVisible(false);
        win.dispose();
        System.exit(0);
    }
}
```

Figure 9.14 shows the custom option pane that displays a progress bar.

Figure 9.14 Custom option pane.

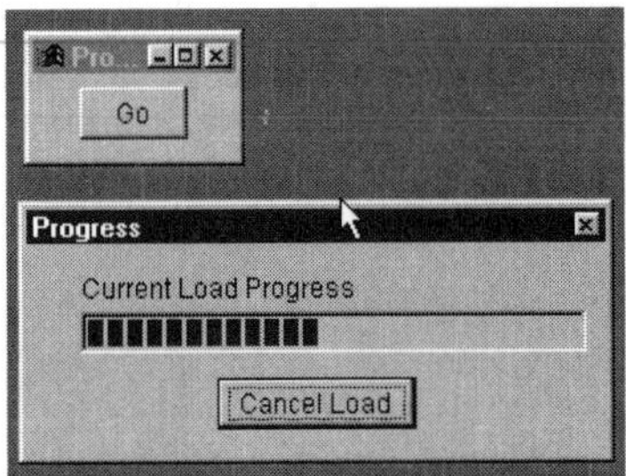

This example ignores the return value from the option pane because we always want to stop the timer if the option pane is closed.

Creating an Option Dialog

The final technique for dealing with option panes is to create them from scratch. This is actually a useful technique because it allows you to get a handle on the option pane itself and its dialog or internal frame. You may have noticed in the last example that the progress pane stays on screen even though the progress is completed. In our simple case, we don't have a handle to the dialog. Without this handle we can't tell it to close. By creating our own option pane, we can grab a handle to the dialog and close it at will.

Creating an option pane is a four-step process:

1. Create the option pane using a constructor, and initialize it.
2. Create a dialog for the pane.
3. Show the dialog.
4. Determine and act on the results.

There are several constructors for creating an option pane, as listed in Table 9.12.

The next step is to configure the option pane and create a dialog or internal frame for the pane. You ask the pane to create a holder for you. Use either of the following methods to create this holder:

```
public JDialog createDialog(Component parentComponent,
                            String title);

public JInternalFrame createInternalFrame(Component parentComponent,
                                          String title);
```

Both methods take a parent component and a title for the dialog or frame. The return value of these methods gives you a handle to the pane's dialog or frame. Use this handle to show the dialog or internal frame. In Chapter 14, we discuss internal frames in detail. Basically, internal frames are windows that live inside another window. In general, your application displays all of its windows separately or in internal frames. Based on this initial decision, you may choose to use the internal version of the option panes rather than the dialog version. We have stayed with dialogs for consistency.

When the show method returns, you want to get the user's selection. Because the dialog doesn't give this information to you, you have to ask the option pane for it using the getValue() method:

```
public Object getValue();
```

This method returns the object JOptionPane.UNINITIALIZED_VALUE if the user hasn't made a value or null if there is no appropriate value, due to a cancel or close. If the user actually made a selection, this value is probably an Integer object that represents the index of the selected value.

The following example, pictured in Figure 9.15, creates a simple dialog using the techniques we just discussed. This dialog has an OK and a Cancel button. A message is printed based on the user's selection.

Table 9.12 JOptionPane Constructors

Constructor	Function
JOptionPane()	Creates an option pane with a test message.
JOptionPane(Object message)	Creates an option pane with the specified message.
JOptionPane(Object message, int messageType)	Creates an option pane with the specified message and message type.
public JOptionPane(Object message, int messageType, int optionType)	Creates an option pane with the specified message, message type, and option type.
public JOptionPane(Object message, int messageType, int optionType, Icon icon)	Creates an option pane with the specified message, message type, option type, and icon.
public JOptionPane(Object message, int messageType, int optionType, Icon icon, Object options[])	Creates an option pane with the specified message, message type, option type, icon, and set of options.
public JOptionPane(Object message, int messageType, optionType, Icon icon, Object options[], Object initialValue)	Creates an option pane with the specified message, message type, option type, icon, and set of options. Selects the specified initial value from the options.

```
import com.sun.java.swing.*;
import java.awt.event.*;

import java.awt.*;
import java.lang.*;

public class ConstructExample extends JPanel
implements ActionListener
{
    public ConstructExample()
    {
        JButton go = new JButton("Go");
        go.addActionListener(this);
        add(go);
    }

    public void actionPerformed(ActionEvent e)
    {
        String msg[] = {"A file error has occurred."
                        ,"Continue?"};

        JOptionPane pane= new JOptionPane(msg
                                    ,JOptionPane.ERROR_MESSAGE
                                    ,JOptionPane.OK_CANCEL_OPTION);
        JDialog dialog;
        Object result;

        dialog = pane.createDialog(this,"Error");

        dialog.show();

        result = pane.getValue();

        if(result instanceof Integer)
        {
            int intResult=((Integer)result).intValue();

            if(intResult == JOptionPane.OK_OPTION)
            {
                System.out.println("Got OK");
            }
            else
            {
```

```
                System.out.println("Cancelled/Closed");
            }
        }
        else if(result == null)
        {
            System.out.println("Cancelled/Closed");
        }
    }

    public Dimension getPreferredSize()
    {
        return new Dimension(100, 60);
    }

    public static void main(String s[])
    {
        JFrame frame = new JFrame("Constructor");
        ConstructExample panel = new ConstructExample();

        frame.setForeground(Color.black);
        frame.setBackground(Color.lightGray);
        frame.addWindowListener(new WindowCloser());
        frame.getContentPane().add(panel,"Center");

        frame.setSize(panel.getPreferredSize());
        frame.setVisible(true);
    }
}
```

Our example uses the WindowCloser class to handle the close box. This class is included in the same file and inherits the import statements.

```
class WindowCloser extends WindowAdapter
{
    public void windowClosing(WindowEvent e)
    {
        Window win = e.getWindow();
        win.setVisible(false);
        win.dispose();
        System.exit(0);
    }
}
```

Figure 9.15 shows a confirm dialog created with an option pane.

Figure 9.15 Option pane created with constructor.

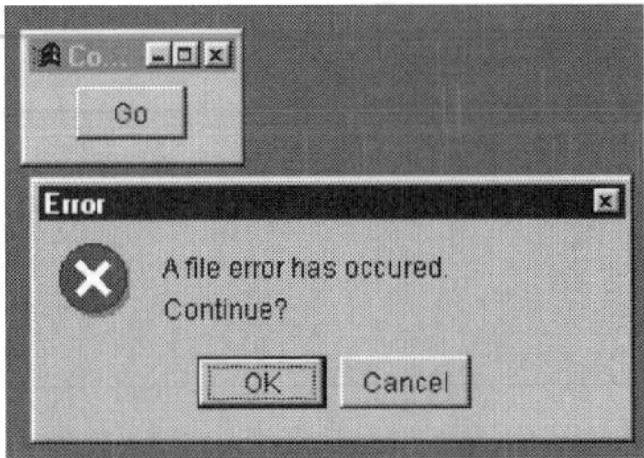

Style Guidelines

JOptionPane is extremely configurable. You can use an option pane to create most of your dialogs. As a result, rely on the option type and message type whenever possible to define the icon and buttons. This allows the current look and feel to modify the pane for the current platform.

Choose your message type and option type based on the meaning of the dialog. For example, use a yes-no dialog to ask a question, but an OK-cancel dialog for warnings and errors. For the message type you may use INFORMATION_MESSAGE to display a simple comment, but use ERROR_MESSAGE if something unexpected has occurred. Users have become accustomed to judging the importance of a dialog by these icons. If you use the wrong one, a user may quickly press OK to remove the dialog from the screen and inadvertently lose data.

Because option panes are so easy to use, often needing just one line of code, use them whenever appropriate. For example, use an error message dialog if an exception occurs. Users appreciate the standard user interface that an option pane represents, and it doesn't take much work on your part.

Finally, dialogs are intended for windows that must be dealt with and then go away. Use frames when you create windows that will linger on the screen, like document windows, tool bars, and tool inspectors.

TIMERS AND PROGRESS BARS

10

Applications often need to have events occur at regular intervals. Maybe you want an icon to blink every second or a graphic to move across the screen. Swing provides a timer object that notifies its action listeners of action events on a timed basis. The timer supports both a configurable delay between events and an initial delay and a flag that indicates if the timer should repeat.

One common use of timers is to keep track of the status of a process that happens in some other thread. You have probably seen applications display progress bars that show how far a loading or calculation process has advanced. In this case, the application checks the status of the process periodically and then updates the progress bar to represent graphically how far the process has gotten. To make this common activity even easier, Swing provides a progress bar component. This progress bar can be used to display a progress indicator that updates as a particular action is completed. Along with the progress bar, there is a progress monitor that displays a progress bar on a panel. This monitor actually waits for a specified amount of time before it activates. This makes it easy for you, as a programmer, to provide a progress bar for lengthy operations and still avoid busying the interface if the operation occurs quickly. A special filter stream is also provided to work with a progress monitor when you read from a stream.

Timers

The Swing Timer creates and posts action events based on three configuration parameters. First, there is an initial delay. The timer waits for the specified initial delay before firing any action events. Next, a flag indicates if the timer should repeat. If this flag is true, the timer continues to fire action events based on the final parameter, a delay. Both delays are specified in milliseconds, so a delay of 1000 is a delay of one second.

To manage the parameters for a timer, use the methods shown in Table 10.1.

You can also set the delay in the timer's constructor with the following method:

```
public Timer(int delay, ActionListener listener);
```

Table 10.1 Methods That Manage the Parameters for a Timer

Method	Function
public void setDelay(int delay)	Sets the amount of time in milliseconds between timer events sent to listeners.
public int getDelay()	Returns the current timer delay.
public void setInitialDelay (int initialDelay)	Sets the delay before the first timer action is executed. After the first execution, the standard setDelay is used.
public int getInitialDelay()	Returns the initial delay.
public void setRepeats (boolean flag)	Tells the timer to send only one event to the listeners if the Boolean is false. If the Boolean is set to true then the timer continues to send messages at regular delay intervals.
public boolean repeats()	Returns a Boolean that specifies if the timer is set to repeat.

In this case, the initial delay is 0, the timer repeats, and the specified ActionListener is added to the timer's list. This is the only constructor for Timer.

When a timer posts an action event, it posts the event into the main event queue. If you recall our earlier discussion of the event queue in Chapter 2, this means that the ActionEvents from a timer are handed to their appropriate listeners in the same thread that user and paint events are processed. This is often a useful feature because the timer is used to create animations and other timed activities without your worrying about multithreaded code. We see in our discussion of progress monitor input streams later in this chapter, however, a situation where this is not the preferred behavior. In particular, if you start a timer and expect it to warn you if a process has taken too long, this warning is noticeable only if you actively check for it in the event queue or if you perform the timely operation in another thread. The action event doesn't "interrupt" the event queue thread to notify action listeners. Basically, a thread can do only one thing at a time. If you use a button press to initiate a lengthy operation in your actionPerformed method, no other events are processed until that method is returned. This includes timer notifications and paint events.

To start a timer, or to stop it, use the following methods:

```
public void start();
public void stop();
```

You can also check if a timer is running with the isRunning() method:

```
public boolean isRunning();
```

To restart a timer and tell it to wait for the initial delay again, before sending any more notifications, use the following method:

```
public void restart();
```

Timers provide one more feature, *coalescing*, that causes the timer to wait until its current notification event is processed before it fires another one. For example, if you tell the timer to fire every second, but the program is performing time-intensive, event-handling operations and the notification sits in the queue for three seconds, the timer won't add another event until the first one is processed. Coalescing is on by default, but you can turn it off using the setCoalesce method, as shown here:

```
public void setCoalesce(boolean flag);
```

If coalescing is off, many ActionEvents may pile up in your event queue if it takes a long time to process each one. Users prefer performing time-intensive operations in another thread, however, so that the event queues thread provides a quick response.

The following example, pictured in Figure 10.1, demonstrates a timer that uses action commands. In this example, the user enters a number in a text field and an alarm sounds when the specified time has passed. A check box indicates if the alarm needs to repeat.

This example is implemented in the form of a subclass of JPanel. A main class method creates a Frame for the panel and then displays it. A helper class called WindowCloser is used to close the window when the close box is selected.

```
import java.util.*;
import java.awt.*;
import java.awt.event.*;
import com.sun.java.swing.*;
import com.sun.java.swing.text.*;

public class Timers extends JPanel
implements ActionListener
{
    JTextField delayField;
    JCheckBox repeat;
    Timer clock;

    final static String SET="set";
    final static String ALARM="alarm";

    public Timers()
    {
        JLabel label;
        GridLayout grid;
```

```
        setBackground(Color.lightGray);

        grid = new GridLayout(1,3,10,10);
        setLayout(grid);

        label = new JLabel("Delay (ms)");
        add(label);

        delayField = new JTextField();
        delayField.addActionListener(this);
        delayField.setActionCommand(SET);
        add(delayField);

        repeat = new JCheckBox("Repeat");
        repeat.addActionListener(this);
        repeat.setActionCommand(SET);
        add(repeat);

        clock = new Timer(1000,this);
        clock.setRepeats(false);
        clock.stop();
    }

    public void actionPerformed(ActionEvent e)
    {
        String command;

        command = e.getActionCommand();

        if (SET.equals(command))
        {
            int delayTime;

            delayTime = Integer.parseInt(delayField.getText());

            clock.stop();
            clock.setDelay(delayTime);
            clock.setInitialDelay(delayTime);

            if(repeat.isSelected())
            {
                clock.setRepeats(true);
            }
            else
            {
```

```
                clock.setRepeats(false);
            }

            clock.start();

            delayField.selectAll();
        }
        else if(e.getSource() == clock)
        {
            System.out.println("ALARM!");
            getToolkit().beep();
        }
    }

    public Dimension getPreferredSize()
    {
        return new Dimension(300, 50);
    }

    public static void main(String s[])
    {
        JFrame frame = new JFrame("Timers");
        Timers panel = new Timers();

        frame.setForeground(Color.black);
        frame.setBackground(Color.lightGray);
        frame.addWindowListener(new WindowCloser());
        frame.getContentPane().add(panel,"Center");

        frame.setSize(panel.getPreferredSize());
        frame.setVisible(true);
    }
}

class WindowCloser extends WindowAdapter
{
    public void windowClosing(WindowEvent e)
    {
        Window win = e.getWindow();
        win.setVisible(false);
        win.dispose();
        System.exit(0);
    }
}
```

Figure 10.1 A timer that uses action commands.

Figure 10.1 shows a dialog that allows you to set an alarm with a timer.

Another side effect for those timers that use the event queue is that its ActionEvent is posted as close to the specified time as possible. If the processor is too busy, or if the event queue is slow to process, the ActionEvent may be processed at a time later than the one specified. For example, if you set the timer to fire every second and another event ties up the processor for two seconds, the ActionEvent won't process for at least two seconds. If you don't use coalescing, these delays can actually cause the addition of several action events to the queue before the first one is handled.

> **NOTE**
>
> Timers actually post their event from a thread other than the event-processing thread. All events, regardless of how they get to the queue, are processed in the same thread.

The following example, pictured in Figure 10.2, implements and displays a subclass of JComponent called DigitalClock. This clock component uses a timer to repaint itself with the current time. To make sure that the actual time is displayed, we use two techniques. First, the timer is set to fire every 200 milliseconds rather than every second. This finer granularity smoothes out any hiccups in the event-processing thread. By default, the Timer coalesces events so there are no extra timer actions in the queue.

The second technique we utilize is to use the actual time for our display, rather than assume that the timer fired every 200 milliseconds. This ensures that when a timer event arrives and we repaint, it is the correct time. The clock can have the wrong time only if a timer event is delayed for more than one second. This technique is obvious in a clock application, but it is also necessary in games, simulations, and animations where the user expects smooth operations. Essentially, all timer-based operations should use real time to determine what to do; they should never assume that the timer event arrived on time.

The main code in bold for the DigitalClock class is in the paint method. This method gets the current time and creates a string from it. This string is displayed in the appropriate font, centered in the component. You may notice two issues when you create the string. First, we have to deal with adding a 0 before any single-digit numbers for minutes or seconds. Second, we display a ":" when the seconds are odd and a "." when they are even. This trick creates a visual indicator to the user of the clock ticking. The constructor creates the timer, and the actionPerformed method that receives timer notifications calls repaint. There are also several convenience methods for starting and stopping the clock.

```
import java.util.*;
import java.awt.*;
import java.awt.event.*;
import com.sun.java.swing.*;
import com.sun.java.swing.text.*;

public class DigitalClock extends JComponent
 implements ActionListener
{
    Timer ticker;
    boolean showSeconds;

    public DigitalClock()
    {
        showSeconds = false;
        ticker = new Timer(200,this);

        setDoubleBuffered(true);
        resume();
    }

    public void resume()
    {
        ticker.start();
    }

    public void suspend()
    {
        ticker.stop();
    }

    public boolean running()
    {
        return ticker.isRunning();
    }

    public void setShowSeconds(boolean tf)
    {
        showSeconds = tf;
```

```
    repaint();
}

public Dimension getPreferredSize()
{
    Font theFont;
    FontMetrics fm=null;
    Dimension retVal;

    theFont = getFont();
    if(theFont != null) fm = getToolkit().getFontMetrics(theFont);

    if(fm != null)
    {
        retVal =
            new Dimension(fm.stringWidth("00:00:00"),fm.getHeight());
    }
    else
    {
        retVal = new Dimension(75,25);
    }

    return retVal;
}

public void paint(Graphics g)
{
    String timeString;
    GregorianCalendar realDate;
    Font theFont;
    FontMetrics fm=null;
    Dimension curSize;
    int h,m,s;

    theFont = getFont();
    if(theFont != null) fm = getToolkit().getFontMetrics(theFont);

    if((fm != null) && isEnabled() && running())
    {
        realDate = new GregorianCalendar();
        h = realDate.get(Calendar.HOUR_OF_DAY);
        h = h%12;
```

```
            m = realDate.get(Calendar.MINUTE);
            s = realDate.get(Calendar.SECOND);

            timeString = ""+h;

            if(s%2==0) timeString+=":";
            else timeString+=".";

            if((m>0)&&(m<10)) timeString+="0";
            timeString += m;
            if(m==0) timeString+="0";

            if(showSeconds)
            {
                if(s%2==0) timeString+=":";
                else timeString+=".";

                if((s>0)&&(s<10)) timeString+="0";
                timeString += s;
                if(s==0) timeString+="0";
            }

            curSize = getSize();

            g.setColor(getBackground());
            g.fillRect(0,0,curSize.width,curSize.height);

            g.setColor(getForeground());
            g.setFont(theFont);

                //Center the string
            g.drawString(timeString,
                (curSize.width-
                            fm.stringWidth(timeString.replace(' ',':')))/2,
                (curSize.height + fm.getAscent())/2);
        }
    }

    public void actionPerformed(ActionEvent evt)
    {
        if(evt.getSource()==ticker) repaint();
    }
}
```

Figure 10.2 Clock example.

To see the DigitalClock in action we created a little example, pictured in Figure 10.2. This example creates a frame with a clock on it. A WindowCloser is assigned to the frame to handle the close box.

```
import java.util.*;
import java.awt.*;
import java.awt.event.*;
import com.sun.java.swing.*;
import com.sun.java.swing.text.*;

public class Clocks extends JPanel
{
    public Clocks()
    {
        DigitalClock clock = new DigitalClock();

        setBackground(Color.lightGray);
        setLayout(new FlowLayout(FlowLayout.CENTER));

        clock.setFont(new Font("Serif",Font.BOLD,24));
        clock.setShowSeconds(true);

        add(clock);
    }

    public Dimension getPreferredSize()
    {
        return new Dimension(200, 70);
    }

    public static void main(String s[])
    {
        JFrame frame = new JFrame("Clocks");
        Clocks panel = new Clocks();

        frame.setForeground(Color.black);
        frame.setBackground(Color.lightGray);
```

```
            frame.addWindowListener(new WindowCloser());
            frame.getContentPane().add(panel,"Center");

            frame.setSize(panel.getPreferredSize());
            frame.setVisible(true);
        }
}

class WindowCloser extends WindowAdapter
{
    public void windowClosing(WindowEvent e)
    {
        Window win = e.getWindow();
        win.setVisible(false);
        win.dispose();
        System.exit(0);
    }
}
```

Progress Bar

For many of us, the increasing speed of computers has been met and even surpassed by an increase in work for the computer to do. Even though the computers are faster, computing still feels as if it takes a long time. Humans are impatient so they need some sort of cue, usually visual, to let them know the computer is making progress. When we think progress is being made we are far more forgiving and patient. Applications now use an updating progress bar that displays the current extent of their progress in completing a time-consuming task. In other words, progress bars provide a visual indication of how much time a user has until he or she can get back to work.

JFC provides a simple progress bar component, like the one pictured in Figure 10.3, as well as some supporting classes that make using progress bars even easier.

Figure 10.3 Progress bar.

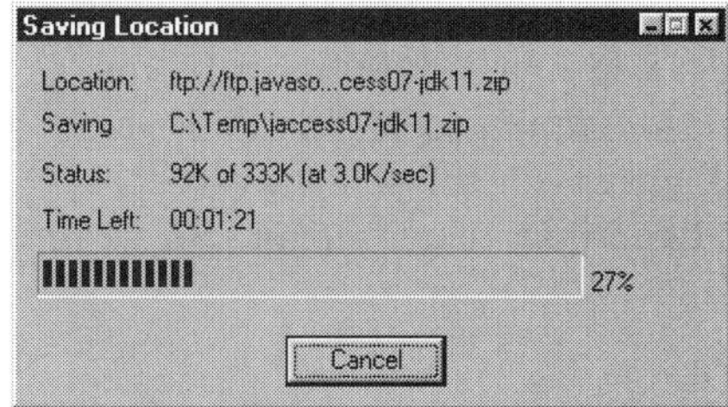

The progress bar component is implemented in the JProgressBar class. These components use a BoundedRangeModel to hold their data. This is the same type of model used by sliders, and it manages a minimum value, a maximum value, and a current value. Interacting with a progress bar is a four-part process:

1. Create the progress bar.
2. Set the bar's orientation to JProgressBar.HORIZONTAL or JProgressBar.VERTICAL.
3. Set the bar's minimum and maximum values.
4. Set the bar's current value, and update this value as necessary.

To create a progress bar, use the following constructor:

```
public JProgressBar();
```

This creates a horizontal progress bar with a border. If you want to assign the bar's orientation use the setOrientation() method, as shown here:

```
public void setOrientation(int newOrientation);
```

Pass in one of the following JProgressBar static variables to set the orientation of the progress bar to either horizontal or vertical.

```
JProgressBar.VERTICAL
JProgressBar.HORIZONTAL
```

The next step is to assign a minimum and maximum value. The progress bar is like a slider: It displays the current value as it relates to the minimum and maximum value. For example, if you set the current value to the maximum value, the entire bar is filled. If you set the value to the number halfway between the minimum and maximum values, then half of the bar is filled. To manage the minimum and maximum values, use the following methods:

```
public void setMaximum(int n);
public void setMinimum(int n);
public int getMaximum();
public int getMinimum();
```

These methods actually assign or return the progress bar's model's values.

The current value for a progress bar is used to change the bar's position. This value is updated, from the minimum to eventually the maximum value, throughout the operation that is tracked. For example, if you process 100 records, you can set the progress bar's minimum to 0 and the maximum to 100 and initialize the current value to 0. As a record is processed, increment the current value that shows the user how many records are processed and how many remain. To set or retrieve the current value, use these methods:

```
public void setValue(int n);
public int getValue();
```

Figure 10.4 Progress bar example.

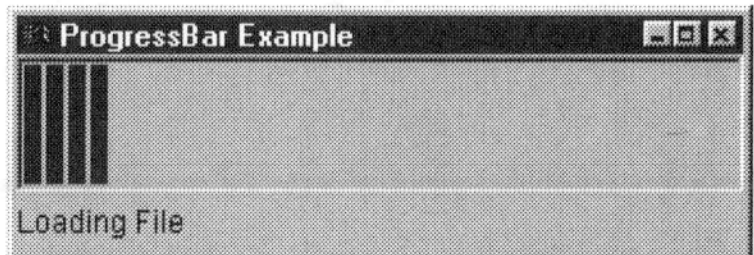

Again, these methods are actually forwarded to the bar's model.

You can have the JProgressBar paint its border or background. Normally, you paint both of these; this is the default. JProgressBar has a method setOpaque that, when passed true, tells the progress bar to fill its background when it paints. It also has a method setBorderPainted that, when set to true, tells the progress bar to paint its border. If these methods are set to false, then the progress bar won't paint the background or its border, respectively. The progress bar also has methods for retrieving the current setting of these values. All four methods are as follows:

```
public void setOpaque(boolean opaque);
public boolean isOpaque();
public void setBorderPainted(boolean b);
public boolean isBorderPainted();
```

Our example for JProgressBar, pictured in Figure 10.4, loads a file from disk as it sleeps. As the file loads, a progress bar is updated to reflect the current percentage of the file loaded. This example shows how to initialize a progress bar and how to update its value. We have highlighted some of the important techniques for using JProgressBar within the code. The first bold code block shows the progress bar constructed and having its parameters set. Keep in mind that we track a percentage in this case, so the minimum is 0 and the maximum is 100. In the next bold code block we check to make sure that the file exists and if it does we store the length of the file. We do this so we can calculate what percentage we have loaded as loading and the progress bar can reflect an actual percentage of the file loaded. The formula i*100/max is used to set the progress bar value. This value is a number between 0 and 100. Note in the next bold code that we set the value of the progress bar to 100 when we finish loading. Note that the percentage is a fractional value and may never actually reach 100. We want the progress bar visually to complete so finalizing at 100 guarantees the user will see the operation actually complete, regardless of the file size or how often we update the progress bar.

```
import java.util.*;
import java.io.*;
import java.awt.*;
import java.awt.event.*;
import com.sun.java.swing.*;
import com.sun.java.swing.border.*;
```

```
public class Progress extends JPanel
{
    JProgressBar progBar;
    Label status;

    public Progress()
    {
        setBackground(Color.lightGray);
        setLayout(new BorderLayout());

        progBar = new JProgressBar();
        progBar.setMinimum(0);
        progBar.setMaximum(100);
        progBar.setValue(0);

        status = new Label("");

        add(progBar,"Center");
        add(status,"South");
    }

    public void go()
    {
        FileInputStream fileIn=null;
        int curByte;
        int i,max;
        File file;

        status.setText("Loading File");

        try
        {
            file = new File("Progress.java");
            fileIn = new FileInputStream("Progress.java");

            if(file.exists()) max = (int) file.length();
            else max = 0;

            for(i=0;i<max;i++)
            {
                curByte = fileIn.read();

                //Show status as a percent
```

```
                progBar.setValue((i*100)/max);

                //Make sure to takes a few seconds
                Thread.sleep(5);
            }

            status.setText("Load completed");
            progBar.setValue(100);
        }
        catch(Exception exp)
        {
            status.setText("Read failed");
        }
        finally
        {
            try
            {
                if(fileIn != null) fileIn.close();
            }
            catch(Exception exp2)
            {
            }
        }
    }

    public Dimension getPreferredSize()
    {
        return new Dimension(300, 100);
    }

    public static void main(String s[])
    {
        JFrame frame = new JFrame("ProgressBar Example");
        Progress panel = new Progress();

        frame.setForeground(Color.black);
        frame.setBackground(Color.lightGray);
        frame.addWindowListener(new WindowCloser());
        frame.getContentPane().add(panel,"Center");

        frame.setSize(panel.getPreferredSize());
        frame.setVisible(true);

        panel.go();
```

```
    }
}

class WindowCloser extends WindowAdapter
{
    public void windowClosing(WindowEvent e)
    {
        Window win = e.getWindow();
        win.setVisible(false);
        win.dispose();
        System.exit(0);
    }
}
```

You may have noticed that we set the bar's value to 100 after the file is totally copied. This is a useful technique because it ensures that the bar displays completion, on completion, regardless of any round-off errors in calculating the current percentage.

The Progress Bar's Model

Remember that most of the components in Swing are designed to use the model-view-controller architecture. As we mentioned earlier in this section, a JProgressBar uses a BoundedRangeModel to store its data. This is the same type of model that a slider uses. The actual model object for both sliders and progress bars can be shared between the two components.

As a simple demonstration of this powerful technique, we created a small example that displays a slider and a progress bar that share the same model. This example is pictured in Figure 10.5. Admittedly, the example is quite simple and not necessarily useful in a real program, but the technique it represents can reduce code and increase the functionality of your Swing programs immensely. A more powerful example may be to use the same model for several text areas in a word processor, allowing the user to create multiple views of a document. Because models are often defined with an interface rather than a class, you can create a model that provides data for a tree or a list. All of these examples show how the separation of a model from a component can be used to reduce the amount of data stored in a program by centralizing it into a single model or a group of shared models.

The code for this example creates a progress bar and a slider. The bar's values are initialized, and its default model is assigned to the slider. The slider inherits these initial values from the model. If you run this example from the CD-ROM you see that when the slider is moved the progress bar updates automatically. These updates are the result of change events coming from the model to the two components.

```
import java.util.*;
import java.io.*;
import java.awt.*;
import java.awt.event.*;
import com.sun.java.swing.*;
import com.sun.java.swing.border.*;

public class ProgressModel extends JPanel
{
    public ProgressModel()
    {
        JProgressBar progBar;
        JSlider slider;
        BoundedRangeModel model;

        setBackground(Color.lightGray);
        setLayout(new GridLayout(2,1,10,10));

        progBar = new JProgressBar();
        progBar.setMinimum(0);
        progBar.setMaximum(100);
        progBar.setValue(0);

        slider = new JSlider();

        model = progBar.getModel();
        slider.setModel(model);

        add(progBar);
        add(slider);
    }

    public Dimension getPreferredSize()
    {
        return new Dimension(300, 100);
    }

    public static void main(String s[])
    {
        JFrame frame = new JFrame("ProgressModel Example");
        ProgressModel panel = new ProgressModel();

        frame.setForeground(Color.black);
```

```
        frame.setBackground(Color.lightGray);
        frame.addWindowListener(new WindowCloser());
        frame.getContentPane().add(panel,"Center");

        frame.setSize(panel.getPreferredSize());
        frame.setVisible(true);
    }
}

class WindowCloser extends WindowAdapter
{
    public void windowClosing(WindowEvent e)
    {
        Window win = e.getWindow();
        win.setVisible(false);
        win.dispose();
        System.exit(0);
    }
}
```

Progress Monitors

JFC also provides a number of classes that automatically displays progress bars and update them during lengthy operations. The ProgressMonitor class is used to display a progress bar on an option pane whenever a certain time has passed. The ProgressMonitorInputStream uses a progress monitor to monitor the calls to read its data and displays a progress bar if the stream takes too long to read.

Interacting with a ProgressMonitor relies on two concepts. First, you must manage the actual progress as you do with a progress bar. Second, you must assign an initial delay. When the monitor is created it starts counting. If the initial delay is reached, without the progress achieving the maximum value, a progress panel is displayed and it is updated to show the monitor's current value. An example of this panel is pictured in Figure 10.6.

If you process 100 records, you may set the minimum and maximum values for the progress monitor to 0 and 100. Then, as your progress records you can update the current value to the number of records processed. When you have

Figure 10.5 Shared model for creating a progress bar and a slider.

Figure 10.6 Progress monitor.

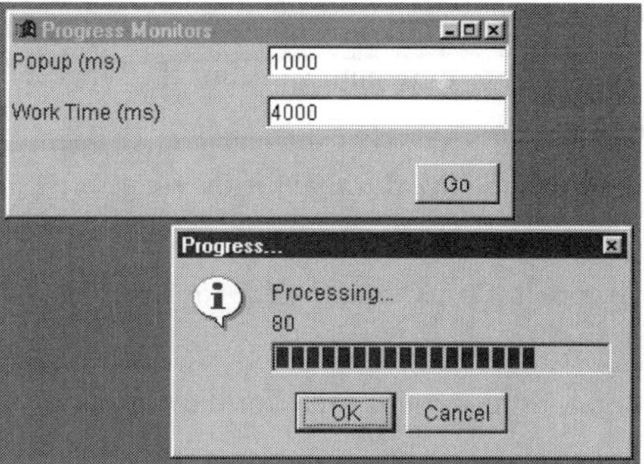

processed 10 records, set the value to 10. When you hit 11 records, set the value to 11. If the initial delay is set to one second and it takes three seconds to process all the records, the monitor pops up a window that shows the current progress. If the delay is set to one second and it takes 500 milliseconds to process the records, no progress is displayed. Basically, the monitor is used to display operations that take long enough that they require user feedback. If the operation doesn't take very long, then there is no need to display the same feedback.

To create a monitor, use the following constructor:

```
public ProgressMonitor(Component parentComponent,
                       Object message, String note,
                       int min, int max)
```

This method requires an initial minimum and maximum value as well as a note. Because the monitor may display a dialog, you must provide a component to the constructor. The frame that contains this component is used to construct the dialog. Finally, a message is provided to the constructor. This message is used as the title on the progress dialog.

The methods that manage the monitor's progress are shown in Table 10.2.

You are expected to update the progress regularly, just as you would for a progress bar, without a monitor. When you complete an operation, tell the monitor that it is done using the method:

```
public void close();
```

This closes the progress dialog if it is displayed.

There is also a note displayed on the progress dialog. You can assign this note using the following method:

```
public void setNote(String note);
```

Table 10.2 Methods That Manage the Monitor's Progress

Method	Function
public int getMinimum()	Returns the monitor's minimum value for the range it is tracking.
public void setMinimum(int m)	Sets the monitor's minimum value for the range it is tracking.
public int getMaximum()	Returns the monitor's maximum value for the range it is tracking.
public void setMaximum(int m)	Sets the monitor's maximum value for the range it is tracking.
public void setProgress(int p)	Sets the current value of the monitor in the range set with the methods above.

To assign the initial delay, you actually assign two values: millisToDecideToPopup and millisToPopup. The first value is used as a delay. If this time is not passed from the creation of the monitor to the current time, the monitor won't check to see if it needs to pop up. The second value is used to determine if it's time to pop up the progress dialog. The monitor calculates the current time it takes to update the progress. If this time looks as if it will exceed the millisToPopup, the progress window is displayed. You can manage these values using the following methods:

```
public void setMillisToDecideToPopup(int millisToDecideToPopup);
public int getMillisToDecideToPopup();
public void setMillisToPopup(int millisToPopup);
public int getMillisToPopup();
```

By default, both values are 0, so you can set just one if you want the window to pop up after a specified time. You can use both if you want the monitor to wait before checking the time; even then, you may want to see if the ultimate time is long enough to warrant a progress dialog.

In Figure 10.6, you can see that the dialog displayed by a progress monitor has OK and Cancel buttons. If the user clicks either button the dialog is removed from the screen. If the Cancel button is clicked, the current operation stops. The progress monitor doesn't notify you of this event. Instead, you must determine that the monitor was canceled by sending it the message:

```
public boolean isCancelled();
```

This returns "true" if the cancel button was pressed; "false" is returned if the dialog is still visible, was never displayed, or the OK button was used to remove it from the screen.

Figure 10.6 was created using the following example. In this example, a simple user interface is used to set several values. The first value is the delay for a progress monitor. The second value is a delay for a timer. When the program is told to go, the timer updates the monitor's progress at a rate equal to 10 percent for every one-tenth of the timer delay time. In other words, the progress continues to 100 percent based on the value for the timer's delay. The progress monitor displays a dialog if the time for the timer to reach 100 percent is greater than its delay. For example, if the monitor delay is set to 1000 milliseconds and the timer is set to 2000 milliseconds, then the progress dialog displays when the progress is approximately 50 percent.

This example also checks for the Cancel button and stops the timer if the user chooses this option. A message is printed to the console for a canceled operation, and three system beeps are sounded for a completed operation. A system beep is sounded each time the progress is updated to provide some feedback in the situation where you set the monitor delay to a value greater than the timer delay.

```
import java.util.*;
import java.awt.*;
import java.awt.event.*;
import com.sun.java.swing.*;
import com.sun.java.swing.text.*;

public class Monitor extends JPanel
implements ActionListener
{
    JTextField delayField;
    JTextField popupField;
    Timer clock;
    int ticks;
    ProgressMonitor monitor;

    final static String GO="go";

    public Monitor()
    {
        JLabel label;
        JPanel tmpPanel;
        JButton go;

        setBackground(Color.lightGray);

        tmpPanel = new JPanel();
        tmpPanel.setLayout(new GridLayout(2,2,10,10));

        label = new JLabel("Popup (ms)");
```

```
        tmpPanel.add(label);

        popupField = new JTextField();
        tmpPanel.add(popupField);

        label = new JLabel("Work Time (ms)");
        tmpPanel.add(label);

        delayField = new JTextField();
        tmpPanel.add(delayField);

        setLayout(new BorderLayout());
        add(tmpPanel,"North");

        tmpPanel = new JPanel();
        tmpPanel.setLayout(new FlowLayout(FlowLayout.RIGHT));

        go = new JButton("Go");
        go .addActionListener(this);
        go .setActionCommand(GO);

        tmpPanel.add(go);

        add(tmpPanel,"South");

        clock = new Timer(1000,this);
        clock.setRepeats(false);
        clock.stop();
    }

    public void actionPerformed(ActionEvent e)
    {
        String command;

        command = e.getActionCommand();

        if (GO.equals(command))
        {
            int delayTime;
            int popupTime;

            clock.stop();
            if(monitor != null) monitor.close();
```

```
            delayTime = Integer.parseInt(delayField.getText());
            popupTime = Integer.parseInt(popupField.getText());

            ticks = 0;

            clock.setDelay(delayTime/10);
            clock.setRepeats(true);

            monitor = new
                    ProgressMonitor(this,"Processing...","Started",0,100);
            monitor.setMillisToDecideToPopup(popupTime);
            clock.start();
        }
        else if(e.getSource() == clock)
        {
            if(monitor.isCancelled())
            {
                clock.stop();
                System.out.println("Cancelled");
            }
            if(ticks < 100)
            {
                ticks+=10;
                monitor.setProgress(ticks);
                monitor.setNote(String.valueOf(ticks));
                getToolkit().beep();
            }
            else //Got to 100
            {
                clock.stop();
                monitor.close();

                //Three beeps to end
                try
                {
                    getToolkit().beep();
                    Thread.sleep(200);
                    getToolkit().beep();
                    Thread.sleep(200);
                    getToolkit().beep();
                }
                catch(Exception exp){}
            }
        }
```

```
    }

    public Dimension getPreferredSize()
    {
        return new Dimension(300, 120);
    }

    public static void main(String s[])
    {
        JFrame frame = new JFrame("Progress Monitors");
        Monitor panel = new Monitor();

        frame.setForeground(Color.black);
        frame.setBackground(Color.lightGray);
        frame.addWindowListener(new WindowCloser());
        frame.getContentPane().add(panel,"Center");

        frame.setSize(panel.getPreferredSize());
        frame.setVisible(true);
    }
}

class WindowCloser extends WindowAdapter
{
    public void windowClosing(WindowEvent e)
    {
        Window win = e.getWindow();
        win.setVisible(false);
        win.dispose();
        System.exit(0);
    }
}
```

Note that we have used Thread.sleep during our triple beep. This is purely cosmetic and does not relate to timers or progress monitors in any way. It's there to separate the beeps from each other and for no other purpose.

Progress Monitor Input Streams

One of the common uses for a progress bar is to indicate progress while reading a file. Although you can provide this feedback manually, as we did for Figure 10.4, you can also use a ProgressMonitorInputStream to manage it automatically. The ProgressMonitorInputStream is a subclass of FilterInputStream. The main functionality that the ProgressMonitorInputStream adds is the creation of a Progress-Monitor. To use a ProgressMonitorInputStream, create it as a filter stream, access its progress monitor to set any initial delay values, and start reading. The ProgressMonitorInputStream sets the progress monitor's minimum, maximum, and current values, based on the size of the stream and the number of bytes that are read from it.

To create a ProgressMonitorInputStream use the following constructor:

```
public ProgressMonitorInputStream(Component parentComponent,
                                  Object message, InputStream in)
```

The parent component's frame is used to create the progress dialog. The message is used as the title for the progress dialog, and the input stream is the data source. This constructor is very similar to the constructor for ProgressMonitor, except that the minimum and maximum values are provided based on the input stream's data.

To retrieve the stream's ProgressMonitor, use the following method:

```
public ProgressMonitor getProgressMonitor();
```

Otherwise, use the stream normally.

> **NOTE**
>
> Unfortunately, there is one issue when using a ProgressMonitorInput-Stream. Remember that paint requests and events are handled in the same thread in Swing. If you try to read a stream as the result of an event notification, this can hinder future paint requests as well as other events. This may result in the progress dialog not repainting properly. To avoid this conflict, you need to perform lengthy operations in a second thread. You can still use the progress monitor to provide feedback, but don't try to do the actual reading in the event thread.

The following example, pictured in Figure 10.7, demonstrates how to create a monitor stream. In this example a stream is read in a background thread that uses a ProgressMonitorInputStream. The background thread checks if the progress monitor is canceled and stops reading in this case.

Figure 10.7 Monitor streams.

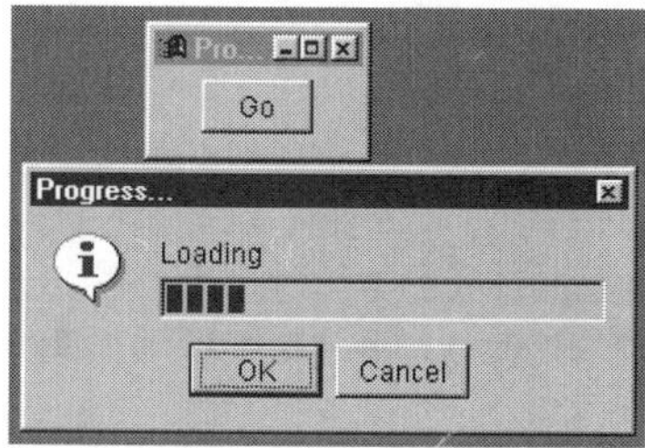

```
import java.applet.*;
import java.util.*;
import java.io.*;
import java.awt.*;
import java.awt.event.*;
import com.sun.java.swing.*;
import com.sun.java.swing.border.*;

public class ProgStream extends JPanel
implements ActionListener, Runnable
{
    Thread kicker;

    public ProgStream()
    {
        JButton go;

        setBackground(Color.lightGray);
        setLayout(new FlowLayout());

        go = new JButton("Go");
        go.addActionListener(this);
        add(go);
    }

    public void actionPerformed(ActionEvent evt)
    {
        kicker = new Thread(this);
        kicker.start();
    }

    public void run()
    {
        FileInputStream fileIn=null;
        ProgressMonitorInputStream progIn=null;
        int curByte;
        ProgressMonitor progMon;

        try
        {
            fileIn = new FileInputStream("ProgStream.java");
            progIn = new ProgressMonitorInputStream(this,"Loading",fileIn);
```

```
            progMon = progIn.getProgressMonitor();
            progMon.setMillisToDecideToPopup(10);

            while((curByte = progIn.read()) != -1)
            {
                Thread.sleep(5);

                if(progMon.isCancelled())
                {
                    getToolkit().beep();
                    Thread.sleep(200);//pause for next beep
                    break;
                }
            }

            getToolkit().beep();
        }
        catch(Exception exp)
        {
        }
        finally
        {
            try
            {
                if(progIn != null) progIn.close();
            }
            catch(Exception exp2)
            {
            }
        }
    }

    public Dimension getPreferredSize()
    {
        return new Dimension(100,60);
    }

    public static void main(String s[])
    {
        JFrame frame = new JFrame("Progress Stream Example");
        ProgStream panel = new ProgStream();

        frame.setForeground(Color.black);
        frame.setBackground(Color.lightGray);
```

```
        frame.addWindowListener(new WindowCloser());
        frame.getContentPane().add(panel,"Center");

        frame.setSize(panel.getPreferredSize());
        frame.setVisible(true);
    }
}

class WindowCloser extends WindowAdapter
{
    public void windowClosing(WindowEvent e)
    {
        Window win = e.getWindow();
        win.setVisible(false);
        win.dispose();
        System.exit(0);
    }
}
```

Style Guidelines

Based on our discussion about timers and progress bars in this chapter, there are several important style guidelines to keep in mind.

1. When you use a timer, base each timing calculation on the current time. Don't assume that the timer will fire exactly when you want it to fire.
2. When you finish an operation that is tracked by a progress bar or monitor, set the progress to the maximum value. This ensures that regardless of round-off errors, the user sees the bar indicate total completion.
3. Always perform lengthy operations in a background thread. This prevents delays in the event-processing thread that also initiates drawing.

Any program that performs lengthy operations must provide feedback to the user. If it's convenient to place a progress bar on an existing window, then use this bar to indicate work in progress. This technique is used in many Web browsers to indicate progress when a file loads. If there is no good place to display a progress bar, you can use a ProgressMonitor. In this case, set the delay to some value less than two seconds. The user definitely notices a one- to two-second delay, and you need to provide feedback before he or she starts wondering what is taking so long. As a last resort, you can create your own progress dialog. This technique is also used with some Web browsers to indicate the progress of files that are downloaded.

TREES

11

One of the more popular and complex components to make its way into the current user interface experience is the *tree* component. A tree, as pictured in Figure 11.1, is usually displayed as a set of hierarchical nodes. Each node can contain an icon and a text label. The nodes can also display some form of graphic to indicate if it contains child nodes and lines that join the children nodes to their parent nodes. Swing provides a tree component in the form of JTree and a set of accompanying classes.

At a fundamental level, a tree displays a hierarchical collection of objects or nodes. The top of this hierarchy is called the *root*. Below the root are zero or more children. Each child can have zero or more of its own children. An element of the hierarchy that does not want or have children is called a *leaf*. The hierarchy is also constrained by the fact that each element can be a child for only one other element—its parent. This means that there is exactly one path from the root node to any leaf. This path uniquely identifies a node and is used by JTree to identify nodes.

The nodes for a JTree are managed with a TreeModel. This model can use any type of object to represent an element in the tree. A special object called the TreeCellRenderer is responsible for converting the object to a visual representation. This means that you can create your own models and renderers to display them. Later in this section, we create a tree model for a file system. We also create a renderer that displays program-specified icons along with a title for each node.

Figure 11.1 An example tree.

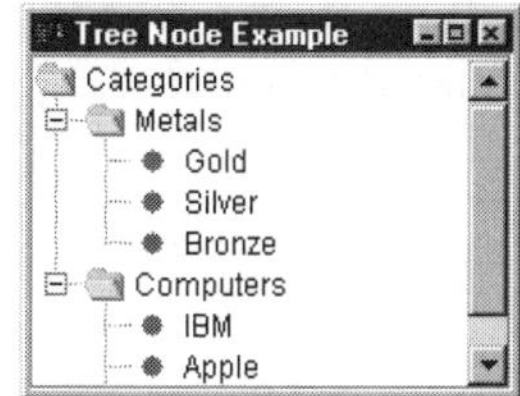

Table 11.1 TreeModel Methods

Method	Function
Public Object getRoot()	Returns the root node of the tree.
Public Object getChild (Object parent, int index)	Returns the child at index for the specified parent node.
Public int getChildCount(Object parent)	Returns the number of children for the specified parent node.
Public boolean isLeaf(Object node)	Returns true if the specified node is a leaf and won't have children.
Public void valueForPathChanged (TreePath path, Object newValue)	Used by the JTree to notify the model that a node was edited.
Public int getIndexOfChild (Object parent, Object child)	Returns the index of the specified child for the specified parent.
Public void addTreeModelListener (TreeModelListener l)	Adds an object to the model's list of TreeListeners.
Public void removeTreeModelListener (TreeModelListener l)	Removes an object to the model's list of TreeListeners.

Creating a Tree

To create a tree you must first define its data by creating a TreeModel. A TreeModel is an interface, defined in the package com.sun.java.swing.tree, that defines eight methods. The eight methods are used with the tree to access its nodes, as shown in Table 11.1. As you inspect the TreeModel's methods, notice that the nodes are always treated as objects. It is the renderer's responsibility to convert this object to a meaningful graphical display.

JTree provides a set of constructors for creating a tree with specified data, as shown in Table 11.2. All of these constructors create a com.sun.java.swing.tree .DefaultTreeModel to act as their model and initialize it with the data you provide.

In the following example, pictured in Figure 11.2, we create a tree from a Vector that contains several strings. Notice that the tree does not display a root node because a value for the root node is not supplied. We have also placed the tree in a JScrollPane. This is a common practice with trees because they often display large amounts of information.

```
import com.sun.java.swing.*;

import java.awt.event.*;
import java.awt.*;
```

Table 11.2 JTree Constructors

Constructor	Function
public JTree()	Creates a new tree with a sample model.
public JTree(Object value[])	Creates a new tree with the objects in value as children of the root node.
public JTree(Vector value)	Creates a new tree with the objects in value as children of the root node.
public JTree(Hashtable value)	Creates a new tree with the values in the value Hashtable as children of the root node.
public JTree(TreeNode root)	Creates a new tree with the specified root node.
public JTree(TreeNode root, boolean asksAllowsChildren)	Creates a new tree with the specified root node. Leafiness for the elements is determined with the message isLeaf or getAllowsChildren, depending on the value of asksAllowsChildren.
public JTree(TreeModel newModel)	Creates a new tree with the specified TreeModel.

```
import java.util.*;

public class SimpleTreeExample extends JPanel
{
    public SimpleTreeExample()
    {
        JTree tree;
        Vector data;
        Font f;

        f = new Font("SanSerif",Font.PLAIN,24);
        setFont(f);
        setLayout(new BorderLayout());

        data = new Vector();
        data.addElement("Gold");
        data.addElement("Silver");
        data.addElement("Bronze");
        data.addElement("Copper");
        data.addElement("Iron");
        data.addElement("Platinum");
        data.addElement("Titanium");
```

```
        tree = new JTree(data);
        tree.setFont(f);

        add(new JScrollPane(tree),"Center");
    }

    public Dimension getPreferredSize()
    {
        return new Dimension(200, 120);
    }

    public static void main(String s[])
    {
        JFrame frame = new JFrame("Simple Tree Example");
        SimpleTreeExample panel = new SimpleTreeExample();

        frame.setDefaultCloseOperation(JFrame.DO_NOTHING_ON_CLOSE);
        frame.setForeground(Color.black);
        frame.setBackground(Color.lightGray);
        frame.getContentPane().add(panel,"Center");

        frame.setSize(panel.getPreferredSize());
        frame.setVisible(true);
        frame.addWindowListener(new WindowCloser());
    }
}
```

This example uses a WindowCloser object to manage the window's close box. This class is included in the example file and relies on the same import statements.

```
class WindowCloser extends WindowAdapter
{
    public void windowClosing(WindowEvent e)
    {
        Window win = e.getWindow();
        win.setVisible(false);
        win.dispose();
        System.exit(0);
    }
}
```

Figure 11.2 shows a simple tree example.

Figure 11.2 Simple tree example.

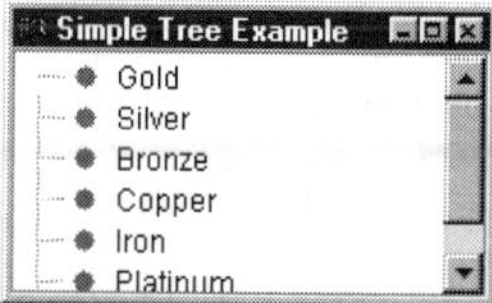

Tree Nodes

The default tree model uses objects called TreeNodes to represent each node in the tree. TreeNode is an interface that defines seven methods, as shown in Table 11.3.

Although you can create your own TreeNode classes, JavaSoft provides a powerful node class called DefaultMutableTreeNode. This node class is used by default for the default tree model.

DefaultMutableTreeNode provides a method for accessing its parent and children including methods to get the first leaf or last child. More importantly, a mutable tree node keeps track of another object called the user object. As a programmer, you can use this user object to manage your data in the context of the default tree model. Simply create your objects and attach them to tree nodes using the methods:

```
public void setUserObject(Object o);
public Object getUserObject();
```

You can also assign this object in the constructor. The three constructors you can use to do this are listed in Table 11.4.

Table 11.3 TreeNode Methods

Method	Function
public TreeNode getChildAt(int childIndex)	Returns the child node at the specified index.
public int getChildCount()	Returns the number of children for this node.
public TreeNode getParent()	Gets the parent for this node.
public int getIndex(TreeNode node)	Gets the index for a child of this node.
public boolean getAllowsChildren()	Returns true if this node allows children, not whether it has any.
public boolean isLeaf()	Returns true if this node doesn't have or want children.
public Enumeration children()	Returns an enumernation of the nodes children.

Table 11.4 DefaultMutableTreeNode Constructors

Constructor	Function
Public DefaultMutableTreeNode()	Creates a tree node with no user object.
Public DefaultMutableTreeNode (Object userObject)	Creates a tree node with the specified user object.
Public DefaultMutableTreeNode (Object userObject, Boolean allowsChildren)	Creates a node with the specified user object and indicates whether it allows children.

The tree node relies on its user object to construct its string value for the toString method. This allows the default cell renderer for a JTree to take advantage of the user object when it displays data.

The following example creates a tree that uses DefaultMutableTreeNodes. The user objects for the nodes are the strings that we want displayed in the tree. We have created a tree with a root node, two parent nodes, and three children for each parent. Notice that the parents appear with a different icon by default, and they can be expanded by the user to view or hide their children.

```
import com.sun.java.swing.*;
import com.sun.java.swing.tree.*;
import java.awt.event.*;
import java.awt.*;
import java.util.*;

public class TreeNodeExample extends JPanel
{
    public TreeNodeExample()
    {
        JTree tree;
        DefaultMutableTreeNode rootNode;
        DefaultMutableTreeNode parentNode;
        DefaultMutableTreeNode node;
        Font f;

        f = new Font("SanSerif",Font.PLAIN,24);
        setFont(f);
        setLayout(new BorderLayout());

        rootNode = new DefaultMutableTreeNode("Categories");

        parentNode = new DefaultMutableTreeNode("Metals");
```

```
node = new DefaultMutableTreeNode("Gold",false);
parentNode.add(node);

node = new DefaultMutableTreeNode("Silver",false);
parentNode.add(node);

node = new DefaultMutableTreeNode("Bronze",false);
parentNode.add(node);

node = new DefaultMutableTreeNode("Copper",false);
parentNode.add(node);

node = new DefaultMutableTreeNode("Iron",false);
parentNode.add(node);

node = new DefaultMutableTreeNode("Platinum",false);
parentNode.add(node);

node = new DefaultMutableTreeNode("Titanium",false);
parentNode.add(node);

rootNode.add(parentNode);

@!@Companies seemed more appropriate since NeXT is dead.@!@

parentNode = new DefaultMutableTreeNode("Companies");

node = new DefaultMutableTreeNode("Paradigm Research",false);
parentNode.add(node);

node = new DefaultMutableTreeNode("JavaSoft",false);
parentNode.add(node);

node = new DefaultMutableTreeNode("Wiley Press",false);
parentNode.add(node);

node = new DefaultMutableTreeNode("Your Name Here",false);
parentNode.add(node);

rootNode.add(parentNode);

tree = new JTree(rootNode);
tree.setFont(f);
```

```
        add(new JScrollPane(tree),"Center");
    }

    public Dimension getPreferredSize()
    {
        return new Dimension(200, 120);
    }

    public static void main(String s[])
    {
        JFrame frame = new JFrame("Tree Node Example");
        TreeNodeExample panel = new TreeNodeExample();

        frame.setDefaultCloseOperation(JFrame.DO_NOTHING_ON_CLOSE);
        frame.setForeground(Color.black);
        frame.setBackground(Color.lightGray);
        frame.getContentPane().add(panel,"Center");

        frame.setSize(panel.getPreferredSize());
        frame.setVisible(true);
        frame.addWindowListener(new WindowCloser());
    }
}
```

This example uses a WindowCloser object to manage the window's close box. This class is included in the example file and relies on the same import statements.

```
class WindowCloser extends WindowAdapter
{
    public void windowClosing(WindowEvent e)
    {
        Window win = e.getWindow();
        win.setVisible(false);
        win.dispose();
        System.exit(0);
    }
}
```

Figure 11.3 shows a tree that contains several nodes.

Tree Model Listeners

Once you have created a DefaultTreeModel with tree nodes, you can add and remove nodes using the following methods:

Figure 11.3 TreeNode example.

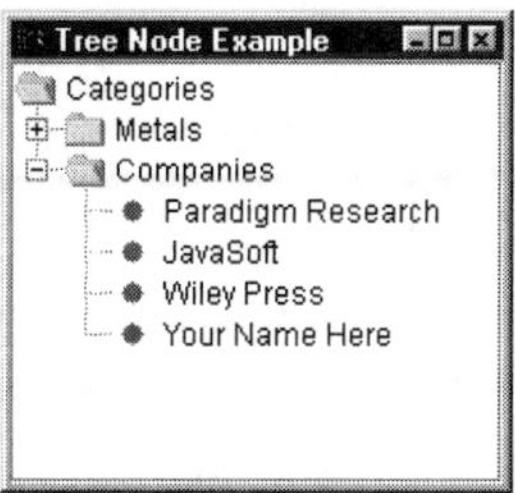


```
public void removeNodeFromParent(MutableTreeNode node);
public void insertNodeInto(MutableTreeNode newChild,
                           MutableTreeNode parent,
                           int index)
```

These methods trigger notifications to objects listening to the model, including the tree itself. To listen for changes to a tree model, implement the TreeModelListener interface. This interface defines four methods as shown in Table 11.5.

Add your tree listener to the tree model using the following methods:

```
public void addTreeModelListener(TreeModelListener l);
public void removeTreeModelListener(TreeModelListener l);
```

The JTree automatically adds itself to the model as a listener. Updates to the model are reflected automatically in the tree based on these notifications.

Tree Model Events

The TreeModelListener methods are called with the tree model at the appropriate time. The argument to all of the methods is a TreeModelEvent object. This event

Table 11.5 TreeModelListener Methods

Method	Function
Public void treeNodesChanged (TreeModelEvent e)	One or more nodes were changed in the tree. The value for a node possibly changed.
Public void treeNodesInserted (TreeModelEvent e)	One or more nodes were inserted into the tree.
Public void treeNodesRemoved (TreeModelEvent e)	One or more nodes were removed from the tree.
Public void treeStructureChanged (TreeModelEvent e)	The tree's structure underwent a major change.

Table 11.6 TreeModelEvent Methods

Method	Function
public TreePath getTreePath()	Returns the tree path that contains effected nodes.
public Object[] getPath()	Returns the array representation of the tree path.
public Object[] getChildren()	Returns an array of the affected child nodes; these nodes may not have a parent if they are removed.
public int[] getChildIndices()	Returns the indices of the affected child nodes.

contains information about the nodes that are affected by the current action. This information is accessed via four methods, as shown in Table 11.6.

The TreeModelEvent uses TreePath objects to represent locations in the tree. A TreePath is basically an array of objects that locates a node. The first element in the array is the root node. Each element after the root is a parent to the following element, culminating in the final element, the node itself. To create a TreePath you first create the array of nodes and then use the following constructor:

```
public TreePath(Object[] thePath);
```

In most cases, you won't need to create your own tree paths. You usually receive tree paths from other tree objects, like the TreeModelEvent. Once you have a tree path, you can access its data with five methods, as shown in Table 11.7.

Table 11.7 TreePath Methods

Method	Function
public Object getLastPathComponent()	Returns the last object in the path, the deepest child.
public int getPathCount()	Returns the number of objects in the path.
public Object getPathComponent (int element)	Retrieves the object at the specified index.
public boolean isDescendant (TreePath aTreePath)	Returns true if the target path is a descendant of a TreePath. This is true if a TreePath targets a node that is ultimately a child of the target path.
public Object[] getPath()	Returns the complete array representation of the path.

Custom Tree Models

You can create your own tree model as well. In the following example we define a tree model for the file system. This tree model takes a File object as the root and creates a file system tree below this root. To make our job easier we defined a helper class called FileHolder to act as the object for each node of the tree. The FileHolder class is not a TreeNode object, and it won't work with the DefaultTreeModel. We have created it specifically for our model. A FileHolder manages a single file object and can return a Vector that contains the children for this file object. The toString method is implemented to return the name of the file; it allows the default tree cell renderer to display file names in the tree.

```
import java.io.*;
import java.util.*;


class FileHolder
{
    File myFile;
    Vector children;

    public FileHolder(File f)
    {
        myFile = f;
    }

    public File getFile()
    {
        return myFile;
    }

    public Vector getChildren()
    {
        if(myFile.isDirectory()
            &&(children == null))
        {
            int i,max=0;
            String list[];
            File curFile;
            FileHolder curHolder;

            children = new Vector();

            list = myFile.list();
```

```
            if(list != null) max = list.length;

            for(i=0;i<max;i++)
            {
                curFile = new File(myFile,list[i]);
                curHolder = new FileHolder(curFile);
                children.addElement(curHolder);
            }
        }

        return children;
    }

    public String toString()
    {
        return myFile.getName();
    }
}
```

The tree model is implemented in the class FileSystemTreeModel. For simplicity we have implemented this path to ignore edits and TreeModelListeners. In a later example, we update this model to allow editing and to fire TreeEvents appropriately. Notice that it is fairly easy to create a tree from custom data. The main work involves defining a root node and determining its children, as well as the children for other nodes. Keep in mind that although we used FileHolder objects for each node, you can use any type of object for this task.

```
import com.sun.java.swing.*;
import com.sun.java.swing.tree.*;
import com.sun.java.swing.event.*;
import java.io.*;
import java.util.*;

class FileSystemTreeModel implements TreeModel
{
    protected FileHolder root;
    protected Vector listeners;

    public FileSystemTreeModel(File r)
    {
        root = new FileHolder(r);
        listeners = new Vector();
    }

    public Object getRoot()
```

```
    {
        return root;
    }

    public Object getChild(Object parent,
                                int index)
    {
        Object retVal = null;
        Vector children;

        if(parent instanceof FileHolder)
        {
            children = ((FileHolder)parent).getChildren();

            if(children != null)
            {
                if(index < children.size())
                {
                    retVal = children.elementAt(index);
                }
            }
        }

        return retVal;
    }

    public int getChildCount(Object parent)
    {
        int retVal = 0;
        Vector children;

        if(parent instanceof FileHolder)
        {
            children = ((FileHolder)parent).getChildren();

            if(children != null)
            {
                retVal = children.size();
            }
        }

        return retVal;
    }
```

```
public boolean isLeaf(Object node)
{
    boolean retVal = true;
    File file;

    if(node instanceof FileHolder)
    {
        file = ((FileHolder)node).getFile();

        retVal = file.isFile();
    }

    return retVal;
}

public void valueForPathChanged(TreePath path,Object newVal)
{
    //Do Nothing
}

public int getIndexOfChild(Object parent,
                                    Object child)
{
    int retVal = -1;
    Vector children;

    if(parent instanceof FileHolder)
    {
        children = ((FileHolder)parent).getChildren();

        if(children != null)
        {
            retVal = children.indexOf(child);
        }
    }

    return retVal;
}

public void addTreeModelListener(TreeModelListener l)
{
    if((l != null)&&!listeners.contains(l)) listeners.addElement(l);
}
```

```
    public void removeTreeModelListener(TreeModelListener l)
    {
        listeners.removeElement(l);
    }
}
```

To test our tree model we created a program that builds a tree, initialized from the command line, and then displays it. This example is pictured in Figure 11.4. To set the model for a tree we use the setModel() method:

```
public void setModel(TreeModel newModel);
```

This method updates the tree and tells it to register for notifications if the model changes.

```
import com.sun.java.swing.*;

import java.awt.event.*;
import java.awt.*;
import java.io.*;
import java.util.*;

public class FileTree extends JPanel
{
    public FileTree(String startPath)
    {
        JTree tree;
        FileSystemTreeModel model;
        File root;
        Font f;

        f = new Font("SanSerif",Font.PLAIN,24);
        setFont(f);
        setLayout(new BorderLayout());

        root = new File(startPath);
        model = new FileSystemTreeModel(root);

        tree = new JTree();
        tree.setModel(model);
        tree.setFont(f);

        add(new JScrollPane(tree),"Center");
    }

    public Dimension getPreferredSize()
```

```
    {
        return new Dimension(250, 200);
    }

    public static void main(String s[])
    {
        JFrame frame = new JFrame("File Tree Example");
        FileTree panel;

        if(s.length > 0)
            panel = new FileTree(s[0]);
        else
            panel = new FileTree("/");

        frame.setDefaultCloseOperation(JFrame.DO_NOTHING_ON_CLOSE);
        frame.setForeground(Color.black);
        frame.setBackground(Color.lightGray);
        frame.getContentPane().add(panel,"Center");

        frame.setSize(panel.getPreferredSize());
        frame.setVisible(true);
        frame.addWindowListener(new WindowCloser());
    }
}
```

This example uses a WindowCloser object to manage the window's close box. This class is included in the example file and relies on the same import statements.

```
class WindowCloser extends WindowAdapter
{
    public void windowClosing(WindowEvent e)
    {
        Window win = e.getWindow();
        win.setVisible(false);
        win.dispose();
        System.exit(0);
    }
}
```

Figure 11.4 shows a tree displaying files on your file system.

If you expect your model to hold a large amount of data, pass "true" to the tree method setLargeModel. This tells the tree to prepare for a large data set. The method looks like this:

```
public void setLargeModel(boolean newValue);
```

Figure 11.4 File system tree model.

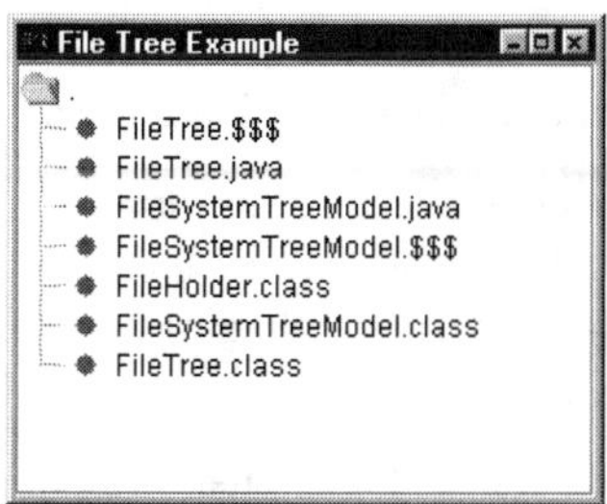

When true is passed to this method the tree attempts to optimize its behavior for large data sets. Optimization can provide a smoother UI response but may be more memory intensive. For most cases, it presents an acceptable trade-off of memory versus speed of UI update.

Tree Selections

Once you create a tree to display data, the next step is to use the tree as an interactive component. This brings us to the concept of tree selections. A user interacts with a tree in two ways: by expanding paths and by making selections. These selections can take one of three forms: a single selected path, a set of continuous paths, or a disjoint set of paths. Because of this complexity, JTree uses an object called a TreeSelectionModel to keep track of its current selection. You can interact with this model directly or retrieve information about the current selection from the JTree itself.

To get the selection model from a tree, use the following method:

```
public TreeSelectionModel getSelectionModel();
```

This returns an object that implements the TreeSelectionModel interface. By default, this is an instance of com.sun.java.swing.tree.DefaultTreeSelectionModel. You can set the model for a tree using the setSelectionModel method:

```
public void setSelectionModel(TreeSelectionModel selectionModel);
```

Perhaps the first order of business with the tree's selection model is to set the selection mode. This mode can have one of the three values listed in Table 11.8. Each of these values is a static variable of the TreeSelectionModel class.

The selection mode's default value is DISCONTIGUOUS_TREE_SELECTION. To set the mode for a selection model, use the following method and pass in one of the available values.

```
public void setSelectionMode(int mode);
```

Once the mode is set, the tree is ready to accept selections.

Table 11.8 Tree Selection Modes

Mode	Function
SINGLE_TREE_SELECTION	Only a single node can be selected at a time.
CONTIGUOUS_TREE_SELECTION	Multiple nodes can be selected, but they must have paths that are next to each other. For example, two adjacent children of the same parent can be selected.
DISCONTIGUOUS_TREE_SELECTION	Any number or nodes can be selected, without limitation, beyond the general constraint that you can't select a node that is not visible.

The easiest way to track a user selection is with tree paths. Depending on the selection mode, the tree has zero or more currently selected paths. You can get these paths using the same methods for JTree or TreeSelectionModel, as shown here:

```
public TreePath getSelectionPath();
public TreePath[] getSelectionPaths();
```

If you ask for a single path, when multiple paths are selected, the first selected path is returned. You can also check for the number of selected paths using the getSelectionCount() method:

```
public int getSelectionCount();
```

You can check if there already is a selection by using the following method:

```
public boolean isSelectionEmpty();
```

To check if a specific path is selected use:

```
public boolean isPathSelected(TreePath path);
```

This method uses the TreePaths equal method to check if two paths are equal, and it does not rely on string-object reference equality.

The flip side of retrieving the selection is setting it. You can change a tree's path by either setting the path specifically or adding to the path. In both cases, the JTree and TreeSelectionModel provide methods to perform the alteration using a single path or an array.

```
public void setSelectionPath(TreePath path)
public void setSelectionPaths(TreePath pPaths[])
public void addSelectionPath(TreePath path)
public void addSelectionPaths(TreePath paths[])
```

Trees and selection models also provide methods to clear the current selection. You can also remove one or more paths from the current selection using the following three methods:

```
public void clearSelection()
public void removeSelectionPath(TreePath path)
public void removeSelectionPaths(TreePath paths[])
```

Trees also provide an interface for interacting with the current selection as a collection of rows. These rows depend on the currently expanded nodes.

Tree Selection Listeners

Trees notify TreeSelectionListeners when their selection changes. This type of listener defines a single method, as shown here:

```
public void valueChanged(TreeSelectionEvent e)
```

The argument to valueChanged is a TreeSelectionEvent. This event defines six methods for accessing the paths related to the change event, as shown in Table 11.9. As with lists, the paths related to a change can involve the paths added as well as the paths removed. Methods are provided to check if a path is added or not.

In general, you will probably want to access the current selection from the tree, or selection model, directly rather than using the event. The event contains information about paths added to or removed from the selection rather than the entire selection.

To add your object to a JTree as a selection listener use the following method:

```
public void addTreeSelectionListener(TreeSelectionListener tsl);
```

This method also works on the selection model.

Table 11.9 TreeSelectionEvent Methods

Methods	**Functions**
Public TreePath[] getPaths()	Returns the paths added or removed from the selection.
Public TreePath getPath()	Returns the first path added or removed from the selection.
Public boolean isAddedPath()	Returns true if the first path was added to the selection.
Public boolean IsAddedPath(TreePath path)	Checks if a path was added to the selection as part of this event.
Public TreePath GetOldLeadSelectionPath()	Return the path that was previously first.
Public TreePath GetNewLeadSelectionPath()	Return the path that is currently first.

Our next example, pictured in Figure 11.5, displays a tree that supports a single selection. When the user changes the selection, the currently selected path is formatted and displayed in a text field.

```
import com.sun.java.swing.*;
import com.sun.java.swing.tree.*;
import com.sun.java.swing.event.*;
import java.awt.event.*;
import java.awt.*;
import java.util.*;

public class TreeSelExample extends JPanel
implements TreeSelectionListener
{
    JTextField selField;
    JTree tree;

    public TreeSelExample()
    {
        DefaultMutableTreeNode rootNode;
        DefaultMutableTreeNode parentNode;
        DefaultMutableTreeNode node;
        TreeSelectionModel selModel;
        Font f;

        f = new Font("SanSerif",Font.PLAIN,24);
        setFont(f);
        setLayout(new BorderLayout());

        rootNode = new DefaultMutableTreeNode("Categories");

        parentNode = new DefaultMutableTreeNode("Metals");

        node = new DefaultMutableTreeNode("Gold",false);
        parentNode.add(node);

        node = new DefaultMutableTreeNode("Silver",false);
        parentNode.add(node);

        node = new DefaultMutableTreeNode("Bronze",false);
        parentNode.add(node);

        node = new DefaultMutableTreeNode("Copper",false);
        parentNode.add(node);
```

```
        node = new DefaultMutableTreeNode("Iron",false);
        parentNode.add(node);

        node = new DefaultMutableTreeNode("Platinum",false);
        parentNode.add(node);

        node = new DefaultMutableTreeNode("Titanium",false);
        parentNode.add(node);

        rootNode.add(parentNode);

        parentNode = new DefaultMutableTreeNode("Companies");

        node = new DefaultMutableTreeNode("Paradigm Research",false);
        parentNode.add(node);

        node = new DefaultMutableTreeNode("JavaSoft",false);
        parentNode.add(node);

        node = new DefaultMutableTreeNode("Wiley Press",false);
        parentNode.add(node);

        node = new DefaultMutableTreeNode("Your name here",false);
        parentNode.add(node);

        rootNode.add(parentNode);

        tree = new JTree(rootNode);
        tree.setFont(f);

        tree.addTreeSelectionListener(this);

        selModel = tree.getSelectionModel();
        selModel.setSelectionMode(TreeSelectionModel.SINGLE_TREE_SELECTION);

        add(new JScrollPane(tree),"Center");

        selField = new JTextField(20);
        add(selField,"South");
    }

    public void valueChanged(TreeSelectionEvent e)
    {
        TreePath path = tree.getSelectionPath();
```

```
        Object pathObj[] = path.getPath();
        int i,max;
        String formattedPath = "";

        max = pathObj.length;

        for(i=0;i<max;i++)
        {
            formattedPath+="/";
            formattedPath+=pathObj[i].toString();
        }

        selField.setText(formattedPath);
    }

    public Dimension getPreferredSize()
    {
        return new Dimension(200, 120);
    }

    public static void main(String s[])
    {
        JFrame frame = new JFrame("Tree Selection Example");
        TreeSelExample panel = new TreeSelExample();

        frame.setDefaultCloseOperation(JFrame.DO_NOTHING_ON_CLOSE);
        frame.setForeground(Color.black);
        frame.setBackground(Color.lightGray);
        frame.getContentPane().add(panel,"Center");

        frame.setSize(panel.getPreferredSize());
        frame.setVisible(true);
        frame.addWindowListener(new WindowCloser());
    }
}
```

This example uses a WindowCloser object to manage the window's close box. This class is included in the example file and relies on the same import statements.

```
class WindowCloser extends WindowAdapter
{
    public void windowClosing(WindowEvent e)
    {
        Window win = e.getWindow();
        win.setVisible(false);
```

```
            win.dispose();
            System.exit(0);
        }
    }
```

Figure 11.5 shows a tree with a single selection.

The example in Figure 11.6 is similar to Figure 11.5, but it supports multiple selection paths. In this case, the current selection is printed in a text area, one path to a line.

```
import com.sun.java.swing.*;
import com.sun.java.swing.tree.*;
import com.sun.java.swing.event.*;
import java.awt.event.*;
import java.awt.*;
import java.util.*;

public class TreeMSelExample extends JPanel
implements TreeSelectionListener
{
    JTextArea selArea;
    JTree tree;

    public TreeMSelExample()
    {
        DefaultMutableTreeNode rootNode;
        DefaultMutableTreeNode parentNode;
        DefaultMutableTreeNode node;
        TreeSelectionModel selModel;
        Font f;

        f = new Font("SanSerif",Font.PLAIN,24);
```

Figure 11.5 Single tree selection.

```
setFont(f);
setLayout(new BorderLayout(10,10));

rootNode = new DefaultMutableTreeNode("Categories");

parentNode = new DefaultMutableTreeNode("Metals");

node = new DefaultMutableTreeNode("Gold",false);
parentNode.add(node);

node = new DefaultMutableTreeNode("Silver",false);
parentNode.add(node);

node = new DefaultMutableTreeNode("Bronze",false);
parentNode.add(node);

node = new DefaultMutableTreeNode("Copper",false);
parentNode.add(node);

node = new DefaultMutableTreeNode("Iron",false);
parentNode.add(node);

node = new DefaultMutableTreeNode("Platinum",false);
parentNode.add(node);

node = new DefaultMutableTreeNode("Titanium",false);
parentNode.add(node);

rootNode.add(parentNode);

parentNode = new DefaultMutableTreeNode("Companies");

node = new DefaultMutableTreeNode("Paradigm Research",false);
parentNode.add(node);

node = new DefaultMutableTreeNode("JavaSoft",false);
parentNode.add(node);

node = new DefaultMutableTreeNode("Wiley Press",false);
parentNode.add(node);

node = new DefaultMutableTreeNode("Your name here",false);
parentNode.add(node);
```

```
        rootNode.add(parentNode);

        tree = new JTree(rootNode);
        tree.setFont(f);

        tree.addTreeSelectionListener(this);

        selModel = tree.getSelectionModel();
        selModel.setSelectionMode(
                        TreeSelectionModel.DISCONTIGUOUS_TREE_SELECTION);

        add(new JScrollPane(tree),"Center");

        selArea = new JTextArea(5,20);
        add(new JScrollPane(selArea),"South");
    }

    public void valueChanged(TreeSelectionEvent e)
    {
        TreePath paths[] = tree.getSelectionPaths();
        Object pathObj[];
        int i,max;
        int j,numPaths;
        String formattedPath = "";

        numPaths = paths.length;

        for(j=0;j<numPaths;j++)
        {
            pathObj = paths[j].getPath();
            max = pathObj.length;

            for(i=0;i<max;i++)
            {
                formattedPath+="/";
                formattedPath+=pathObj[i].toString();
            }

            formattedPath+="\n";
        }

        selArea.setText(formattedPath);
    }
```

```
    public Dimension getPreferredSize()
    {
        return new Dimension(200, 200);
    }

    public static void main(String s[])
    {
        JFrame frame = new JFrame("Tree Multi-Selection Example");
        TreeMSelExample panel = new TreeMSelExample();

        frame.setDefaultCloseOperation(JFrame.DO_NOTHING_ON_CLOSE);
        frame.setForeground(Color.black);
        frame.setBackground(Color.lightGray);
        frame.getContentPane().add(panel,"Center");

        frame.setSize(panel.getPreferredSize());
        frame.setVisible(true);
        frame.addWindowListener(new WindowCloser());
    }
}
```

This example uses a WindowCloser object to manage the window's close box. This class is included in the example file and relies on the same import statements.

```
class WindowCloser extends WindowAdapter
{
    public void windowClosing(WindowEvent e)
    {
        Window win = e.getWindow();
        win.setVisible(false);
        win.dispose();
        System.exit(0);
    }
}
```

Figure 11.6 shows a tree that supports the selection of multiple nodes.

Tree Expansion Listeners

For applications that need to know when the user expands or contracts a tree node, the JTree supports the concept of an *expansion listener*. These listeners implement the TreeSelectionListener interface. TreeSelectionListener defines two methods: treeExpanded() and treeCollapsed().

Figure 11.6 Multiple tree selection.

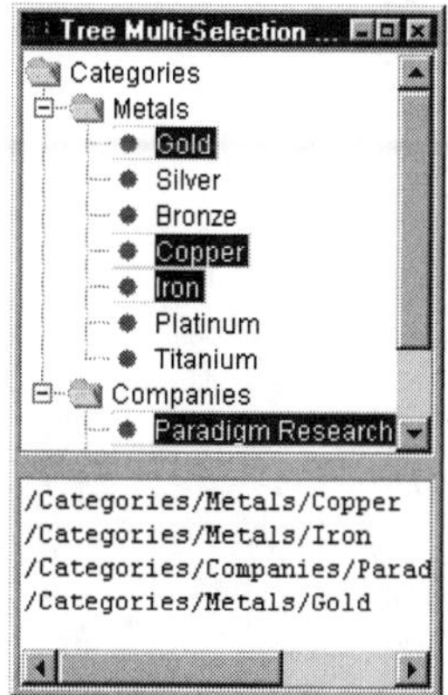


```
public abstract void treeExpanded(TreeExpansionEvent event);
public abstract void treeCollapsed(TreeExpansionEvent event);
```

The argument to these methods is a TreeExpansionEvent. A TreeExpansionEvent has a single method for returning the tree path that was expanded or contracted, as shown here:

```
public TreePath getPath();
```

You can assign a listener to a tree using the following method:

```
public void addTreeExpansionListener(TreeExpansionListener tel);
```

In the following example, pictured in Figure 11.7, we assign an expansion listener to a tree. When the tree expands or collapses a path, the listener updates a text field with the path's contents.

```
import com.sun.java.swing.*;
import com.sun.java.swing.tree.*;
import com.sun.java.swing.event.*;
import java.awt.event.*;
import java.awt.*;
import java.util.*;

public class TreeExpExample extends JPanel
implements TreeExpansionListener
{
    JTextField selField;
    JTree tree;

    public TreeExpExample()
    {
```

```
DefaultMutableTreeNode rootNode;
DefaultMutableTreeNode parentNode;
DefaultMutableTreeNode node;
TreeSelectionModel selModel;
Font f;

f = new Font("SanSerif",Font.PLAIN,24);
setFont(f);
setLayout(new BorderLayout());

rootNode = new DefaultMutableTreeNode("Categories");

parentNode = new DefaultMutableTreeNode("Metals");

node = new DefaultMutableTreeNode("Gold",false);
parentNode.add(node);

node = new DefaultMutableTreeNode("Silver",false);
parentNode.add(node);

node = new DefaultMutableTreeNode("Bronze",false);
parentNode.add(node);

node = new DefaultMutableTreeNode("Copper",false);
parentNode.add(node);

node = new DefaultMutableTreeNode("Iron",false);
parentNode.add(node);

node = new DefaultMutableTreeNode("Platinum",false);
parentNode.add(node);

node = new DefaultMutableTreeNode("Titanium",false);
parentNode.add(node);

rootNode.add(parentNode);

parentNode = new DefaultMutableTreeNode("Companies");

node = new DefaultMutableTreeNode("Paradigm Research",false);
parentNode.add(node);

node = new DefaultMutableTreeNode("JavaSoft",false);
parentNode.add(node);
```

```
        node = new DefaultMutableTreeNode("Wiley Press",false);
        parentNode.add(node);

        node = new DefaultMutableTreeNode("Your name here",false);
        parentNode.add(node);

        rootNode.add(parentNode);

        parentNode = new DefaultMutableTreeNode("Trucks");

        node = new DefaultMutableTreeNode("S10",false);
        parentNode.add(node);

        node = new DefaultMutableTreeNode("Ranger",false);
        parentNode.add(node);

        node = new DefaultMutableTreeNode("Frontier",false);
        parentNode.add(node);

        rootNode.add(parentNode);

        tree = new JTree(rootNode);
        tree.setFont(f);

        tree.addTreeExpansionListener(this);

        add(new JScrollPane(tree),"Center");

        selField = new JTextField(20);
        add(selField,"South");
    }

    public void treeCollapsed(TreeExpansionEvent e)
    {
        TreePath path = e.getPath();
        Object pathObj[] = path.getPath();
        int i,max;
        String formattedPath = "";

        max = pathObj.length;

        for(i=0;i<max;i++)
        {
            formattedPath+="/";
```

```
            formattedPath+=pathObj[i].toString();
        }

        selField.setText("Collapsed: "+formattedPath);
    }

    public void treeExpanded(TreeExpansionEvent e)
    {
        TreePath path = e.getPath();
        Object pathObj[] = path.getPath();
        int i,max;
        String formattedPath = "";

        max = pathObj.length;

        for(i=0;i<max;i++)
        {
            formattedPath+="/";
            formattedPath+=pathObj[i].toString();
        }

        selField.setText("Expanded: "+formattedPath);
    }

    public Dimension getPreferredSize()
    {
        return new Dimension(200, 120);
    }

    public static void main(String s[])
    {
        JFrame frame = new JFrame("Tree Expansion Example");
        TreeExpExample panel = new TreeExpExample();

        frame.setDefaultCloseOperation(JFrame.DO_NOTHING_ON_CLOSE);
        frame.setForeground(Color.black);
        frame.setBackground(Color.lightGray);
        frame.getContentPane().add(panel,"Center");

        frame.setSize(panel.getPreferredSize());
        frame.setVisible(true);
        frame.addWindowListener(new WindowCloser());
    }
}
```

Figure 11.7 Tree expansion listener example.

This example uses a WindowCloser object to manage the window's close box. This class is included in the example file and relies on the same import statements.

```
class WindowCloser extends WindowAdapter
{
    public void windowClosing(WindowEvent e)
    {
        Window win = e.getWindow();
        win.setVisible(false);
        win.dispose();
        System.exit(0);
    }
}
```

Figure 11.7 shows the example for the expansion listener that handles the expansion event.

Tree Cell Renderers

Like JList and JComboBox, JTree uses renderers to perform the drawing for each node. In the case of a tree, the renderer must implement the interface TreeCellRenderer. This interface defines only a single method, shown here:

```
public Component getTreeCellRendererComponent(JTree tree,
                                              Object value,
                                              boolean selected,
                                              boolean expanded,
                                              boolean leaf,
                                              int row,
                                              boolean hasFocus)
```

This method returns a component that can draw the node with the specified value, for the specified tree, with the specified attributes. When the tree needs to draw a node, it asks its renderer for the renderer component and then tells this component to paint in the appropriate location.

The tree's default cell renderer displays icons based on the current look and feel and displays the string returned from a node by sending it the toString method. You can create your own renderers by implementing the TreeCellRenderer interface, creating an object of your new renderer class, and telling the tree to use the custom renderer by calling the setCellRenderer() method, as shown here:

```
public void setCellRenderer(TreeCellRenderer x);
```

This renderer must display the main content of the node's cell. The tree's UI object is responsible for drawing any other accoutrements for the node, such as an "x" to indicate that it can expand or a "-" to indicate that it can contract.

In the next example, pictured in Figure 11.8, we use a custom renderer that displays text and an icon for each node. The renderer also makes sure that each node appears in the correct font and that selected nodes are highlighted. To provide icons for each node, we created an object called a TreeData that we use as the user object for each node in the tree. This TreeData object can have a title and an icon. Basically, it's a holder. In a larger application you may use an object that represented a file, a person, or some other data in your program as the user objects for nodes. A renderer in this program uses methods in the user object to customize the display.

```
import com.sun.java.swing.*;

import java.awt.event.*;
import java.awt.*;

class TreeData
{
    protected Icon icon;
    protected String title;

    public TreeData(String t,Icon i)
    {
        icon = i;
        title = t;
    }

    public Icon getIcon()
    {
        return icon;
    }

    public String getTitle()
    {
        return title;
    }
}
```

Figure 11.8 Custom TreeCellRenderer.

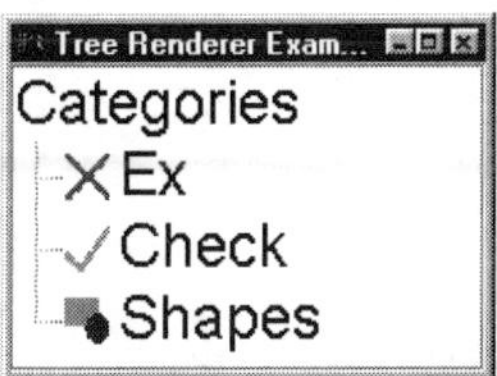

Our custom renderer uses a JLabel as its rendering component. When the label is requested, the renderer initializes it with the data from the current node. If this node is a TreeData object, then the node's icon and title are used. Otherwise, the icon is set to null, and the label's text is set to the value returned by the node's toString method. The label's font is set to the tree's font, and its colors are set to reflect the tree's colors. We reverse the foreground and background to indicate highlighting. In some cases, it may be too harsh to have white on black, so you may want to use another background color. To make sure that the label's background is filled, we set it to opaque in the renderer's constructor.

```
import java.lang.*;
import com.sun.java.swing.*;
import com.sun.java.swing.tree.*;
import java.awt.*;

public class TreeIconRenderer extends Object
implements TreeCellRenderer
{
    JLabel theLabel;

    public TreeIconRenderer()
    {
        theLabel = new JLabel();
        theLabel.setOpaque(true);
    }

    public Component getTreeCellRendererComponent(JTree tree,
                              Object value,
                              boolean selected,
                              boolean expanded,
                              boolean leaf,
                              int row,
                              boolean hasFocus)

    {
```

```
TreeData data=null;

theLabel.setFont(tree.getFont());

if(selected)
{
    theLabel.setForeground(tree.getBackground());
    theLabel.setBackground(tree.getForeground());
}
else
{
    theLabel.setBackground(tree.getBackground());
    theLabel.setForeground(tree.getForeground());
}



if(value instanceof TreeData)
{
    data = (TreeData) value;
}

else if(value instanceof DefaultMutableTreeNode)
{
    DefaultMutableTreeNode node;

    node = (DefaultMutableTreeNode) value;

    if(node.getUserObject() instanceof TreeData)
    {
        data = (TreeData) node.getUserObject();
    }
}

if(data != null)
{
    theLabel.setIcon(data.getIcon());
    theLabel.setText(data.getTitle());
}
else
{
    theLabel.setIcon(null);
    theLabel.setText(value.toString());
}
```

```
            return theLabel;
        }
    }
```

The example for this renderer creates three nodes with icons. Because the renderer can change height based on the tree's current font we set the trees row height to 0. This causes the tree to check with the renderer's component to determine the actual height of each node that is displayed. Remember that the tree thinks of rows as the visible nodes. To set the row height, use the following method:

```
public void setRowHeight(int rowHeight);
```

Using a height of 0 makes the height dependent on the renderer's component.

```
import com.sun.java.swing.*;
import com.sun.java.swing.tree.*;
import java.awt.event.*;
import java.awt.*;
import java.util.*;

public class TreeRenderExample extends JPanel
{
    public TreeRenderExample()
    {
        JTree tree;
        Font f;
        DefaultMutableTreeNode rootNode;
        DefaultMutableTreeNode parentNode;
        DefaultMutableTreeNode node;
        TreeIconRenderer treeR;
        TreeData data;
        ImageIcon icon;

        f = new Font("SanSerif",Font.PLAIN,24);
        setFont(f);
        setLayout(new BorderLayout());

        rootNode = new DefaultMutableTreeNode("Categories");

        icon = new ImageIcon("images/ex.gif");
        data = new TreeData("Ex",icon);
        node = new DefaultMutableTreeNode(data,false);
        rootNode.add(node);

        icon = new ImageIcon("images/check.gif");
        data = new TreeData("Check",icon);
```

```
        node = new DefaultMutableTreeNode(data,false);
        rootNode.add(node);

        icon = new ImageIcon("images/shapes.gif");
        data = new TreeData("Shapes",icon);
        node = new DefaultMutableTreeNode(data,false);
        rootNode.add(node);

        tree = new JTree(rootNode);
        tree.setFont(f);

        treeR = new TreeIconRenderer();
        tree.setCellRenderer(treeR);

        tree.setRowHeight(0);//let the renderer handle it

        add(new JScrollPane(tree),"Center");
    }

    public Dimension getPreferredSize()
    {
        return new Dimension(200, 120);
    }

    public static void main(String s[])
    {
        JFrame frame = new JFrame("Tree Renderer Example");
        TreeRenderExample panel = new TreeRenderExample();

        frame.setDefaultCloseOperation(JFrame.DO_NOTHING_ON_CLOSE);
        frame.setForeground(Color.black);
        frame.setBackground(Color.lightGray);
        frame.getContentPane().add(panel,"Center");

        frame.setSize(panel.getPreferredSize());
        frame.setVisible(true);
        frame.addWindowListener(new WindowCloser());
    }
}
```

This example uses a WindowCloser object to manage the window's close box. This class is included in the example file and relies on the same import statements.

```
class WindowCloser extends WindowAdapter
{
```

```
    public void windowClosing(WindowEvent e)
    {
        Window win = e.getWindow();
        win.setVisible(false);
        win.dispose();
        System.exit(0);
    }
}
```

Tree Display Attributes

Trees are configured to display or hide their root node. They can also be told to display a handle from parent nodes to the children. Figure 11.9 shows two trees. Both use the same model, but the one on the left shows its root and root handles. The one on the right shows neither.

To control these attributes, use the following methods:

```
public void setRootVisible(boolean rootVisible);
public void setShowsRootHandles(boolean newValue) ;
```

In the example used to create Figure 11.9, notice that the same tree model is used for both trees. This is an interesting technique, one that can prove valuable in applications with a lot of data and a large user interface. The example creates two trees with the same model. One is initialized to show the root node and handles; the other is initialized to hide the same features. The trees are placed in a grid for display.

```
import com.sun.java.swing.*;
import com.sun.java.swing.tree.*;
import java.awt.event.*;
import java.awt.*;
import java.util.*;

public class TreeRootExample extends JPanel
```

Figure 11.9 Trees and their root handles.

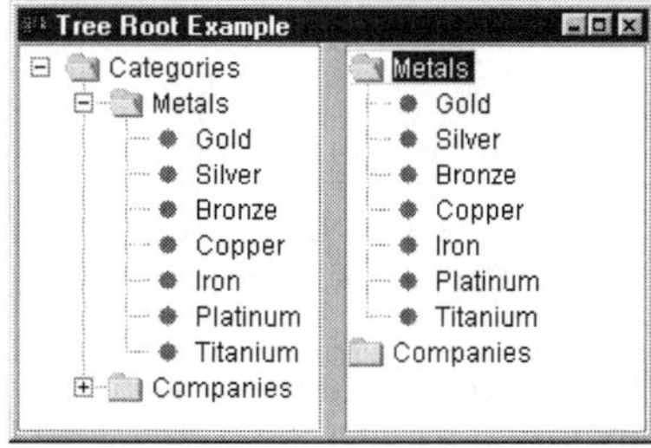

```
{
    public TreeRootExample()
    {
        JTree tree1,tree2;
        DefaultMutableTreeNode rootNode;
        DefaultMutableTreeNode parentNode;
        DefaultMutableTreeNode node;
        Font f;

        f = new Font("SanSerif",Font.PLAIN,24);
        setFont(f);
        setLayout(new GridLayout(1,2,10,10));

        rootNode = new DefaultMutableTreeNode("Categories");

        parentNode = new DefaultMutableTreeNode("Metals");

        node = new DefaultMutableTreeNode("Gold",false);
        parentNode.add(node);

        node = new DefaultMutableTreeNode("Silver",false);
        parentNode.add(node);

        node = new DefaultMutableTreeNode("Bronze",false);
        parentNode.add(node);

        node = new DefaultMutableTreeNode("Copper",false);
        parentNode.add(node);

        node = new DefaultMutableTreeNode("Iron",false);
        parentNode.add(node);

        node = new DefaultMutableTreeNode("Platinum",false);
        parentNode.add(node);

        node = new DefaultMutableTreeNode("Titanium",false);
        parentNode.add(node);

        rootNode.add(parentNode);

        parentNode = new DefaultMutableTreeNode("Companies");

        node = new DefaultMutableTreeNode("Paradigm Research",false);
```

```
        parentNode.add(node);

        node = new DefaultMutableTreeNode("JavaSoft",false);
        parentNode.add(node);

        node = new DefaultMutableTreeNode("Wiley Press",false);
        parentNode.add(node);

        node = DefaultMutableTreeNode("Your name here",false);
        parentNode.add(node);

        rootNode.add(parentNode);

        tree1 = new JTree(rootNode);
        tree1.setFont(f);

        tree1.setRootVisible(true);
        tree1.setShowsRootHandles(true);

        tree2 = new JTree();
        tree2.setModel(tree1.getModel());
        tree2.setFont(f);

        tree2.setRootVisible(false);
        tree2.setShowsRootHandles(false);

        add(new JScrollPane(tree1));
        add(new JScrollPane(tree2));
    }

    public Dimension getPreferredSize()
    {
        return new Dimension(300, 200);
    }

    public static void main(String s[])
    {
        JFrame frame = new JFrame("Tree Root Example");
        TreeRootExample panel = new TreeRootExample();

        frame.setDefaultCloseOperation(JFrame.DO_NOTHING_ON_CLOSE);
        frame.setForeground(Color.black);
```

```
        frame.setBackground(Color.lightGray);
        frame.getContentPane().add(panel,"Center");

        frame.setSize(panel.getPreferredSize());
        frame.setVisible(true);
        frame.addWindowListener(new WindowCloser());
    }
}
```

This example uses a WindowCloser object to manage the window's close box. This class is included in the example file and relies on the same import statements.

```
class WindowCloser extends WindowAdapter
{
    public void windowClosing(WindowEvent e)
    {
        Window win = e.getWindow();
        win.setVisible(false);
        win.dispose();
        System.exit(0);
    }
}
```

Editable Trees

Trees support cell editors that allow the user to edit the value for a cell in place. Swing provides a default editor for this purpose that uses a text field to allow the user to alter the current value. To initiate the default editor use the JTree method:

```
public void setEditable(boolean flag);
```

The user can double- or triple-click the tree to activate the editor. When the editor is done editing, possibly because the user pressed the Return key, it sends the message valueForPathChanged to the tree's model. It is the model's responsibility to alter the underlying data and notify all of the TreeModelListeners. The tree or its UI object is one of these listeners; it then updates the display.

To demonstrate the default editor, we have updated the FileSystemTreeModel to implement valueForPathChanged and rename the changed file to match the new value. The model then fires a TreeModelEvent to notify listeners. This event requires the path for the parent and arrays that contain the children that changed as well as their index. A lot of our code for valueForPathChanged is used to create this information, and it is unrelated to the value changing itself. We have highlighted the code that is primarily focused on changing the value and initiating notification. This is the model FileHolder object from the previous FileTree example.

```
import com.sun.java.swing.*;
import com.sun.java.swing.tree.*;
import com.sun.java.swing.event.*;
import java.io.*;
import java.util.*;

class FileSystemTreeModel implements TreeModel
{
    protected FileHolder root;
    protected Vector listeners;

    public FileSystemTreeModel(File r)
    {
        root = new FileHolder(r);
        listeners = new Vector();
    }

    public Object getRoot()
    {
        return root;
    }

    public Object getChild(Object parent,
                                    int index)
    {
        Object retVal = null;
        Vector children;

        if(parent instanceof FileHolder)
        {
            children = ((FileHolder)parent).getChildren();

            if(children != null)
            {
                if(index < children.size())
                {
                    retVal = children.elementAt(index);
                }
            }
        }

        return retVal;
    }
```

```
public int getChildCount(Object parent)
{
    int retVal = 0;
    Vector children;

    if(parent instanceof FileHolder)
    {
        children = ((FileHolder)parent).getChildren();

        if(children != null)
        {
            retVal = children.size();
        }
    }

    return retVal;
}

public boolean isLeaf(Object node)
{
    boolean retVal = true;
    File file;

    if(node instanceof FileHolder)
    {
        file = ((FileHolder)node).getFile();

        retVal = file.isFile();
    }

    return retVal;
}

public void valueForPathChanged(TreePath path,Object newVal)
{
    FileHolder holder;
    File file;
    File newFile;

    try
    {
        holder= (FileHolder) path.getLastPathComponent();
        file = holder.getFile();
```

```
//Create a file for the new path
newFile = new File(file.getParent(),newVal.toString());

if(file.renameTo(newFile))
{
    Object objPath[];
    Object pobjPath[];
    TreePath parentPath;
    FileHolder parentHolder;
    Vector files;
    int i,max;
    int childInd[];
    Object child[];

    //Change the file for the holder
    holder.setFile(newFile);

    //Notify listeners
    objPath = path.getPath();

    max = objPath.length - 1;
    pobjPath = new Object[max];

    for(i=0;i<max;i++)
    {
        pobjPath[i] = objPath[i];
    }

    parentPath = new TreePath(pobjPath);

    parentHolder = (FileHolder)
                parentPath.getLastPathComponent();

    files = parentHolder.getChildren();

    childInd = new int[1];
    childInd[0] = files.indexOf(holder);

    child = new Object[1];
    child[0] = holder;

    fireValueChanged(parentPath,childInd,child);
```

```
            }
        }
        catch(Exception exp)
        {
            //ignore the change
        }
    }

    public int getIndexOfChild(Object parent,
                                        Object child)
    {
        int retVal = -1;
        Vector children;

        if(parent instanceof FileHolder)
        {
            children = ((FileHolder)parent).getChildren();

            if(children != null)
            {
                retVal = children.indexOf(child);
            }
        }

        return retVal;
    }

    public void addTreeModelListener(TreeModelListener l)
    {
        if((l != null)&&!listeners.contains(l)) listeners.addElement(l);
    }

    public void removeTreeModelListener(TreeModelListener l)
    {
        listeners.removeElement(l);
    }

    protected void fireValueChanged(TreePath path,int[] ind,
                                        Object[] children)
    {
        TreeModelEvent evt;
        int i,max;
```

```
        TreeModelListener curL;

        evt = new TreeModelEvent(this,path,ind,children);

        max = listeners.size();

        for(i=0;i<max;i++)
        {
            curL = (TreeModelListener) listeners.elementAt(i);

            curL.treeNodesChanged(evt);
        }
    }
}
```

To test the new model we update the earlier example to use an editable tree.

```
import com.sun.java.swing.*;

import java.awt.event.*;
import java.awt.*;
import java.io.*;
import java.util.*;

public class EditableFileTree extends JPanel
{
    public EditableFileTree(String startPath)
    {
        JTree tree;
        FileSystemTreeModel model;
        File root;
        Font f;

        f = new Font("SanSerif",Font.PLAIN,24);
        setFont(f);
        setLayout(new BorderLayout());

        root = new File(startPath);
        model = new FileSystemTreeModel(root);

        tree = new JTree();
        tree.setModel(model);
        tree.setFont(f);
        tree.setEditable(true);
```

```
        add(new JScrollPane(tree),"Center");
    }

    public Dimension getPreferredSize()
    {
        return new Dimension(250, 200);
    }

    public static void main(String s[])
    {
        JFrame frame = new JFrame("Editable File Tree");
        EditableFileTree panel;

        if(s.length > 0)
            panel = new EditableFileTree(s[0]);
        else
            panel = new EditableFileTree("/");

        frame.setDefaultCloseOperation(JFrame.DO_NOTHING_ON_CLOSE);
        frame.setForeground(Color.black);
        frame.setBackground(Color.lightGray);
        frame.getContentPane().add(panel,"Center");

        frame.setSize(panel.getPreferredSize());
        frame.setVisible(true);
        frame.addWindowListener(new WindowCloser());
    }
}
```

This example uses a WindowCloser object to manage the window's close box. This class is included in the example file and relies on the same import statements.

```
class WindowCloser extends WindowAdapter
{
    public void windowClosing(WindowEvent e)
    {
        Window win = e.getWindow();
        win.setVisible(false);
        win.dispose();
        System.exit(0);
    }
}
```

When run, this example looks like Figure 11.10.

Figure 11.10 Editable file tree.

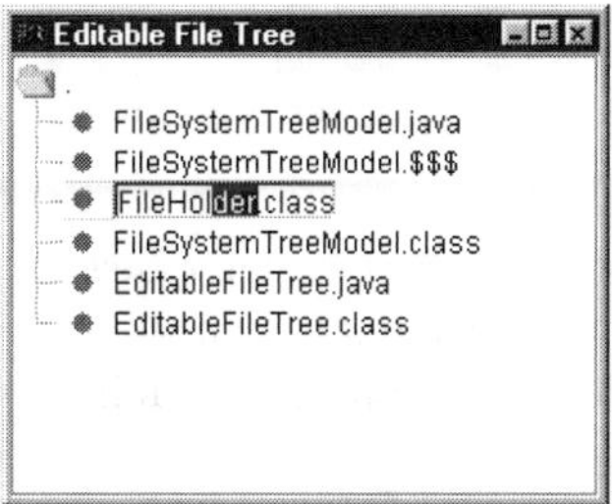

Custom Tree Cell Editors

You can create your own tree cell editor by implementing the TreeCellEditor interface. This interface defines a single method:

```
public Component getTreeCellEditorComponent(JTree tree,
                                            Object value,
                                            boolean isSelected,
                                            boolean expanded,
                                            boolean leaf,
                                            int row)
```

Like the renderer, the getTreeCellEditorComponent method is expected to initialize and return a component that performs the actual editing. TreeCellEditor also inherits a number of methods for the editor to implement. These are defined in the interface CellEditor and are listed in Table 11.10.

The CellEditor methods fall into three basic categories. First, one method asks the editor if an event needs to initiate the editor. Second, another method tells the editor to start editing. Third, some other events tell the editor to stop editing. The tree initiates these methods when the tree's data changes or the selection changes. For editors that don't accept any value, the stopCellEditing method returns false and continues editing. Normally, the tree doesn't use this method and cancels editing instead. To tell the tree to delegate the decision to stop editing to the editor, use the following method:

```
public void setInvokesStopCellEditing(boolean newValue);
```

There are also two methods to manage CellEditorListeners for the editor:

```
public void editingStopped(ChangeEvent e);
public void editingCanceled(ChangeEvent e);
```

Both methods take a single ChangeEvent with the editor as its source. This is a notification event only and contains no other data.

To assign your custom editor to a tree, use the setCellEditor() method shown here:

Table 11.10 CellEditor Methods

Method	Function
public Object getCellEditorValue()	Returns the editor's current value, like the string in a text field.
public boolean isCellEditable (EventObject anEvent)	Returns true if the editor can start editing based on the provided event. For example, you might start editing only if the event is part of a double mouse click.
public boolean shouldSelectCell (EventObject anEvent)	Tells the editor to start editing and provides the initiating event. The editor can use this event to initialize itself, possibly the current selection. If this method returns true, the tree will select the edited cell. If not, the old selection will be maintained, even after the editing is complete.
public boolean stopCellEditing()	Tells the editor to stop editing. The editor can return false not to stop and avoid an invalid entry.
public void cancelCellEditing()	Immediately stops the editor, regardless of the current value.
public void addCellEditorListener (CellEditorListener l)	Adds a CellEditorListener to the editor.
public void removeCellEditorListener (CellEditorListener l)	Removes a CellEditorListener from the editor.

```
public void setCellEditor(TreeCellEditor cellEditor);
```

To turn on editing use the setEditable() method:

```
public void setEditable(boolean flag);
```

If you want to keep track of the current editor, you can access it using the following method:

```
public TreeCellEditor getCellEditor();
```

In Figure 11.11 we use a custom editor and renderer. The renderer displays an icon based on the type of node: leaf, expanded, or collapsed. As with our earlier renderer, the majority of the work is performed with a JLabel.

```
import java.lang.*;
import com.sun.java.swing.*;
import com.sun.java.swing.tree.*;
```

```
import java.awt.*;

public class SimpleTreeRenderer extends Object
implements TreeCellRenderer
{
    JLabel theLabel;
    Icon open;
    Icon closed;
    Icon leaf;

    public SimpleTreeRenderer()
    {
        theLabel = new JLabel();
        theLabel.setOpaque(true);

        open = new ImageIcon("images/check.gif");
        closed = new ImageIcon("images/ex.gif");
        leaf = new ImageIcon("images/shapes.gif");
    }

    public Component getTreeCellRendererComponent(JTree tree,
                                Object value,
                                boolean selected,
                                boolean expanded,
                                boolean isleaf,
                                int row,
                                boolean hasFocus)

    {
        theLabel.setFont(tree.getFont());

        if(selected)
        {
            theLabel.setForeground(tree.getBackground());
            theLabel.setBackground(tree.getForeground());
        }
        else
        {
            theLabel.setBackground(tree.getBackground());
            theLabel.setForeground(tree.getForeground());
        }

        if(isleaf)
        {
```

```
                theLabel.setIcon(leaf);
            }
            else if(expanded)
            {
                theLabel.setIcon(open);
            }
            else
            {
                theLabel.setIcon(closed);
            }

            theLabel.setText(value.toString());

            return theLabel;
        }
}
```

Figure 11.11 shows our custom tree editor.

The editor uses a text field with the tree's current font to edit the string values in the tree. Editing is initiated by double-clicking the mouse on a cell. The editor updates the cell's value if the text field notifies it of an action event. This happens only if the user presses the Return key while editing a value. If the user starts editing and then changes the selection, the editor won't change the current value.

```
import java.awt.*;
import java.awt.event.*;
import com.sun.java.swing.*;
import com.sun.java.swing.event.*;
import com.sun.java.swing.tree.*;
import java.util.*;

public class TreeFieldEditor
implements TreeCellEditor, ActionListener
{
    JTextField theField;
    JTree theTree;
    Vector listeners;
```

Figure 11.11 Custom tree editor.

```
public TreeFieldEditor()
{
    listeners = new Vector();
    theField = new JTextField();
    theField.addActionListener(this);
}

public Component getTreeCellEditorComponent(JTree tree,
                                            Object value,
                                            boolean isSelected,
                                            boolean expanded,
                                            boolean leaf,
                                            int row)
{
    theTree = tree;

    theField.setFont(tree.getFont());
    theField.setText(value.toString());
    theField.selectAll();

    return theField;
}

public Object getCellEditorValue()
{
    return theField.getText();
}

public boolean shouldSelectCell(EventObject anEvent)
{
    theField.selectAll();
    theField.requestFocus();

    return true;
}

public boolean isCellEditable(EventObject anEvent)
{
    boolean retVal = false;

    if(anEvent instanceof MouseEvent)
    {
        MouseEvent me = (MouseEvent) anEvent;

        if(me.getClickCount()==2)
```

```
            {
                retVal = true;
            }
        }

        return retVal;
    }

    public boolean stopCellEditing()
    {
        fireEditingStopped();
        return true;
    }

    public void cancelCellEditing()
    {
        fireEditingCanceled();
    }

    public void addCellEditorListener(CellEditorListener l)
    {
        if(!listeners.contains(l))
            listeners.addElement(l);
    }

    public void removeCellEditorListener(CellEditorListener l)
    {
        listeners.removeElement(l);
    }

    protected void fireEditingStopped()
    {
        int i,max;
        CellEditorListener curL;
        ChangeEvent evt;

        max = listeners.size();

        evt = new ChangeEvent(this);

        for (i = 0;i < max; i++)
        {
            curL = (CellEditorListener)listeners.elementAt(i);
```

```
            curL.editingStopped(evt);
        }
    }

    protected void fireEditingCanceled()
    {
        int i,max;
        CellEditorListener curL;
        ChangeEvent evt;

        max = listeners.size();

        evt = new ChangeEvent(this);

        for (i = 0;i < max; i++)
        {
            curL = (CellEditorListener)listeners.elementAt(i);
            curL.editingCanceled(evt);
        }
    }

    public void actionPerformed(ActionEvent e)
    {
        String value;
        DefaultMutableTreeNode node=null;
        Object selItem;
        TreePath path;

        value = theField.getText();
        path = theTree.getSelectionPath();
        selItem = path.getLastPathComponent();

        if(selItem instanceof DefaultMutableTreeNode)
            node = (DefaultMutableTreeNode)selItem;

        if(node != null)
        {
            node.setUserObject(value);
        }

        fireEditingStopped();
    }
}
```

The example we used to create Figure 11.11 builds a small tree, sets the renderer and editor, and then adds the tree to a scroll pane before displaying it. A default model is used to describe the tree's data, and strings are used as values.

```
import com.sun.java.swing.*;
import com.sun.java.swing.tree.*;
import java.awt.event.*;
import java.awt.*;
import java.util.*;

public class CustomEditorExample extends JPanel
{
    public CustomEditorExample()
    {
        JTree tree;
        Font f;
        DefaultMutableTreeNode rootNode;
        DefaultMutableTreeNode parentNode;
        DefaultMutableTreeNode node;
        TreeCellRenderer treeR;
        TreeCellEditor treeE;
        ImageIcon icon;

        f = new Font("SanSerif",Font.PLAIN,24);
        setFont(f);
        setLayout(new BorderLayout());

        rootNode = new DefaultMutableTreeNode("Colors");

        node = new DefaultMutableTreeNode("Red",false);
        rootNode.add(node);

        node = new DefaultMutableTreeNode("Green",false);
        rootNode.add(node);

        node = new DefaultMutableTreeNode("Blue",false);
        rootNode.add(node);

        tree = new JTree(rootNode);
        tree.setFont(f);

        treeR = new SimpleTreeRenderer();
        tree.setCellRenderer(treeR);
```

```
        treeE = new TreeFieldEditor();
        tree.setCellEditor(treeE);
        tree.setEditable(true);
        tree.setInvokesStopCellEditing(true);

        tree.setRowHeight(0);//let the renderer handle it

        add(new JScrollPane(tree),"Center");
    }

    public Dimension getPreferredSize()
    {
        return new Dimension(200, 120);
    }

    public static void main(String s[])
    {
        JFrame frame = new JFrame("Custom Editor Example");
        CustomEditorExample panel = new CustomEditorExample();

        frame.setDefaultCloseOperation(JFrame.DO_NOTHING_ON_CLOSE);
        frame.setForeground(Color.black);
        frame.setBackground(Color.lightGray);
        frame.getContentPane().add(panel,"Center");

        frame.setSize(panel.getPreferredSize());
        frame.setVisible(true);
        frame.addWindowListener(new WindowCloser());
    }
}
```

This example uses a WindowCloser object to manage the window's close box. This class is included in the example file and relies on the same import statements.

```
class WindowCloser extends WindowAdapter
{
    public void windowClosing(WindowEvent e)
    {
        Window win = e.getWindow();
        win.setVisible(false);
        win.dispose();
        System.exit(0);
    }
}
```

Tree Mouse Events

Like any JComponent, JTree supports mouse and keyboard event listeners. If you want to create an interface that allows the user to perform special actions on a tree's data using the mouse or keyboard, use event listeners to do so. The following example prints a message whenever the user double-clicks the mouse on an item. A subclass of the MouseAdapter called DoubleClicker is used to listen for mouse events. When a double-click event occurs the listener converts the mouse's location to a path and displays the value of this path.

To convert a location to a path, use either of these two methods:

```
public TreePath getPathForLocation(int x, int y)
public TreePath getClosestPathForLocation(int x, int y)
```

Use the second method to get the path closest to a location. Both methods return null if no path is appropriate or available.

When run our double-clicker example looks like the program in Figure 11.12.

```
import com.sun.java.swing.*;
import com.sun.java.swing.tree.*;
import java.awt.event.*;
import java.awt.*;
import java.util.*;

public class TreeClickExample extends JPanel
{
    public TreeClickExample()
    {
        JTree tree;
        Vector data;
        Font f;

        f = new Font("SanSerif",Font.PLAIN,24);
        setFont(f);
        setLayout(new BorderLayout());

        data = new Vector();
        data.addElement("Gold");
        data.addElement("Silver");
        data.addElement("Bronze");
        data.addElement("Copper");
        data.addElement("Iron");
        data.addElement("Platinum");
        data.addElement("Titanium");
```

```
        tree = new JTree(data);
        tree.setFont(f);

        tree.addMouseListener(new DoubleClicker());

        add(new JScrollPane(tree),"Center");
    }

    public Dimension getPreferredSize()
    {
        return new Dimension(200, 120);
    }

    public static void main(String s[])
    {
        JFrame frame = new JFrame("Tree Clicks Example");
        TreeClickExample panel = new TreeClickExample();

        frame.setDefaultCloseOperation(JFrame.DO_NOTHING_ON_CLOSE);
        frame.setForeground(Color.black);
        frame.setBackground(Color.lightGray);
        frame.getContentPane().add(panel,"Center");

        frame.setSize(panel.getPreferredSize());
        frame.setVisible(true);
        frame.addWindowListener(new WindowCloser());
    }
}
```

This example uses a WindowCloser object to manage the window's close box. This class is included in the example file and relies on the same import statements.

```
class WindowCloser extends WindowAdapter
{
    public void windowClosing(WindowEvent e)
    {
        Window win = e.getWindow();
        win.setVisible(false);
        win.dispose();
        System.exit(0);
    }
}
```

For simplicity, we have included the DoubleClicker class in the example file so that it will use the same import statements.

Figure 11.12 Tree double clicker.

```
class DoubleClicker extends MouseAdapter
{
    public void mouseClicked(MouseEvent e)
    {
        if(e.getClickCount() == 2)
        {
            JTree tree;
            Object item;
            TreePath path;

            tree = (JTree) e.getSource();
            path = tree.getPathForLocation(e.getX(), e.getY());
            item = path.getLastPathComponent();

            System.out.println("Double clicked on " + item);

            tree.scrollPathToVisible(path);
        }
    }
}
```

Figure 11.12 shows the handling of a double click of a tree node.

The double clicker in this example also scrolls the current path to visible using the following method:

```
public void scrollPathToVisible(TreePath path);
```

In general, if a user can see a path to click on it, then this method won't do much. If you are selecting paths programmatically, however, this is an important technique.

Style Guidelines

Trees are a great for displaying hierarchical data. Keep in mind that the tree's display is provided by a data model. It's fairly easy to create your own tree models that generate data based on some other aspect of your program, such as the file system or a relational database. In our example we created data from the file system, but you could use any other appropriate data. By creating your own tree model, you can also create notification schemes that update the tree automatically when data changes.

If you control a tree's selection programmatically, use the scrollPathToVisible method to make sure that at least the first path in the selection is visible. This reduces confusion for the user.

Custom tree cell renderers are a great way to add information to a tree by providing custom icons or other graphics. If you use a custom renderer, keep in mind that the tree may add its own graphics to indicate expandable cells or root handles.

Finally, as with all components, take advantage of the event listeners if you need to add event-based functionality. It's unlikely that you will need to create your own subclass of JTree. JTree is quite extensible via delegated events, cell renderers, cell editors, and the tree model.

TABLES

12

A table is one of the most versatile of the more complex UI elements found in Swing. A spreadsheet is a table of formulas; a price list is a table of products and their prices. A table is often used to show the user what is in a relational database. Swing includes a powerful object for displaying tabular data called JTable, which displays rows and columns of data. Each entry in the table is called a *cell* and is located uniquely by its row and column. A *header* is used to display the title for each column. This header also allows the user to reorder the columns in a JTable, as pictured in Figure 12.1. The user can select and drag the columns so that their positions are transposed. If you want to sort the data based on these values, you need to do this yourself because sorting is based on the meaning of the cell values.

One of the most powerful features of the JTable implementation is that it hides a lot of the complexity involved with managing a table. Programmers do not have to spend a lot of effort customizing the existing table object. Instead we can focus on creating a TableModel object that feeds data to the table.

Figure 12.1 JTable.

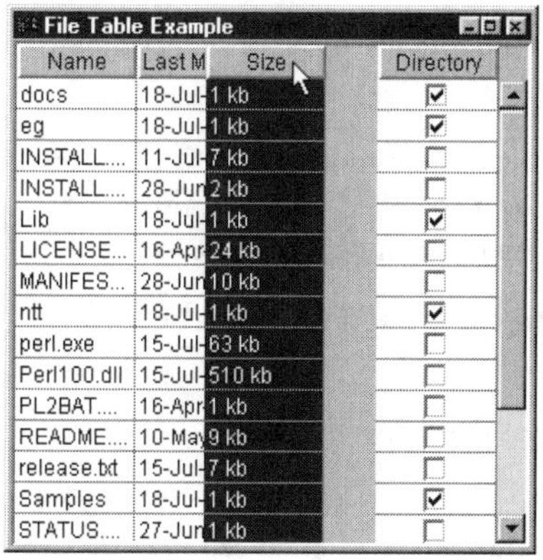

File Table Example

Name	Last M	Size	Directory
docs	18-Jul-	1 kb	☑
eg	18-Jul-	1 kb	☑
INSTALL....	11-Jul-	7 kb	☐
INSTALL....	28-Jun	2 kb	☐
Lib	18-Jul-	1 kb	☑
LICENSE...	16-Apr	24 kb	☐
MANIFES...	28-Jun	10 kb	☐
ntt	18-Jul-	1 kb	☑
perl.exe	15-Jul-	63 kb	☐
Perl100.dll	15-Jul-	510 kb	☐
PL2BAT....	16-Apr	1 kb	☐
README....	10-May	9 kb	☐
release.txt	15-Jul-	7 kb	☐
Samples	18-Jul-	1 kb	☑
STATUS....	27-Jun	1 kb	☐

TableModel

JTables retrieve their data from a TableModel. This model has methods to return the number of rows and columns, information about the type of data in a column, the data for each cell, and the name for each column. The model is also responsible for telling the table if a cell is editable, and if so, the model provides a method to change the data for a cell. Finally, the model is responsible for tracking model listeners to be notified if the table changes. A complete list of these methods is provided in Table 12.1.

As we see in this chapter's examples, creating custom table models that describe any kind of tabular data is easy. It's easy because Swing provides a prebuilt table model called AbstractTableModel that you can subclass. This class manages a list of table model listeners and provides methods to notify those listeners when data changes. The abstract model also returns an object for each column class value and returns false to isCellEditable for all cells. To create a read-only table model you only need to implement the three methods shown in Table 12.2. You can rely on the abstract-table model for the rest.

Table 12.1 TableModel Methods

Method	Function
Public void addTableModelListener (TableModelListener l)	Adds a table model listener to the notification list.
Public void removeTableModelListener (TableModelListener l)	Removes a table model listener from the notification list.
Public int getRowCount()	Returns the number of rows of data.
Public int getColumnCount()	Returns the number of columns to display.
Public String getColumnName (Int columnIndex)	Returns the name for the specified column.
Public Class getColumnClass (Int columnIndex)	Returns the class of object used to describe the data for a specified column. This can be Object.class in the most generic case.
Public boolean isCellEditable (Int rowIndex,Int columnIndex)	Returns true if the specified cell is editable.
Public Object getValueAt (Int rowIndex,Int columnIndex)	Returns the value for a specified cell.
Public void setValueAt(Object aValue, Int rowIndex,Int columnIndex)	Sets the value for a specified cell.

Table 12.2 Methods That Must Be Implemented in Subclasses of AbstractTableModel

Method	Function
public int getRowCount()	Returns the number of data rows in a table model.
public int getColumnCount()	Returns the number of data columns in a table model.
public Object getValueAt(int, int)	Returns an object associated with a specific row and column in a table model.

TableModelListeners

The table and its model interact through the TableModelListener interface. This interface is used to notify objects when the model's data changes. The table uses these notifications to update the display. A TableModelListener must have the following method:

```
public void tableChanged(TableModelEvent evt);
```

The argument to this method is a TableModelEvent object. The same object is used for insert, update, and remove events, so the event object can provide information about its type and the data changed using the methods listed in Table 12.3.

Remember that, in our case, we often trigger these event notifications rather than handle them. The table or its UI handles the events and updates the table's appearance appropriately.

AbstractTableModel provides a number of methods for firing off tableChanged notifications. These are listed in Table 12.4.

Table 12.3 TableModelEvent Methods

Method	Function
Public int getColumn()	Returns the column affected, may be TableModelEvent. ALL_COLUMNS to indicate that all columns are affected for the affected rows.
Public int getFirstRow()	Returns the first row affected. This may be TableModelEvent. HEADER_ROW to indicate that the names, types, or order of columns has changed.
Public int getLastRow()	Returns the last row affected.
Public int getType()	Returns the type of event. This is either TableModelEvent.INSERT, TableModelEvent.UPDATE, or TableModelEvent.DELETE.

Table 12.4 AbstractTableModel Notification Methods

Method	Use
Protected void fireTableDataChanged()	Fires an event that indicates that the table's data has changed.
Protected void fireTableStructureChanged()	Fires an event that indicates that the table's structure has changed. This may include columns added or removed.
Protected void fireTableRowsInserted (int firstRow,Int lastRow)	Fires an event that indicates that the specified rows are inserted.
Protected void fireTableRowsUpdated (int firstRow,Int lastRow)	Fires an event that indicates that the specified rows are udpated.
Protected void fireTableRowsDeleted (int firstRow,Int lastRow)	Fires an event that indicates that the specified rows are deleted.
Protected void fireTableCellUpdated (int row,Int column)	Fires an event that indicates that the specified cell is updated.

When the table receives the tableChanged method, it can either use the same columns or build new ones. Use the following method to tell the table to build new columns when the model's structure changes.

```
public void setAutoCreateColumnsFromModel(boolean createColumns);
```

If you don't set this value to true, then use the following method to perform the same task manually:

```
public void createDefaultColumnsFromModel();
```

The following example implements a table model that displays the files for a directory. For each file, the name, size, and modified time are displayed, as well as an indication of whether the file is a directory. Notice, in Figure 12.2, that the table uses check boxes to show Boolean values. This model returns false to isEditable for all cells, so the table does not allow the user to alter its data.

The first class in this example is FileTableModel. This class extends AbstractTableModel. When a file table model is created it is passed a File object. This File object is supposed to point to a directory because it is used to create a listing of the files in that directory. Each of the table model methods relies on a cached list of the directory files that we create in the constructor and stores them in the variable "files." This model is very similar to the FileTreeModel that we created in Chapter 11. As a subclass of AbstractTableModel, the FileSystemTableModel implements the necessary AbstractTableModel methods, as described in Table

Figure 12.2 File table model.

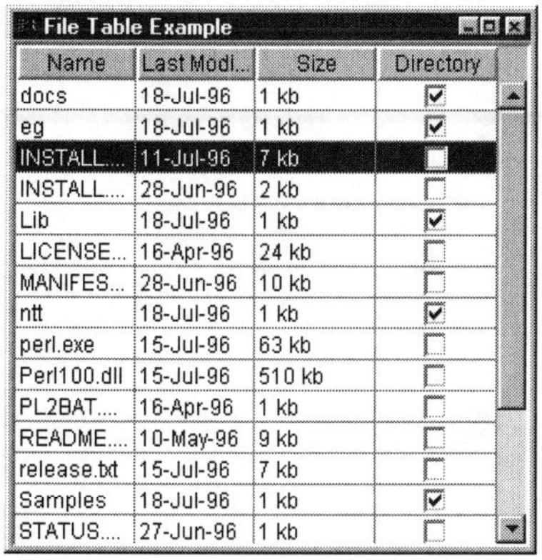

File Table Example

Name	Last Modi...	Size	Directory
docs	18-Jul-96	1 kb	☑
eg	18-Jul-96	1 kb	☑
INSTALL....	11-Jul-96	7 kb	☐
INSTALL....	28-Jun-96	2 kb	☐
Lib	18-Jul-96	1 kb	☑
LICENSE...	16-Apr-96	24 kb	☐
MANIFES...	28-Jun-96	10 kb	☐
ntt	18-Jul-96	1 kb	☑
perl.exe	15-Jul-96	63 kb	☐
Perl100.dll	15-Jul-96	510 kb	☐
PL2BAT....	16-Apr-96	1 kb	☐
README....	10-May-96	9 kb	☐
release.txt	15-Jul-96	7 kb	☐
Samples	18-Jul-96	1 kb	☑
STATUS....	27-Jun-96	1 kb	☐

12.1. The implementation of these methods allows the FileSystemTableModel to describe a data model for a table that includes columns with the headings "Name," "Last Modified," "Size," and "Directory."

```
import com.sun.java.swing.*;
import com.sun.java.swing.table.*;
import com.sun.java.swing.event.*;
import java.io.*;
import java.util.*;

public class FileSystemTableModel extends AbstractTableModel
{
    protected Vector files;

    public FileSystemTableModel(File r)
    {
        String fileNames[];
        File curFile;
        int i,max;

        files = new Vector();

        fileNames = r.list();

        max = fileNames.length;

        for(i=0;i<max;i++)
        {
            curFile = new File(r,fileNames[i]);
```

```
            files.addElement(curFile);
        }
    }

    public int getRowCount()
    {
        return files.size();
    }

    public int getColumnCount()
    {
        return 4;
    }

    public String getColumnName(int columnIndex)
    {
        String retVal = "";

        switch(columnIndex)
        {
            case 0:
                retVal = "Name";
                break;
            case 1:
                retVal = "Last Modified";
                break;
            case 2:
                retVal = "Size";
                break;
            case 3:
                retVal = "Directory";
                break;
            default:
                retVal = "default";
                break;
        }

        return retVal;
    }

    public Class getColumnClass(int columnIndex)
    {
        Class retVal = String.class;
```

```
        if(columnIndex==3) retVal = Boolean.class;

        return retVal;
    }

    public boolean isCellEditable(int rowIndex,
                                        int columnIndex)
    {
        boolean retVal = false;

        return retVal;
    }

    public Object getValueAt(int rowIndex,
                                  int columnIndex)
    {
        Object retVal=null;
        File file=null;

        if(rowIndex < files.size())
        {
            file = (File)files.elementAt(rowIndex);
        }

        if(file == null) return "";

        if(columnIndex == 0)
        {
            retVal = file.getName();
        }
        else if(columnIndex == 1)
        {
            Date d = new Date(file.lastModified());
            java.text.DateFormat df =
                    java.text.DateFormat.getDateInstance();

            retVal = df.format(d);
        }
        else if(columnIndex == 2)
        {
            long sizeInBytes = file.length();
            long sizeInKb = sizeInBytes/1024;
```

```
            if(sizeInKb < 1) sizeInKb = 1;

            retVal = String.valueOf(sizeInKb) + " kb";
        }
        else if(columnIndex == 3)
        {
            retVal = new Boolean(file.isDirectory());
        }
        else
        {
            retVal = file;
        }

        return retVal;
    }

    public void setValueAt(Object aValue,
                                    int rowIndex,
                                    int columnIndex)
    {
        return;
    }
}
```

To test the FileTableModel, we created a simple application that displays a JTable using a FileTableModel. The directory for the model is determined in the main method. To create the table in this example we use the default constructor. We also rely on the following convenience method provided by JTable to create the scroll pane for our table.

```
public static JScrollPane createScrollPaneForTable(JTable aTable);
```

This method creates a scroll pane with the appropriate column header to display the table's column names.

The code for our example program is as follows:

```
import com.sun.java.swing.*;

import java.awt.event.*;
import java.awt.*;
import java.io.*;
import java.util.*;

public class FileTable extends JPanel
{
    public FileTable(String startPath)
```

```
    {
        JTable table;
        FileSystemTableModel model;
        File root;
        Font f;

        f = new Font("SanSerif",Font.PLAIN,24);
        setFont(f);
        setLayout(new BorderLayout());

        root = new File(startPath);
        model = new FileSystemTableModel(root);

        table = new JTable();
        table.setModel(model);
        table.createDefaultColumnsFromModel();
        table.setFont(f);

        add(JTable.createScrollPaneForTable(table)
            ,"Center");
    }

    public Dimension getPreferredSize()
    {
        return new Dimension(300, 300);
    }

    public static void main(String s[])
    {
        JFrame frame = new JFrame("File Table Example");
        FileTable panel;

        if(s.length > 0)
            panel = new FileTable(s[0]);
        else
            panel = new FileTable("/");

        frame.setDefaultCloseOperation(JFrame.DO_NOTHING_ON_CLOSE);
        frame.setForeground(Color.black);
        frame.setBackground(Color.lightGray);
        frame.getContentPane().add(panel,"Center");

        frame.setSize(panel.getPreferredSize());
        frame.setVisible(true);
```

```
        frame.addWindowListener(new WindowCloser());
    }
}
```

This example uses a WindowCloser object to handle the close box. This class is implemented in the same file as the text program, so that it inherits the import statements.

```
class WindowCloser extends WindowAdapter
{
    public void windowClosing(WindowEvent e)
    {
        Window win = e.getWindow();
        win.setVisible(false);
        System.exit(0);
    }
}
```

Table Display Attributes

JTable provides a number of methods that allow the programmer to control how the table displays its data. These methods are listed in Table 12.5, along with a description of their purpose.

Table 12.5 JTable Attribute Methods

Method	Function
public void setIntercellSpacing (Dimension newSpacing)	Sets the spacing between cells.
public Dimension getIntercellSpacing()	Returns the spacing between cells.
public void setGridColor(Color newColor)	Sets the color used to draw the grid.
public Color getGridColor()	Returns the color used to draw the grid.
public void setShowGrid(boolean b)	Sets whether to draw the grid lines.
public boolean getShowGrid()	Returns true if the table draws its grid lines, false otherwise.
public void setAutoResizeMode(int mode)	Tells the table what to do if it is resized. This can be one of the following JTable class variables: AUTO_RESIZE_OFF, AUTO_RESIZE_LAST_COLUMN, AUTO_RESIZE_ALL_COLUMNS.
public int getAutoResizeMode()	Returns the table's resize mode.

Selections

Tables support three kinds of selections.

1. *Row selections* occur when the user selects an entire row.
2. *Column selections* occur when the user selects a column.
3. *Cell selections* occur when the user selects a single cell.

These modes can be turned on or off using the following methods:

```
public void setColumnSelectionAllowed(boolean flag);
public void setRowSelectionAllowed(boolean flag);
public void setCellSelectionEnabled(boolean flag);
```

Our next example enables cell selection, which is off by default, and also sets several of the table's display attributes. A FileSystemTableModel is used to provide data to the table. This is the same model used in the previous example.

```
import com.sun.java.swing.*;

import java.awt.event.*;
import java.awt.*;
import java.io.*;
import java.util.*;

public class CellFileTable extends JPanel
{
    public CellFileTable(String startPath)
    {
        JTable table;
        FileSystemTableModel model;
        File root;
        Font f;

        f = new Font("SanSerif",Font.PLAIN,24);
        setFont(f);
        setLayout(new BorderLayout());

        root = new File(startPath);
        model = new FileSystemTableModel(root);

        table = new JTable();
        table.setModel(model);
        table.createDefaultColumnsFromModel();

        table.setCellSelectionEnabled(true);
```

```
        table.setIntercellSpacing(new Dimension(5,3));
        table.setGridColor(Color.green);
        table.setFont(f);

        add(JTable.createScrollPaneForTable(table)
            ,"Center");
    }

    public Dimension getPreferredSize()
    {
        return new Dimension(300, 300);
    }

    public static void main(String s[])
    {
        JFrame frame = new JFrame("Cell Selection Example");
        CellFileTable panel;

        if(s.length > 0)
            panel = new CellFileTable(s[0]);
        else
            panel = new CellFileTable("/");

        frame.setDefaultCloseOperation(JFrame.DO_NOTHING_ON_CLOSE);
        frame.setForeground(Color.black);
        frame.setBackground(Color.lightGray);
        frame.getContentPane().add(panel,"Center");

        frame.setSize(panel.getPreferredSize());
        frame.setVisible(true);
        frame.addWindowListener(new WindowCloser());
    }
}
```

The file for this example includes the WindowCloser class. A WindowCloser is used to handle the close box on the example window.

```
class WindowCloser extends WindowAdapter
{
    public void windowClosing(WindowEvent e)
    {
        Window win = e.getWindow();
        win.setVisible(false);
        System.exit(0);
    }
}
```

Figure 12.3 Cell selections.

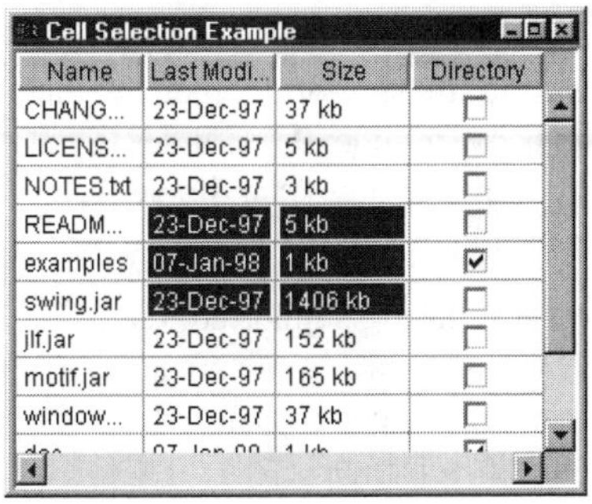

A running version of this example is pictured in Figure 12.3.

You can access much of the information about the current selection directly from the table using the methods in Table 12.6. The table also provides methods to set the selection and check if certain values are selected.

The actual selection for a table is managed by ListSelectionModels. A different model is used to track the current row selection from the current column selection.

Table 12.6 Table Selection Methods

Method	Function
public void selectAll()	Selects the entire table.
public void clearSelection()	Removes all rows, columns, and cells from the selection.
public void setRowSelectionInterval (int index0, int index1)	If row selections are supported, selects all of the rows between index0 and index1, including the rows at index0 and index1.
public void setColumnSelectionInterval (int index0, int index1)	If column selections are supported, selects all of the columns between index0 and index1, including the columns at index0 and index1.
public void addRowSelectionInterval (int index0, int index1)	If row selections are supported, adds all of the rows between index0 and index1, including the rows at index0 and index1, to the selection.
public void addColumnSelectionInterval (int index0, int index1)	If column selections are supported, adds all of the columns between index0 and index1, including the columns at index0 and index1, to the selection.

Continues

Table 12.6 Table Selection Methods *(Continued)*

Method	Function
public void removeRowSelectionInterval (int index0, int index1)	If row selections are supported, removes all of the rows between index0 and index1, including the rows at index0 and index1, from the selection.
public void removeColumnSelectionInterval (int index0, int index1)	If column selections are supported, removes all of the columns between index0 and index1, including the columns at index0 and index1, from the selection.
public int getSelectedRow()	Returns the index of the last selected row, -1 if there is no selection.
public int getSelectedColumn()	Returns the index of the last selected column, -1 if there is no selection.
public int[] getSelectedRows()	Returns an array of indices for all of the selected rows.
public int[] getSelectedColumns()	Returns an array of indices for all of the selected columns.
public int getSelectedRowCount()	Returns the number of selected rows.
public int getSelectedColumnCount()	Returns the number of selected columns.
public boolean isRowSelected(int row)	Returns true if the specified row is selected.
public boolean isColumnSelected (int column)	Returns true if the specified column is selected.
public boolean isCellSelected (int row,int column)	Returns true if the specified cell is selected.

To get the row selection model you can use the JTable method:

```
public ListSelectionModel getSelectionModel();
```

To get the column selection model you have to use the table's column model. We discuss this model more later; for now, just use the following code to get a table's column selection model:

```
table.getColumnModel().getSelectionModel();
```

Once you have these models you can register as ListSelectionListeners to receive notifications as the selection changes. We discussed ListSelectionListeners in Chapter 5. Because the selection may involve rows, columns, or cells, you must retrieve the actual selection from the table, rather than the selection events.

You can also use the selection models to set the selection modes for the table. See our discussion in Chapter 5 about what these modes can be.

The following example demonstrates how you can register for a ListSelectionListener for row and column selection changes. The table in this example uses our FileSystemTableModel and is configured to support cell selections. Whenever the current selection changes, our listener prints the selection to the console. Notice that we use the table to get the real selection, not the events provided to valueChanged. To demonstrate how to change selection modes, we have set the row selection mode to single selection.

```
import com.sun.java.swing.*;
import com.sun.java.swing.event.*;
import com.sun.java.swing.table.*;
import java.awt.event.*;
import java.awt.*;
import java.io.*;
import java.util.*;

public class SelTable extends JPanel
implements ListSelectionListener
{
    JTable table;

    public SelTable(String startPath)
    {
        FileSystemTableModel model;
        File root;
        Font f;
        ListSelectionModel listMod;

        setLayout(new BorderLayout());

        root = new File(startPath);
        model = new FileSystemTableModel(root);

        table = new JTable();
        table.setModel(model);
        table.createDefaultColumnsFromModel();

        table.setCellSelectionEnabled(true);

        table.setIntercellSpacing(new Dimension(5,3));
        table.setGridColor(Color.green);
```

```
    add(JTable.createScrollPaneForTable(table)
        ,"Center");

    listMod = table.getSelectionModel();
    listMod.setSelectionMode(ListSelectionModel.SINGLE_SELECTION);
    listMod.addListSelectionListener(this);

    listMod = table.getColumnModel().getSelectionModel();
    listMod.addListSelectionListener(this);
}

public void valueChanged(ListSelectionEvent e)
{
    int i,maxRows;
    int j,maxCols;
    int[] selRows;
    int[] selCols;
    Object value;

    selRows = table.getSelectedRows();
    selCols = table.getSelectedColumns();

    maxRows = selRows.length;
    maxCols = selCols.length;

    for(i=0;i<maxRows;i++)
    {
        for(j=0;j<maxCols;j++)
        {
            if(j!=0) System.out.print(" ");

            value = table.getValueAt(selRows[i],selCols[j]);

            System.out.print(value);
        }

        System.out.println();
    }
}

public Dimension getPreferredSize()
{
    return new Dimension(300, 300);
}
```

```
    public static void main(String s[])
    {
        JFrame frame = new JFrame("Table Selection Example");
        SelTable panel;

        if(s.length > 0)
            panel = new SelTable(s[0]);
        else
            panel = new SelTable("/");

        frame.setDefaultCloseOperation(JFrame.DO_NOTHING_ON_CLOSE);
        frame.setForeground(Color.black);
        frame.setBackground(Color.lightGray);
        frame.getContentPane().add(panel,"Center");

        frame.setSize(panel.getPreferredSize());
        frame.setVisible(true);
        frame.addWindowListener(new WindowCloser());
    }
}
```

The file for this example includes the WindowCloser class. A WindowCloser is used to handle the close box on the example window.

```
class WindowCloser extends WindowAdapter
{
    public void windowClosing(WindowEvent e)
    {
        Window win = e.getWindow();
        win.setVisible(false);
        System.exit(0);
    }
}
```

A running version of this example is pictured in Figure 12.4.

Editable Tables

Displaying data in a table is a great feature, but most applications need to edit the cells as well. JTables can support editing. It's up to the TableModel to determine if editing is appropriate for a given cell by implementing the isCellEditable method and returning true. If the model supports editing, it must also implement the setValueAt method, which gets called when the value of a cell has changed. The table uses a cell editor, like lists, to perform the actual editing process. Once a new value is determined, the table notifies the model. The model is then

Figure 12.4 Table selection listener.

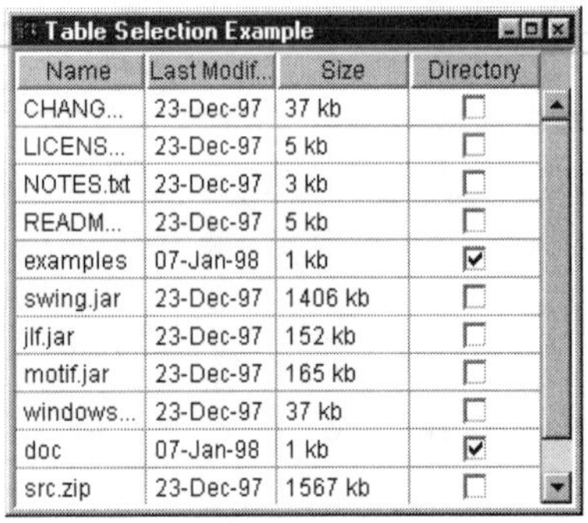

Table Selection Example

Name	Last Modif...	Size	Directory
CHANG...	23-Dec-97	37 kb	☐
LICENS...	23-Dec-97	5 kb	☐
NOTES.txt	23-Dec-97	3 kb	☐
READM...	23-Dec-97	5 kb	☐
examples	07-Jan-98	1 kb	☑
swing.jar	23-Dec-97	1406 kb	☐
jlf.jar	23-Dec-97	152 kb	☐
motif.jar	23-Dec-97	165 kb	☐
windows...	23-Dec-97	37 kb	☐
doc	07-Jan-98	1 kb	☑
src.zip	23-Dec-97	1567 kb	☐

expected to notify its TableModelListeners, including the table itself, to update the user interface.

For the next example we update the FileSystemTableModel to support editing of the file name. When the user edits the file name, the underlying file is renamed to match the new value. FileSystemTableModel is a subclass of AbstractTableModel, so we rely on the inherited methods to perform the actual notification. In this case, we use the fireTableCellUpdated method on the changed cell.

> **WARNING**
>
> This example renames the underlying files. Make sure you don't change anything important.

```
import com.sun.java.swing.*;
import com.sun.java.swing.table.*;
import com.sun.java.swing.event.*;
import java.io.*;
import java.util.*;

public class FileSystemTableModel extends AbstractTableModel
{
    protected Vector files;

    public FileSystemTableModel(File r)
    {
        String fileNames[];
        File curFile;
        int i,max;

        files = new Vector();
```

```
            fileNames = r.list();

            max = fileNames.length;

            for(i=0;i<max;i++)
            {
                curFile = new File(r,fileNames[i]);
                files.addElement(curFile);
            }
        }

        public int getRowCount()
        {
            return files.size();
        }

        public int getColumnCount()
        {
            return 4;
        }

        public String getColumnName(int columnIndex)
        {
            String retVal = "";

            switch(columnIndex)
            {
                case 0:
                    retVal = "Name";
                    break;
                case 1:
                    retVal = "Last Modified";
                    break;
                case 2:
                    retVal = "Size";
                    break;
                case 3:
                    retVal = "Directory";
                    break;
                default:
                    retVal = "default";
                    break;
            }
```

```
        return retVal;
    }

    public Class getColumnClass(int columnIndex)
    {
        Class retVal = String.class;

        if(columnIndex==3) retVal = Boolean.class;

        return retVal;
    }

    public boolean isCellEditable(int rowIndex,
                                        int columnIndex)
    {
        boolean retVal = false;

        if(columnIndex == 0) retVal = true;

        return retVal;
    }

    public Object getValueAt(int rowIndex,
                                   int columnIndex)
    {
        Object retVal=null;
        File file=null;

        if(rowIndex < files.size())
        {
            file = (File)files.elementAt(rowIndex);
        }

        if(file == null) return "";

        if(columnIndex == 0)
        {
            retVal = file.getName();
        }
        else if(columnIndex == 1)
        {
            Date d = new Date(file.lastModified());
            java.text.DateFormat df =
                 java.text.DateFormat.getDateInstance();
```

```
                retVal = df.format(d);
            }
            else if(columnIndex == 2)
            {
                long sizeInBytes = file.length();
                long sizeInKb = sizeInBytes/1024;

                if(sizeInKb < 1) sizeInKb = 1;

                retVal = String.valueOf(sizeInKb) + " kb";
            }
            else if(columnIndex == 3)
            {
                retVal = new Boolean(file.isDirectory());
            }
            else
            {
                retVal = file;
            }

            return retVal;
        }

        public void setValueAt(Object aValue,
                               int rowIndex,
                               int columnIndex)
        {
            File file,newFile;

            if(columnIndex != 0) return;

            file = (File) files.elementAt(rowIndex);

            //Create a file for the new path
            newFile = new File(file.getParent(),aValue.toString());

            if(file.renameTo(newFile))
            {
                files.setElementAt(newFile,rowIndex);
            }

            fireTableCellUpdated(rowIndex,columnIndex);
        }
    }
```

To test this new version of the table model, we provide a simple example that creates a table and displays it with a FileSystemTableModel.

```
import com.sun.java.swing.*;

import java.awt.event.*;
import java.awt.*;
import java.io.*;
import java.util.*;

public class EditFileTable extends JPanel
{
    public EditFileTable(String startPath)
    {
        JTable table;
        FileSystemTableModel model;
        File root;
        Font f;

        f = new Font("SanSerif",Font.PLAIN,24);
        setFont(f);
        setLayout(new BorderLayout());

        root = new File(startPath);
        model = new FileSystemTableModel(root);

        table = new JTable();
        table.setModel(model);
        table.createDefaultColumnsFromModel();

        table.setFont(f);

        add(JTable.createScrollPaneForTable(table)
            ,"Center");
    }

    public Dimension getPreferredSize()
    {
        return new Dimension(300, 300);
    }

    public static void main(String s[])
    {
        JFrame frame = new JFrame("Editable File Table Example");
```

```
        EditFileTable panel;

        if(s.length > 0)
            panel = new EditFileTable(s[0]);
        else
            panel = new EditFileTable("/");

        frame.setDefaultCloseOperation(JFrame.DO_NOTHING_ON_CLOSE);
        frame.setForeground(Color.black);
        frame.setBackground(Color.lightGray);
        frame.getContentPane().add(panel,"Center");

        frame.setSize(panel.getPreferredSize());
        frame.setVisible(true);
        frame.addWindowListener(new WindowCloser());
    }
}
```

The file for this example includes the WindowCloser class. A WindowCloser is used to handle the close box on the example window.

```
class WindowCloser extends WindowAdapter
{
    public void windowClosing(WindowEvent e)
    {
        Window win = e.getWindow();
        win.setVisible(false);
        System.exit(0);
    }
}
```

A running version of this example is shown in Figure 12.5.

Tables and JDBC

One of the classic forms of tabular data is the relational database. Because JavaSoft provides a database connectivity solution—JDBC—we decided to include an example that displays data from a database in a table. This example relies on the JDBCTableModel class, which we wrote to map data from a query into a table. This model is read-only, although you can easily extend it to support editing. If you are unfamiliar with JDBC, you should still find the functionality of this model intriguing. With very little code, we display data from a relational database.

The constructor for this model takes the database connection information as arguments. Then when the programmer wants to perform a query, the arguments call the executeQuery method with a structured query language (SQL) string. This

Figure 12.5 Editable table.

Editable File Table Example

Name	Last Modi...	Size	Directory
docs	18-Jul-96	1 kb	☑
eg	18-Jul-96	1 kb	☑
INSTALL.BA	11-Jul-96	7 kb	☐
INSTALL....	28-Jun-96	2 kb	☐
Lib	18-Jul-96	1 kb	☑
LICENSE...	16-Apr-96	24 kb	☐
MANIFES...	28-Jun-96	10 kb	☐
ntt	18-Jul-96	1 kb	☑
perl.exe	15-Jul-96	63 kb	☐
Perl100.dll	15-Jul-96	510 kb	☐
PL2BAT....	16-Apr-96	1 kb	☐
README....	10-May-96	9 kb	☐
release.txt	15-Jul-96	7 kb	☐
Samples	18-Jul-96	1 kb	☑
STATUS....	27-Jun-96	1 kb	☐

method caches information from the query, including the column names, column types, and actual data returned. Once these values are cached, the TableModel methods are easy to write. They return a value from a Vector. Because the data from a relational database is represented by rows of values and each row is represented by a list of columns, we create a Vector representing each column in the row. We store each row Vector in another Vector. In this way we capture all the values of the relational database table in a Vector that contains Vectors to model the tabular format.

Please note that this is not necessarily the most efficient mechanism for caching database data. But it is easy to understand and serves well for educational purposes in this book.

```
import java.util.*;
import java.sql.*;
import com.sun.java.swing.table.*;
import com.sun.java.swing.event.*;

public class JDBCTableModel extends AbstractTableModel
{
    Connection connection;
    Statement statement;
    ResultSet resultSet;
    Vector names;
    Vector types;
    Vector data;
    ResultSetMetaData metaData;

    public JDBCTableModel(String url, String driverName,
                          String user, String passwd)
    {
```

```
        data = new Vector();
        types = new Vector();
        names = new Vector();

        try
        {
            //load the driver
            Class.forName(driverName);

            connection =
                    DriverManager.getConnection(url, user, passwd);

            statement = connection.createStatement();
        }
        catch (Exception exp)
        {
            System.out.println("Error connecting: "+exp);
        }
    }

    public void executeQuery(String query)
    {
        int i,max;
        Vector rowData;
        int curType;

        try
        {
            data = new Vector();
            types = new Vector();
            names = new Vector();

            resultSet = statement.executeQuery(query);

            metaData = resultSet.getMetaData();

            max =  metaData.getColumnCount();

            //get the column names
            for(i=0;i<max;i++)
            {
                //adjust for meta data index start at 1
                names.addElement(metaData.getColumnLabel(i+1));
            }
```

```
//get the column types
for(i=0;i<max;i++)
{
    try
    {
        curType = metaData.getColumnType(i+1);
    }
    catch (SQLException e)
    {
        //make it a string if we can't get it
        curType = -1;
    }

    switch(curType)
    {
        case Types.CHAR:
        case Types.VARCHAR:
        case Types.LONGVARCHAR:
            types.addElement(String.class);

        case Types.BIT:
            types.addElement(Boolean.class);

        case Types.TINYINT:
        case Types.SMALLINT:
        case Types.INTEGER:
            types.addElement(Integer.class);

        case Types.BIGINT:
            types.addElement(Long.class);

        case Types.FLOAT:
        case Types.DOUBLE:
            types.addElement(Double.class);

        case Types.DATE:
            types.addElement(java.sql.Date.class);

        default:
            types.addElement(Object.class);
    }
}

//load the data
while (resultSet.next())
```

```
            {
                rowData = new Vector();

                for (i=0;i<max;i++)
                {
                    rowData.addElement(resultSet.getObject(i+1));
                }

                data.addElement(rowData);
            }

            fireTableChanged(null);
        }
        catch (Exception exp)
        {
            System.out.println("Error performing query: "+exp);
            exp.printStackTrace();
        }
    }

    public void close() throws SQLException
    {
        resultSet.close();
        statement.close();
        connection.close();
    }

    protected void finalize() throws Throwable
    {
        close();
        super.finalize();
    }

    public String getColumnName(int col)
    {
        String retVal;

        retVal = (String) names.elementAt(col);

        if(retVal == null) retVal = "";

        return retVal;
    }

    public Class getColumnClass(int col)
```

```
    {
        Class retVal;

        retVal = (Class) types.elementAt(col);

        if(retVal == null) retVal = Object.class;

        return retVal;
    }

    public boolean isCellEditable(int row, int col)
    {
        return false;
    }

    public int getColumnCount()
    {
        return names.size();
    }

    public int getRowCount()
    {
        return data.size();
    }

    public Object getValueAt(int row, int col)
    {
        Vector rowData = (Vector)data.elementAt(row);

        return rowData.elementAt(col);
    }

    public void setValueAt(Object value, int row, int col)
    {
        //This model is not editable.
    }
}
```

Our text program for the JDBCTableModel displays a table and a text field. When the user enters data in the text field and presses Return, the table model is told to execute the text in the field as a query. We used an ActionListener to implement this event handling. For our example, we used a Microsoft Access database; it's quite common, and most developers can use it. This program can be altered to work with other databases such as Oracle by changing the highlighted code in the constructor for our custom panel. When the table model is created, pass in different values to connect to a different database.

```
import com.sun.java.swing.*;

import java.awt.event.*;
import java.awt.*;
import java.io.*;
import java.util.*;

public class JDBCTable extends JPanel
implements ActionListener
{
    JTextField queryField;
    JDBCTableModel model;

    public JDBCTable()
    {
        JTable table;
        File root;
        Font f;
        JPanel tmpPanel;

        setLayout(new BorderLayout());

        model = new JDBCTableModel("jdbc:odbc:northwind"
                                   ,"sun.jdbc.odbc.JdbcOdbcDriver"
                                   ,""
                                   ,"");

        table = new JTable();
        table.setModel(model);
        table.createDefaultColumnsFromModel();

        add(JTable.createScrollPaneForTable(table)
            ,"Center");

        tmpPanel = new JPanel();
        tmpPanel.add(new JLabel("Query: "));

        queryField = new JTextField("Enter your query here",30);
        queryField.addActionListener(this);
        queryField.selectAll();
```

```
        tmpPanel.add(queryField);

        add(tmpPanel,"South");
    }

    public void actionPerformed(ActionEvent evt)
    {
        String query = queryField.getText();

        model.executeQuery(query);
        queryField.selectAll();
    }

    public Dimension getPreferredSize()
    {
        return new Dimension(450, 350);
    }

    public static void main(String s[])
    {
        JFrame frame = new JFrame("JDBC Table Example");
        JDBCTable panel = new JDBCTable();

        frame.setDefaultCloseOperation(JFrame.DO_NOTHING_ON_CLOSE);
        frame.setForeground(Color.black);
        frame.setBackground(Color.lightGray);
        frame.getContentPane().add(panel,"Center");

        frame.setSize(panel.getPreferredSize());
        frame.setVisible(true);
        frame.addWindowListener(new WindowCloser());
    }
}
```

The file for this example includes the WindowCloser class. A WindowCloser is used to handle the close box on the example window.

```
class WindowCloser extends WindowAdapter
{
    public void windowClosing(WindowEvent e)
    {
        Window win = e.getWindow();
        win.setVisible(false);
        System.exit(0);
    }
}
```

Figure 12.6 Table with data from a database.

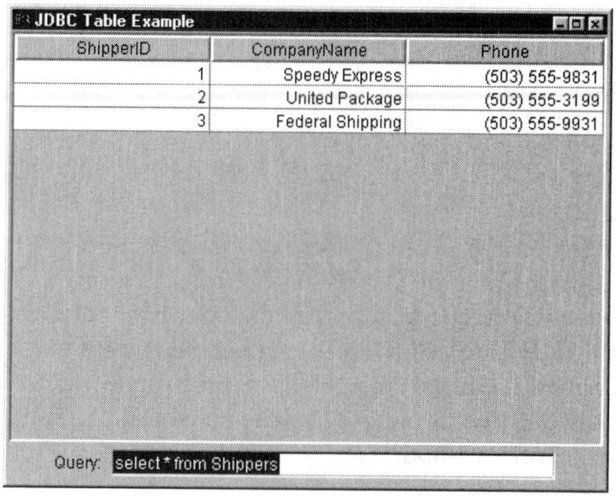

ShipperID	CompanyName	Phone
1	Speedy Express	(503) 555-9831
2	United Package	(503) 555-3199
3	Federal Shipping	(503) 555-9931

JDBC Table Example

Query: select * from Shippers

A running version of this program is pictured in Figure 12.6.

Table Framework

Although tables are relatively easy to use, they have a slightly complex framework underneath the covers. This framework is required to manage the reordering of columns, display various types of data, and support editing of various data types. The classes in the Swing table framework include renderers, editors, a TableHeader component, and TableColumn objects to represent the columns.

Renderers

Tables use an object that implements the TableCellRenderer interface to draw the contents of each cell. This renderer is similar to the tree renderer that we discussed in Chapter 11. The big exception is that the default table-cell renderer uses different components based on the type of data displayed. In fact, rather than using a single renderer, the table keeps a set of renderers. The choice of renderer is based on the class of the data for a particular column. This class is retrieved from the table model using the method getColumnClass. Although you can write your own renderers for a table, it's probably easier to use the existing ones whenever possible. If you do choose to write a renderer, you can register it with the table using the following method:

```
public void setDefaultRenderer(Class columnClass,
                               TableCellRenderer renderer);
```

Keep in mind that your custom renderer must support row and column selections, unless you place it in a table that uses cell selections. This means that your renderer should either render all of the possible data types in your model or create an appearance similar to the default renderer that's used for the types you don't support.

You must also reset the table's row height using the setRowHeight method because this is not changed automatically.

```
public void setRowHeight(int newHeight);
```

Editors

Tables use editor objects to manage the editing process. These editors must implement the TableCellEditor interface that extends the CellEditor interface. Creating a table editor is similar to creating a tree editor, except that the table may have several editors. As with renderers, the editor used for a cell is based on the type of data in that cell. Although you can write your own editors for a table, it's probably easier to use the existing ones whenever possible. If you do choose to write an editor, you can register it with the table using the following method:

```
public void setDefaultEditor(Class columnClass,
                             TableCellEditor editor);
```

TableHeader

Tables use a component called a JTableHeader to draw the column names and to manage the reordering process. The table header provides methods for controlling whether the table allows reordering or resizing of columns by the user. To access the table header, use the JTable method, then use the methods listed in Table 12.7 to alter the header's characteristics.

```
public JTableHeader getTableHeader();
```

Table 12.7 JTableHeader Methods

Method	Function
public void setReorderingAllowed(boolean b)	Used to tell the header if reordering is allowed. Pass in true to turn reordering on.
public void setResizingAllowed(boolean b)	Used to tell the header if column resizing is allowed. Pass in true to turn resizing on.
public void setUpdateTableInRealTime (boolean flag)	Tells the header if the table is updated throughout the drag processing. Passing in false tells the header to update the table once, after the user releases the reordered column header.

Table 12.8 TableColumn Methods

Method	Function
Public void setMaxWidth (Int newMaxWidth)	Sets the maximum width for the column.
Public void setMinWidth (Int newMinWidth)	Sets the minimum width for the column.
Public void setResizable(Boolean flag)	Sets whether the column is resizable.
Public void setCellEditor (TableCellEditor anEditor)	Sets the editor for this column.
Public void setCellRenderer (TableCellRenderer aRenderer)	Sets the renderer for this column.

TableColumns

Tables use an object called a TableColumn to manage the data and appearance for each column. As a programmer, you probably interact with table columns only if you want to assign a minimum or maximum width to a particular column. You can also assign specific renderers and editors to the column instead of using the defaults assigned to the table itself. You may want to create a renderer that displays negative numbers in red. That way, when you apply this renderer to a table column, all negative numbers in that column can be drawn in red instead of black. The table column objects for a table are managed by a TableColumnModel. This model provides methods to retrieve the columns and add, move, and remove them. To get to a TableColumn object use the following JTable method to get the column model:

```
public TableColumnModel getColumnModel();
```

Then use the TableColumnModel method getColumn to retrieve a specific column object or use the method getColumns to retrieve a collection of all columns in the model.

```
public TableColumn getColumn(int columnIndex);
public Enumeration getColumns();
```

Finally, use the methods listed in Table 12.8 to interact with the column.

Style Guidelines

Tables are useful mechanisms for displaying information. A table allows users to view large amounts of information all at once and quickly. Fortunately, the JTable class is easy to use. Use a table if users need to compare two or more pieces of data and if you won't know ahead of time which data they need. In general, you only need to create a default table, create a custom table model, and add your model to the table. Because the AbstractTableModel class implements the majority of the table model infrastructure, you can focus on mapping your data into a tabular format.

Choose labels for columns that accurately reflect the data. Use row labels if rows contain different data. Left justify column and row labels to make reading easier for the user. Don't use a colon after the labels; it's distracting.

Be careful when extending the table framework with custom renderers and editors. The defaults are set up to work well, and they should be used whenever possible. Unlike a list, where the renderer can work independently of other rows, a table-cell renderer must account for the other cells in its row and column. For example, if you highlight the selection in a particular cell with black and the default is blue, this draws attention to that one cell, even if the entire row is selected.

Tabbed and Split Panes

13

Building user interfaces is a hard business. Users want access to more and more data, but monitors and display technologies are limited by cost. User-interface designers have been working on these limitations for some time and are still trying to figure out the best ways to present information. Some general techniques are available, and Swing attempts to provide as many of these techniques as possible. The tree and table components from previous chapters are examples of components designed to display information. The two components in this chapter are designed to make more information available by temporarily hiding information when possible.

The tabbed pane has become a standard in many applications. This component displays a set of named tabs, much like file folders, that the user can select. Selecting a tab displays a different component in the main area of the pane. A split pane displays two components and a divider. The user can move the divider to display different amounts of the two main components. These split panes are common in interfaces that display two types of information simultaneously. One good example of split panes is a spreadsheet that displays the data/table at the top and the available formulas at the bottom. Some spreadsheet programs also use a tabbed pane to separate the available spreadsheets.

JTabbedPane

The Swing engineers have provided an easy-to-use tabbed pane called JTabbedPane. This subclass of JComponent displays a set of tabs, depending on the current look and feel, and a currently selected component. Each tab can have an icon and/or a string description. The tabbed pane even manages separate tool tips for the various tabs.

To create a JTabbedPane, use the default constructor:

```
public JTabbedPane();
```

This creates a new tabbed pane with no tabs.

Next you can add tabs to the pane using several addTab methods, as shown in Table 13.1. Each method takes information about the tab and a component to display when that tab is selected.

Table 13.1 JTabbedPane's addTab Methods

Method	Function
Public void addTab(String title, Component component)	Adds a tab with the specified title and component.
Public void addTab(String title, Icon icon,Component component)	Adds a tab with the specified title, icon, and component.
Public void addTab(String title,Icon icon, Component component,String tip)	Adds a tab with the specified title, icon, component, and tool tip.
Public void insertTab(String title,Icon icon, Component component,String tip,Int index)	Inserts a tab with the specified title, icon, component, and tool tip at the specified index.

To specify a particular tab to alter, you use its index. These indices start at 0 for the left-most tab and increase to the right. The total number of tabs is obtained by using the following method:

```
public int getTabCount();
```

To get the index of a tab, use the methods:

```
public int indexOfTab(String title);
public int indexOfComponent(Component component);
```

The first method, indexOfTab, uses the tab's title to find it. The second method, indexOfComponent, uses the tab's component to find it. You can also get the selected tab by its index or component, as shown here:

```
public int getSelectedIndex();
public Component getSelectedComponent();
```

Similar methods are provided to set the selected tab:

```
public void setSelectedIndex(int index);
public void setSelectedComponent(Component c);
```

The following three examples demonstrate how you can create tabs with text, icons, or both. The first example creates a tabbed pane with three tabs. Each tab has a string title. The tabbed pane is pictured in Figure 13.1.

```
import java.applet.*;
import java.util.*;
import java.awt.*;
import java.awt.event.*;
import com.sun.java.swing.*;
```

```
import com.sun.java.swing.border.*;

public class TextTabs extends JPanel
{
    public TextTabs()
    {
        JTabbedPane pane;
        JPanel panel;

        setBackground(Color.lightGray);
        setLayout(new BorderLayout());

        pane = new JTabbedPane();

        panel = new JPanel();
        panel.add(new Label("First"));
        pane.addTab("First",panel);

        panel = new JPanel();
        panel.add(new Label("Second"));
        pane.addTab("Second",panel);

        panel = new JPanel();
        panel.add(new Label("Third"));
        pane.addTab("Third",panel);

        pane.setSelectedIndex(0);
        add(pane,"Center");
    }

    public Dimension getPreferredSize()
    {
        return new Dimension(200, 200);
    }

    public static void main(String s[])
    {
        JFrame frame = new JFrame("Text Tabs Example");
        TextTabs panel = new TextTabs();

        frame.setForeground(Color.black);
        frame.setBackground(Color.lightGray);
        frame.addWindowListener(new WindowCloser());
        frame.getContentPane().add(panel,"Center");
```

Figure 13.1 Text Tabs.

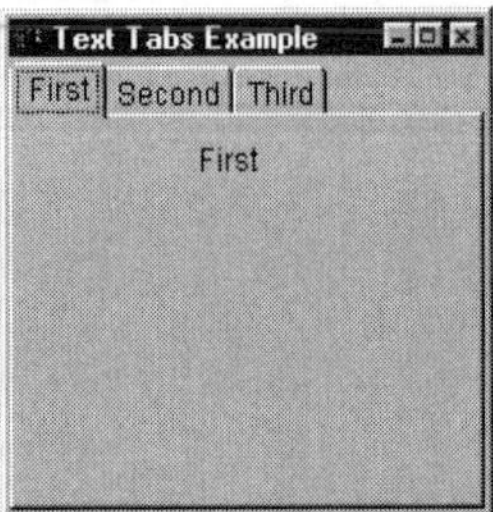


```
        frame.setSize(panel.getPreferredSize());
        frame.show();
    }
}

class WindowCloser extends WindowAdapter
{
    public void windowClosing(WindowEvent e)
    {
        Window win = e.getWindow();
        win.setVisible(false);
        win.dispose();
        System.exit(0);
    }
}
```

Figure 13.1 shows a tabbed pane that contains text tabs.

Our second example creates three tabs, each with an icon and no string associated with it. This example is pictured in Figure 13.2.

```
import java.applet.*;
import java.util.*;
import java.awt.*;
import java.awt.event.*;
import com.sun.java.swing.*;
import com.sun.java.swing.border.*;

public class IconTabs extends JPanel
{
    public IconTabs()
    {
        JTabbedPane pane;
        JPanel panel;
```

```
        ImageIcon icon;

        setBackground(Color.lightGray);
        setLayout(new BorderLayout());

        pane = new JTabbedPane();

        icon = new ImageIcon("images/shapes.gif");
        panel = new JPanel();
        panel.add(new Label("First"));
        pane.addTab(null,icon,panel);

        icon = new ImageIcon("images/check.gif");
        panel = new JPanel();
        panel.add(new Label("Second"));
        pane.addTab(null,icon,panel);

        icon = new ImageIcon("images/ex.gif");
        panel = new JPanel();
        panel.add(new Label("Third"));
        pane.addTab(null,icon,panel);

        pane.setSelectedIndex(0);
        add(pane,"Center");
    }

    public Dimension getPreferredSize()
    {
        return new Dimension(200, 200);
    }

    public static void main(String s[])
    {
        JFrame frame = new JFrame("Icon Tabs Example");
        IconTabs panel = new IconTabs();

        frame.setForeground(Color.black);
        frame.setBackground(Color.lightGray);
        frame.addWindowListener(new WindowCloser());
        frame.getContentPane().add(panel,"Center");

        frame.setSize(panel.getPreferredSize());
        frame.show();
    }
```

```
}

class WindowCloser extends WindowAdapter
{
    public void windowClosing(WindowEvent e)
    {
        Window win = e.getWindow();
        win.setVisible(false);
        win.dispose();
        System.exit(0);
    }
}
```

Figure 13.2 shows a tabbed pane that contains tabs displaying icons.

Our final example for creating a tabbed pane creates three tabs. Each tab contains an icon and a string title and has a tool tip assigned to it. This example is pictured in Figure 13.3.

```
import java.applet.*;
import java.util.*;
import java.awt.*;
import java.awt.event.*;
import com.sun.java.swing.*;
import com.sun.java.swing.border.*;

public class Tabs extends JPanel
{
    public Tabs()
    {
        JTabbedPane pane;
        JPanel panel;
        ImageIcon icon;

        setBackground(Color.lightGray);
```

Figure 13.2 Icon Tabs.

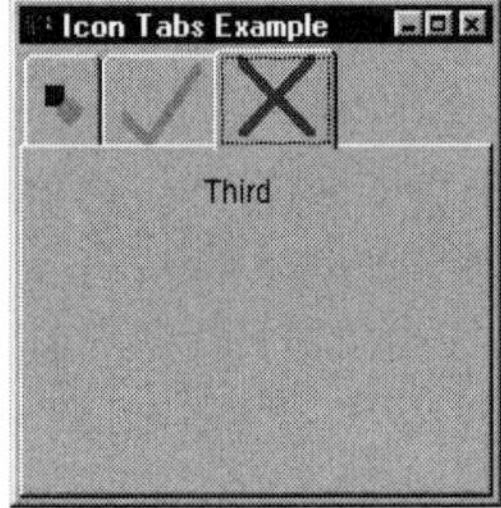

```
        setLayout(new BorderLayout());

        pane = new JTabbedPane();

        icon = new ImageIcon("images/shapes.gif");
        panel = new JPanel();
        panel.add(new Label("First"));
        pane.addTab("First",icon,panel,"Shapes");

        icon = new ImageIcon("images/check.gif");
        panel = new JPanel();
        panel.add(new Label("Second"));
        pane.addTab("Second",icon,panel,"Check");

        icon = new ImageIcon("images/ex.gif");
        panel = new JPanel();
        panel.add(new Label("Third"));
        pane.addTab("Third",icon,panel,"Ex");

        pane.setSelectedIndex(0);
        add(pane,"Center");
    }

    public Dimension getPreferredSize()
    {
        return new Dimension(300, 200);
    }

    public static void main(String s[])
    {
        JFrame frame = new JFrame("Tabs Example");
        Tabs panel = new Tabs();

        frame.setForeground(Color.black);
        frame.setBackground(Color.lightGray);
        frame.addWindowListener(new WindowCloser());
        frame.getContentPane().add(panel,"Center");

        frame.setSize(panel.getPreferredSize());
        frame.show();
    }
}

class WindowCloser extends WindowAdapter
```

```
{
    public void windowClosing(WindowEvent e)
    {
        Window win = e.getWindow();
        win.setVisible(false);
        win.dispose();
        System.exit(0);
    }
}
```

Figure 13.3 shows a tabbed pane that uses tool tips to show the tab's function.

When you run the example programs from the CD-ROM you may notice that when the window is too narrow to display the tabs, the tabs wrap around to form multiple rows. A narrow display is handled by the tabbed pane and is dependent on your look and feel. This wrapping behavior is common for most look-and-feel implementations. In general, the JTabbedPane provides some mechanism for dealing with a narrow display area.

Tab attributes are altered once the tab is added to the tabbed pane. The methods for altering a tab's attributes are setTitleAt, which sets the title of a tab at a certain index position, setIconAt, which sets the icon for a tab at a certain indexed position, and setComponentAt, which adds a component to a tab at an indexed position. The methods look like this:

```
public void setTitleAt(int index,
                       String title);
public void setIconAt(int index,
                      Icon icon);
public void setComponentAt(int index,
                           Component component);
```

The same set of methods is included to retrieve the values for a tab. The method getTitleAt returns the title of a tab at a certain index position, getIconAt returns the icon at a certain tab position, and getComponentAt returns a component associated with a tab at an index position. The methods are as follows:

Figure 13.3 JTabbedPane with tool tips.

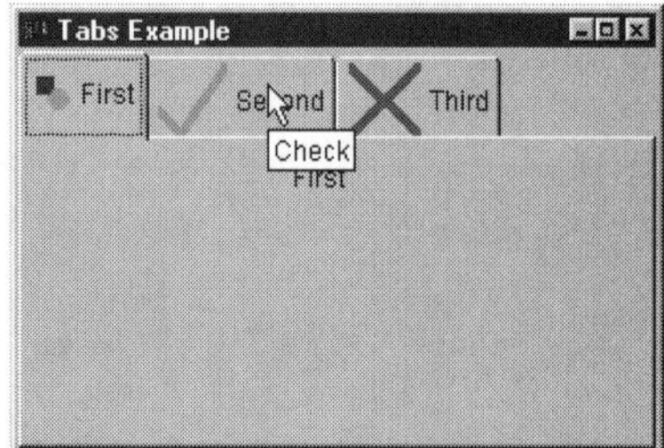

```
public String getTitleAt(int index);
public Icon getIconAt(int index);
public Component getComponentAt(int index);
```

These methods are useful when you want to convert the current selection into an icon or text.

JTabbedPane Change Listener

JTabbedPane uses an object of the type SingleSelectionModel as its model. This model object keeps track of a single, selected item, in this case the current tab. You can listen for changes to the current tab using the ChangeListener interface. Simply implement ChangeListener and add yourself to the tabbed pane's list of listeners. When the current tab changes you are sent the following message:

```
public void stateChanged(ChangeEvent e);
```

The next example creates a tabbed pane with three tabs and prints the new selection whenever the user selects a tab. This example is pictured in Figure 13.4.

```
import java.applet.*;
import java.util.*;
import java.awt.*;
import java.awt.event.*;
import com.sun.java.swing.*;
import com.sun.java.swing.event.*;
import com.sun.java.swing.border.*;

public class TabChanges extends JPanel
implements ChangeListener
{
    JTabbedPane pane;

    public TabChanges()
    {
        JPanel panel;

        setBackground(Color.lightGray);
        setLayout(new BorderLayout());

        pane = new JTabbedPane();

        panel = new JPanel();
        panel.add(new Label("First"));
        pane.addTab("First",panel);

        panel = new JPanel();
```

```
        panel.add(new Label("Second"));
        pane.addTab("Second",panel);

        panel = new JPanel();
        panel.add(new Label("Third"));
        pane.addTab("Third",panel);

        pane.setSelectedIndex(0);

        pane.addChangeListener(this);
        add(pane,"Center");
    }

    public Dimension getPreferredSize()
    {
        return new Dimension(200, 200);
    }

    public void stateChanged(ChangeEvent e)
    {
        int curSelIndex = pane.getSelectedIndex();
        String curPaneTitle = pane.getTitleAt(curSelIndex);

        System.out.println("Selected: "+curPaneTitle);
    }

    public static void main(String s[])
    {
        JFrame frame = new JFrame("Tab Changes Example");
        TabChanges panel = new TabChanges();

        frame.setForeground(Color.black);
        frame.setBackground(Color.lightGray);
        frame.addWindowListener(new WindowCloser());
        frame.getContentPane().add(panel,"Center");

        frame.setSize(panel.getPreferredSize());
        frame.show();
    }
}

class WindowCloser extends WindowAdapter
{
```

Figure 13.4 Tab change listener.

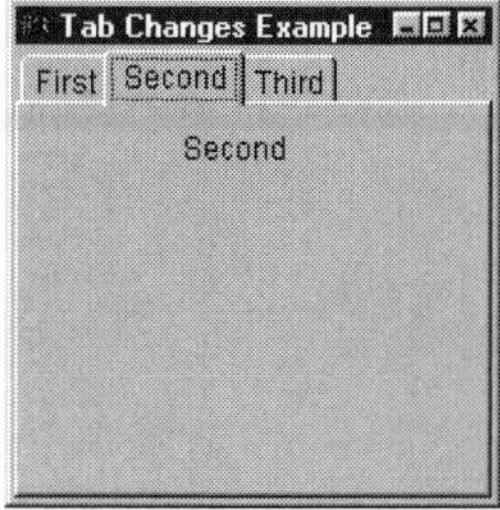


```
        public void windowClosing(WindowEvent e)
        {
            Window win = e.getWindow();
            win.setVisible(false);
            win.dispose();
            System.exit(0);
        }
}
```

Figure 13.4 shows a tabbed pane using a change listener to respond to events.

JSplitPane

JSplitPane defines a container that holds two components. These components are divided by a movable control. When the control is moved, one component is enlarged and the other made smaller. JSplitPanes are created with one of two orientations. This orientation determines the direction of the divider or split. A horizontal split draws the divider from top to bottom, placing the two components on the left and right. A vertical split draws the divider from left to right, placing the components on the top and bottom. Figures 13.5 and 13.6 show these two orientations.

Depending on your preference, the split pane can update its components continuously, as the divider moves, or after the divider stops. If the components are resized continuously, the pane is said to be using *continuous layout.* For simple components this is often more visually appealing. For components that take a while to draw, however, *noncontinuous layout* may perform better. When set to noncontinuous, the split pane draws a line to indicate the new location during dragging. When the user releases the mouse, the divider is updated, and the components resized. The number of resize calculations is reduced to one.

There are several constructors for creating a JSplitPane. These are listed in Table 13.2.

Figure 13.5 Horizontal orientation.

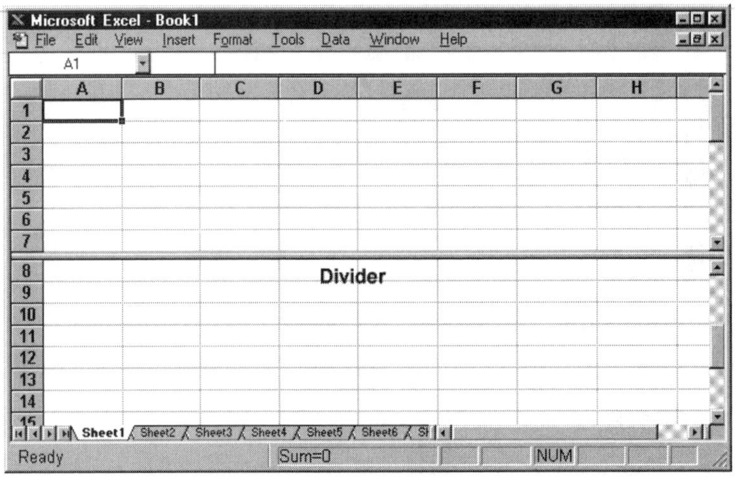

The orientations for a split pane are defined as class variables of JSplitPane:

```
HORIZONTAL_SPLIT
VERTICAL_SPLIT
```

To turn continuous layout on or off, after the split pane is constructed, use the following method:

```
public void setContinuousLayout(boolean tf);
```

Figure 13.6 Vertical orientation.

Table 13.2 JSplitPane Constructors

Constructor	Function
Public JsplitPane()	Creates a new split pane, vertically divided.
Public JsplitPane(int newOrientation)	Creates a new split pane with the specified orientation. Continuous layout is turned off.
Public JsplitPane(int newOrientation, Boolean newContinuousLayout)	Creates a split pane with the specified orientation and with continuous layout turned on or off.
Public JsplitPane(int newOrientation, Component newLeftComponent, Component newRightComponent)	Creates a split pane with the specified orientation and components. These are the top and bottom components for a horizontal divided pane. Continuous layout is turned on.
Public JsplitPane(int newOrientation, Boolean newContinuousLayout, Component newLeftComponent, Component newRightComponent)	Creates a split pane with the specified orientation and components. These are the top and bottom components for a horizontal divided pane. Turns continuous layout on or off based on the Boolean argument.

The following example creates a vertically split JSplitPane with two panels as its contents. These panels are labeled and have a background color to distinguish them.

> **TIP**
>
> The use of color in this example is helpful for illustrating this topic. Color can be an effective tool for drawing attention. In your applications you should be careful how you use color as it can also be distracting if not well planned. Review the style guidelines at the end of this chapter for more information on color use with tabbed panes.

The running version of this example is pictured in Figure 13.7. Continuous layout is turned off for this example.

```
import java.applet.*;
import java.util.*;
import java.awt.*;
import java.awt.event.*;
import com.sun.java.swing.*;
import com.sun.java.swing.border.*;

public class VSplit extends JPanel
```

```
{
    public VSplit()
    {
        JSplitPane pane;
        JPanel top,bottom;
        JLabel label;

        setBackground(Color.lightGray);
        setLayout(new BorderLayout());

        top = new JPanel();
        top.setOpaque(true);
        top.setBackground(Color.red);
        top.setLayout(new BorderLayout());
        label = new JLabel("Top",JLabel.CENTER);
        label.setVerticalAlignment(JLabel.CENTER);
        label.setForeground(Color.white);
        top.add(label,"Center");

        bottom = new JPanel();
        bottom.setOpaque(true);
        bottom.setBackground(Color.blue);
        bottom.setLayout(new BorderLayout());
        label = new JLabel("Bottom",JLabel.CENTER);
        label.setVerticalAlignment(JLabel.CENTER);
        label.setForeground(Color.white);
        bottom.add(label,"Center");


        pane = new JSplitPane(JSplitPane.VERTICAL_SPLIT
                                ,top,bottom);

        pane.setContinuousLayout(false);
        add(pane,"Center");
    }

    public Dimension getPreferredSize()
    {
        return new Dimension(200, 200);
    }

    public static void main(String s[])
    {
        JFrame frame = new JFrame("Vertical Split Example");
```

```
        VSplit panel = new VSplit();

        frame.setForeground(Color.black);
        frame.setBackground(Color.lightGray);
        frame.addWindowListener(new WindowCloser());
        frame.getContentPane().add(panel,"Center");

        frame.setSize(panel.getPreferredSize());
        frame.show();
    }
}

class WindowCloser extends WindowAdapter
{
    public void windowClosing(WindowEvent e)
    {
        Window win = e.getWindow();
        win.setVisible(false);
        win.dispose();
        System.exit(0);
    }
}
```

Figure 13.7 shows a vertical split pane.

The next example is similar to Figure 13.7, except that continuous layout is turned on and the divider is set to horizontal. This example is pictured in Figure 13.8.

```
import java.applet.*;
import java.util.*;
import java.awt.*;
import java.awt.event.*;
import com.sun.java.swing.*;
import com.sun.java.swing.border.*;
```

Figure 13.7 Vertically split JSplitPane.

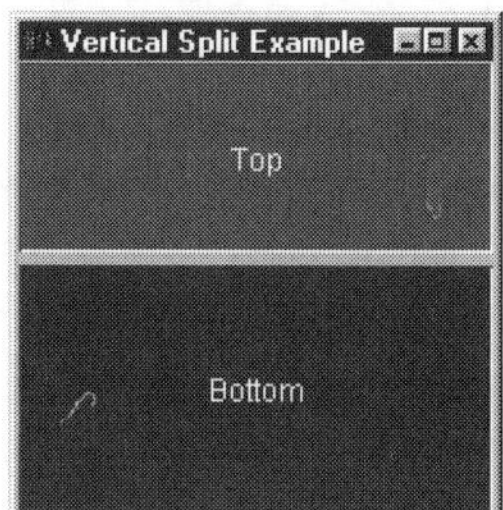

```
public class HSplit extends JPanel
{
    public HSplit()
    {
        JSplitPane pane;
        JPanel left,right;
        JLabel label;

        setBackground(Color.lightGray);
        setLayout(new BorderLayout());

        left = new JPanel();
        left.setOpaque(true);
        left.setBackground(Color.red);
        left.setLayout(new BorderLayout());
        label = new JLabel("Left",JLabel.CENTER);
        label.setForeground(Color.white);
        left.add(label,"Center");

        right = new JPanel();
        right.setOpaque(true);
        right.setBackground(Color.blue);
        right.setLayout(new BorderLayout());
        label = new JLabel("Right",JLabel.CENTER);
        label.setForeground(Color.white);
        right.add(label,"Center");


        pane = new JSplitPane(JSplitPane.HORIZONTAL_SPLIT
                              ,left,right);

        pane.setContinuousLayout(true);
        add(pane,"Center");
    }

    public Dimension getPreferredSize()
    {
        return new Dimension(200, 200);
    }

    public static void main(String s[])
    {
        JFrame frame = new JFrame("Horizontal Split Example");
        HSplit panel = new HSplit();
```

```
            frame.setForeground(Color.black);
            frame.setBackground(Color.lightGray);
            frame.addWindowListener(new WindowCloser());
            frame.getContentPane().add(panel,"Center");

            frame.setSize(panel.getPreferredSize());
            frame.show();
        }
    }

    class WindowCloser extends WindowAdapter
    {
        public void windowClosing(WindowEvent e)
        {
            Window win = e.getWindow();
            win.setVisible(false);
            win.dispose();
            System.exit(0);
        }
    }
```

Figure 13.8 shows a horizontal split pane.

Once a pane is created there are several techniques that you can use to interact with it. First, you can control the components in the split pane. To manage these components you can use the methods shown in Table 13.3.

You can also set the divider location using the setDividerLocation method. There are two techniques to use this method for setting the divider location. The first technique takes an actual integer number of pixels to which it moves the divider. The second technique takes a percentage, and moves the divider to that percentage of the split panes' total size. The two techniques are shown here:

```
public void setDividerLocation(double proportionalLocation);
public void setDividerLocation(int location);
```

Figure 13.8 Horizontal split JSplitPane.

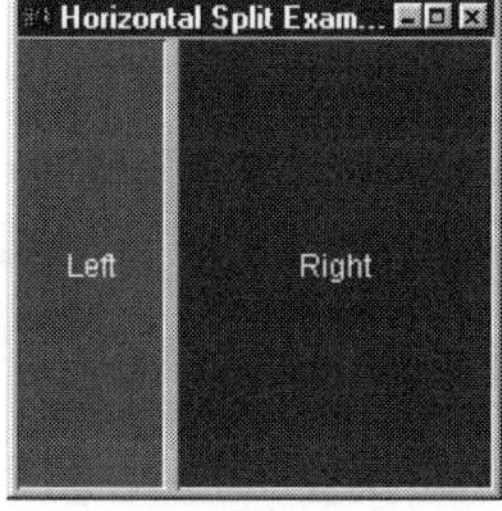

Table 13.3 JSplitPane Component Methods

Method	Function
public Component getLeftComponent()	Gets the component to the left or above the divider.
public void setLeftComponent (Component comp)	Sets the component to the left, or above the divider.
public Component getTopComponent()	Gets the component to the left or above the divider.
public void setTopComponent (Component comp)	Sets the component to the left or above the divider.
public Component getRightComponent()	Gets the component to the right or below the divider.
public void setRightComponent (Component comp)	Sets the component to the right or below the divider.
public Component getBottomComponent()	Gets the component to the right or below the divider.
public void setBottomComponent (Component comp)	Sets the component to the right or below the divider.
public void remove (Component component)	Removes the specified child component.
public void removeAll()	Removes all of the child components.

The actual handling of the divider position is up to the look and feel. If you want to have the split pane try to resize to the content's preferred size, use the following method:

```
public void resetToPreferredSizes();
```

You can also set the size of the divider bar. Use the setDividerSize method and pass in the number of pixels wide that you want the bar to be, as shown here:

```
public void setDividerSize(int newSize);
```

Keep in mind that a wide divider reduces the space available to your components. You may want a wide divider in cases where the components need a good visual break between them, like two images.

The following example, pictured in Figure 13.9, creates a JSplitPane with a wide divider. This split pane is used to divide two other split panes. Remember that a JSplitPane can split any two components, including containers, like panels, and even other split panes. Split panes within split panes are not a common user-interface technique, but we have seen them used effectively in applications such as project management where the user wants to see multiple, related data views, such as resource allocations, project milestones, and performance charts.

```
import java.applet.*;
import java.util.*;
import java.awt.*;
import java.awt.event.*;
import com.sun.java.swing.*;
import com.sun.java.swing.border.*;

public class TwoSplit extends JPanel
{
    public TwoSplit()
    {
        JSplitPane pane;
        JSplitPane topPane,bottomPane;
        JPanel left2,right2;
        JPanel left,right;
        JLabel label;

        setBackground(Color.lightGray);
        setLayout(new BorderLayout());

        left2 = new JPanel();
        left2.setOpaque(true);
        left2.setBackground(Color.cyan);
        left2.setLayout(new BorderLayout());
        label = new JLabel("left2",JLabel.CENTER);
        label.setVerticalAlignment(JLabel.CENTER);
        label.setForeground(Color.black);
        left2.add(label,"Center");

        right2 = new JPanel();
        right2.setOpaque(true);
        right2.setBackground(Color.magenta);
        right2.setLayout(new BorderLayout());
        label = new JLabel("right2",JLabel.CENTER);
        label.setVerticalAlignment(JLabel.CENTER);
        label.setForeground(Color.white);
        right2.add(label,"Center");

        left = new JPanel();
```

```
        left.setOpaque(true);
        left.setBackground(Color.yellow);
        left.setLayout(new BorderLayout());
        label = new JLabel("Left",JLabel.CENTER);
        label.setForeground(Color.black);
        left.add(label,"Center");

        right = new JPanel();
        right.setOpaque(true);
        right.setBackground(Color.black);
        right.setLayout(new BorderLayout());
        label = new JLabel("Right",JLabel.CENTER);
        label.setForeground(Color.white);
        right.add(label,"Center");

        topPane = new JSplitPane(JSplitPane.HORIZONTAL_SPLIT
                            ,left,right);
        topPane.setContinuousLayout(true);

        bottomPane = new JSplitPane(JSplitPane.HORIZONTAL_SPLIT
                            ,left2,right2);
        bottomPane.setContinuousLayout(true);


        pane = new JSplitPane(JSplitPane.VERTICAL_SPLIT
                            ,topPane,bottomPane);
        pane.setContinuousLayout(true);
        pane.setDividerSize(2*bottomPane.getDividerSize());

        add(pane,"Center");
    }

    public Dimension getPreferredSize()
    {
        return new Dimension(200, 200);
    }

    public static void main(String s[])
    {
        JFrame frame = new JFrame("Multiple Split Example");
        TwoSplit panel = new TwoSplit();

        frame.setForeground(Color.black);
        frame.setBackground(Color.lightGray);
```

```
        frame.addWindowListener(new WindowCloser());
        frame.getContentPane().add(panel,"Center");

        frame.setSize(panel.getPreferredSize());
        frame.show();
    }
}

class WindowCloser extends WindowAdapter
{
    public void windowClosing(WindowEvent e)
    {
        Window win = e.getWindow();
        win.setVisible(false);
        win.dispose();
        System.exit(0);
    }
}
```

Figure 13.9 shows multiple split panes.

One-Touch Expandable JSplitPane

Our final example for this chapter demonstrates an interesting feature of JSplitPane. This feature, called *one-touch expandable*, causes the divider to display two small buttons. The appearance of these buttons depends on the look and feel. When the user clicks one of these buttons, it moves the divider based on its current and last position. If the divider is in the middle of the pane, then the up arrow moves it to the top of the pane and the bottom arrow moves it to the bottom. If the divider has already been moved to an edge, the arrow moves it back to its position before it was touched.

You can alter or inspect this last location value programmatically using the following methods:

Figure 13.9 Wide divider and multiple split panes.

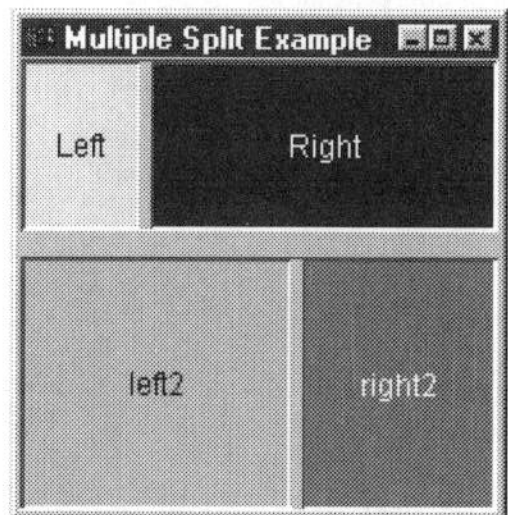

```
public void setLastDividerLocation(int newLastLocation);
public int getLastDividerLocation();
```

Our example creates a simple split pane with one-touch expandable turned on. Run this example from the CD-ROM to see what happens when the small arrows, pictured in Figure 13.10, are pressed.

```
import java.applet.*;
import java.util.*;
import java.awt.*;
import java.awt.event.*;
import com.sun.java.swing.*;
import com.sun.java.swing.border.*;

public class OneTouch extends JPanel
{
    public OneTouch()
    {
        JSplitPane pane;
        JPanel top,bottom;
        JLabel label;

        setBackground(Color.lightGray);
        setLayout(new BorderLayout());

        top = new JPanel();
        top.setOpaque(true);
        top.setBackground(Color.red);
        top.setLayout(new BorderLayout());
        label = new JLabel("Top",JLabel.CENTER);
        label.setVerticalAlignment(JLabel.CENTER);
        label.setForeground(Color.white);
        top.add(label,"Center");

        bottom = new JPanel();
        bottom.setOpaque(true);
        bottom.setBackground(Color.blue);
        bottom.setLayout(new BorderLayout());
        label = new JLabel("Bottom",JLabel.CENTER);
        label.setVerticalAlignment(JLabel.CENTER);
        label.setForeground(Color.white);
        bottom.add(label,"Center");

        pane = new JSplitPane(JSplitPane.VERTICAL_SPLIT
                             ,top,bottom);
```

```
        pane.setContinuousLayout(false);
        pane.setOneTouchExpandable(true);
        add(pane,"Center");
    }

    public Dimension getPreferredSize()
    {
        return new Dimension(200, 200);
    }

    public static void main(String s[])
    {
        JFrame frame = new JFrame("One Touch Split Example");
        OneTouch panel = new OneTouch();

        frame.setForeground(Color.black);
        frame.setBackground(Color.lightGray);
        frame.addWindowListener(new WindowCloser());
        frame.getContentPane().add(panel,"Center");

        frame.setSize(panel.getPreferredSize());
        frame.show();
    }
}

import java.awt.*;
import java.awt.event.*;
class WindowCloser extends WindowAdapter
{
    public void windowClosing(WindowEvent e)
    {
        Window win = e.getWindow();
        win.setVisible(false);
        win.dispose();
        System.exit(0);
    }
}
```

Figure 13.10 shows the use of the one-touch expandable split pane.

Style Guidelines

JTabbedPanes are a great way to provide easy access to multiple user-interface components. Use a tabbed pane only if the components in it are related.

Figure 13.10 One-touch expandable JSplitPane.

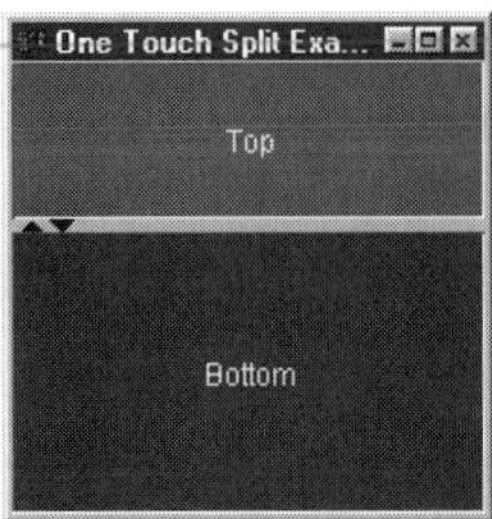

Otherwise, use separate windows to display the components. Another caution with tabbed panes is that you need to keep labels consistent. Having all text, all icons, or all text with icon labels is fine, but using some icons and some text is distracting. This is like having a tool bar with icons and text mixed. It isn't wrong, just distracting. For example, if the Save command is represented by a disk icon, and the Open command is the word "open" this confuses the user. In particular. The user may question the significance of the disk icon.

Along the same lines, color can also be distracting. When labeling tabs, use color carefully. A tab with a red icon draws the user's attention away from other icons. As with all user-interface design, the goal is not to add brighter colors to all tabs, but to use color carefully, in a subdued fashion.

JSplitPanes are useful if the components in them resize gracefully. They are not suggested for forms or other user interfaces that can't really resize. JSplitPanes do work well with JScrollPanes as their contents because the scroll pane takes care of size changes. Of course, this assumes that the contents of the scroll pane are appropriate, meaning that the contents of the scroll pane can be scrolled over, like a document or Web page, but probably not a form. Finally, when using split panes, set the divider to a reasonable visual size. A divider that's too thick can distract the user from the components that are displayed.

ROOT PANES, LAYERS, AND INTERNAL FRAMES

14

As we discussed in Chapter 2, and as we have used in all of our examples, JFrames and JApplets have a JRootPane as their main child component. A JRootPane manages the contents of the frame or applet by providing several functions that include a layout for internal components and an optional menu bar. All of the other children are added to a content pane inside this root. The motivation behind this separation is to support *internal frames* and *layers*. Internal frames are windows that live inside another window or applet. Their internal frames are organized into different layers to position them in front of each other. Figure 14.1 shows an example of this layered relationship. Layers are also used to position pop-up menus relative to the other components.

Figure 14.1 Layered internal frames.

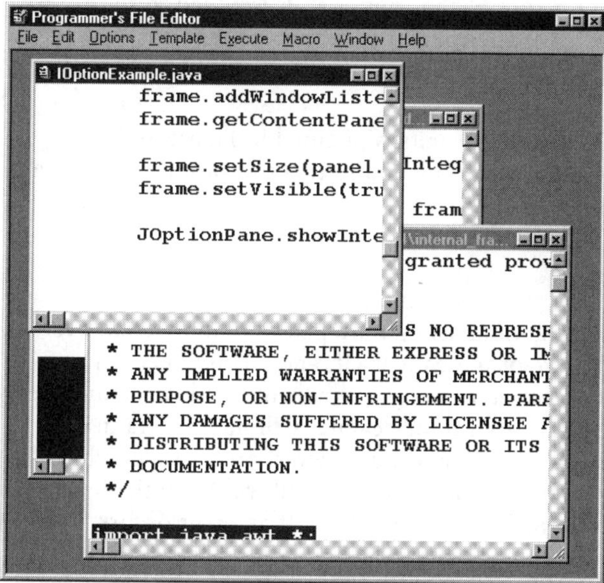

In this chapter, we discuss the concepts and implementations of the root pane and the layered pane. With these concepts we then discuss and build several examples using internal frames.

JRootPane

A JRootPane is a holder for several other components. These other components consist of the following:

GlassPane. This pane fills the root pane's bounds. It is added to the root pane first, to allow it to grab mouse events for the root pane. A root pane always has a glass pane. If you try to set the glass pane to null it always throws an exception. The glass pane is not visible by default; it's a hidden implementation component rather than a visual one. When the root pane needs to grab mouse events, it shows the transparent glass pane.

LayeredPane. This pane, as we discuss in the next section, manages the layers for the root pane. The layered pane is the parent for the rest of the root pane's other children. It cannot be set to null without throwing an exception.

ContentPane. This pane is a basic container that fills the layered pane's bounds at what is called the *frame content layer*. All of your components are added to this content pane, or to the layered pane, above the content layer.

MenuBar. The menu bar for a root pane is optional. It is added to the layered pane at the same layer as the content pane, except that it is placed at the top of the pane. This positioning is, of course, dependent on the current look and feel.

The relationship between these components is pictured in Figure 14.2.

JRootPane provides methods for accessing and setting the various root-pane components. These are listed in Table 14.1.

JLayeredPane

JLayeredPane is used to manage components that are placed in numbered, overlapping layers. Each layer is the size of the pane itself, and a component in a higher numbered layer *always* draws on top of a component in a lower numbered layer. This fact makes a layered pane useful for dealing with internal frames as well as pop-up menus. For example, you can create a word processor in which all of the documents appear as windows inside the main window. When the user selects a document, it is displayed in front of the others. If an error occurs, however, the alert dialog floats above all documents, including the selected one.

Within each layer a component has a position. This position defaults to the reverse order that items are added: The component added to the layer last appears

Figure 14.2 RootPane components.

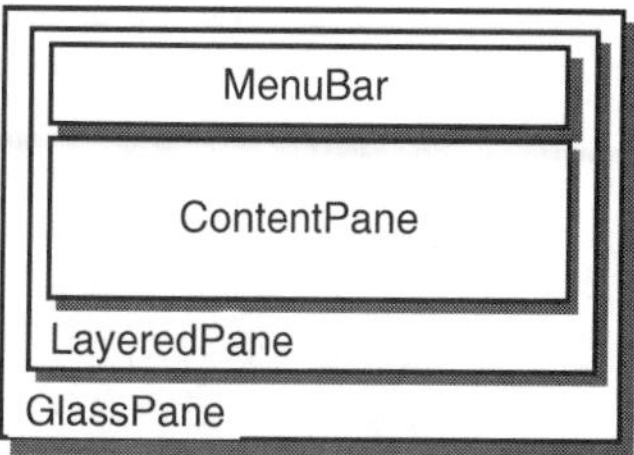

on top of the other components in that layer if they overlay. The top component is at position 0.

The example pictured in Figure 14.3 shows what happens if two components are added to the same layer and a third is added to another higher layer.

To add a component to a layered pane in a specific layer, use the standard add method, but provide an Integer object as a constraint. For example, the following code snippet adds a component to the 0 layer of a layered pane.

```
layers.add(component,new Integer(0));
```

There are actually several named layers. These are defined for use by the library, and you can use them within your own application. By using these named layers, your applications can work well with Swing and reduce the user confusion for having too many layers. The named layers are listed in Table 14.2 in the order that they appear from back to front. The drag layer is closest to the user.

Table 14.1 JRootPane Methods

Method	Function
Public Component getGlassPane()	Returns the glass pane.
Public void setGlassPane(Component glass)	Sets the glass pane.
Public JLayeredPane getLayeredPane()	Returns the layered pane.
Public void setLayeredPane (JLayeredPane layered)	Sets the layered pane.
Public Container getContentPane()	Returns the content pane.
Public void setContentPane (Container content)	Sets the content pane.
Public JMenuBar getMenuBar()	Returns the menu bar.
Public void setMenuBar(JMenuBar menu)	Sets the menu bar.

Figure 14.3 Layers and positions.

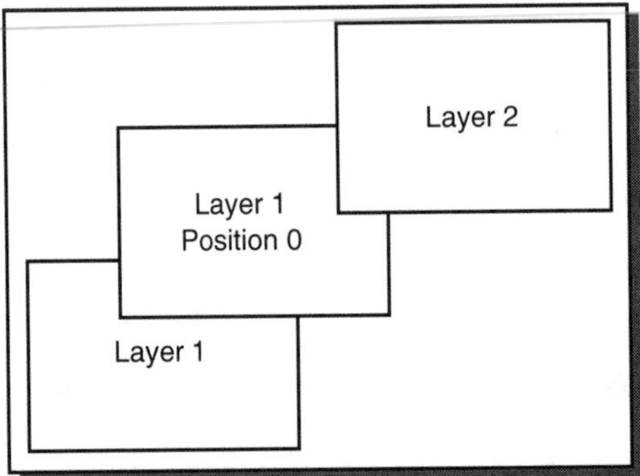

The numerical values for these layers are stored in JLayeredPane static variables with the name of the layer. JLayeredPane.DEFAULT_LAYER is an Integer object with value for the default layer.

JLayeredPane provides a number of methods for managing the layer and position of its components. These are listed in Table 14.3.

JInternalFrame

Internal frames are frames that live inside a container. Some windowing systems and applications use this style of frame to organize an application's windows into a single container. You may want to use internal frames for an applet that needs to organize its user interface into frames. Remember that JApplet uses a root pane, so it can have internal frames in its layered pane the same way that a JFrame can.

Table 14.2 Named Layers

Layer Name	Use
FRAME_CONTENT_LAYER	Used by the root pane for the content pane and menu bar.
DEFAULT_LAYER	The layer used if one is not assigned to the component when it is added.
PALETTE_LAYER	Contains inspector dialogs and tool boxes.
MODAL_LAYER	Used for modal dialogs like option panes.
POPUP_LAYER	Contains pop-up menus.
DRAG_LAYER	Used for dragging; items dragged appear above all other named layers.

Table 14.3 JLayeredPane Methods

Method	Function
public int getLayer(JComponent c)	Returns the layer for a component.
public void setLayer(Component c, int layer)	Sets the layer for a component. This method is used before the component is added to the layered pane. You can also set this value when adding the component with the add method.
public void setLayer(Component c, int layer, int position)	Sets the component layer and position. This method is used before it is added to the layered pane.
public void moveToFront(Component c)	Moves a component to the front-most position in its layer.
public void moveToBack(Component c)	Moves a component to the rear-most position in its layer.
public Component[] getComponentsInLayer(int layer)	Returns the components in the specified layer.

Figure 14.4 shows an example of a program that uses internal frames to organize the open documents.

One of the common features for a regular frame is the ability to miniaturize, or sometimes referred to as *iconify*, itself. To support this mechanism, Swing provides a set of Desktop classes that work with internal frames to manage their icons. These classes are usually provided by the look and feel, and they are listed in Table 14.4.

Programs that want to support the iconify operation and maintain look-and-feel independence should reset the layered pane to a JDesktopPane. This is particularly true for applications that organize their entire interface into internal frames. You can also use a desktop pane as a child of the content pane to create a tool bar at the top style interface, with children in internal frames below the tool bar.

Internal frames are much like JFrames. They have a root pane, with a content pane for their contents, and a menu bar. The methods to access the root pane's contents are the same for internal frames as frames. In particular, the getContentPane() method returns the content pane, as shown here:

```
public Container getContentPane();
```

The setMenuBar() method sets the menu bar, as shown here:

```
public void setMenuBar(JMenuBar m);
```

Internal frames are packed to the smallest size that fits their children's preferred size. To pack an internal frame, use the following method:

Figure 14.4 Internal frames.

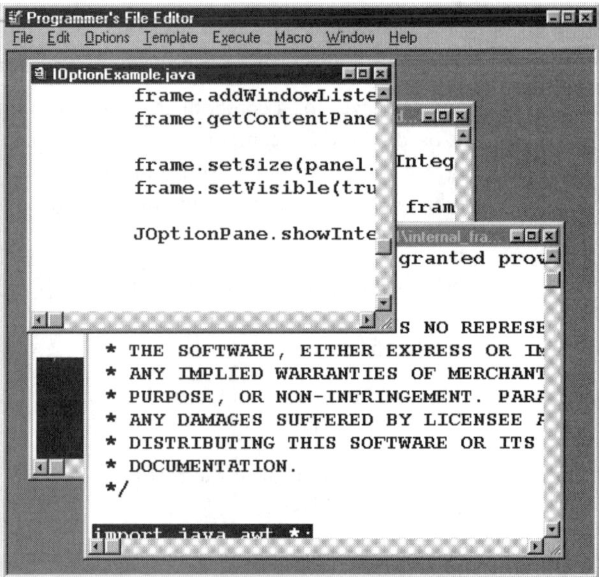


```
public void pack();
```

Normally you pack internal frames before displaying them to ensure that they can fit their contents.

An internal frame also has several attributes that determine the controls on the frame's title bar. The appearance of these controls is look-and-feel dependent, but you set them with the JInternalFrame methods shown in Table 14.5.

Because an application may have several internal frames in the same layer, Swing provides the concept of a selected internal frame. This frame may draw differently based on the look and feel, and it will be moved to the front of its layer. To control the selected frame, use the method:

```
public void setSelected(boolean selected) throws PropertyVetoException
```

Table 14.4 Desktop Classes

Class	Function
DesktopManager	A class that manages look-and-feel specific actions for the DesktopPane.
JDesktopPane	A layered-pane subclass that manages desktop icons for internal frames.
JDesktopIcon	A component that represents the iconified window.

You can also check if a frame is selected using the isSelected() method, as shown here:

```
public boolean isSelected();
```

You may have noticed that many of the methods that change a frame's appearance can throw exceptions. This is to support property change listeners as

Table 14.5 JInternalFrame Methods

Method	Function
public void setClosable(boolean b)	Sets whether the frame is closed by the user.
public boolean isClosable()	Returns whether the frame is closed by the user.
public boolean isClosed()	Checks if the frame is closed.
public void setClosed(boolean b)	Closes the frame.
public void setResizable(boolean b)	Sets whether the frame can be resized by the user.
public boolean isResizable()	Returns whether the frame can be resized by the user.
public void setIconifiable(boolean b)	Sets whether the frame can be iconified by the user.
public boolean isIconifiable()	Returns whether the frame can be iconified by the user.
public boolean isIcon()	Checks if the frame is iconified.
public void setIcon(boolean b)	Iconifies the frame; may throw an exception.
public void setMaximizable(boolean b)	Sets whether the frame can be maximized by the user.
public boolean isMaximizable()	Returns whether the frame can be maximized by the user.
public boolean isMaximum()	Checks if the frame is maximized.
public void setMaximum(boolean b)	Maximizes the frame; may throw an exception.
public void setTitle(String title)	Sets the frame's title to the specified String.
public String getTitle()	Returns the frame's title.
public void setFrameIcon(Icon icon)	Sets the frame's icon.
public Icon getFrameIcon()	Returns the frame's icon.

Table 14.6 JInternalFrame Constructors

Constructor	Initialization
JInternalFrame()	Creates an internal frame with no title.
public JInternalFrame(String title)	Creates a frame with the specified title string.
public JInternalFrame(String title, boolean resizable)	Creates a frame with the specified title string and sets the resizable attribute based on the Boolean parameter.
public JInternalFrame(String title, boolean resizable, boolean closable)	Creates a frame with the specified title string and sets the resizable and closable attributes based on the Boolean parameters.
public JInternalFrame(String title, boolean resizable, boolean closable, boolean maximizable)	Creates a frame with the specified title string and sets the resizable, closable, and maximizable attributes based on the Boolean parameters.
public JInternalFrame(String title, boolean resizable, boolean closable, boolean maximizable, boolean iconifiable)	Creates a frame with the specified title string and sets the resizable, closable, maximizable, and iconifiable attributes based on the Boolean parameters.

defined by the JavaBeans specification. For more information on JavaBeans, see Sun's Web site at http://java.sun.com/beans/.

JInternalFrame provides several constructors that are used to set the initial attributes for a frame. These constructors are shown in Table 14.6.

The next example, pictured in Figure 14.5, creates several internal frames, with some of the JInternalFrame constructors. Notice that based on the attributes, different controls are available to the user on the frame. We have tiled the frames using a simple counter for the x and y location to make the frames easier to see. This location is relative to the frame's parent, the layered pane. All of the frames are added to the default layer.

```
import java.awt.*;
import java.awt.event.*;
import com.sun.java.swing.*;
import com.sun.java.swing.border.*;

public class IFrames extends JFrame
{
    public IFrames()
    {
```

```
JInternalFrame frame;
JMenuBar bar;
JMenu menu;
JMenuItem tmp;
JPanel panel;
int x,y;
Dimension prefSize;
JLayeredPane layers;

setTitle("Internal Frame Example");

layers = new JDesktopPane();
setLayeredPane(layers);

//Keep a running origin, to tile iframes
x = 0;
y = 0;

//Create a default internal Frame
frame = new JInternalFrame();

panel = new JPanel();
panel.add(new JLabel("Label"));
panel.add(new JButton("Button"));
frame.getContentPane().add(panel,"Center");

frame.setLocation(x,y);
frame.pack();
layers.add(frame);

x+=50;
y+=50;

//Create an internal Frame with a title
//and a menu
frame = new JInternalFrame("Frame 2");

panel = new JPanel();
panel.add(new JLabel("Label"));
panel.add(new JButton("Button"));
frame.getContentPane().add(panel,"Center");

bar = new JMenuBar();
```

```
menu = new JMenu("Levels");

tmp = new JMenuItem("Primary");
menu.add(tmp);

tmp = new JMenuItem("Secondary");
menu.add(tmp);

tmp = new JMenuItem("Tertiary");
menu.add(tmp);

bar.add(menu);
frame.setMenuBar(bar);

frame.setLocation(x,y);
frame.pack();
layers.add(frame);

x+=50;
y+=50;

//Create an internal Frame with a title
//that is resizable and closable
frame = new JInternalFrame("Frame 3",true,true);

panel = new JPanel();
panel.add(new JLabel("Label"));
panel.add(new JButton("Button"));
frame.getContentPane().add(panel,"Center");

frame.setLocation(x,y);
frame.pack();

layers.add(frame);

x+=50;
y+=50;

//Create an internal Frame with a title
//that is resizable and closable
//maximizable and iconizable
frame = new JInternalFrame("Frame 4",true,true,true,true);
```

```
            panel = new JPanel();
            panel.add(new JLabel("Label"));
            panel.add(new JButton("Button"));
            frame.getContentPane().add(panel,"Center");

            frame.setLocation(x,y);
            frame.pack();

            layers.add(frame);
        }

        public Dimension getPreferredSize()
        {
            return new Dimension(400, 400);
        }

        public static void main(String s[])
        {
            JFrame frame = new IFrames();

            frame.setForeground(Color.black);
            frame.setBackground(Color.lightGray);
            frame.addWindowListener(new WindowCloser());

            frame.setSize(frame.getPreferredSize());
            frame.setVisible(true);
        }
    }

    This example file includes the WindowCloser class to act as a window
    listener for the main frame.
    class WindowCloser extends WindowAdapter
    {
        public void windowClosing(WindowEvent e)
        {
            Window win = e.getWindow();
            win.setVisible(false);
            win.dispose();
            System.exit(0);
        }
    }
```

Figure 14.5 shows an example of internal frames with various features enabled.

Figure 14.5 Internal frames example.

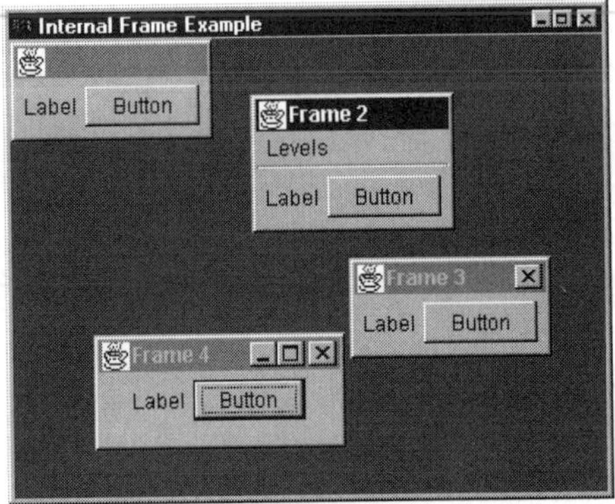

Internal OptionPanes

In Chapter 9, we discussed how JOptionPane creates internal windows instead of dialogs. To support internal dialogs, JInternalFrames can be set to modal. Unlike dialogs, you must control the modality of the internal frames manually with the startModal and stopModal methods:

```
public synchronized void startModal();
public synchronized void stopModal();
```

Of course, if you use the option pane to create a dialog, it manages this process for you.

The following example creates a form in the content pane and displays an internal alert. Figure 14.6 shows the form without the alert, and Figure 14.7 shows the alert in the frame. Because the majority of code in this example is used to create the form, we have highlighted the section that creates an internal option pane.

```
import com.sun.java.swing.*;
import java.awt.event.*;

import java.awt.*;
import java.lang.*;

public class IOptionExample extends JPanel
{
    public IOptionExample()
    {
        JTextField field;
        JLabel label;
        JPanel tmpPanel;
        Font font;
```

```
/*
 * Use a grid layout, and turn on buffering to reduce flicker.
 */
setLayout(new GridLayout(4,1,10,10));
setBackground(Color.lightGray);
setDoubleBuffered(true);

label = new JLabel("Name:");
field = new JTextField(25);

tmpPanel = new JPanel();
tmpPanel.setLayout(new FlowLayout(FlowLayout.LEFT));

tmpPanel.add(label);
tmpPanel.add(field);
add(tmpPanel);

label = new JLabel("Address:");
field = new JTextField(25);

tmpPanel = new JPanel();
tmpPanel.setLayout(new FlowLayout(FlowLayout.LEFT));

tmpPanel.add(label);
tmpPanel.add(field);
add(tmpPanel);

tmpPanel = new JPanel();
tmpPanel.setLayout(new FlowLayout(FlowLayout.LEFT));


label = new JLabel("State:");
field = new JTextField(4);
tmpPanel.add(label);
tmpPanel.add(field);

label = new JLabel("Zip:");
field = new JTextField(12);
tmpPanel.add(label);
tmpPanel.add(field);
add(tmpPanel);

label = new JLabel("Phone:");
field = new JTextField(25);
```

```
        tmpPanel = new JPanel();
        tmpPanel.setLayout(new FlowLayout(FlowLayout.LEFT));

        tmpPanel.add(label);
        tmpPanel.add(field);
        add(tmpPanel);
    }

    public Dimension getPreferredSize()
    {
        return new Dimension(380, 160);
    }

    public static void main(String s[])
    {
        JFrame frame = new JFrame("Info Internal Frame");
        IOptionExample panel = new IOptionExample();

        frame.setForeground(Color.black);
        frame.setBackground(Color.lightGray);
        frame.addWindowListener(new WindowCloser());
        frame.getContentPane().add(panel,"Center");

        frame.setSize(panel.getPreferredSize());
        frame.setVisible(true);

        JOptionPane.showInternalMessageDialog(panel
                              ,"Something Important Has Happened."
                              ,"Important"
                              ,JOptionPane.INFORMATION_MESSAGE);
    }
}
```

This example file includes the WindowCloser class to act as a window listener for the main frame.

```
class WindowCloser extends WindowAdapter
{
    public void windowClosing(WindowEvent e)
    {
        Window win = e.getWindow();
        win.setVisible(false);
        win.dispose();
```

```
            System.exit(0);
        }
    }
```

Figure 14.6 shows a form after the alert is displayed.

Figure 14.7 shows the example form with the alert.

Remember that all of the showDialog methods in JOptionPane come with an internal version.

Internal Frames and Layers

Our final example for this section, pictured in Figure 14.8, creates a number of internal frames in various layers. As in the previous example, we use a counter to tile the frames across and down the window. We have added frames to every 40th layer to show how these layers compare to the named layers.

```
import java.awt.*;
import java.awt.event.*;
import com.sun.java.swing.*;
import com.sun.java.swing.border.*;

public class Layers extends JFrame
{
    public Layers()
    {
        JInternalFrame frame;
        JPanel panel;
        JLayeredPane layers;
        int i;
        Dimension prefSize;

        setTitle("Layered Pane Example");

        layers = getLayeredPane();
```

Figure 14.6 Form without an alert.

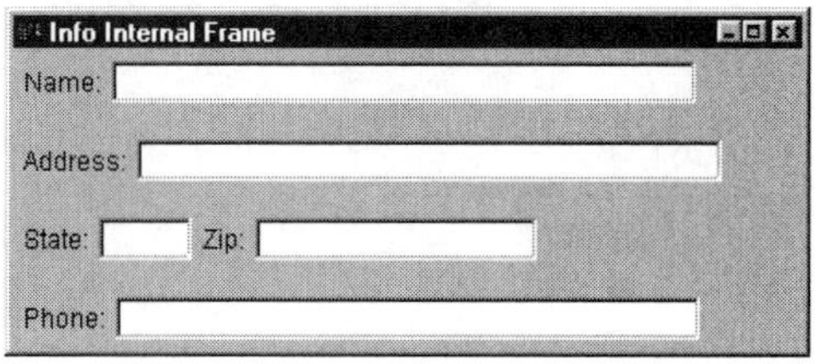

Figure 14.7 Form with an alert.

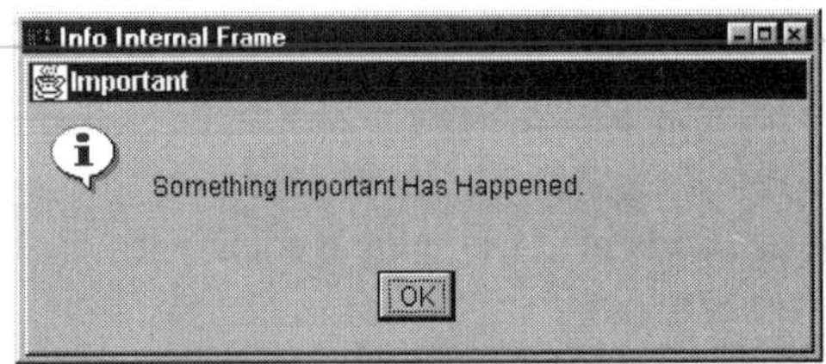


```
//Add a frame to the 0th layers
frame = new JInternalFrame();

panel = new JPanel();
panel.add(new JLabel("0th Layer"));
frame.getContentPane().add(panel,"Center");

frame.setLocation(50,10);
frame.pack();

layers.add(frame,new Integer(0));

//Make a few internal frames at various layers

for(i=0;i<10;i+=2)
{
    frame = new JInternalFrame();

    panel = new JPanel();
    panel.add(new JLabel("Layer "+(i*40)));
    frame.getContentPane().add(panel,"Center");

    frame.setLocation(i*20,i*20);
    frame.pack();

    layers.add(frame,new Integer(i*40));
}

//Add a frame to the Pallette layers
frame = new JInternalFrame();

panel = new JPanel();
panel.add(new JLabel("Palette Layer"));
frame.getContentPane().add(panel,"Center");
```

```
        frame.setLocation((i++)*20,(i++)*20);
        frame.pack();

        layers.add(frame,JLayeredPane.PALETTE_LAYER);

        //Add a frame to the popup layers
        frame = new JInternalFrame();

        panel = new JPanel();
        panel.add(new JLabel("Popup Layer"));
        frame.getContentPane().add(panel,"Center");

        frame.setLocation((i++)*20,(i++)*20);
        frame.pack();

        layers.add(frame,JLayeredPane.POPUP_LAYER);

        //Add a frame to the drag layers
        frame = new JInternalFrame();

        panel = new JPanel();
        panel.add(new JLabel("Drag Layer"));
        frame.getContentPane().add(panel,"Center");

        frame.setLocation((i++)*20,(i++)*20);
        frame.pack();

        layers.add(frame,JLayeredPane.DRAG_LAYER);
    }

    public Dimension getPreferredSize()
    {
        return new Dimension(400, 400);
    }

    public static void main(String s[])
    {
        JFrame frame = new Layers();

        frame.setForeground(Color.black);
        frame.setBackground(Color.lightGray);
        frame.addWindowListener(new WindowCloser());

        frame.setSize(frame.getPreferredSize());
```

Figure 14.8 Layers example.

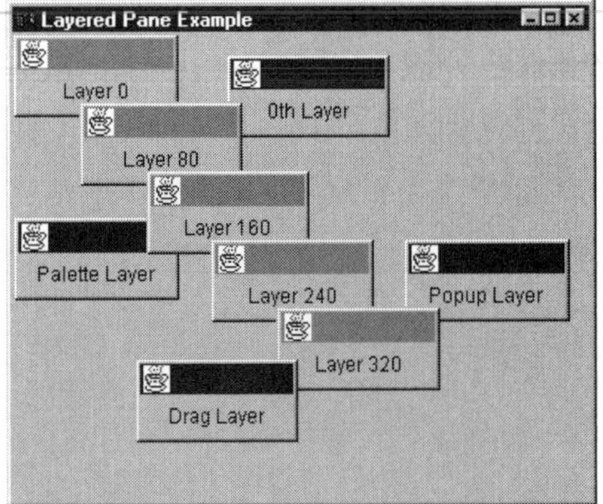


```
        frame.setVisible(true);
    }
}
```

This example file includes the WindowCloser class to act as a window listener for the main frame.

```
class WindowCloser extends WindowAdapter
{
    public void windowClosing(WindowEvent e)
    {
        Window win = e.getWindow();
        win.setVisible(false);
        win.dispose();
        System.exit(0);
    }
}
```

This example is pictured in Figure 14.8.

Style Guidelines

Layers are designed for windows that pop up based on user actions, managing objects that are dragged and working with internal frames. The majority of your user interface should still be placed in the content pane for an applet, internal frame, or frame. When you first design your interface, decide whether to use internal frames. This is really a toss-up depending on the platform you work on. For example, in Microsoft Windows, most word processors use internal frames for each document, while Netscape's browser uses a regular frame for each browser you open. Usually, internal frames make an application less window-intensive because there may be only one window. They make it hard, however, to view several documents at the same time. You should also consider using regular frames for windows with different functions. For example, Netscape uses separate windows for browsers and e-mail. If you are going to use internal frames, then some part of the interface must be used exclusively for these frames and cannot contain normal components. Basically, you don't want to float a frame on top of buttons and text fields in a normal window. They distract the user.

When you use layers, try to use the named layers when possible. You may also want to create one other layer that you use for your frames, but don't create hundreds. By keeping the number of layers to a minimum your program makes the best use of the selected frame. If you're not using internal frames, it's highly unlikely that you should use layers; instead you should place all components in the content pane of the root pane.

STYLED TEXT

15

Managing styled text is arguably the most complex issue when designing an application, in any environment. It requires efficient tracking of information that includes font kerning, colors, styles, selections, events, and much more. Swing provides a complete framework for implementing styled-text components. It also provides five text components that you can use in your applications: JTextField, JPasswordField, JTextArea, JTextPane, and JEditorPane. We discussed the first three of these components in Chapter 7. In this chapter, we discuss the text and editor panes. We also introduce the text framework that Swing provides.

This chapter begins by introducing the text framework design, provides some examples of how the design functions in practice, and then discusses the remaining two styled-text components. The first step in this discussion involves a number of definitions. If you don't plan to extend the text framework, skip ahead to the discussions on JTextPane and JEditorPane. Later, when you see how easy the text framework is to use, come back and read about how the components are implemented.

Basic Text Framework Design

The design for the Swing text framework centers on the com.sun.java.swing.text .JTextComponent class. This class defines an abstract text component and the relationships between it and the other elements of the text framework. The model for a text component is called a *Document.* This Document is responsible for storing information about the text, including styles, fonts, or other attributes. The UI object for a text component must be a subclass of TextUI. This class is responsible for displaying the information in a Document and responding to user events in the text component. An object called a *caret* and another called a *highlighter* draw the current selection for a text component, and a *keymap* stores the actions to perform for each key press. These actions are implementations of the Swing Action interface, so they can be shared between text components and even used in menus and tool bars.

Figure 15.1 shows the relationships between JTextComponent and its model and UI. Chapter 7 contains a table (Table 7.3) that lists many of the JTextComponent methods that are shared between all of its subclasses. In the same way that you use these methods with text fields, you use them with the other text components.

Document

As we mentioned, the concept of a Document, or text model, is defined in the com.sun.java.swing.text.Document interface. This interface defines methods for retrieving text, setting text, and listening for changes to the model. All of the text components use an implementation of Document to store their data. The implementation for Document can range in complexity from a simple string with a font to a parsed representation of HTML depending on the underlying data and the component that uses the Document. The data that makes up a Document is stored in elements. These elements have attributes associated with them. This relationship is pictured in Figure 15.2.

Elements are hierarchical, and the top-level element is called the *root element*. A simple Document can only have a root element with no children, while a complex Document can have several root elements that represent different representations of the same data. For example, a document for a source code control system might keep track of each version of the code as a separate root element.

Elements

Each element in a document represents a subset of the Document's data. An element can have attributes associated with it like a font size or color. The element is also responsible for keeping track of its position in the document as an offset.

Figure 15.1 JTextComponent design.

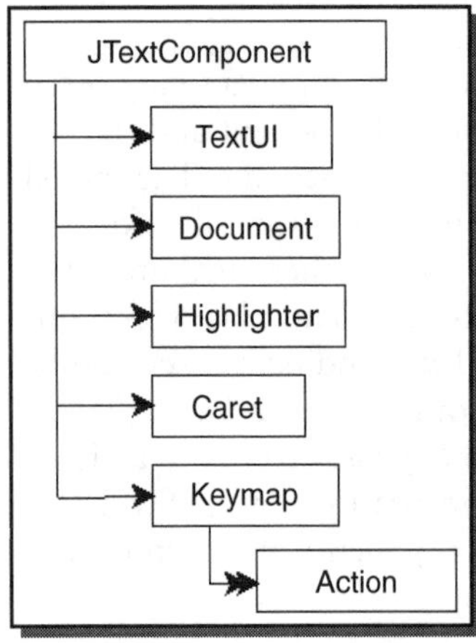

Figure 15.2 Document design.

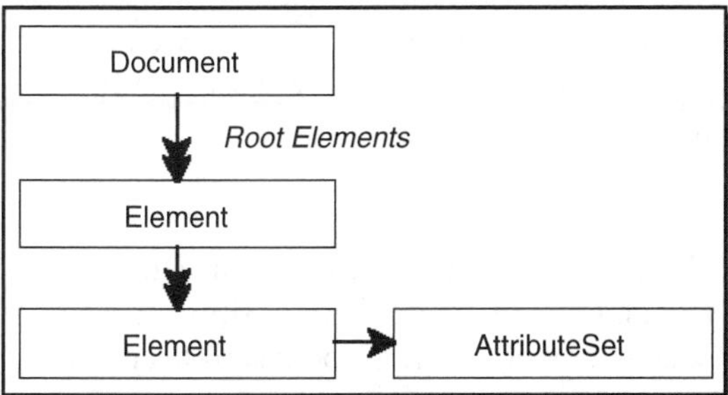

Elements can exist in a hierarchy. An element is responsible for knowing if it has children and if so what elements they are. For example, a paragraph element is responsible for the various lines and words it contains (see Figure 15.3). In general, an element is something that the Document needs to treat separately from other parts of the data to make it easier to edit or display them. For example, for a styled Document, the elements can represent runs of characters that have the same font and color.

All elements are expected to implement the com.sun.java.swing.text.Element interface.

Attributes

Attributes for a Document's elements are stored in objects that implement the com.sun.java.swing.text.AttributeSet interface. An AttributeSet stores a set of name-value pairs. These pairs are used to determine the characteristics of a document element. For example, the Font Family attribute has a font name as its value, while the Font Size attribute stores an integer size. In either case, it's up to the Document to define what attribute names are valid.

Figure 15.3 Element example.

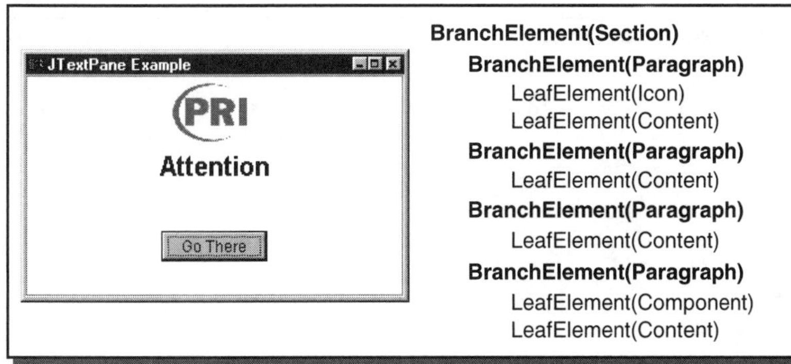

Later in this chapter we discuss styled documents and provide an example that creates several attribute sets before applying them to a JTextPane. In our case we use the SimpleAttributeSet class, which implements AttributeSet as well as the MutableAttributeSet interfaces. MutableAttributeSets are attribute sets that provide methods for changing the attributes.

Positions

For applications that need to keep track of a particular location in that Document, Swing provides position objects. The Document can create these positions based on an index into the data. Once created, the position object updates to keep track of its original position, even if the data has changed. For example, a position object set to the end of the document remains at the end even if data is inserted. A position object set to follow the "o" in "Hello," as pictured in Figure 15.4, remains after the "o" even if the word "Well" is placed in front of "Hello."

The implementation for a position object is Document dependent, but the position implements com.sun.java.swing.text.Position.

Segments

A segment is a character array used to improve performance during the manipulation of the text component. Documents use segments to hand data to the programmer rather than strings. Although this array is mutable, the programmer is not supposed to change it. For performance purposes, the raw information is returned rather than converting the mutable string into a nonmutable string. Changing the data, however, breaks the contract between programmer and Document and can lead to indeterminable results such as a Document method that runs past the end of the document's content and throws an exception.

Document Events

Objects can register with a document to receive notification if the document changes. These DocumentListeners must implement the com.sun.java.swing.event .DocumentListener interface. A different message is sent to the document's listeners

Figure 15.4 Positions in action.

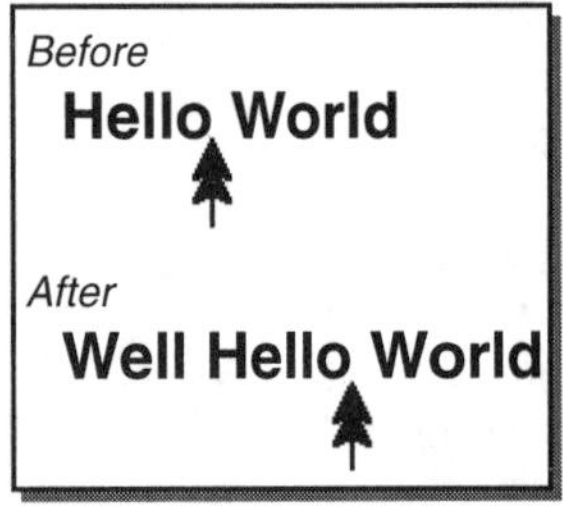

based on whether the change is from inserted data, removed data, or a change of attributes. These methods are listed in Table 15.1.

The argument to a DocumentListener method is a DocumentEvent. This object provides information not only about the document that changed but also the position and extent of the change.

Available Document Types

Swing provides two document implementations. A *plain document* represents a single string of information with a font associated with it. Plain documents are used with text areas and text fields to store their data. The PlainDocument class is a basic implementation of Document that provides a single font and color for the text content. *Styled documents*, and in particular DefaultStyledDocuments, store multiple runs of characters, each with their own attributes. A styled document can use multiple fonts, colors, and alignments to describe their data.

StyledDocument A styled document provides a method for setting the attributes for a character or paragraph. This document also provides the concept of a logical style for characters that do not have a specified style. Styled documents are defined as an interface, com.sun.java.swing.text.StyledDocument, but Swing provides an implementation called DefaultStyledDocument. When the user types or enters text, the styled document applies the current style, or attribute set, to the new text. Programmers can also add text using a particular set of attributes. These attributes are contained in a class called StyleConstants, described in the next section.

StyleConstants All of the attributes for a styled document are named. Instead of making programmers remember the available names for font color or alignment, the names have been attached to a class called *StyleConstants*. This class has class variables for keeping track of the correct name for the common styles. The class also provides static methods for adding a particular attribute name-value pair to an attribute set. Some of these more commonly used methods are listed in Table 15.2.

We use the StyleConstants class in our example of the JTextPane later in this chapter.

Table 15.1 DocumentListener Methods

Method	Function
Public void insertUpdate(DocumentEvent e)	Data was inserted.
Public void removeUpdate(DocumentEvent e)	Data was removed.
Public void changedUpdate(DocumentEvent e)	Attributes were changed.

Table 15.2 Commonly Used StyleConstants Methods

Method	Function
Public static void setFontFamily (MutableAttributeSet a,String fam)	Sets the font family name to the string for an attribute set defined by a MutableAttributeSet.
Public static void setFontSize (MutableAttributeSet a,Int s)	Sets the font size to the int value for a specified attribute set.
Public static void setBold (MutableAttributeSet a,Boolean b)	Tells the specified attribute set that the current font is bold if the Boolean is "true".
Public static void setItalic (MutableAttributeSet a,Boolean b)	Tells the specified attribute set that the current font is italic if the Boolean is "true".
Public static void setForeground (MutableAttributeSet a,Color fg)	Sets the foreground color for the specified attribute set.

TextUI

The appearance of a text component, like the other Swing components that we've discussed, is defined with a UI object. In the case of JTextComponent, the class TextUI is used to describe the user interface. Each of the JTextComponent subclasses uses its own subclass of TextUI to define its appearance. For example, JTextField wants a TextFieldUI to define its appearance, but TextFieldUI is a special kind of TextUI. Swing provides a default UI object called DefaultTextUI that is used as the superclass of look-and-feel-specific UI implementations.

A TextUI object is responsible for displaying the information in a text component's model. To do this, the TextUI maps the data in the model into views. These views each display a particular kind of data. For example, one view may display a paragraph and another an image. These views are ultimately associated with elements in the document model.

To create views and manage the various formats of text documents, a TextUI relies on an object called the EditorKit. This kit loads documents from files and creates a ViewFactory that generates views for the document's elements.

The TextUI also relies on an object called the TextController to manage the user input for a text component.

The high-level design for the TextUI is pictured in Figure 15.5.

The UI is not responsible for displaying the current selection. This is the responsibility of a component's highlighter.

Views

Each element in a document is mapped on to a view. This view must extend the com.sun.java.swing.text.View class. A view can draw itself and provide information

Figure 15.5 TextUI design.

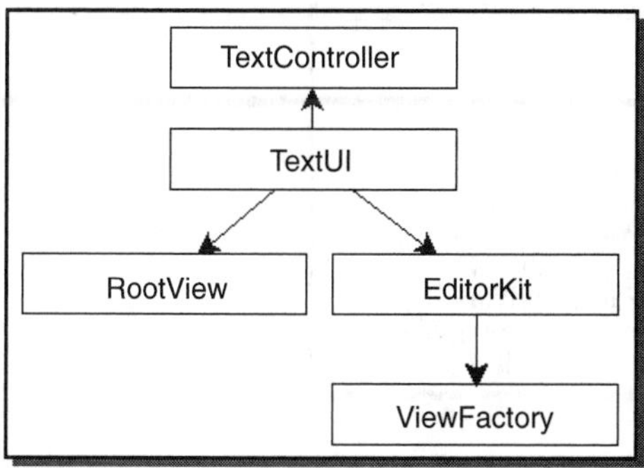

about its current size, much as a component does. Like a container, views can hold other views. Unlike a component, a view must also be able to break itself into pieces if the user's editing causes a break in the underlying element.

Swing provides a number of default views, as listed in Table 15.3.

The UI object uses a single view to represent the top level of the display and the root element from the document object. This root view contains children as necessary to display the various child elements. An example of how views are used is pictured in Figure 15.6.

Table 15.3 Available Views

Class	Function
BoxView	A composite view that organizes its children into a box. This may create a vertical collection of lines, for instance.
ComponentView	Displays a single lightweight component.
CompositeView	Contains other views.
FieldView	Extends PlainView to support a single line of text. This view is used by JTextField.
IconView	Displays an Icon.
LabelView	Displays a styled chunk of text.
ParagraphView	A special BoxView that implements line wrapping and supports multiple fonts, colors, and attributes.
PasswordView	View used in JPasswordFields. All contents are rendered as an echo character.
PlainView	Displays a line of text with a single font and color.

Figure 15.6 View example.

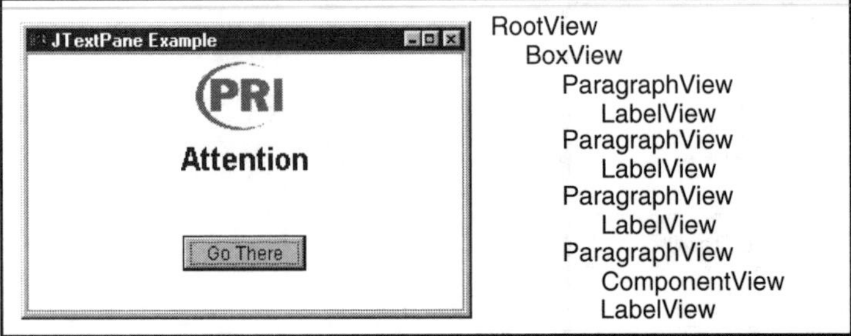

ViewFactory

The views for a text UI are created with a ViewFactory object. This factory is a simple object that returns a view given an element. Basically, the view factory is a mapping between elements and the view class that represents them. For example, the ViewFactor for a text UI that displays HTML creates IconView objects for the images in an HTML page. The same factory could create ComponentViews for the HTML form elements. Each view depends on the data it displays, according to the underlying document format.

EditorKit

Perhaps the heart of the text framework is the *editor kit*. This object is responsible for setting up the defaults for a text UI object, creating documents from streams, and writing documents to streams. The editor kit is also responsible for creating a ViewFactory that is appropriate for the documents it reads in. JavaSoft provides several editor kits with Swing, including one for generic styled documents, one for Rich Text Format, and one for HTML. We take advantage of these kits in our JEditorPane examples found later in this chapter.

Text Controller

The final element in the TextUI family is the *text controller*. This object is defined by the com.sun.java.swing.text.TextController interface as an object that implements the MouseListener, MouseMotionListener, FocusListener, and KeyListener interfaces. The UI object creates a text controller to handle events for the text component. Swing provides a default implementation of this interface in the form of the DefaultTextController class. The DefaultTextController uses a text component's keymap to determine what action to take for each event.

Caret and Highlighter

The insertion mark, or caret, for a text component is drawn and managed by an object that implements the com.sun.java.swing.text.Caret interface. Swing provides an implementation of this interface called DefaultCaret. This caret works with the component's highlighter. As we've mentioned previously, a highlighter object is responsible for displaying the current selection in a highlighted fashion. Swing provides an implementation of the com.sun.java.swing.text.Highlighter interface called DefaultHighlighter. A caret draws the "|" symbol that appears at the current location, and a highlighter draws the blue box around a selection.

KeyMap

Each JTextComponent has a keymap defined by an object that implements the com.sun.java.swing.text.Keymap interface. This keymap is responsible for mapping KeyStroke objects to actions. The KeyStroke stores a character code. The text controller uses this keycode to identify a keystroke and its associated action, allowing the text controller to determine what action to take based on the user's typing.

Actions

The actions stored by the KeyMap are actually action objects we have used in creating menus and tool bars. These actions all implement the ActionListener interface and provide some form of text and/or icon to represent them. TextComponents use actions to represent all of their interactive functionality. This can include inserting a character, paging down, and event copying data to the clipboard.

The actions used by text components are subclasses of TextAction. TextAction is a subclass of AbstractAction, which provides a method for accessing the currently focused component and retrieving the list of keystrokes that triggered the action to be invoked.

The Editor Kit is responsible for adding actions to a text component's key map. The DefaultEditorKit provides a wide range of default actions, as shown in Table 15.4, as well as others. There are actually more than 20 default actions. Instead of listing all of them, one of the examples in this chapter provides a menu that is used to invoke all of the default actions for a JTextPane. Running this example allows you to see what each action does and its name.

Depending on the editor kit that a UI object uses, some or all of these actions may be installed. For example, the UI for a text field uses the default editor kit, but it doesn't install the pageUpAction because the text field shows only a single line. The TextAreaUI class, on the other hand, also uses the default editor kit and does install the pageUpAction. An editor kit can use different actions than the defaults or provide more, depending on the type of document it supports.

Because the actions on a text component are managed with action objects, you can use the same actions to handle a copy menu item that the text controller uses to initiate a copy sequence. The potential for code reuse is amazing. We provide an example of this technique in the section on JTextPane.

Table 15.4 Examples of Default Actions

Action	Function
copyAction	Copies the current selection to the clipboard.
defaultKeyTypedAction	Used when there are no actions for a key.
deleteNextCharAction	Deletes the character after the caret, usually mapped to the Delete key.
deletePrevCharAction	Deletes the character before the caret, usually mapped to the Backspace key.
forwardAction	Moves the caret forward one character, usually mapped to the right arrow.
insertContentAction	Inserts content into the document, often used for the alphanumeric and punctuation keys.
insertBreakAction	Inserts a line or paragraph break.
pageUpAction	Goes up one page. Usually mapped to the Page Up key.
readOnlyAction	Tells the component to stop being editable.
writableAction	Tells the component to be editable.

How the Framework Works

As you have guessed, the Swing text framework has a lot of classes and levels. Digging through these classes is a long process, and it is not always necessary if you just want to use the JEditorPane to display HTML. To help explain how these classes work, let's walk through two examples. The first is how the framework opens a file, and the second is how it handles a key press.

Opening a File

When you request that the JEditorPane open a file, it relies on the editor kit for most of the work. First, the editor kit opens a stream to the data. Next, the editor kit reads the data and creates a model for it. This model is then assigned to the component. The component's UI object is notified that the model changed. This causes it to update its root view. Finally, the new root view is created with the ViewFactory provided by the editor kit. This process is pictured in Figure 15.7.

Handling a Key Press

Let's look at how a styled-text component such as JTextPane handles a key press.

Figure 15.7 Opening a file.

1. Programmer set the file to open.
2. Editor pane finds the correct kit to open the file.
3. Pane tells the kit to read the file.
4. Kit creates a document from the file and assigns it to the pane.
5. UI receives notification of the model change and updates.

First, when the text pane is created it generates both a UI and model object. The UI object creates a TextController and uses the EditorKit class to create a key map for the text pane. The text controller is assigned to the text component as a key listener. When the user presses a key, the controller is notified. Next, the controller checks for the key in the keymap. Based on the results of this search, the controller can either do nothing if the key isn't there or notify the action that an event has occurred. For instance, if the "a" key is pressed, the action inserts an "a" at the current selection. If the Page Down key is pressed, and if an action is mapped to it, the component may be told to scroll down one page, and the caret is moved.

The steps for this example are pictured in Figure 15.8.

Figure 15.8 Handling a key press.

a. UI created Keymap

b. UI creates TextController and assigns it as an event listener of the TextComponent

1. Controller receives event notification
2. Controller uses KeyMap to find an Action for the key event
3. Controller triggers Action.
4. Action alters text

JTextPane

The JTextPane class is a text component that, when placed in a scroll pane, provides much of the same functionality as a basic word processor. The text pane supports multiple styles and can even display components and icons within the text. You can use text panes to act as multiline labels or display messages, except input messages.

Text panes use a StyledDocument object for their model and provide convenience methods for accessing the model's styles. Text panes manage their styles in two forms: style objects and AttributeSets. Style object is an extension of MutableAttributeSet that supports change listeners, so a style is treated like an AttributeSet. The text pane stores styles by name, so that the program using the pane can use them to provide a style-sheet-type interface common to modern word processors. For example, you may define a *code style* that uses a Courier 12-point font and a *header style* that uses a serif font in 18 point. Then you can assign these styles to characters, input messages, or paragraphs.

Use an object with the AttributeSet interface to define the attributes and their settings. *Character attributes* and styles, like a font or color choice, affect individual characters. *Paragraph attributes,* like alignment, affect the entire paragraph. *Input attributes* affect any text that's added to the text pane. To set these values for a text pane's attributes, use the following methods:

```
public void setCharacterAttributes(AttributeSet attr,
                                   boolean replace);
public void setParagraphAttributes(AttributeSet attr,
                                   boolean replace);
```

Both of these methods either affect the current selection of the text pane, or if no selection is made, set the attributes for any text that is entered into the text pane following calls to the setCharacterAttributes method or setParagraphAttributes method. For instance, if you set a character attribute for bold, then all text typed after this setting is in bold. The Boolean parameter of the setCharacterAttributes method and setParagraphAttributes method indicates whether these attributes must completely replace the current input attributes or be added to them. If the Boolean is set to "true," the pane replaces the current attribute settings with these new settings. If the value of the Boolean parameter is set to "false," then the new attribute set is added to the existing set. Only attributes with the same name are replaced.

To add text to a text pane programatically, use the replaceSelection method:

```
public void replaceSelection(String content);
```

This method replaces the current selection. If you set the current selection to 0 width, by placing the caret using the setCaretPosition() method, the replaceSelection method appends the content at the current position, as shown here:

```
public void setCaretPosition(int pos);
```

The styles for the new content are determined by the text pane's input attributes.

To insert an icon or a component, use the following methods:

```
public void insertIcon(Icon g);
public void insertComponent(Component c);
```

These methods embed the item in the current text at the current selection.

The following example, shown in Figure 15.9, shows three styles: bold, normal, and small. These styles are used to define character attributes in the next program. The center style is used for paragraph attributes. The example program adds items to a text pane using all of these styles. We use the text pane's document object to provide us with its current length so that we can always move the caret to the end before performing a replace. To create each attribute set we instantiate a SimpleAttributeSet and use the StyleConstants class to add attributes to it. Then, as we add text to the pane, we update the current character and paragraph attributes to the four styles that we defined.

```
import java.util.*;
import java.awt.*;
import java.awt.event.*;
import com.sun.java.swing.*;
import com.sun.java.swing.text.*;

public class TextPaneExample extends JPanel
{
    public TextPaneExample()
    {
        JTextPane area;
        MutableAttributeSet normalStyle;
        MutableAttributeSet boldStyle;
        MutableAttributeSet smallStyle;
        MutableAttributeSet centerStyle;
        Document doc;

        setLayout(new BorderLayout());
        setBackground(Color.lightGray);
        setDoubleBuffered(true);

        area = new JTextPane();

        doc = area.getDocument();

        normalStyle = new SimpleAttributeSet();

        StyleConstants.setFontFamily(normalStyle,"SanSerif");
```

```
        StyleConstants.setFontSize(normalStyle,14);

        boldStyle = new SimpleAttributeSet(normalStyle);
        StyleConstants.setBold(boldStyle,true);
        StyleConstants.setFontSize(boldStyle,20);

        smallStyle = new SimpleAttributeSet(normalStyle);
        StyleConstants.setFontSize(smallStyle,10);

        centerStyle = new SimpleAttributeSet();
        StyleConstants.setAlignment(centerStyle
                                ,StyleConstants.ALIGN_CENTER);

        area.setCaretPosition(0);
        area.setParagraphAttributes(centerStyle,true);
        area.insertIcon(new ImageIcon("images/logo.gif"));
        area.replaceSelection("\n");

        area.setCaretPosition(doc.getLength());
        area.setParagraphAttributes(centerStyle,true);
        area.setCharacterAttributes(boldStyle,false);
        area.replaceSelection("Attention\n\n");

        area.setCaretPosition(doc.getLength());
        area.setCharacterAttributes(normalStyle,true);
        area.replaceSelection("Free Stuff Available\n\n");

        area.setCaretPosition(doc.getLength());
        area.setCharacterAttributes(smallStyle,true);
        area.replaceSelection("One at this price.\n\n");

        area.setCaretPosition(doc.getLength());
        area.setParagraphAttributes(centerStyle,true);
        area.insertComponent(new JButton("Go There"));

        add(new JScrollPane(area),"Center");
    }

    public Dimension getPreferredSize()
    {
        return new Dimension(300, 150);
    }

    public static void main(String s[])
```

```
    {
        JFrame frame = new JFrame("JTextPane Example");
        TextPaneExample panel = new TextPaneExample();

        frame.setDefaultCloseOperation(JFrame.DO_NOTHING_ON_CLOSE);
        frame.setForeground(Color.black);
        frame.setBackground(Color.lightGray);
        frame.addWindowListener(new WindowCloser());
        frame.getContentPane().add(panel,"Center");

        frame.setSize(panel.getPreferredSize());
        frame.setVisible(true);
    }
}
```

This example uses a window closer object to handle the window's close box.

```
class WindowCloser extends WindowAdapter
{
    public void windowClosing(WindowEvent e)
    {
        Window win = e.getWindow();
        win.setVisible(false);
        System.exit(0);
    }
}
```

Text components use actions to describe their functionality. As an experiment and learning exercise, we create a small program that creates a text pane and displays it in a window. Then we create a menu for that window that contains all the actions that the text pane supports. Look at Figure 15.10, and notice that a styled-text pane has a lot of actions. So many, in fact, that we had to clip the

Figure 15.9 TextPane example.

image to fit it in the book. JTextPane not only supports a fair number of features, it uses actions for everything including the Delete key and for typing a character. Depending on your screen size, this menu may get too big. In this case, you can update the example to add 10 actions each to several menus.

When you run this example from the CD-ROM you will see that you can move the caret, copy text, enable the text pane, disable the text pane, set the font, and perform the other actions, all from the menu. This is a great demonstration of the power of the Swing text framework and the code management opportunities of using actions to encapsulate functionality.

```
import java.util.*;
import java.awt.*;
import java.awt.event.*;
import com.sun.java.swing.*;
import com.sun.java.swing.text.*;

public class TextActions extends JPanel
{
    public TextActions(JFrame frame)
    {
        JTextPane area;

        setLayout(new BorderLayout());
        setBackground(Color.lightGray);
        setDoubleBuffered(true);

        area = new JTextPane();

        add(new JScrollPane(area),"Center");

        buildMenu(frame,area);
    }

    public void buildMenu(JFrame frame,JTextComponent text)
    {
        Action[] actions;
        int i,max;
        JMenuBar bar;
        JMenu menu;

        bar = new JMenuBar();
        menu = new JMenu("Actions");

        actions = text.getActions();
```

```
            max = actions.length;

            for(i=0;i<max;i++)
            {
                menu.add(actions[i]);
            }

            bar.add(menu);

            frame.setJMenuBar(bar);
        }

        public Dimension getPreferredSize()
        {
            return new Dimension(300, 150);
        }

        public static void main(String s[])
        {
            JFrame frame = new JFrame("Text Actions Example");
            TextActions panel = new TextActions(frame);

            frame.setDefaultCloseOperation(JFrame.DO_NOTHING_ON_CLOSE);
            frame.setForeground(Color.black);
            frame.setBackground(Color.lightGray);
            frame.addWindowListener(new WindowCloser());
            frame.getContentPane().add(panel,"Center");

            frame.setSize(panel.getPreferredSize());
            frame.setVisible(true);
        }
    }
```

This example code includes and uses the WindowCloser class.

```
class WindowCloser extends WindowAdapter
{
    public void windowClosing(WindowEvent e)
    {
        Window win = e.getWindow();
        win.setVisible(false);
        System.exit(0);
    }
}
```

The running version of this example is pictured in Figure 15.10.

Figure 15.10 Text actions.

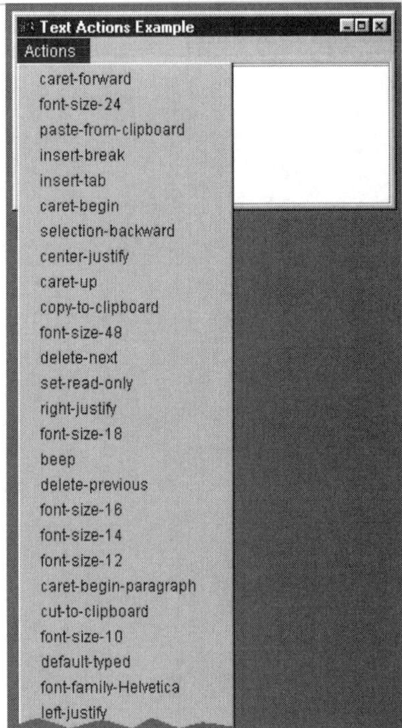

JEditorPane

Another styled text component provided by Swing is the JEditorPane. This component provides a fairly simple interface that uses the concept of a current page to display information. When you want to display text in the editor pane, you set its page by calling the setPage method and passing a URL object or a string that contains a URL. The methods are as follows:

```
public void setPage(URL page) throws IOException
public void setPage(String url) throws IOException
```

Notice that both of these methods can throw exceptions if the page is invalid in some way.

The editor pane keeps a map between content types, as defined for the World Wide Web and editor kits. The types are listed in Table 15.5.

Based on the content type of the page's URL, the editor pane resets its editor kit to match the URL before the editor kit loads the file. You can also set the content type manually using the following method and passing in one of the strings found in Table 15.5.

```
public void setContentType(String type);
```

Table 15.5 EditorPane Content Types

Type	Meaning
text/plain	Regular text, with no attributes.
text/rtf	Text in the Rich Text Format (RTF).
text/html	Text defined by HTML.

If you plan to set the text of an editor pane using the setText method, set the content type to text/plain first.

The following example loads a text file into an editor pane. This example shows three important techniques:

1. We set the content type of the pane.
2. We set the page for the editor pane.
3. We create a file URL based on this content.

Keep in mind that you always set the pane's current page with a URL. Therefore, to set the pane to a file you must create a file URL. For testing purposes, the main method in this example checks to see if there is a file name on the command line and displays one if there is. If no file is provided, a default file name of "Constitution.txt" is used.

```
import java.util.*;
import java.awt.*;
import java.io.*;
import java.net.*;
import java.awt.event.*;
import com.sun.java.swing.*;
import com.sun.java.swing.text.*;

public class PlainExample extends JPanel
{
    public PlainExample(String fileName)
    {
        JEditorPane area;
        URL url;

        setLayout(new BorderLayout());
        setBackground(Color.lightGray);
        setDoubleBuffered(true);

        area = new JEditorPane();

        area.setContentType("text/plain");
```

```
        try
        {
            url = new URL("file",null,fileName);
            area.setPage(url);
        }
        catch(Exception exp)
        {
            area.setText("Error loading page.\n" + exp);
        }

        add(new JScrollPane(area),"Center");
    }

    public Dimension getPreferredSize()
    {
        return new Dimension(300, 300);
    }

    public static void main(String s[])
    {
        JFrame frame = new JFrame("Plain Text Example");
        PlainExample panel;

        if(s.length > 0) panel = new PlainExample(s[0]);
        else panel = new PlainExample("Constitution.txt");

        frame.setDefaultCloseOperation(JFrame.DO_NOTHING_ON_CLOSE);
        frame.setForeground(Color.black);
        frame.setBackground(Color.lightGray);
        frame.addWindowListener(new WindowCloser());
        frame.getContentPane().add(panel,"Center");

        frame.setSize(panel.getPreferredSize());
        frame.setVisible(true);
    }
}
```

This example uses a WindowCloser object to handle the window's close box.

```
class WindowCloser extends WindowAdapter
{
    public void windowClosing(WindowEvent e)
    {
        Window win = e.getWindow();
        win.setVisible(false);
```

```
            System.exit(0);
        }
    }
```

The running version of this example is pictured in Figure 15.11.

Because JEditorPane supports HTML, the designers decided to provide a notification mechanism for when the user activates hyperlinks. This mechanism is based on the use of HyperlinkListeners. To define a HyperlinkListener, you implement the single method and register with the editor pane as a HyperlinkListener.

```
public void hyperlinkUpdate(HyperlinkEvent e);
```

The editor pane calls this method when a link is activated. The argument to the method is a HyperlinkEvent. You can use the getURL method to retrieve the URL for the link from the event.

```
public URL getURL();
```

If you want to support links, the listener must use this URL to update the editor pane's current page.

The following example, pictured in Figure 15.12, displays an editor pane with the URL provided on the command line. The content type for the URL is determined by the URL itself. If an error occurs, the content type is set to text/plain and a message is printed to the editor pane. We have implemented the HyperlinkListener interface and updated the current page appropriately.

If you run this example you will see that we have not provided any user feedback during the page load. Please wait for pages to load when you select a link; this can take some time depending on your computer and network connection.

Figure 15.11 Editor pane that displays a plain text document.

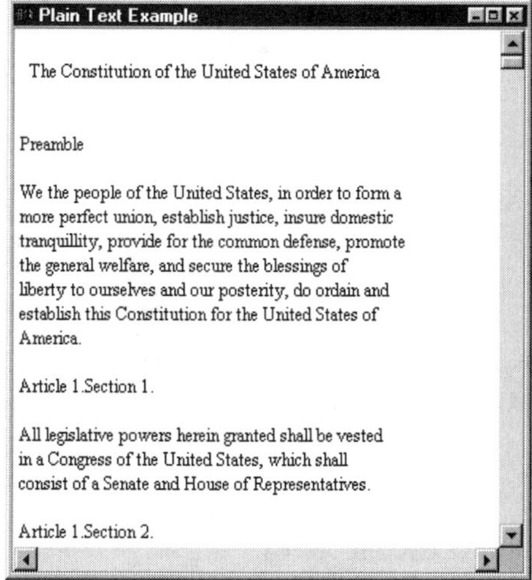

```
import java.util.*;
import java.awt.*;
import java.io.*;
import java.net.*;
import java.awt.event.*;
import com.sun.java.swing.*;
import com.sun.java.swing.event.*;
import com.sun.java.swing.text.*;

public class HTMLExample extends JPanel
implements HyperlinkListener
{
    JEditorPane area;

    public HTMLExample(String urlText)
    {
        URL url;

        setLayout(new BorderLayout());
        setBackground(Color.lightGray);
        setDoubleBuffered(true);

        area = new JEditorPane();

        add(new JScrollPane(area),"Center");

        area.addHyperlinkListener(this);

        try
        {
            if(urlText != null)
            {
                url = new URL(urlText);
                area.setPage(url);
            }
        }
        catch(Exception exp)
        {
            area.setContentType("text/plain");
            area.setText("Error loading page.\n" + exp);
        }
    }

    public void hyperlinkUpdate(HyperlinkEvent evt)
    {
```

```
            try
            {
                area.setPage(evt.getURL());
            }
            catch(Exception exp)
            {
                area.setContentType("text/plain");
                area.setText("Error loading page.\n" + exp);
            }
        }

        public Dimension getPreferredSize()
        {
            return new Dimension(300, 300);
        }

        public static void main(String s[])
        {
            JFrame frame = new JFrame("HTML Text Example");
            HTMLExample panel;

            if(s.length > 0) panel = new HTMLExample(s[0]);
            else panel = new HTMLExample(null);

            frame.setDefaultCloseOperation(JFrame.DO_NOTHING_ON_CLOSE);
            frame.setForeground(Color.black);
            frame.setBackground(Color.lightGray);
            frame.addWindowListener(new WindowCloser());
            frame.getContentPane().add(panel,"Center");

            frame.setSize(panel.getPreferredSize());
            frame.setVisible(true);
        }
    }
```

This example uses a WindowCloser object to handle the window's close box.

```
class WindowCloser extends WindowAdapter
{
    public void windowClosing(WindowEvent e)
    {
        Window win = e.getWindow();
        win.setVisible(false);
        System.exit(0);
    }
}
```

Figure 15.12 Editor pane with HTML.

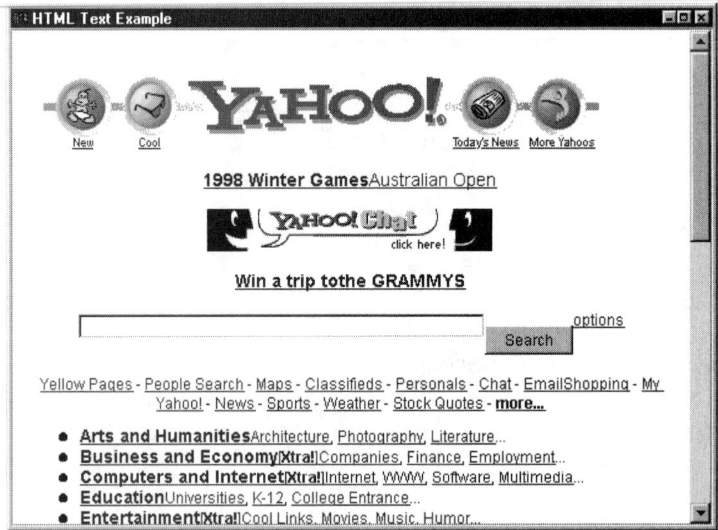

The running version of this example is pictured in Figure 15.12.

Style Guidelines

Styled text is a great way to display information. Using the text or editor panes in your application allows you to provide HTML-style online help as well as rich-text license agreements and information screens. Be careful to minimize the number of fonts you use in these messages. It can distract the user if the font changes for every word.

Finally, be sure to set an editor pane's content type to text/plain before setting its text, and keep in mind that the editor pane will throw exceptions if the page that you send it to is invalid in some way.

Creating Custom JFC Components

16

As you have seen in previous chapters, JFC provides numerous components that simplify the development of application user interfaces. JFC not only provides a number of useful components, it provides programmers with a foundation for creating their own components as well. More over, custom components are considered to be on an equal footing with the components provided by JavaSoft. There are several ways to create custom components. We list them here from the easiest method to the most complex.

1. Create custom components by adding listeners to existing components. Event listeners were introduced in Chapter 2, but they have been used throughout the book.
2. Create custom models for existing objects. We discuss creating custom models in Chapters 11, 12, and 17.
3. Subclass an existing component class. All of our examples have used subclassing, but Chapter 6 provides a specific example of a custom component that draws itself.
4. Create a custom component from scratch.

Because we have used most of the other techniques in our examples from previous chapters, this chapter focuses on creating complete, custom components from scratch.

Once you have decided to create a component from scratch, keep in mind that the task of writing a truly reusable component is noticeably more complex than writing a simple, one-shot component. For example, reusable components should use the JFC model-view-controller architecture. This means you have to create at least three classes, where one class may be sufficient for a one-shot component.

We have broken the process for creating custom components into nine steps. The choice of steps is arbitrary, and you may find that some are optional, depending on your design decisions. We thought it important to provide a framework and process for creating components that is generic enough to use in everyday programming.

The nine steps for creating a component are as follows:

1. Determine the component's functionality.
2. Decide on a UI object and a model object.
3. Determine the methods provided by the model and UI.
4. Define the model as an interface.
5. Define the UI as an interface.
6. Implement the main component, relying on your UI and model interfaces.
7. Implement at least one UI object that implements your UI interface.
8. Implement at least one version of your model.
9. Test your component.

The remainder of this chapter discusses each of these steps in order.

Step 1: Determine the Component's Functionality

For our example used throughout the nine-step process we create a class called TouchScreen. A touch-screen object is a component that acts like an HTML image map, except that it highlights the selected area. Essentially, the touch-screen object displays an image. Some of the areas found on this image are marked "special" by the programmer. When a user selects an important area, an Action event is fired.

Determining the functionality for our touch-screen object or your own component is a process of requirements gathering. Use whatever design methodology you are familiar with. In your projects, you need to plan to spend time with users and domain experts to determine whether a custom component is required and, if yes, what it needs to look and act like. Keep in mind that it's always easier to use existing components than to create new ones, assuming that they perform the task that you need. You also need to discuss with the users and domain experts whether the component could be used in other projects. It's important to decide if you plan to reuse the component before you design it.

If you don't plan to reuse a component, or if it will be used only on a specific look and feel, you may want to ignore some of the pluggable look-and-feel infrastructure. This decision can reduce your code considerably. You may consider implementing the component as a subclass of JComponent and implement paint and event handling directly in the component or in one of its listeners.

In our touch-screen example, we want to create a component that displays an image and allows the user to select regions of that image. The selected region highlights, and then an action is triggered whenever the selected region changes. We also have the regions highlight as the user moves the mouse over them. An example of this touch-screen component is shown in Figure 16.1.

Figure 16.1 Touch-screen component.

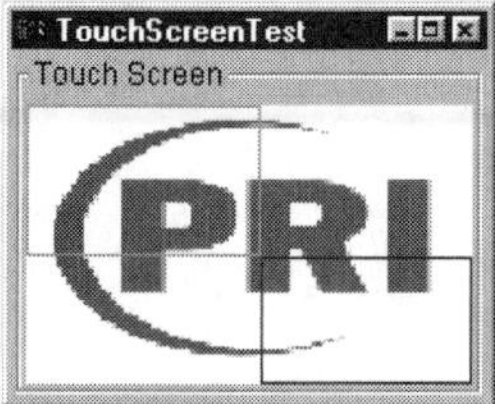

> **NOTE**
>
> For the sake of creating an educational example, we have made trade-offs between simplicity and functionality. Please don't consider this to be the best touch-screen component that can be built. It's intended as a teaching tool and as a basis for a real touch-screen component. That said, you should find the component useful in its current implementation as well.

Step 2: Decide on a UI Object and a Model Object

We want our touch-screen component to be reusable so we divided it into the UI-component-model architecture. In general, you want to break a component into these pieces when you think that one of the pieces may be changed or reused. For example, we design a model interface for our touch-screen object that supports arbitrary shapes, but we implement a model that handles only polygons and rectangles. Another model based on our interface could provide support for circles and arbitrary paths, motivating a separate model object. Our UI is a simple one that scales the image and supports borders. Another UI object may make the selected region flash or blink. Again, this is just another reason to separate the UI from the component. We create a UI interface and a model interface that supports the requirements of our touch-screen component in later steps. The important point in this step is that we identified from evaluating our requirements that there isn't an existing model or UI that we can use as is. We must create a custom UI and model, but we went through the process of looking for existing interfaces that may have provided this functionality already so we wouldn't reinvent something that we already had.

Ultimately, we create five classes and interfaces. These are pictured in Figure 16.2.

You probably won't want to reuse the model or UI for the touch-screen component in another object, but some components do use models that can be reused. For example, all of the button classes in JFC share the same model type, and a number of classes use the BoundedRangeModel and SingleSelectionModel. If you

Figure 16.2 Touch-screen classes.

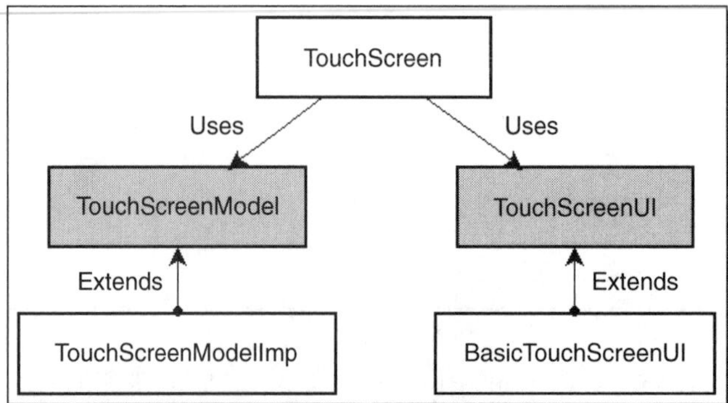

create a component or set of components that can share a model, this is also a good motivation for separating it from the component itself.

Step 3: Determine the Methods Provided by the Model and UI

The next step in the process is to determine the methods you need to provide the required functionality, as determined in Step 1. This is really a two-part process. First, you need to determine what methods the UI object requires; second, you need to determine what methods the model object needs. In our case, the UI object doesn't have any special responsibilities so it can be a generic subclass of ComponentUI. That said, we are going to implement the UI object to register as a MouseListener with its associated TouchScreen component to implement the look and feel of the custom component. Ultimately, our UI object must implement MouseListener and MouseMotionListener.

Our model requires a few methods. We need methods that provide a way to do the following:

- Set and retrieve the image (setImage(Image), getImage())
- Retrieve the available regions (regions())
- Add and remove regions (addRegion(Shape), removeRegion(Shape))
- Retrieve the selected regions (getRegionForPoint(Point), getSelectedRegion())
- Select a region (selectRegion(Shape), selectRegionForPoint(Point))

To improve the interface, we decided to include a method for selecting a region, given a point. This method is called:

```
public Shape getRegionForPoint(Point p);
```

Remember that models do not have to know about components. Instead, components register a ChangeListener with the model to receive notifications when the model changes. This requires methods in the model that support the adding and removal of ChangeListeners. In our example, we use the standard ChangeListener interface. You may find it necessary to define your own model listener type. The JFC ListSelectionModel defines its own listener interface in the form of the ListSelectionListener to gain this flexibility. Our touch-screen model notifies change listeners when the selection changes or the image changes. This allows the UI object to update the component if the image changes.

Step 4: Define the Model as an Interface

Now that you know the model's function and the methods you need to implement, it's time to define the methods in Java using an interface. By defining the methods in an interface you allow other programmers freedom in their implementation. The Document interface, for example, allowed JFC to define both a simple string text model and a more complex and rich styled-text model. In a network application, you could create one model that gets data from a local source and another that loads data from the network. Using interfaces gives programmers implementation freedom. If the model is defined as a class, the programmer may have to write a lot of support code because if he or she wants to create a model that behaves quite differently from the original, the model can't inherit from it. Using an interface you define a set of methods without confining the implementation. You can provide default implementations with convenience methods, but a programmer doesn't have to subclass these implementations. The programmer can write his or her own. For example, both JTree and JTable define their models by an interface. The table model we implemented was an object subclass. The table models extended AbstractTableModel and took advantage of its code.

Our model is defined in the interface TouchScreenModel. Notice that we have tried to provide all of the functionality, with a minimum number of methods, to make it easy for programmers to create new model types.

```
import java.util.*;
import java.awt.*;
import java.awt.event.*;
import com.sun.java.swing.*;
import com.sun.java.swing.event.*;
import com.sun.java.swing.text.*;

public interface TouchScreenModel
{
    public void setImage(Image i);
    public Image getImage();
```

```
    public void addRegion(Shape s);
    public void removeRegion(Shape s);
    public void selectRegion(Shape s);
    public void selectRegionForPoint(Point p);
    public Shape getRegionForPoint(Point p);
    public Shape getSelectedRegion();
    public Enumeration regions();

    public void addChangeListener(ChangeListener x);
    public void removeChangeListener(ChangeListener x);
}
```

Some extensions to this model could include associating separate ActionListeners for each region or providing a tool tip for each region.

Step 5: Define the UI as an Interface

Our UI is just a subtype of ComponentUI with no new functionality. We need to define it so that we can perform type checking. The UI, however, doesn't provide any other functionality. As a result of its simplicity, the UI is very easy to define.

```
import java.util.*;
import java.awt.*;
import java.awt.event.*;
import com.sun.java.swing.*;
import com.sun.java.swing.plaf.*;
import com.sun.java.swing.text.*;

public abstract class TouchScreenUI extends ComponentUI
{
}
```

Keep in mind that we implement the necessary methods from ComponentUI in our actual UI class so although this interface is trivial, the actual UI requires some work because it involves implementing the painting and event-handling code.

Step 6: Implement the Main Component, Relying on Your UI and Model Interfaces

Given the interfaces for the UI and model objects, we are ready to define the TouchScreen component. To simplify this discussion, we break the component's methods down into categories. A complete version of the code is included at the end of this section. The categories we describe include:

1. The TouchScreen constructor
2. UI object accessor methods
3. Model object accessor methods
4. Touch-screen action listeners
5. Methods delegated to the Model and UI object
6. The touch screen's change listener

The class declaration for our TouchScreen class is this:

```
public class TouchScreen extends JComponent
```

At the top of the class we define instance variables. The TouchScreen class requires a string to hold its action command, a variable for both the model and the UI, the color to use when highlighting, a change listener for the model, and finally a vector to track action listeners. We chose to use a vector so that we can support multiple action listeners. Some components may find it more appropriate to support a single listener.

```
{
protected String actionCmd;
TouchScreenModel model;
TouchScreenUI ui;
Color hilightColor;
protected ChangeListener changeList;
protected Vector actList;
```

TouchScreen Constructor

Next, we define a constructor. Notice that we use methods to create the change listener, default model, and default user interface. This allows subclasses to override the default functionality. The default user interface is actually created in the updateUI method. The default change listener we use is defined in the same file as the TouchScreen class.

```
public TouchScreen()
{
    changeList = createChangeListener();
    actList = new Vector();
    hilightColor = Color.green;

    setModel(createDefaultModel());

    updateUI();
}
```

```
protected ChangeListener createChangeListener()
{
    return new DefTSChangeListener(this);
}

protected TouchScreenModel createDefaultModel()
{
    return new TouchScreenModelImp();
}

protected TouchScreenUI createDefaultUI()
{
    return BasicTouchScreenUI.createUI(this);
}
```

UI Accessor Methods

Now we need to define the methods used to support pluggable look and feels. The updateUI method is used with the UIManager class to notify a component that the current look and feel has changed. We implement it here just in case, although we doubt that there is a look and feel for the touch-screen UI in the Swing release. Along with updateUI, the component is expected to provide the name of its UI class, which is TouchScreenUI. JFC requires that we ask the UI object to install itself on the component in the set method and uninstall from the component when it no longer is used. This makes the set method more lengthy than the trivial get method. The final step for setting the UI is to invalidate the component so that it's reintegrated in its parent and redrawn. Notice that we don't do anything if the UI we are given is our existing UI. This prevents excess work.

```
public void updateUI()
{
    TouchScreenUI ui;

    ui = (TouchScreenUI)UIManager.getUI(this);

    if(ui == null) ui = createDefaultUI();

    setUI(ui);
}


public String getUIClassID()
{
    return "TouchScreenUI";
}
```

```
public TouchScreenUI getUI()
{
    return ui;
}

public void setUI(TouchScreenUI newUI)
{
    TouchScreenUI oldUI = getUI();

    if(oldUI == newUI) return;//don't do anything

    if(oldUI != null) oldUI.uninstallUI(this);

    ui = newUI;

    if(ui != null) ui.installUI(this);

    invalidate();
}
```

Model Accessor Methods

Once the UI accessor methods are defined, we can define the model accessor methods. These are similar to the UI methods above except that a change listener is added to the model in place of the UI installation. Similarly, when the model is no longer needed, the change listener is removed.

```
public TouchScreenModel getModel()
{
    return model;
}

public void setModel(TouchScreenModel newModel)
{
    TouchScreenModel oldModel = getModel();

    if (oldModel != null)
    {
        oldModel.removeChangeListener(changeList);
    }

    model = newModel;

    if (newModel != null)
    {
```

```
        newModel.addChangeListener(changeList);
    }
}
```

Our touch screen keeps track of its own highlight color. We have provided accessor methods to set and retrieve this value:

```
public void setHilightColor(Color c)
{
    hilightColor = c;
}

public Color getHilightColor()
{
    return hilightColor;
}
```

Managing ActionListeners

We want our touch-screen component to support action listeners. This requires methods to add and remove listeners, but we have also included a convenience method that causes the touch-screen object to notify its action listeners that an action has been invoked. Again, this method is a convenience and is provided only to improve code reuse. There are also methods to retrieve and set the touch-screen action command, called setActionCommand and getActionCommand. These methods are accessors for the action command. When a listener is notified on an action event, the action command is used to distinguish the intention of the event.

```
public void setActionCommand(String cmd)
{
    actionCmd = cmd;
}

public String getActionCommand()
{
    return actionCmd;
}

//Use a vector to support multiple listeners
public void addActionListener(ActionListener al)
{
    if(!actList.contains(al)) actList.addElement(al);
}

public void removeActionListener(ActionListener al)
{
    actList.addElement(al);
```

```
}

//Method to notify action listeners
void notifyListeners()
{
    int i,max;
    ActionEvent evt;
    ActionListener curListener;

    evt = new ActionEvent(this,ActionEvent.ACTION_PERFORMED
                                              ,actionCmd);

    max = actList.size();

    for(i=0;i<max;i++)
    {
        curListener = (ActionListener) actList.elementAt(i);

        curListener.actionPerformed(evt);
    }
}
```

Methods Delegated to the Model and UI Object

Now that we have defined the basic housekeeping methods of the TouchScreen class, we define the methods that are delegated to the UI object. These are operations that could be handled by our touch-screen component but are instead forwarded to our UI object so that it's easily extended or replaced by another UI object. In the same way, we also provide a set of methods that delegate model-related responsibility to the model. This allows a programmer who uses the component to ignore the model and UI if he or she wants to and work directly with the TouchScreen object.

Methods Delegated to the Model Object

First, let's look at the methods delegated to the model. Again, these are not required; they are provided to make the API simpler. All of these methods rely on the TouchScreenModel interface defined earlier and simply forward requests to the model. These methods look familiar because they mimic the ones in our TouchScreenModel interface, described earlier.

```
public void setImage(Image i)
{
    if(model != null) model.setImage(i);
}

public Image getImage()
{
```

```
        Image retVal = null;

        if(model != null) retVal = model.getImage();

        return retVal;
    }

    public void addRegion(Shape s)
    {
        if(model != null) model.addRegion(s);
    }

    public void removeRegion(Shape s)
    {
        if(model != null) model.removeRegion(s);
    }

    public void selectRegion(Shape s)
    {
        if(model!=null) model.selectRegion(s);
    }

    public void selectRegionForPoint(Point p)
    {
        if(model!=null) model.selectRegionForPoint(p);
    }

    public Shape getSelectedRegion()
    {
        Shape retVal = null;

        if(model != null) retVal = model.getSelectedRegion();

        return retVal;
    }

    public Enumeration regions()
    {
        Enumeration retVal = null;

        if(model != null) retVal = model.regions();

        return retVal;
    }
```

Methods Delegated to the UI Object

Now let's look at the methods delegated to the UI object. This is a little tricky. First, we want to provide valid return values if no UI object is available. Second, we need to make sure to call the super.paint method after we have the user interface paint the contents. This causes all of the component's children to be painted. You should include this step even if you don't plan to put children on this component. This way, if someone uses your component and adds children to it, the children behave correctly. The methods to determine our preferred, minimum and maximum size are also delegated to the UI object. Because the TouchScreenUI is simply a subtype of ComponentUI, we rely on ComponentUI methods during this stage of development.

```
public void paint(Graphics g)
{
    if (ui != null)
    {
        ui.paint(g, this);
    }

    super.paint(g);  // paint children if any
}

public Dimension getPreferredSize()
{
    Dimension retVal = null;

    if(ui != null) retVal = ui.getPreferredSize(this);
    else retVal = new Dimension();

    return retVal;
}

public Dimension getMinimumSize()
{
    Dimension retVal = null;

    if(ui != null) retVal = ui.getMinimumSize(this);
    else retVal = new Dimension();

    return retVal;
}

public Dimension getMaximumSize()
{
```

```
        Dimension retVal = null;

        if(ui != null) retVal = ui.getMaximumSize(this);
        else retVal = new Dimension();

        return retVal;
    }
```

The Touch Screen's ChangeListener

Finally, we need to implement the default ChangeListener for the model. Our implementation repaints the screen when a change occurs and, if there is a selected region, tells the TouchScreen object to notify its action listeners. Remember, one of these objects was created in the constructor, via a convenience method.

```
class DefTSChangeListener implements ChangeListener
{
    TouchScreen screen;

    public DefTSChangeListener(TouchScreen ts)
    {
        screen = ts;
    }

    public void stateChanged(ChangeEvent e)
    {
        if(screen != null)
        {
            TouchScreenModel mod;
            mod = screen.getModel();

            screen.repaint();

            if(mod.getSelectedRegion() != null)
            {
                screen.notifyListeners();
            }
        }
    }
}
```

Complete TouchScreen.java File

That's it. The completed TouchScreen.java file looks like this:

```
import java.util.*;
import java.awt.*;
import java.awt.event.*;
import com.sun.java.swing.*;
import com.sun.java.swing.event.*;
import com.sun.java.swing.text.*;

public class TouchScreen extends JComponent
{
    protected Vector actList;
    protected ChangeListener changeList;
    protected String actionCmd;
    TouchScreenModel model;
    TouchScreenUI ui;
    Color hilightColor;

    public TouchScreen()
    {
        changeList = createChangeListener();
        actList = new Vector();
        hilightColor = Color.green;

        setModel(createDefaultModel());

        updateUI();
    }

    /**
     * Notification from the UIFactory that the L&F
     * has changed.
     */
    public void updateUI()
    {
        TouchScreenUI ui;

        ui = (TouchScreenUI)UIManager.getUI(this);

        if(ui == null) ui = createDefaultUI();

        setUI(ui);
    }


    /**
```

```
 * Returns a string that specifies the name of the L&F class
 * that renders this component.
 */
public String getUIClassID()
{
    return "TouchScreenUI";
}

public TouchScreenUI getUI()
{
    return ui;
}

public void setUI(TouchScreenUI newUI)
{
    TouchScreenUI oldUI = getUI();

    if(oldUI == newUI) return;//don't do anything

    if(oldUI != null) oldUI.uninstallUI(this);

    ui = newUI;

    if(ui != null) ui.installUI(this);

    invalidate();
}

public TouchScreenModel getModel()
{
    return model;
}

public void setModel(TouchScreenModel newModel)
{
    TouchScreenModel oldModel = getModel();

    if (oldModel != null)
    {
        oldModel.removeChangeListener(changeList);
    }

    model = newModel;

    if (newModel != null)
```

```
        {
            newModel.addChangeListener(changeList);
        }
    }

    public void setActionCommand(String cmd)
    {
        actionCmd = cmd;
    }

    public String getActionCommand()
    {
        return actionCmd;
    }

    //Use a vector to support multiple listeners
    public void addActionListener(ActionListener al)
    {
        if(!actList.contains(al)) actList.addElement(al);
    }

    public void removeActionListener(ActionListener al)
    {
        actList.addElement(al);
    }

    //Method to notify action listeners
    void notifyListeners()
    {
        int i,max;
        ActionEvent evt;
        ActionListener curListener;

        evt = new ActionEvent(this,ActionEvent.ACTION_PERFORMED,actionCmd);

        max = actList.size();

        for(i=0;i<max;i++)
        {
            curListener = (ActionListener) actList.elementAt(i);

            curListener.actionPerformed(evt);
        }
    }
```

```
/*
 * Hilight color accessors
 */
public void setHilightColor(Color c)
{
    hilightColor = c;
}

public Color getHilightColor()
{
    return hilightColor;
}

/*
 * Methods delegated to the model
 */

public void setImage(Image i)
{
    if(model != null) model.setImage(i);
}

public Image getImage()
{
    Image retVal = null;

    if(model != null) retVal = model.getImage();

    return retVal;
}

public void addRegion(Shape s)
{
    if(model != null) model.addRegion(s);
}

public void removeRegion(Shape s)
{
    if(model != null) model.removeRegion(s);
}

public void selectRegion(Shape s)
{
    if(model!=null) model.selectRegion(s);
}
```

```
    public void selectRegionForPoint(Point p)
    {
        if(model!=null) model.selectRegionForPoint(p);
    }

    public Shape getSelectedRegion()
    {
        Shape retVal = null;

        if(model != null) retVal = model.getSelectedRegion();

        return retVal;
    }

    public Enumeration regions()
    {
        Enumeration retVal = null;

        if(model != null) retVal = model.regions();

        return retVal;
    }

    /*
     * Methods to delegate to the ui object
     */
    public void paint(Graphics g)
    {
        if (ui != null)
        {
            ui.paint(g, this);
        }

        super.paint(g);  // paint children if any
    }

    public Dimension getPreferredSize()
    {
        Dimension retVal = null;

        if(ui != null) retVal = ui.getPreferredSize(this);
        else retVal = new Dimension();

        return retVal;
    }
```

```
    public Dimension getMinimumSize()
    {
        Dimension retVal = null;

        if(ui != null) retVal = ui.getMinimumSize(this);
        else retVal = new Dimension();

        return retVal;
    }

    public Dimension getMaximumSize()
    {
        Dimension retVal = null;

        if(ui != null) retVal = ui.getMaximumSize(this);
        else retVal = new Dimension();

        return retVal;
    }

    /*
     * Methods to help subclasses.
     */
    protected ChangeListener createChangeListener()
    {
        return new DefTSChangeListener(this);
    }

    protected TouchScreenModel createDefaultModel()
    {
        return new TouchScreenModelImp();
    }

    protected TouchScreenUI createDefaultUI()
    {
        return BasicTouchScreenUI.createUI(this);
    }
}

class DefTSChangeListener implements ChangeListener
{
    TouchScreen screen;

    public DefTSChangeListener(TouchScreen ts)
```

```
        {
            screen = ts;
        }

        public void stateChanged(ChangeEvent e)
        {
            if(screen != null)
            {
                TouchScreenModel mod;
                mod = screen.getModel();

                screen.repaint();

                if(mod.getSelectedRegion() != null)
                {
                    screen.notifyListeners();
                }
            }
        }
    }
```

Step 7: Implement at Least One UI Object

At this point we need to implement at least one class that implements TouchScreenUI. Let's call it BasicTouchScreenUI. Because we want the UI to define the feel of our component, we have created it to act as a MouseListener—updating the model when a mouse event occurs. The UI object also acts as a MouseMotionListener for the touch screen to highlight regions as the user drags the mouse.

The UI object is also responsible for defining the component's look. This means defining the preferred, maximum, and minimum sizes as well as the paint method. The sizes are determined from the current image and the border, if any. The paint method paints the image scaled to fit inside the border, then draws the selected and/or highlighted regions. Notice that if the region is a rectangle, it's intersected with the bounds so that it fits in the available area.

A convenience method, getBorderInsets, is used to calculate a nonnull set of insets based on the component's border. If the component doesn't have a border these insets are 0.

Finally, the UI object must implement the installUI and deinstallUI methods. These methods are called by the pluggable look-and-feel framework when the look and feel for a component changes. This includes the first time a component is assigned a look and feel. In our implementation we add and remove the UI as a MouseListener during these methods.

NOTE

For simplicity, this UI object doesn't take into account scaling when calculating the regions to draw and hit test. This means that if you change the default size of the component's content, further calculations are required to determine where the mouse actually clicked on the image.

The completed BasicTouchScreenUI is defined as follows:

```
import java.util.*;
import java.awt.*;
import java.awt.event.*;
import com.sun.java.swing.*;
import com.sun.java.swing.border.*;
import com.sun.java.swing.text.*;

public class BasicTouchScreenUI extends TouchScreenUI
implements MouseListener, MouseMotionListener
{
    Shape hilightRegion;

    /*
     * Method for creating ui objects
     */
    public static BasicTouchScreenUI createUI(TouchScreen ts)
    {
        return new BasicTouchScreenUI();
    }

    /*
     * Mouse listener method.
     */
    public void mouseClicked(MouseEvent evt)
    {
    }

    public void mousePressed(MouseEvent evt)
    {
    }

    public void mouseReleased(MouseEvent evt)
    {
        TouchScreenModel mod;
        TouchScreen screen;
```

```
        screen = (TouchScreen) evt.getSource();
        mod = screen.getModel();

        mod.selectRegionForPoint(evt.getPoint());
    }

    public void mouseEntered(MouseEvent evt)
    {
    }

    public void mouseExited(MouseEvent evt)
    {
        TouchScreen screen;

        screen = (TouchScreen) evt.getSource();
        hilightRegion = null;
        screen.repaint();
    }

    /*
     * Mouse motion methods.
     */

    public void mouseDragged(MouseEvent evt)
    {
    }

    public void mouseMoved(MouseEvent evt)
    {
        TouchScreenModel mod;
        TouchScreen screen;

        screen = (TouchScreen) evt.getSource();
        mod = screen.getModel();

        hilightRegion = mod.getRegionForPoint(evt.getPoint());
        screen.repaint();
    }

    /*
     * Overriden ComponentUI methods.
     */
    public void paint(Graphics g,JComponent c)
    {
```

```
Image img;
TouchScreenModel mod;
TouchScreen screen;
Shape selRegion;
Color clr;
Dimension size = c.getSize();
Rectangle bounds;
Rectangle imageBounds;
Insets border = getBorderInsets(c);

screen = (TouchScreen) c;
mod = screen.getModel();
img = mod.getImage();

imageBounds = new Rectangle();
imageBounds.width = size.width-border.left-border.right;
imageBounds.height = size.height-border.top-border.bottom;
imageBounds.x = border.left;
imageBounds.y = border.top;

/*
 * This is a simple version that assumes the
 * component is big enough, and there is no border.
 */
if(img != null)
{
     g.drawImage(img,imageBounds.x
                     ,imageBounds.y
                     ,imageBounds.width
                     ,imageBounds.height
                     ,c);
}

if(hilightRegion != null)
{
    g.setColor(((TouchScreen)c).getHilightColor());

    if(hilightRegion instanceof Polygon)
    {
        g.drawPolygon((Polygon)hilightRegion);
    }
    else
    {
        bounds = hilightRegion.getBounds();
```

```
                bounds = bounds.intersection(imageBounds);

                //Subtract 1 for round off
                g.drawRect(bounds.x,bounds.y
                              ,bounds.width-1,bounds.height-1);
            }
        }

        selRegion= mod.getSelectedRegion();

        if(selRegion != null)
        {
            clr = c.getForeground();
            g.setColor(clr);

            if(selRegion instanceof Polygon)
            {
                g.drawPolygon((Polygon)selRegion);
            }
            else
            {
                bounds = selRegion.getBounds();

                bounds = bounds.intersection(imageBounds);

                //Subtract 1 for round off
                g.drawRect(bounds.x,bounds.y
                              ,bounds.width-1,bounds.height-1);
            }
        }

    }

    public Dimension getPreferredSize(JComponent c)
    {
        Dimension retVal = new Dimension();
        Image img;
        TouchScreenModel mod;
        TouchScreen screen;
        Insets border = getBorderInsets(c);

        screen = (TouchScreen) c;
        mod = screen.getModel();
        img = mod.getImage();
```

```
        if(img != null)
        {
            retVal.width = img.getWidth(c);
            retVal.height = img.getHeight(c);
        }

        if(border != null)
        {
            retVal.width += border.left + border.right;
            retVal.height += border.top + border.bottom;
        }

        return retVal;
    }

    public Dimension getMinimumSize(JComponent c)
    {
        return getPreferredSize(c);
    }

    public Dimension getMaximumSize(JComponent c)
    {
        return getPreferredSize(c);
    }

    protected Insets getBorderInsets(JComponent c)
    {
        Border b = c.getBorder();
        Insets retVal;

        if(b != null)
        {
            retVal = b.getBorderInsets(c);
        }
        else
        {
            retVal = new Insets(0,0,0,0);
        }

        return retVal;
    }

    /*
     * Methods for adding and removing the ui
     */
```

```
    public void installUI(JComponent c)
    {
        TouchScreen screen;

        screen = (TouchScreen)c;
         screen.addMouseListener(this);
         screen.addMouseMotionListener(this);
    }

    public void uninstallUI(JComponent c)
    {
        TouchScreen screen;

        screen = (TouchScreen)c;
         screen.removeMouseListener(this);
         screen.removeMouseMotionListener(this);
    }
}
```

Step 8: Implement at Least One Version of the Model

The next-to-last step in defining our custom component is to create at least one model. We create a model called TouchScreenModelImp that stores a vector of regions and selects regions by bounds or selects polygons by containment for efficiency. The region also keeps track of the image for a touch-screen component and the currently selected region. Whenever the current selection changes, a ChangeEvent is fired. Notice that our support for ChangeListeners is very similar to the component's support for ActionListeners. This is a standard code pattern that you can use over and over again in custom components. Programs can add and remove regions, select a region, and get the region for a specific point.

```
import java.util.*;
import java.awt.*;
import java.awt.event.*;
import com.sun.java.swing.*;
import com.sun.java.swing.event.*;
import com.sun.java.swing.text.*;

public class TouchScreenModelImp implements TouchScreenModel
{
    protected Image img;
    protected Vector regions;
    protected Vector changeList;
```

```
protected Shape selectedRegion;

public TouchScreenModelImp()
{
    regions = new Vector();
    changeList = new Vector();
}

public void setImage(Image i)
{
    if(img != i)
    {
        img = i;
        notifyListeners();
    }
}

public Image getImage()
{
    return img;
}

public void addRegion(Shape s)
{
    if(! regions.contains(s)) regions.addElement(s);
}

public void removeRegion(Shape s)
{
    regions.removeElement(s);
}

public void selectRegion(Shape s)
{
    if((s == null) || regions.contains(s))
    {
        selectedRegion = s;
        notifyListeners();
    }
}

public void selectRegionForPoint(Point p)
{
    selectRegion(getRegionForPoint(p));
}
```

```
public Shape getRegionForPoint(Point p)
{
    Enumeration regions = regions();
    Shape curRegion=null;
    Rectangle bounds;

    if(p == null) return null;

    while(regions.hasMoreElements())
    {
        curRegion = (Shape) regions.nextElement();

        if(curRegion instanceof Polygon)
        {
            if(((Polygon)curRegion).contains(p))
            {
                break;
            }
        }
        else
        {
            bounds = curRegion.getBounds();
            if(bounds.contains(p))
            {
                break;
            }
            else
            {
                curRegion = null;
            }
        }
    }

    return curRegion;
}

public Shape getSelectedRegion()
{
    return selectedRegion;
}

public Enumeration regions()
{
    return regions.elements();
}
```

```
    /*
     * use a vector to support multiple listeners
     */
    public void addChangeListener(ChangeListener cl)
    {
        if(!changeList.contains(cl)) changeList.addElement(cl);
    }

    public void removeChangeListener(ChangeListener cl)
    {
        changeList.removeElement(cl);
    }

    protected void notifyListeners()
    {
        ChangeEvent evt;
        int i,max;
        ChangeListener curListener;

        evt = new ChangeEvent(this);

        max= changeList.size();

        for(i=0;i<max;i++)
        {
            curListener = (ChangeListener) changeList.elementAt(i);
            curListener.stateChanged(evt);
        }
    }
}
```

Custom implementations of TouchScreenModel could include support for other region shapes and tool tips for the various regions.

Step 9: Test Your Component

At last, you have a custom component. The final step is to test it. Certainly if you plan to deploy your component to customers, you want to test it thoroughly. The first step in the testing process is to create a simple program that displays the component and interacts with it. For our example we simply add a screen component with a border to a panel, add several regions to it, and print messages when action events are received. This example test is shown in Figure 16.3.

```
import java.util.*;
import java.awt.*;
```

Figure 16.3 Touch-screen test.

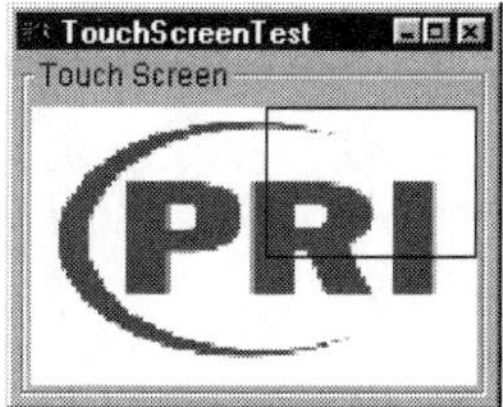


```
import java.awt.event.*;
import com.sun.java.swing.*;
import com.sun.java.swing.text.*;
import com.sun.java.swing.border.*;

public class TouchScreenTest extends JPanel
implements ActionListener
{
    TouchScreen screen;

    public TouchScreenTest()
    {
        Toolkit kit = Toolkit.getDefaultToolkit();
        Image img;
        TouchScreenModel mod;

        setBackground(Color.lightGray);
        /*
         * Turn on buffering to reduce flicker.
         */
        setDoubleBuffered(true);

        setLayout(new BorderLayout());

        img = kit.getImage("images/logo.gif");

        screen = new TouchScreen();
        screen.setForeground(Color.blue);
        screen.addActionListener(this);
        screen.setActionCommand("Screen Action");

        screen.setBorder(new TitledBorder("Touch Screen"));

        add(screen,"Center");
```

```
        mod = screen.getModel();

        mod.setImage(img);
        mod.addRegion(new Rectangle(0,0,100,80));
        mod.addRegion(new Rectangle(0,80,100,80));
        mod.addRegion(new Rectangle(100,0,100,80));
        mod.addRegion(new Rectangle(100,80,100,80));
    }

    public void actionPerformed(ActionEvent e)
    {
        String cmd;
        TouchScreen source;
        TouchScreenModel mod;
        Shape curReg;
        Rectangle bounds=null;

        source = (TouchScreen) e.getSource();
        cmd = e.getActionCommand();
        mod = screen.getModel();

        curReg = mod.getSelectedRegion();
        if(curReg != null)
        {
            bounds = curReg.getBounds();
        }

        System.out.println("Action: "+cmd);
        if(bounds != null) System.out.println("\t Sel region: "+bounds);
    }

    public Dimension getPreferredSize()
    {
        return new Dimension(200,160);
    }

    public static void main(String s[])
    {
        JFrame frame = new JFrame("TouchScreenTest");
        TouchScreenTest panel = new TouchScreenTest();

        frame.setForeground(Color.black);
        frame.setBackground(Color.lightGray);
```

```
        frame.addWindowListener(new WindowCloser());
        frame.getContentPane().add(panel,"Center");

        frame.setSize(panel.getPreferredSize());
        frame.setVisible(true);
    }
}
```

We included the WindowCloser class with the TouchScreenTest to handle the close box.

```
class WindowCloser extends WindowAdapter
{
    public void windowClosing(WindowEvent e)
    {
        Window win = e.getWindow();
        win.setVisible(false);
        win.dispose();
        System.exit(0);
    }
}
```

To run this test on your computer you may need to update the file path for the touch-screen component's image. This image, pictured in Figure 16.3, is provided on the CD-ROM along with the entire code from this example.

Conclusions

Our touch-screen component is a fairly usable object. JFC is a large, feature-rich library. You may not find it necessary to support every feature in your components. You can create custom components that look the same in all interfaces or components that change. Components can use models or store their own data. It's up to you. If you decide that you need a custom component that supports the MVC model and pluggable look and feels, then create one with our nine-step process.

Depending on your intentions and decisions throughout the process, you can collapse this process into fewer steps by combining the UI and component, model and component, or all three into one class.

17 Other JFC Topics

Several topics did not quite fit into the other chapters, yet we didn't want to leave them out of this book. As a result, this chapter discusses a collection of topics that are not all related.

Here are the topics that we discuss in this chapter:

- Pluggable look-and-feel architecture (expected to change from JFC versions 1.1 to 1.2 so we didn't want to spend an entire chapter on it)
- Animated icons
- Headers on Scroll panes
- Custom list models
- SwingUtilities class
- The Undo framework

Combined with the previous chapters and the examples in the next two chapters, we hope that this eclectic collection of topics rounds out your JFC 1.1 and Swing education and provides the foundation that will allow you to write some great programs with Swing.

Pluggable Look-and-Feel Architecture

We have mentioned the pluggable look-and-feel feature of Swing several times throughout this book. Because the look-and-feel architecture is expected to change, we thought it would be worth introducing the features without diving into too much detail. We also provide a simple example that changes its look and feel.

> **WARNING**
>
> JavaSoft has officially stated that the APIs for the pluggable look-and-feel architecture may change. We doubt that the UI objects will change much, but the implementations provided by JavaSoft probably will.

Pluggable look-and-feel architectures are supported by the UI objects that components use, as well as the LookAndFeel class. This class acts as a parent to all other classes that want to define a new look and feel. For a programmer to create a new look and feel, he or she must extend the LookAndFeel class or one of the existing subclasses such as the WindowsLookAndFeel class. The look-and-feel object maps the UI types like ButtonUI to a specific class, like com.sun.java.swing.basic.BasicUI. This mapping is handled with a UIDefaults object.

The next step for the adventurous programmer who wants to create a custom look and feel is to implement your own version of the UI objects. Because Swing has a lot of components, you may want to extend an existing look and feel and take advantage of its UI objects for components for which you don't need to modify the look and feel. If you think writing a look and feel sounds like a lot of work, you're right. Unless you can leverage an existing look and feel, you need to write more than 40 classes to create a unique look and feel. That doesn't include all of the model changes and event listeners required to make the look and feel respond to user input. It's a big job. JavaSoft provides several look and feels with Swing. The current look and feels include a Windows, Macintosh, Motif, and platform-neutral look and feel. This means that most users will see Java programs that look like any other program on their desktop. In general, creating a custom look and feel is probably something that large companies will find useful to create a consistent, enterprise-specific, cross-platform style for their programs.

Because we don't want to start people down the hard road of creating look and feels, we at least wanted to show how the look and feel is changed programmatically. This example uses the Windows and Motif look and feels provided by JavaSoft. Depending on licensing issues, it may not run on a non-Microsoft platform. As a result, check the documentation for available look and feels and feel free to edit the example before you run it from the CD-ROM. Because this is a legal issue, it may not be decided until the last minute, or later. To be safe, you should plan to use a non-Windows look and feel if you are not on a Windows platform.

An object called the UIManager is responsible for keeping track of the current look and feel. When a JComponent is told to updateUI or get a new UI object, it checks with the UIManager. Therefore, to change the look and feel, we change the UIManager's current look and feel and tell all of our components to updateUI. In this example we use a convenience method in the SwingUtilities class to call updateUI on the components. This method takes a component, called updateUI, on it and then calls updateUI on its children and their children, as shown here:

```
SwingUtilities.updateComponentTreeUI(Component c);
```

The interface for our example includes a number of components, just so you can see the look and feel change, and a set of radio buttons for changing the look and feel. When a radio button is pressed, both the UIManager and our components are updated. To make sure that our main panel is displayed correctly in the new look and feel, we validate it, to cause a layout and repaint. This ensures that each component's UI is redrawn in the new look and feel.

```
import java.util.*;
import java.awt.*;
import java.awt.event.*;
import com.sun.java.swing.*;
import com.sun.java.swing.text.*;

public class Windows2Motif extends JPanel
implements ActionListener
{
    public Windows2Motif()
    {
        JTextField field;
        AbstractButton button;
        JSlider slider;
        JRadioButton radioButton;
        ButtonGroup grp;
        JPanel topPanel, bottomPanel;

        setLayout(new BorderLayout());
        setBackground(Color.lightGray);

        topPanel = new JPanel();
        topPanel.setLayout(new GridLayout(3,2,5,5));

        field = new JTextField("TextField",10);
        topPanel.add(field);

        button = new JButton("Button");
        topPanel.add(button);

        button = new JCheckBox("Checkbox");
        topPanel.add(button);

        button = new JRadioButton("RadioButton");
        topPanel.add(button);

        slider = new JSlider(JSlider.HORIZONTAL,0,100,50);
        slider.setMajorTickSpacing(10);
        slider.setPaintTicks(true);
        topPanel.add(slider);

        add(topPanel,"Center");

        bottomPanel = new JPanel();
        bottomPanel.setLayout(new FlowLayout(FlowLayout.CENTER,5,5));
```

```
        grp = new ButtonGroup();

        radioButton =  new JRadioButton("Windows",true);
        radioButton.addActionListener(this);
        radioButton.setActionCommand("Windows");
        grp.add(radioButton);
        bottomPanel.add(radioButton);

        radioButton =  new JRadioButton("Motif",false);
        radioButton.addActionListener(this);
        radioButton.setActionCommand("Motif");
        grp.add(radioButton);
        bottomPanel.add(radioButton);

        add(bottomPanel,"South");
    }

    public void actionPerformed(ActionEvent e)
    {
        String cmd;

        cmd = e.getActionCommand();

        if(cmd.equals("Windows")) setUI2Windows();
        else if(cmd.equals("Motif")) setUI2Motif();
    }

    public void setUI2Motif()
    {
        try
        {
            Container parent;
            String cn = "com.sun.java.swing.";

            cn+="motif.MotifLookAndFeel";

            parent = getParent();

            if(parent != null)
            {
                UIManager.setLookAndFeel(cn);

                SwingUtilities.updateComponentTreeUI(this);
                parent.validate();
                parent.repaint();
            }
```

```
        }
        catch(Exception e)
        {
            System.out.println(e);
            e.printStackTrace(System.out);
        }
    }

    public void setUI2Windows()
    {
        try
        {
            Container parent;
            String cn = "com.sun.java.swing.";

            cn+="windows.WindowsLookAndFeel";

            parent = getParent();

            if(parent != null)
            {
                UIManager.setLookAndFeel(cn);

                SwingUtilities.updateComponentTreeUI(this);
                parent.validate();
                parent.repaint();
            }
        }
        catch(Exception e)
        {
            System.out.println(e);
            e.printStackTrace(System.out);
        }
    }

    public Dimension getPreferredSize()
    {
        return new Dimension(200, 200);
    }

    public static void main(String s[])
    {
        JFrame frame = new JFrame("Windows2Motif");
        Windows2Motif panel = new Windows2Motif();
        String cn = "com.sun.java.swing.";
```

```
            cn+="windows.WindowsLookAndFeel";

            frame.setForeground(Color.black);
            frame.setBackground(Color.lightGray);
            frame.addWindowListener(new WindowCloser());
            frame.getContentPane().add(panel,"Center");

            try
            {
                UIManager.setLookAndFeel(cn);
                SwingUtilities.updateComponentTreeUI(frame);
            }
            catch(Exception exp)
            {
                System.out.println(exp);
            }

            frame.setSize(panel.getPreferredSize());
            frame.setVisible(true);
        }
}
```

This example includes the WindowCloser class to manage the close box.

```
class WindowCloser extends WindowAdapter
{
    public void windowClosing(WindowEvent e)
    {
        Window win = e.getWindow();
        win.setVisible(false);
        System.exit(0);
    }
}
```

Figure 17.1 shows this program with each look and feel.

Animated Icons

As we worked on this book we planned to write a custom icon that handled animations. It turns out that the ImageIcon class already does this. If an ImageIcon object is created for a gif89-animated image, it displays the animation. As you may already know, GIF stands for Graphical Interchange Format. The gif89 format is a graphic format that succeeded the gif87a specification. The gif89 specification, written in 1989 by CompuServe, allows layering of images in a single file so that animation is possible. The specification is robust enough to provide a description of animation timing, image interlacing, image transparency, and more.

Figure 17.1 Switching the look and feel.

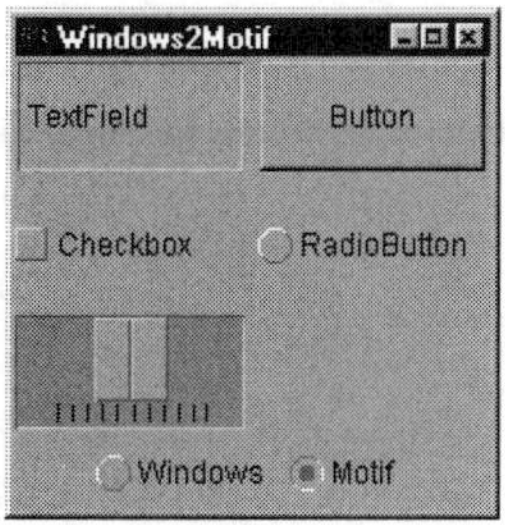

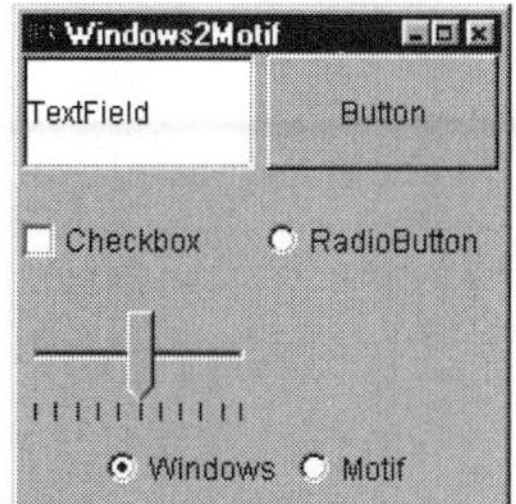

To test the ImageIcon class, and to show how easy it is to create an animated icon, we created the following example. This example uses an icon on a label. You can also put an animated icon in a text pane or on a button. Although it's not necessary, notice that our program tells the ImageIcon to use the component we add it to as an ImageObserver, which may be useful to some components that want information about the image loading or animating.

```
import com.sun.java.swing.*;
import java.awt.event.*;

import java.awt.*;
import java.lang.*;

public class AnimExample extends JPanel
{
    JLabel label;

    public AnimExample()
    {
        ImageIcon icon;

        setBackground(Color.white);

        icon = new ImageIcon("images/plane.gif");

        label = new JLabel(icon,JLabel.CENTER);
        icon.setImageObserver(label);

        add(label,"Center");
    }

    public Dimension getPreferredSize()
    {
        return label.getPreferredSize();
```

```
    }

    public static void main(String s[])
    {
        JFrame frame = new JFrame("AnimatedIcon");
        AnimExample panel = new AnimExample();

        frame.setForeground(Color.black);
        frame.setBackground(Color.lightGray);
        frame.addWindowListener(new WindowCloser());
        frame.getContentPane().add(panel,"Center");

        frame.setSize(panel.getPreferredSize());
        frame.setVisible(true);
    }
}
```

This example includes the WindowCloser class to manage the close box.

```
import java.awt.*;
import java.awt.event.*;
class WindowCloser extends WindowAdapter
{
    public void windowClosing(WindowEvent e)
    {
        Window win = e.getWindow();
        win.setVisible(false);
        System.exit(0);
    }
}
```

When run, this application looks like the one pictured in Figure 17.2.

Scroll Pane Headers

JScrollPane provides seven different areas that you can control. In Chapter 6, we focused on the main area of the scroll pane called the viewport view. The pane

Figure 17.2 Animated icon.

can also place components in its four corners and provide headers for the rows and columns. To set these components, use the following three methods:

```
public void setRowHeaderView(Component view);
public void setColumnHeaderView(Component view);
public void setCorner(String key,
                        Component x);
```

In general, the row header is displayed on the right side and the column header on the top of the scroll pane's area. The corners are positioned in the four corners based on named positions. These positions are defined in JScrollPane static variables:

```
LOWER_LEFT_CORNER
LOWER_RIGHT_CORNER
UPPER_LEFT_CORNER
UPPER _RIGHT_CORNER
```

The components in these named corners are displayed whenever their associated scroll bar is visible.

To demonstrate these headers and corners we have created three classes. The first, HRuler, defines a component that is approximately one foot long and displays tick marks every quarter of an inch—basically, a horizontal ruler. The HRuler is also a MouseMotionListener. When assigned an object to watch, the HRuler displays a highlighted tick mark at the current mouse location. The code for HRuler looks like this:

```
import com.sun.java.swing.*;
import java.awt.event.*;

import java.awt.*;

public class HRuler extends JComponent
implements MouseMotionListener
{
    int curX;

    public void paint(Graphics g)
    {
        Dimension curSize=getSize();
        int i,max;

        g.setColor(getBackground());
        g.fillRect(0,0,curSize.width,curSize.height);

        g.setColor(Color.black);

        max = curSize.width/72;

        for(i=0;i<max;i++)
```

```
        {
            g.drawLine(i*72,curSize.height,i*72,0);
            g.drawLine(i*36,curSize.height/2,i*36,0);
            g.drawLine(i*18,curSize.height/4,i*18,0);
            g.drawLine(i*54,curSize.height/4,i*54,0);
        }

        if(curX > 0)
        {
            g.setColor(Color.blue);
            g.drawLine(curX,curSize.height,curX,0);
        }
    }

    public void mouseDragged(MouseEvent evt)
    {
        curX = evt.getX();
        repaint();
    }

    public void mouseMoved(MouseEvent evt)
    {
        curX = evt.getX();
        repaint();
    }

    public Dimension getPreferredSize()
    {
        return new Dimension(72*12, 16);
    }
}
```

We also created a vertical version of the HRuler called VRuler. This is basically the same code, turned sideways.

```
import com.sun.java.swing.*;
import java.awt.event.*;

import java.awt.*;

public class VRuler extends JComponent
implements MouseMotionListener
{
    int curY;

    public void paint(Graphics g)
    {
```

```
        Dimension curSize=getSize();
        int i,max;

        g.setColor(getBackground());
        g.fillRect(0,0,curSize.width,curSize.height);

        g.setColor(Color.black);

        max = curSize.height/72;

        for(i=0;i<max;i++)
        {
            g.drawLine(0,i*72,curSize.width,i*72);
            g.drawLine(0,i*36,curSize.width/2,i*36);
            g.drawLine(0,i*18,curSize.width/4,i*18);
            g.drawLine(0,i*54,curSize.width/4,i*54);
        }

        if(curY > 0)
        {
            g.setColor(Color.blue);
            g.drawLine(0,curY,curSize.width,curY);
        }
    }

    public void mouseDragged(MouseEvent evt)
    {
        curY = evt.getY();
        repaint();
    }

    public void mouseMoved(MouseEvent evt)
    {
        curY = evt.getY();
        repaint();
    }

    public Dimension getPreferredSize()
    {
        return new Dimension(16,72*12);
    }
}
```

For the corners we implemented a class called Corner. A corner object is a 16 × 16 square that draws a blue circle in its center. The corner is also a mouse listener and keeps track of the scroll pane's main view. When the corner is pressed, it checks which location it's in and scrolls that corner of the main view to visible. To handle the scrolling, we use the JComponent method scrollRectToVisible. Based on the corner location, we create a 1×1 rectangle to pass to this method that is in the correct location.

```
import com.sun.java.swing.*;
import java.awt.event.*;

import java.awt.*;

public class Corner extends JComponent
implements MouseListener
{
    JComponent toScroll;
    String position;

    public Corner(JComponent ts,String pos)
    {
        position = pos;
        toScroll = ts;
        addMouseListener(this);
    }

    public void paint(Graphics g)
    {
        Dimension curSize=getSize();
        int i,max;

        g.setColor(getBackground());
        g.fillRect(0,0,curSize.width,curSize.height);

        g.setColor(Color.blue);
        g.fillOval(0,0,curSize.width,curSize.height);
    }

    public Dimension getPreferredSize()
    {
        return new Dimension(16,16);
    }

    public void mouseClicked(MouseEvent e)
    {
        Rectangle rect= new Rectangle();
        Dimension size = toScroll.getSize();
```

```
        if(position.equals(JScrollPane.UPPER_LEFT_CORNER))
        {
            rect.x = 0;
            rect.y = 0;
            rect.width = 1;
            rect.height = 1;
        }
        else if(position.equals(JScrollPane.LOWER_LEFT_CORNER))
        {
            rect.x = 0;
            rect.y = size.height-1;
            rect.width = 1;
            rect.height = 1;
        }
        else if(position.equals(JScrollPane.UPPER_RIGHT_CORNER))
        {
            rect.x = size.width-1;
            rect.y = 0;
            rect.width = 1;
            rect.height = 1;
        }
        else if(position.equals(JScrollPane.LOWER_RIGHT_CORNER))
        {
            rect.x = size.width-1;
            rect.y = size.height-1;
            rect.width = 1;
            rect.height = 1;
        }

        toScroll.scrollRectToVisible(rect);
    }

    public void mousePressed(MouseEvent e)
    {
    }

    public void mouseReleased(MouseEvent e)
    {
    }

    public void mouseEntered(MouseEvent e)
    {
    }

    public void mouseExited(MouseEvent e)
```

```
    {
    }
}
```

Finally, we create an example that generates a scroll pane that contains a label with an image icon. The headers are set to rulers and the corners to corner objects.

```
import com.sun.java.swing.*;
import java.awt.event.*;

import java.awt.*;

public class RulerExample extends JPanel
{
    public RulerExample()
    {
        JScrollPane scroller;
        JLabel mainView;
        HRuler hRuler;
        VRuler vRuler;
        String pos;

        setLayout(new BorderLayout());

        mainView = new JLabel(new ImageIcon("logo.gif"));

        hRuler = new HRuler();
        mainView.addMouseMotionListener(hRuler);

        vRuler = new VRuler();
        mainView.addMouseMotionListener(vRuler);

        scroller = new JScrollPane(mainView);

        scroller.setColumnHeaderView(hRuler);
        scroller.setRowHeaderView(vRuler);

        pos = JScrollPane.UPPER_LEFT_CORNER;
        scroller.setCorner(pos,new Corner(mainView,pos));

        pos = JScrollPane.LOWER_LEFT_CORNER;
        scroller.setCorner(pos,new Corner(mainView,pos));

        pos = JScrollPane.UPPER_RIGHT_CORNER;
        scroller.setCorner(pos,new Corner(mainView,pos));
```

```
            pos = JScrollPane.LOWER_RIGHT_CORNER;
            scroller.setCorner(pos,new Corner(mainView,pos));

            add(scroller,"Center");
        }

        public Dimension getPreferredSize()
        {
            return new Dimension(600, 600);
        }

        public static void main(String s[])
        {
            JFrame frame = new JFrame("Ruler Example");
            RulerExample rulers = new RulerExample();

            frame.setDefaultCloseOperation(JFrame.DO_NOTHING_ON_CLOSE);
            frame.setForeground(Color.black);
            frame.setBackground(Color.lightGray);
            frame.addWindowListener(new WindowCloser());
            frame.getContentPane().add(rulers,"Center");

            frame.setSize(new Dimension(300,300));
            frame.setVisible(true);
        }
    }
```

This example includes the WindowCloser class to handle the close box.

```
class WindowCloser extends WindowAdapter
{
    public void windowClosing(WindowEvent e)
    {
        Window win = e.getWindow();
        win.setVisible(false);
        System.exit(0);
    }
}
```

The running version of this example is pictured in Figure 17.3. Pay special attention to the rulers in this figure. Notice that they indicate the current mouse position with blue tick marks.

Custom List Models

As we wrote this book we included a tree and table model that retrieves its data from the file system. As an example of a custom list model, we figured we would

Figure 17.3 JScrollPane headers.

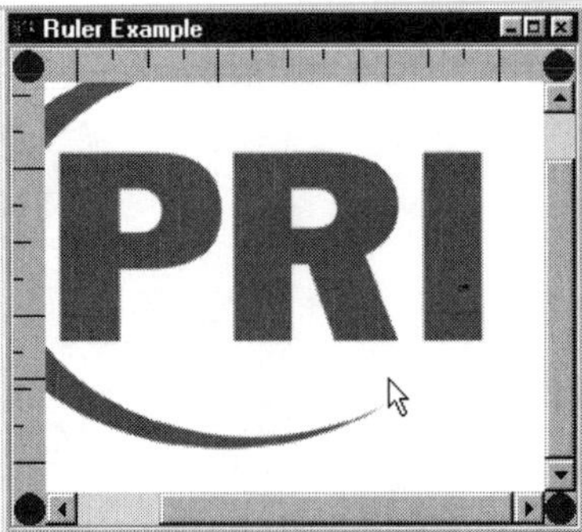

use the same data source here. To create a custom list model, you implement the ListModel interface. This interface defines the methods listed in Table 17.1.

Swing provides a template implementation called AbstractListModel that you can subclass. This class includes methods to notify the list data listeners of changes to the model. These listeners expect to receive the methods in Table 17.2 at appropriate times.

When you subclass AbstractListModel, you can use the methods found in Table 17.3 to notify your listeners.

The code in the abstract model keeps track of the listeners, creates event objects, and sends the appropriate messages.

Our file-system list model is a subclass of AbstractListModel. We construct the list model with a directory and determine the number of elements and objects for each element from the names of the files in this directory.

```
import com.sun.java.swing.*;
import com.sun.java.swing.table.*;
import com.sun.java.swing.event.*;
import java.io.*;
import java.util.*;
```

Table 17.1 ListModel Methods

Method	Function
public int getSize()	Returns the number of items in the list.
public Object getElementAt(int index)	Returns the item at the specified index.
public void addListDataListener (ListDataListener l)	Adds a ListDataListener to the model.
public void removeListDataListener (ListDataListener l)	Removes a ListDataListener from the model.

Table 17.2 ListDataListener Methods

Method	Function
public void intervalAdded(ListDataEvent e)	Notification that data was added.
public void intervalRemoved(ListDataEvent e)	Notification that data was removed.
public void contentsChanged(ListDataEvent e)	Notification that data changed in a way that exceeds a simple addition or removal.

```
public class FileSystemListModel extends AbstractListModel
{
    protected String[] fileNames;

    public FileSystemListModel(File r)
    {
       fileNames = r.list();
    }

    public int getSize()
    {
        int retVal = 0;

        if(fileNames != null) retVal = fileNames.length;

        return retVal;
    }

    public Object getElementAt(int i)
    {
        Object retVal = null;

        if(fileNames != null) retVal = fileNames[i];
```

Table 17.3 AbstractListModel Methods

Method	Usage
protected void fireContentsChanged (Object source,int index0,int index1)	Notifies listeners that the contents have changed.
protected void fireIntervalAdded (Object source,int index0,int index1)	Notifies listeners that an interval was added.
protected void fireIntervalRemoved (Object source,int index0,Int index1)	Notifies listeners that an interval was removed.

```
        return retVal;
    }
}
```

To test our list model we created a program that creates a list with a FileSystemListModel. The directory for the model is determined by the command-line arguments. The list is displayed in a scroll pane.

```
import com.sun.java.swing.*;

import java.awt.event.*;
import java.awt.*;
import java.io.*;
import java.util.*;

public class FileList extends JPanel
{
    public FileList(String startPath)
    {
        JList list;
        FileSystemListModel model;
        File root;

        setLayout(new BorderLayout());

        root = new File(startPath);
        model = new FileSystemListModel(root);

        list = new JList();
        list.setModel(model);

        add(new JScrollPane(list),"Center");
    }

    public Dimension getPreferredSize()
    {
        return new Dimension(300, 300);
    }

    public static void main(String s[])
    {
        JFrame frame = new JFrame("File List Example");
        FileList panel;

        if(s.length > 0)
            panel = new FileList(s[0]);
```

```
        else
            panel = new FileList("/");

        frame.setDefaultCloseOperation(JFrame.DO_NOTHING_ON_CLOSE);
        frame.setForeground(Color.black);
        frame.setBackground(Color.lightGray);
        frame.getContentPane().add(panel,"Center");

        frame.setSize(panel.getPreferredSize());
        frame.setVisible(true);
        frame.addWindowListener(new WindowCloser());
    }
}
```

The WindowCloser class is included in this file to handle window close events.

```
class WindowCloser extends WindowAdapter
{
    public void windowClosing(WindowEvent e)
    {
        Window win = e.getWindow();
        win.setVisible(false);
        System.exit(0);
    }
}
```

The running version of this example is pictured in Figure 17.4.

SwingUtilities

Swing includes a class called SwingUtilities that provides a number of useful methods. All of these methods are static, so you can simply invoke them using the SwingUtilities class. Table 17.4 contains some of the key methods in this class.

The Undo Framework

A common feature of most modern applications is undo. The user likes to know that if he or she makes a mistake, like deleting the wrong word, he or she can undo this mistake. Undo can be tricky to implement. You have to define what can be "undone" in your program and track all user actions so that the data that gets modified can be unmodified later. Swing provides a framework for implementing undo behavior in your programs. This framework is provided in the com.sub.java.swing.undo packages and includes classes and interfaces that help manage undo. At the heart of the undo framework is the UndoableEdit interface. Objects that implement this interface must implement the methods in Table 17.5.

Figure 17.4 File ListModel example.

Table 17.4 Key SwingUtilities Methods

Method	Function
public static void invokeAndWait (Runnable obj) throws InterruptedException, InvocationTargetException	Blocks its thread, waiting for the object's run method to invoke in the event-dispatch thread after all currently queued events are processed.
public static void invokeLater(Runnable obj)	Calls the object's run method in the event-dispatch thread after all currently queued events are processed. This call does not block.
public static Window windowForComponent (Component aComponent)	Returns the Window object that contains the specified component.
public static JRootPane getRootPane (Component c)	Returns the RootPane, if any, that contains the specified component.
public static void updateComponentTreeUI (Component c)	Sends updateUI to the Component object passed int and all of its descendants.
public static int computeStringWidth (FontMetrics fm,String str)	Computes the width of the given string with the specified font metrics. Depending on the font and string, this may be more efficient than asking the font metrics to make the same calculation.
public static boolean isEventDispatchThread()	Returns true if the current thread is the dispatch thread.

An undoable edit should be created each time the user edits the data in a program. The level of granularity for undo depends on the extent of a change that an undoable edit captures. For example, you may want to catch each key press or only the changes since the last save. This depends on the program that you write.

To make creating edit classes easier, the undo package includes a class called AbstractUndoableEdit. This class implements the UndoableEdit interface. When

Table 17.5 UndoableEdit Methods

Method	Function
public boolean addEdit (UndoableEdit anEdit)	Combines the receiving edit with the specified edit and returns true. If the new edit cannot be combined with the previous one, then the method returns false. This method is used to combine smaller edits, like a key press, into larger ones, like a set of key presses.
public boolean replaceEdit (UndoableEdit anEdit)	Replace a combined edit with the new one.
public boolean isSignificant()	Returns true if this edit is significant. This is an arbitrary status applied by the programmer, but it is intended to mark important edits. For example, typing may be significant, but moving the cursor may not.
public String getPresentationName()	Shows by what name is this edit known, for example, "insert item."
public String getUndoPresentationName()	Shows how you describe the undo action for this edit; for example, "undo insert item."
public String getRedoPresentationName()	Shows how you describe the undo action for this edit, for example, "redo insert item."
public void undo() throws CannotUndoException	Tells the edit to undo. May throw a com.sun.java.swing.undo.CannotUndoException if undoing this edit is not possible based on the current state of your application.
public boolean canUndo()	Tests whether the edit can undo.
public void redo() throws CannotRedoException	Tells the edit to redo. May throw a com.sun.java.swing.undo.CannotRedoException. It is up to the particular edit class to determine when this exception is thrown.
public boolean canRedo()	Tests whether the edit can redo.
public void die()	Tells the edit that it won't be used and cleans up any resources that it's using.

Table 17.6 Undo Classes

Class	Purpose
CompoundEdit	An edit that contains child edits. Undoing the parent undoes the children.
StateEdit	An edit that uses Hashtables to store data for an object. The object must implement the StateEditable interface. When the edit is undone the old values for the object are applied.
StateEditable	Interface that retrieves information from an object into a Hashtable and then resets the object's state using a Hashtable.
UndoManager	A CompoundEdit that manages an undo stack. Calling undo undoes the last edit on the stack.
UndoableEditEvent	Represents an activity by an edit.
UndoableEditListener	Interface for objects that want to listen for edit events.
UndoableEditSupport	Class that posts edit events and manages a list of UndoableEditListeners.

you subclass AbstractUndoableEdit, you should use super to call the inherited versions of undo and redo before performing your custom actions.

The other classes and interfaces in the undo framework are listed in Table 17.6.

Perhaps the key class that you use is the UndoManager. This class extends CompoundEdit and manages a set of edits. When you tell the undo manager to undo, it undoes the last edit. If there are three edits to undo, calling undo twice undoes the last two edits. Using the UndoManager you can implement a multilevel undo rather than letting the user undo only the last edit. The UndoManager even provides a method to set a limit on the number of edits it holds, as shown here:

```
public synchronized void setLimit(int l);
```

When the manager becomes full it tells the old edits to die and replaces them with new edits.

Undo Example

For our undo example, we implement a custom UndoableEdit that tracks keys that are typed in a text field. When you tell this edit to undo, it removes the character that was added. When you tell it to redo, it adds the character back. This class, KeyEdit, uses instance variables to keep track of the character added, the text field, and the index at which the character was added. Notice that we call super.undo and super.redo appropriately.

```
import com.sun.java.swing.*;
import com.sun.java.swing.undo.*;
```

```
public class KeyEdit extends AbstractUndoableEdit
{
    char key;
    JTextField field;
    int index;

    public KeyEdit(JTextField t,char c,int i)
    {
        key = c;
        field = t;
        index = i;
    }

    public void undo() throws CannotUndoException
    {
        super.undo();

        field.select(index-1,index);
        field.replaceSelection("");
        field.setCaretPosition(index);
    }

    public void redo() throws CannotRedoException
    {
        super.redo();
        field.setCaretPosition(index);
        field.replaceSelection(""+key);
    }
}
```

To test this example we created a simple program with a text field and two buttons. The object that creates the user interface also acts as a KeyListener for the text field and an action listener for the buttons. When a key is pressed, a KeyEdit is created and added to an UndoManager. When the undo button is pressed, the manager is told to undo. When the redo button is pressed, the manager is told to redo. If you press undo more times than there are edits, exceptions are thrown.

```
import com.sun.java.swing.*;
import com.sun.java.swing.undo.*;
import java.awt.event.*;

import java.awt.*;
import java.lang.*;

public class UndoExample extends JPanel
implements KeyListener,ActionListener
```

```
{
    JTextField field;
    UndoManager manager;

    public UndoExample()
    {
        JButton undo,redo;

        setBackground(Color.white);

        manager = new UndoManager();

        field = new JTextField(15);
        field.addKeyListener(this);

        undo = new JButton("Undo");
        undo.setActionCommand("undo");
        undo.addActionListener(this);

        redo = new JButton("Redo");
        redo.setActionCommand("redo");
        redo.addActionListener(this);

        add(field);
        add(undo);
        add(redo);
    }

    public void keyTyped(KeyEvent evt)
    {
        KeyEdit edit;
        int ind;

        ind = field.getCaretPosition();

        edit = new KeyEdit(field,evt.getKeyChar(),ind);

        manager.addEdit(edit);
    }

    public void keyPressed(KeyEvent evt)
    {
    }

    public void keyReleased(KeyEvent evt)
```

```
    {
    }

    public void actionPerformed(ActionEvent evt)
    {
        String cmd = evt.getActionCommand();

        try
        {
            if("undo".equals(cmd))
            {
                manager.undo();
            }
            else
            {
                manager.redo();
            }
        }
        catch(Exception exp)
        {
            System.out.println("Error during undo: "+exp);
        }
    }

    public Dimension getPreferredSize()
    {
        return new Dimension(400,70);
    }

    public static void main(String s[])
    {
        JFrame frame = new JFrame("Undo");
        UndoExample panel = new UndoExample();

        frame.setForeground(Color.black);
        frame.setBackground(Color.lightGray);
        frame.addWindowListener(new WindowCloser());
        frame.getContentPane().add(panel,"Center");

        frame.setSize(panel.getPreferredSize());
        frame.setVisible(true);
    }
}
```

Figure 17.5 Undo key edits.

```
class WindowCloser extends WindowAdapter
{
    public void windowClosing(WindowEvent e)
    {
        Window win = e.getWindow();
        win.setVisible(false);
        System.exit(0);
    }
}
```

The running version of this example is pictured in Figure 17.5.

Style Guidelines

If you create a user interface with a document in a scroll pane, consider using the column and row headers to act as rulers, or use any other feedback mechanism that is appropriate for the document. You can also use the corner objects to store controls. This is a common technique. Many programs provide controls for paging through a document or changing the current view of a document as corner-style objects.

If you decide to use animated icons, be conservative with them. Using too many animated icons can be very distracting, not to mention resource draining. Keep in mind that a moving icon draws attention to itself, and use them for that purpose. For example, animate a wait icon or maybe an icon that indicates a problem has occurred or a message has arrived.

The undo framework makes it easy to add undo to your application. To use undo, you must encapsulate each change to an application's data into an UndoableEdit object. This technique, like Actions, is a useful way to organize and departmentalize your code. Remember that if you support undo, you should provide logical edits. For example, allow the user to undo a selection change and not a data change. Finally, you can use the presentation names from an UndoableEdit to update menu items. For example, you might display "Undo Insert" when the user has just inserted a value and "Redo Insert" if the user just undid the insert. Updating the menu this way is especially useful in programs that support only one level of undo.

Finally, be very careful about working with the pluggable look-and-feel architecture in the current release of JFC. Although the implementation is solid, JavaSoft plans to change some things in the next release. It's probably not worth it to create all of the code necessary for a look and feel at this point.

ZIP AND JAR VIEWER EXAMPLE 18

For an example of a larger JFC program, we have created an application that views JAR and ZIP files. When the user selects a file to open, the contents of this file are mapped into a JTable. Each entry in the current file can be extracted to a directory of the user's choice. The user interface for this application is pictured in Figure 18.1. Notice that a menu is provided as well as a tool bar with options for the two main operations, opening a file and extracting entries from that file. There are also a progress bar and a status label that can be used to display the current status of an extraction process.

We created this example to show three main techniques with Swing.

1. This application organizes work into actions. These actions provide user-interface information and contain the actual code for program functionality.
2. This program uses a progress bar to notify the user of work in progress.
3. We have implemented a custom table model to minimize the work for displaying data.

We also chose this example because it uses a number of other Swing components such as a menu, tool bar, and table.

The JarViewer Application's Design

There are two major objects in the JarViewer application. The JarTableModel maps the entries in a zip/jar file into a table format. The columns for this table display the file name for each entry, their size, modification time, and comment, if any. The JJarViewer manages the current file and interface. Whenever the current zip file changes, the JJarViewer creates a new JarTableModel instance to define the table's data. The table model loads a java.util.zip.ZipFile for the new file and reads its entries. These entries are used to produce the actual data.

There are four custom Action objects in the JJarViewer class. These actions represent the open, close, quit, and extract functions of the program. Each action is implemented as a subclass of AbstractAction. The open and extract actions also provide an icon for the tool bar.

Figure 18.1 JarViewer in action.

swing.jar

File Actions

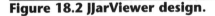

Name	Time	Size	Comment
com/sun/java/swing/JProgressBarBeanInfo.class	19-Dec-97	2 kb	
com/sun/java/swing/text/rtf/RTFReader$Discardi...	19-Dec-97	1 kb	
com/sun/java/swing/basic/BasicToolTipUI.class	19-Dec-97	2 kb	
com/sun/java/swing/text/ParagraphView$Chunk.c...	19-Dec-97	1 kb	
com/sun/java/swing/JRadioButton.class	19-Dec-97	1 kb	
com/sun/java/swing/Action.class	19-Dec-97	1 kb	
com/sun/java/swing/basic/BasicRadioButtonMen...	19-Dec-97	7 kb	
com/sun/java/swing/text/TextAction.class	19-Dec-97	1 kb	
com/sun/java/swing/JTree$AccessibleJTree.class	19-Dec-97	2 kb	
com/sun/java/swing/beaninfo/images/JToolTipC...	19-Dec-97	1 kb	
com/sun/java/swing/basic/BasicComboBoxEditor...	19-Dec-97	1 kb	
com/sun/java/swing/DefaultSingleSelectionMode...	19-Dec-97	2 kb	
com/sun/java/swing/text/html/html32.class	19-Dec-97	86 kb	
com/sun/java/accessibility/AccessibleBundle.class	19-Dec-97	1 kb	

Extracting: ...

A high-level view of this design is pictured in Figure 18.2

One thing to note about the design of this program is that we've created a great deal of cohesion between the actions and the main object, the JJarViewer. These classes were designed to build a program, not for use as reusable components. Because we use actions to organize program functionality, this type of interobject relationship is a common Swing design pattern.

JarTableModel

The JarTableModel object extends AbstractTableModel. When a JarTableModel is created it comes with a File object. The jar model stores this file in an instance

Figure 18.2 JJarViewer design.

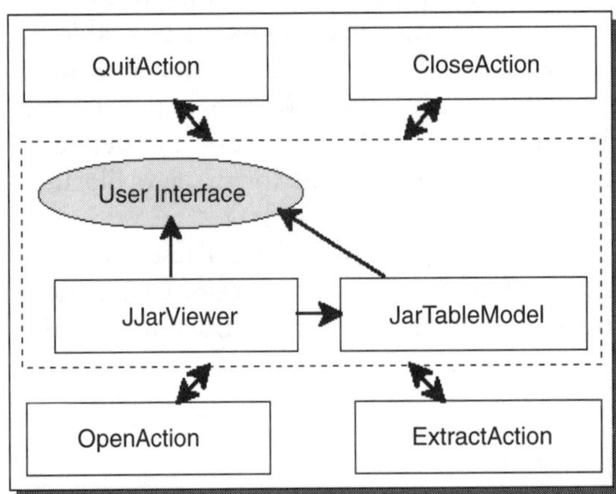

variable and creates a ZipFile object from it. Then the model creates a Vector that contains the ZipFile's entries. The model can access each entry quickly when the table requests data from it. Aside from implementing the TableModel methods to return data from the ZipFile, the JarTableModel also provides accessor methods that allow other objects in the program to get to the current file, zip file, and zip file entries.

JarTableModel supports only four columns of information: name, modification time, size, and comments. In most cases the comments column is empty. A date formatter is used to display the date for an entry, while the size is converted to a string and displayed with its units in kilobytes (kb).

```
import java.io.*;
import java.util.*;
import java.util.zip.*;
import com.sun.java.swing.*;
import com.sun.java.swing.border.*;
import com.sun.java.swing.tree.*;
import com.sun.java.swing.table.*;
import com.sun.java.swing.event.*;
import java.awt.event.*;
import java.awt.*;

public class JarTableModel extends AbstractTableModel
{
    protected File myFile;
    protected ZipFile myZipFile;
    protected Vector entries;

    public JarTableModel(File f)
    {
        myFile = f;
        entries = new Vector();

        try
        {
            if(myFile != null) myZipFile=new ZipFile(myFile);
        }
        catch(Exception exp)
        {
            myZipFile = null;
        }

        updateEntries();
    }

    protected void updateEntries()
```

```
    {
        Enumeration enum;

        if(myZipFile != null)
        {
            enum = myZipFile.entries();

            entries.removeAllElements();

            while(enum.hasMoreElements())
            {
                entries.addElement(enum.nextElement());
            }
        }
    }

    public int getRowCount()
    {
        return entries.size();
    }

    public int getColumnCount()
    {
        return 4;
    }

    public String getColumnName(int columnIndex)
    {
        String retVal = "";

        switch(columnIndex)
        {
            case 0:
                retVal = "Name";
                break;
            case 1:
                retVal = "Time";
                break;
            case 2:
                retVal = "Size";
                break;
            case 3:
                retVal = "Comment";
                break;
            default:
```

```
                retVal = "default";
                break;
        }

        return retVal;
    }

    public Class getColumnClass(int columnIndex)
    {
        return String.class;
    }

    public boolean isCellEditable(int rowIndex,
                                        int columnIndex)
    {
        boolean retVal = false;

        return retVal;
    }

    public Object getValueAt(int rowIndex,
                                   int columnIndex)
    {
        Object retVal=null;
        ZipEntry entry=null;

        if(rowIndex < entries.size())
        {
            entry = (ZipEntry)entries.elementAt(rowIndex);
        }

        if(entry == null) return "";

        if(columnIndex == 0)
        {
            retVal = entry.getName();
        }
        else if(columnIndex == 1)
        {
            Date d = new Date(entry.getTime());
            java.text.DateFormat df =
                java.text.DateFormat.getDateInstance();

            retVal = df.format(d);
        }
        else if(columnIndex == 2)
```

```
        {
            long sizeInBytes = entry.getSize();
            long sizeInKb = sizeInBytes/1024;

            if(sizeInKb < 1) sizeInKb = 1;

            retVal = String.valueOf(sizeInKb) + " kb";
        }
        else if(columnIndex == 3)
        {
            retVal = entry.getComment();
        }

        return retVal;
    }

    public void setValueAt(Object aValue,
                                    int rowIndex,
                                    int columnIndex)
    {
        return;
    }

    public ZipFile getZipFile()
    {
        return myZipFile;
    }

    public File getFile()
    {
        return myFile;
    }

    public Vector getEntries()
    {
        return entries;
    }
}
```

Notice that this model does not support editable tables.

Actions

As we mentioned previously, JJarViewer uses four action objects. All of these actions take a handle to the JJarViewer object in their constructor. This provides them with access to the main program data.

The Open Action

The first action class, OpenAction, is responsible for opening a new zip/jar file. This action initializes its name and icon in the constructor. When the user activates the action, via a menu or toolbar, it requests a file from the user and tells the JJarViewer object to use this file as the new current zip/jar file. We use the AWT FileDialog in this example. Ultimately, Swing will have its own FileChooser but it's not scheduled for release with JFC 1.1. For efficiency, we keep track of the dialog in the JJarViewer object so that if another action needs it, the same dialog can be shared.

```
import java.awt.*;
import java.io.*;
import java.util.*;
import com.sun.java.swing.*;
import com.sun.java.swing.border.*;
import com.sun.java.swing.tree.*;
import com.sun.java.swing.table.*;
import com.sun.java.swing.event.*;
import java.awt.event.*;
import java.awt.*;

public class OpenAction extends AbstractAction
{
    protected JJarViewer jjar;

    public OpenAction(JJarViewer j)
    {
        jjar = j;

        Icon img = new ImageIcon("images/open.gif");
        setIcon(Action.SMALL_ICON,img);
        setIcon(Action.DEFAULT,img);
        setText(Action.DEFAULT,"Open Archive");
    }

    public void actionPerformed(ActionEvent evt)
    {
        FileDialog chooser;

        chooser = jjar.getFileChooser();

        chooser.show();

        File fileToOpen = new File(chooser.getDirectory(),
                                   chooser.getFile());
```

```
        jjar.setFile(fileToOpen);
    }
}
```

The Close Action

The second action in this program is the CloseAction. This action is responsible for closing the current zip/jar file. Aside from initializing its text, this action tells the JJarViewer to close the current file when it is activated.

```
import java.awt.*;
import java.io.*;
import java.util.*;
import com.sun.java.swing.*;
import com.sun.java.swing.border.*;
import com.sun.java.swing.tree.*;
import com.sun.java.swing.table.*;
import com.sun.java.swing.event.*;
import java.awt.event.*;
import java.awt.*;

public class CloseAction extends AbstractAction
{
    protected JJarViewer jjar;

    public CloseAction(JJarViewer j)
    {
        jjar = j;

        setText(Action.DEFAULT,"Close Archive");
    }

    public void actionPerformed(ActionEvent evt)
    {
        jjar.closeFile();
    }
}
```

The Quit Action

The third action for this program is called QuitAction and is used as a window or action listener. In this program we associate the quit action with the quit menu item, and we assign it to the JJarViewer as a WindowListener. When the user selects the close box or chooses the quit menu item, this action sets the current file to null, hides the JJarViewer window, and exits the program.

```
import java.awt.*;
import java.io.*;
import java.util.*;
import com.sun.java.swing.*;
import com.sun.java.swing.border.*;
import com.sun.java.swing.tree.*;
import com.sun.java.swing.table.*;
import com.sun.java.swing.event.*;
import java.awt.event.*;
import java.awt.*;

public class QuitAction extends AbstractAction
implements WindowListener
{
    protected JJarViewer jjar;

    public QuitAction(JJarViewer j)
    {
        jjar = j;

        setText(Action.DEFAULT,"Quit");
    }

    public void actionPerformed(ActionEvent evt)
    {
        doQuit();
    }

    public void doQuit()
    {
        jjar.setFile(null);

        jjar.setVisible(false);

        System.exit(0);
    }

    public void windowOpened(WindowEvent e){}

    public void windowClosing(WindowEvent e)
    {
        doQuit();
    }

    public void windowClosed(WindowEvent e){}
```

```
    public void windowIconified(WindowEvent e){}

    public void windowDeiconified(WindowEvent e){}

    public void windowActivated(WindowEvent e){}

    public void windowDeactivated(WindowEvent e){}
}
```

The Extract Action

Our fourth and final action, called ExtractAction, extracts entries from the current zip file. This action is also the most complex:

1. It initializes itself with text and an icon.
2. When it receives an ActionEvent, the ExtractAction uses a JOptionPane to request the user for a directory to extract to.
3. It validates the user's entry and displays an error message if a file error occurs.
4. If the directory is valid, the ExtractAction creates a background thread, with itself as the Runnable object, and starts the thread.

We use a background thread to perform the extraction so that we can update the JarViewer's progress bar as we read entries from the zip file. Remember that the action event that notified our ExtractAction came from the event queue thread. If we process the request in the same thread, then as we update the progress bar it makes paint requests that are held in the queue until we return. In other words, the progress bar won't repaint until we return.

If we extract files in a background thread, the actionPerformed method does not block, thereby allowing other events to be processed. While the event-processing thread is looking for events, our background thread updates the progress bar, which, in turn, generates paint events. These events are processed in the event-processing thread, simultaneously with our file activity. This is a perfect example of how threads are used to multiplex user and paint events with file input/output.

The ExtractAction's run method implements the extraction by reading the files from the zip file and writing them to the requested destination. Any necessary directories are created in the process. As each entry is processed, the progress bar is updated to the total number processed. We set the maximum to the total number to extract, so this provides an accurate view of the current extraction progress. We also update the status label with the file name for the current entry.

When the extraction is complete, we reset the progress bar to 0, so that it's empty, and reset the status label to the empty string.

```
import java.awt.*;
import java.io.*;
import java.util.*;
```

```
import java.util.zip.*;
import com.sun.java.swing.*;
import com.sun.java.swing.border.*;
import com.sun.java.swing.tree.*;
import com.sun.java.swing.table.*;
import com.sun.java.swing.event.*;
import java.awt.event.*;
import java.awt.*;

public class ExtractAction extends AbstractAction
implements Runnable
{
    protected JJarViewer jjar;
    Thread kicker;
    File dest;
    int rows[];

    public ExtractAction(JJarViewer j)
    {
        jjar = j;

        Icon img = new ImageIcon("images/extract.gif");
        setIcon(Action.SMALL_ICON,img);
        setIcon(Action.DEFAULT,img);
        setText(Action.DEFAULT,"Extract Files");
    }

    public void actionPerformed(ActionEvent evt)
    {
        if((kicker == null)
            && isEnabled())
        {
            JTable table = jjar.getTable();
            String result=null;

            result = JOptionPane.showInputDialog(jjar
                        ,"Where do you want to extract to?"
                        ,"Destination"
                        ,JOptionPane.QUESTION_MESSAGE);

            if(result != null) dest = new File(result);

            if(dest == null)
            {
                //do nothing;
```

```
            }
            if(!dest.exists())
            {
                JOptionPane.showMessageDialog(jjar
                                        ,"That is not a valid directory."
                                        ,"File Error"
                                        ,JOptionPane.ERROR_MESSAGE);

            }
            else
            {
                rows = table.getSelectedRows();

                kicker = new Thread(this);
                kicker.start();
            }
        }
    }

    public synchronized void run()
    {
        int i,max;
        ZipEntry entry;
        File realDest;
        FileOutputStream fileOut;
        BufferedOutputStream bufOut;
        BufferedInputStream bufIn;
        InputStream zipIn;
        String entryPath;
        int cur;
        JarTableModel tmodel = jjar.getTableModel();
        File myFile = tmodel.getFile();
        Vector entries = tmodel.getEntries();
        JProgressBar progBar = jjar.getProgressBar();
        JLabel status = jjar.getStatus();

        if(!dest.isDirectory())
        {
            dest = new File(dest.getParent());
        }

        max = rows.length;

        progBar.setMinimum(0);
        progBar.setMaximum(max);
```

```
progBar.setValue(0);

for(i=0;i<max;i++)
{
    entry = (ZipEntry)entries.elementAt(rows[i]);

    entryPath = entry.getName();
    entryPath = entryPath.replace('/',File.separatorChar);
    entryPath = entryPath.replace('\\',File.separatorChar);

    realDest = new File(dest,entryPath);

    status.setText("Extracting: "+entryPath);

    if(status.getParent() != null)
    {
        status.getParent().validate();
    }

    if(entry.isDirectory())
    {
        realDest.mkdirs();
    }
    else
    {
        new File(realDest.getParent()).mkdirs();

        try
        {
            zipIn = tmodel.getZipFile().getInputStream(entry);
            bufIn = new BufferedInputStream(zipIn);

            fileOut = new FileOutputStream(realDest);
            bufOut = new BufferedOutputStream(fileOut);

            while((cur = bufIn.read()) != -1)
            {
                bufOut.write(cur);
            }

            bufOut.close();
            bufIn.close();
        }
        catch(Exception exp)
        {
```

```
                }
            }

            progBar.setValue(i);
        }

        //reset on completion
        status.setText("");
        progBar.setValue(0);
        kicker = null;
    }
}
```

Notice that the ExtractAction ignores ActionEvents if it's disabled. This ensures that regardless of the user interface that triggers the action, it won't fire unless it's supposed to fire. We use the JJarViewer class to keep this action enabled or disabled based on the current file.

JJarViewer Class

The JJarViewer object is at the heart of this application. JJarViewer is a subclass of JFrame. It provides the main method and creates the user interface. JJarViewer also keeps track of the current file and updates the JarTableModel appropriately. This object acts as an information hub for the other objects in the program.

The import statements for JJarViewer and its class declaration look like this:

```
import java.awt.*;
import java.io.*;
import java.util.*;
import com.sun.java.swing.*;
import com.sun.java.swing.border.*;
import com.sun.java.swing.tree.*;
import com.sun.java.swing.table.*;
import com.sun.java.swing.event.*;
import java.awt.event.*;
import java.awt.*;

public class JJarViewer extends JFrame
{
```

The instance variables are as follows:

```
protected FileDialog sharedChooser;
protected JTable table;
protected JarTableModel tmodel;
JProgressBar progBar;
```

```
JLabel statusField;
Action extractAction;
```

These variables are used to keep track of the user interface, the shared FileDialog, the JarTableModel, and the ExtractAction. We keep this action enabled and disabled based on the state of the current file, so we keep a handle to it as an instance variable.

Building the User Interface

JJarViewer builds the user interface in its constructor where it also initializes the current file to null. The interface has a menu bar, a toolbar at the north of a border layout, a table in a scroll pane in the center of a border layout, and a panel with a progress bar and label at the south of a border layout. The panel at the bottom uses a bevel border to separate it visually from the table. This interface is pictured in Figure 18.3. The actions we just discussed are used to define the menu items and toolbar controls. This ensures that they share the same descriptions.

```
public JJarViewer()
{
    JMenuBar bar = new JMenuBar();
    JMenu fileM,actionM;
    JMenuItem tmp;
    Action action;
    JToolBar tools;
    JPanel status;

    setDefaultCloseOperation(JFrame.DO_NOTHING_ON_CLOSE);
```

Figure 18.3 JJarViewer interface.

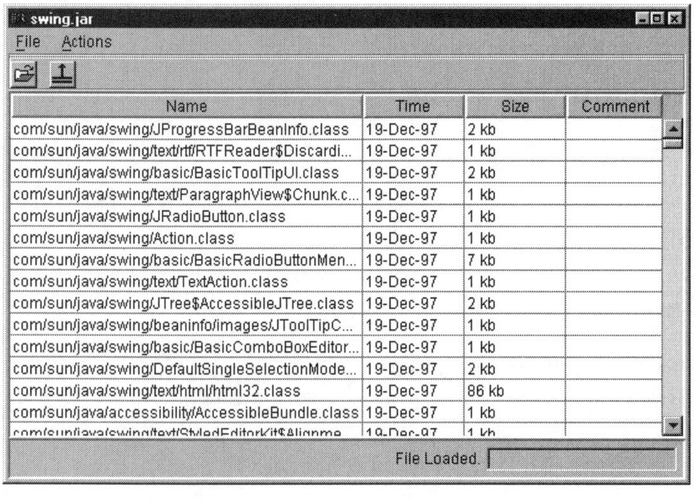

```
table = new JTable();
table.setBackground(Color.white);

getContentPane().add(JTable.createScrollPaneForTable(table), "Center");

tools = new JToolBar();

fileM = new JMenu("File");
fileM.setKeyAccelerator('F');

//Add the open action to the menu
//and toolbar
action = new OpenAction(this);
tmp = fileM.add(action);
tmp.setKeyAccelerator('o');
tools.add(action);

//Add the close action to the menu
action = new CloseAction(this);
tmp = fileM.add(action);
tmp.setKeyAccelerator('c');

fileM.addSeparator();

//Add the quit action to the menu
//and as a window listener
action = new QuitAction(this);
tmp = fileM.add(action);
tmp.setKeyAccelerator('q');

addWindowListener((QuitAction)action);

bar.add(fileM);

tools.addSeparator();

//Build the actions menu
actionM = new JMenu("Actions");
actionM.setKeyAccelerator('A');

extractAction = new ExtractAction(this);
tmp = actionM.add(extractAction);
tmp.setKeyAccelerator('x');
tools.add(extractAction);
```

```
        bar.add(actionM);

        setJMenuBar(bar);
        getContentPane().add(tools,"North");

        status = new JPanel();
        status.setBorder(new BevelBorder(BevelBorder.LOWERED));
        status.setLayout(new FlowLayout(FlowLayout.RIGHT));

        statusField = new JLabel("Select a File to View.");
        status.add(statusField);

        progBar = new JProgressBar();
        status.add(progBar);

        getContentPane().add(status,"South");

        //initialize the file to null

        setFile(null);
    }
```

The JJarViewer class has three methods for accessing the status label, progress bar, and file dialog. These methods are included to allow actions to update the user interface, if necessary.

```
    public JProgressBar getProgressBar()
    {
        return progBar;
    }

    public JLabel getStatus()
    {
        return statusField;
    }

    public FileDialog getFileChooser()
    {
        if(sharedChooser == null)
        {
            sharedChooser = new java.awt.FileDialog(this);
        }

        return sharedChooser;
    }
```

Centralizing Data

The JJarViewer class provides access to the table through the getTable method and table model through the getTableModel method for actions that need the information they contain.

```
public JarTableModel getTableModel()
{
    return tmodel;
}

public JTable getTable()
{
    return table;
}
```

Managing the Current File

The JJarViewer class provides three methods for interacting with the current zip/jar file. Use the setFile method when you set the file, the getFile method to retrieve the file, and the closeFile method to close the file.

Setting the current file causes the viewer to create a new JarTableModel object. If the file is not valid, this model describes a table with four columns and no data. If the file is valid, the model describes the entries in that file. After the model is created it is assigned to the table. The table's selection is also cleared, to avoid confusion between files, and the table is told to rebuild its display based on the new model. Next, the viewer updates three items based on the current file. If the file is null, the status label is set to reflect this, as is the viewer's title. For a null file, the extract action is disabled. This automatically disables the menu and tool bar items, so that the user cannot try to extract something from an empty file. If the file is not null, the title and status bars are updated and the extract action enabled.

```
public void setFile(File f)
{
    tmodel = new JarTableModel(f);
    table.clearSelection();
    table.setModel(tmodel);
    table.createDefaultColumnsFromModel();

    if(f != null)
    {
        setTitle(f.getName());
        statusField.setText("File Loaded.");
        extractAction.setEnabled(true);
    }
    else
```

```
        {
            setTitle("JJar");
            statusField.setText("Select a file to load.");
            extractAction.setEnabled(false);
        }
    }
```

If an object requests the current file, the viewer gets it from the JarTableModel and returns it.

```
public File getFile()
{
    return tmodel.getFile();
}
```

To close the current file, the viewer sets the current file to null. Because this is just a viewer, we never save or change information so there is no need to check for that here.

```
public void closeFile()
{
    setFile(null);
}
```

SetVisible and Main

The JJarViewer class overrides the setVisible method to center itself when it is displayed.

```
public void setVisible(boolean tf)
{
    if(tf)
    {
        Dimension screenSize =
            getToolkit().getScreenSize();
        Dimension curSize;
        int x,y;

        this.pack();

        curSize = getSize();

        curSize.width = Math.max(400,curSize.width);
        curSize.height = Math.max(300,curSize.height);

        x = (screenSize.width-curSize.width)/2;
        y = (screenSize.height-curSize.height)/2;
```

```
            setBounds(x,y,curSize.width,curSize.height);
        }
        super.setVisible(tf);
    }
```

The main method creates a JJarViewer instance and displays the following:

```
public static void main(String s[])
{
    JJarViewer frame = new JJarViewer();

    frame.setForeground(Color.black);
    frame.setBackground(Color.lightGray);

    frame.setVisible(true);
}
```

Of course, the last line of this example is the ending curly bracket:

```
}
```

Summary

Actions provide a great mechanism for organizing program functionality. They define the code to invoke and the text and icon to describe this code. By using actions to perform the major functions for our application, we have created a program that can easily be extended by adding other actions and their accompanying menu items.

Providing a progress bar is helpful to the user during lengthy operations. Because these operations often involve file input/output, you often need to perform the main action in a background thread. This allows the progress bar to update in the event-processing/painting thread. In Chapter 19, we discuss another large example that uses this technique.

Finally, Swing's model-view-controller design makes it easy to display data by creating custom models. In this example, we implemented less than 180 lines of code, including import statements, to map a zip file to a table. This is an incredible time saver; we hope that it improves future application design and reduces development time.

SEARCH PROGRAM EXAMPLE 19

This chapter discusses the design and implementation of a complete JFC program. This program, called DocSearch, is used to index and search a directory of HTML documents. We created this application for searching the Swing documentation. To search documents quickly, we created a simple index format. When the user chooses to search a new directory, an index is created. Later, the original index is used. It's up to the user to remove an index file if he or she wants to rebuild the index. Searches against the index are very fast, and they provide a list of files that contain the search word, as pictured in Figure 19.1. By selecting a file, the user can view it in the editor pane at the bottom of the window.

Keep in mind that this example was created for educational purposes. It does not contain every feature that you may want, but it should prove useful for searching HTML documentation. We tried to keep it simple enough to explain, while making it complete enough to provide several good learning examples. We believe this program should solidify many of the programming issues discussed in this book. Some of the techniques that you should observe in this example are as follows:

- A File index
- Using actions to handle menu events
- Managing threads with Swing
- Using various Swing components
- Using listeners to handle UI-generated events
- User-interface management
- Data management

Design of DocSearch

The basic design for DocSearch separates the functionality into four main categories:

1. The file index
2. Specific user functions

3. User-interface management
4. Data management

The index, both in memory and on disk, is managed with a class called HTMLIndex. This class knows how to index a directory of HTML files and write that index to disk. HTMLIndex objects can read the index from disk into memory. This capability allows the user to search quickly with memory-based information.

Specific user functions include setting the directory to search, quitting the program, setting the current page, and loading the index. These functions are all handled with separate objects.

The user interface and data are managed with the core object that is an instance of DocSearch. DocSearch is a subclass of JFrame that provides a main method to create the user interface. The DocSearch object is also responsible for handling user events, performing the search, displaying the results, and updating the current selection.

The relationship between the objects that make up this program is diagrammed in Figure 19.2.

Figure 19.1 DocSearch example.

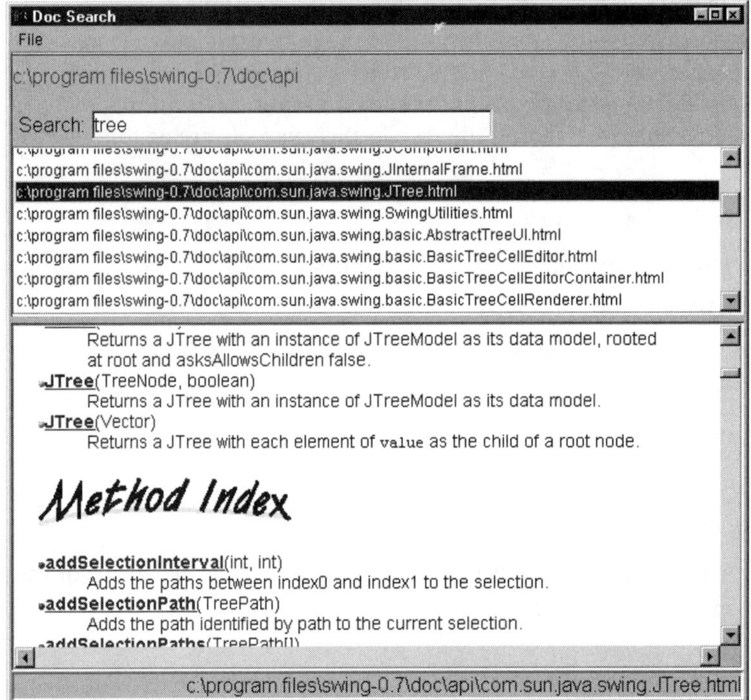

Figure 19.2 DocSearch basic design.

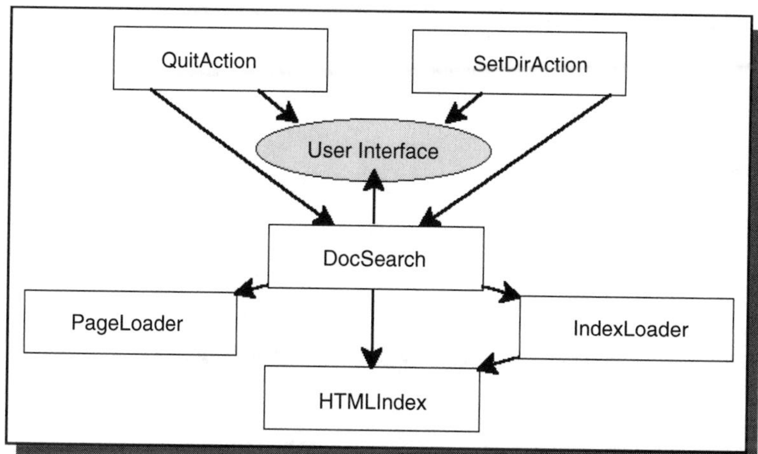

The Index

HTMLIndex uses a simple index format. The index includes an ordered list of files and a list of unique words contained in those files. Along with each word is a list of indices for the files that contain this word. This index supports only regular word searches, although it can be extended to support Boolean and other searches. In our professional lives, we have created an index with full Boolean searching based on the same simple principals of the HTMLIndex.

The indexing process is focused on a directory. All of the .html and .htm files in this directory or subdirectories are indexed. Anything between the < and > characters is ignored, as are the main nonalphanumeric characters. Again, this is a simple version and should not be considered optimal. That said, we created an index for 500 HTML files, totaling over 5MB of data, that is under 400kb.

The in-memory version of the index is a Vector of file names and a hash table of word keys with Vector values. The values are all Integer objects that represent indices into the file name Vector. Again, this is not an attempt to be optimal, but it's simple and works quickly and reliably.

All of the words in the index are converted to lowercase before they are stored to disk and before a search is performed. We found this to be useful when searching for words in the documentation. You can easily remove this code to support case-sensitive searches.

The index is also responsible for returning the files that contain a word, making the HTMLIndex class encapsulate the process of creating, storing, reading, and searching the index.

When an HTMLIndex object is created for a directory, it first checks to see if an index already exists. If one does, it's loaded; otherwise, an index is built and loaded. The name for the index file is defined by the class variable INDEX_FILE _NAME and is currently set to .htmlindex.

The code for HTMLIndex is as follows:

```
import java.util.*;
import java.io.*;

public class HTMLIndex
{
    Vector files;
    Hashtable theIndex;
    boolean indexLoaded;

    public static final String INDEX_FILE_NAME=".htmlindex";

    /*
     * Looks for an index file and creates one if necessary.
     * doesn't log the build process.
     */
    public HTMLIndex(File dir)
    {
        this(dir,false);
    }

    /**
     * Looks for an index file and creates one if necessary.
     * If log is "true" then the indexing progress is logged
     * to the console.
     */
    public HTMLIndex(File dir,boolean log)
    {
        File indexFile;

        theIndex = new Hashtable();
        files = new Vector();

        indexFile = new File(dir,INDEX_FILE_NAME);

        if(!indexFile.exists())
        {
            HTMLIndex.buildIndex(dir,log);
        }

        loadIndexFile(indexFile);
    }
```

```
    /**
     * Private method that loads the index file.
     */
    protected void loadIndexFile(File indexFile)
    {
        FileReader fileIn;
        LineNumberReader lineIn;
        String curLine;
        StringTokenizer cursor;
        String word,curId;
        Vector entryForWord;
        Integer newEntry;

        try
        {
            fileIn = new FileReader(indexFile);
            lineIn = new LineNumberReader(fileIn);

            //Read the file names

            while(((curLine = lineIn.readLine()) != null)
                    &&(curLine.length()>0))
            {
                files.addElement(curLine);
            }

            //Read the words

            while(((curLine = lineIn.readLine()) != null)
                    &&(curLine.length()>0))
            {
                cursor= new StringTokenizer(curLine,"|");

                word = cursor.nextToken();
                entryForWord = new Vector();

                while(cursor.hasMoreTokens())
                {
                    curId = cursor.nextToken();
                    newEntry = new Integer(curId);

                    if(!entryForWord.contains(newEntry))
                        entryForWord.addElement(newEntry);
                }
```

```
                theIndex.put(word,entryForWord);
            }

            lineIn.close();
            fileIn.close();

            indexLoaded = true;
        }
        catch(Exception exp)
        {

            indexLoaded = false;
        }
    }

    /**
     * Return true if the index is loaded.
     */
    public boolean getIndexLoaded()
    {
        return indexLoaded;
    }

    public Enumeration files()
    {
        return files.elements();
    }

    public Enumeration words()
    {
        return theIndex.keys();
    }

    public Vector filesForWord(String word)
    {
        Vector dataForWord;
        Vector results = new Vector();

        dataForWord = (Vector) theIndex.get(word.toLowerCase());

        if(dataForWord != null)
        {
            int i,max;
            int fileIndex;
```

```
                max = dataForWord.size();

                for(i=0;i<max;i++)
                {
                    fileIndex =

    ((Integer)dataForWord.elementAt(i)).intValue();
                    results.addElement(files.elementAt(fileIndex));
                }
            }

            return results;
        }

        /**
         * Private method to index a directory
         */
        public static void buildIndexForDir(File dir
                                            ,Vector files
                                            ,Hashtable entries
                                            ,boolean log)
        {
            String[] list;
            File curFile;
            int i,max;

            list = dir.list();

            if(log) System.out.println("Indexing Directory: "+dir);

            max = list.length;

            for(i=0;i<max;i++)
            {
                curFile = new File(dir,list[i]);

                if(curFile.isDirectory())
                {
                    buildIndexForDir(curFile,files,entries,log);
                }
                else if(list[i].endsWith(".html")
                        ||list[i].endsWith(".htm"))
                {
                    if(log) System.out.println("Indexing file: "+curFile);
```

```
                buildIndexForFile(curFile,files,entries);
            }
        }
    }

    /**
     * Private method to index a file
     */
    public static void buildIndexForFile(File file
                                        ,Vector files
                                        ,Hashtable entries)
    {
        FileReader fileIn;
        BufferedReader bufIn;
        int cur;
        int fileInd;
        boolean inTag;
        StringBuffer curWord;
        String curString;
        Vector entryForWord;
        Integer newEntry;

        try
        {
            files.addElement(file);

            fileInd = files.indexOf(file);

            fileIn = new FileReader(file);
            bufIn = new BufferedReader(fileIn);

            inTag = false;

            curWord = new StringBuffer();

            while((cur = bufIn.read()) != -1)
            {
                if(cur == '<')
                {
                    inTag = true;
                }
                else if(cur == '>')
                {
                    inTag = false;
                }
```

```
else if((Character.isWhitespace((char)cur)
            ||(cur == '.')
            ||(cur == ',')
            ||(cur == '[')
            ||(cur == ']')
            ||(cur == '{')
            ||(cur == '}')
            ||(cur == '(')
            ||(cur == ')')
            ||(cur == '=')
            ||(cur == ';')
            ||(cur == ':')
            ||(cur == '=')
            ||(cur == '-')
            ||(cur == '/')
            ||(cur == '\\'))
            && !inTag)
{
    if(curWord.length()>0)
    {
        curString =
                    curWord.toString().toLowerCase();
        curWord.setLength(0);

        entryForWord = (Vector)
                            entries.get(curString);

        if(entryForWord == null)
        {
            entryForWord = new Vector();

            entries.put(curString,entryForWord);
        }

        newEntry = new Integer(fileInd);

        if(!entryForWord.contains(newEntry))
            entryForWord.addElement(newEntry);
    }
}
else if(!inTag)
{
    //Don't add the separator
```

```
                    //or quotes
                    if(cur == '|')
                    {
                        curWord.append('-');
                    }
                    else if((cur != '\"')
                            &&(cur != '\''))
                    {
                        curWord.append((char)cur);
                    }
                }
            }

            if(curWord.length()>0)
            {
                curString = curWord.toString().toLowerCase();
                curWord.setLength(0);

                entryForWord = (Vector) entries.get(curString);

                if(entryForWord == null)
                {
                    entryForWord = new Vector();

                    entries.put(curString,entryForWord);
                }

                newEntry = new Integer(fileInd);

                if(!entryForWord.contains(newEntry))
                    entryForWord.addElement(newEntry);
            }

            bufIn.close();
            fileIn.close();
        }
        catch(Exception exp)
        {
            //skip this file
        }
    }

    /**
     * Private method write the index file
     */
```

```
public static void writeIndex(File dir
                              ,Vector files
                              ,Hashtable entries)
{
    FileWriter fileOut;
    BufferedWriter bufOut;
    PrintWriter printOut;
    File curFile;
    int i,max;
    Enumeration words;
    String curWord;
    Vector entryForWord;
    File file;

    try
    {
        file = new File(dir,INDEX_FILE_NAME);
        fileOut = new FileWriter(file);
        bufOut = new BufferedWriter(fileOut);
        printOut = new PrintWriter(bufOut);

        //Print files in order

        max = files.size();

        for(i=0;i<max;i++)
        {
            curFile = (File) files.elementAt(i);
            printOut.println(curFile.getAbsolutePath());
        }

        //blank line to break files from words

        printOut.println();

        //print words

        words = entries.keys();

        while(words.hasMoreElements())
        {
            curWord = (String) words.nextElement();

            entryForWord = (Vector) entries.get(curWord);
```

```
                max = entryForWord.size();

                printOut.print(curWord);

                for(i=0;i<max;i++)
                {
                    printOut.print('|');
                    printOut.print(entryForWord.elementAt(i));
                }
                //add new line char
                printOut.println();
            }

            printOut.close();
            bufOut.close();
            fileOut.close();
        }
        catch(Exception exp)
        {
            //failed to write index
        }
    }

    /**
     * Builds an index file for a directory
     */
    public static void buildIndex(File dir,boolean log)
    {
        Vector files = new Vector();
        Hashtable entries = new Hashtable();

        buildIndexForDir(dir,files,entries,log);

        if(log) System.out.println("Writing Index");
        writeIndex(dir,files,entries);
    }

    public static void main(String args[])
    {
        if(args.length <= 1)
        {
            System.out.println("usage: java HTMLIndex dir word");
            return;
        }
```

```
        HTMLIndex index = new HTMLIndex(new File(args[0]),true);
        Vector files = index.filesForWord(args[1]);
        int i,max;

        max = files.size();

        if(max == 0) System.out.println("No Files Match Query");
        else System.out.println("Matching Files---------\n");

        for(i=0;i<max;i++)
        {
            System.out.println(files.elementAt(i));
        }
    }
}
```

A main method is included for testing and building indices from the command line.

Actions

We implemented two actions to manage the two menu items for the DocSearch program. The first action, SetDirAction, is used to set the current search directory. The second action, QuitAction, quits the program. Both of these actions are implemented as a subclass of AbstractAction.

SetDirAction displays an option pane when it is notified of an ActionEvent. The option pane is used to get the name of the directory to search. If the user enters a directory name, it is passed to the DocSearch object. Otherwise, the action does nothing.

```
import java.awt.*;
import java.io.*;
import java.util.*;
import com.sun.java.swing.*;
import com.sun.java.swing.border.*;
import com.sun.java.swing.tree.*;
import com.sun.java.swing.table.*;
import com.sun.java.swing.event.*;
import java.awt.event.*;
import java.awt.*;

public class SetDirAction extends AbstractAction
{
    DocSearch searcher;
```

```
    public SetDirAction(DocSearch s)
    {
        searcher = s;
        setText(Action.DEFAULT,"Set Directory");
    }

    public void actionPerformed(ActionEvent evt)
    {
        String result;

        result = JOptionPane.showInputDialog(searcher
                                    ,"Enter a directory"
                                    ,"Search Directory..."
                                    ,JOptionPane.QUESTION_MESSAGE);

        if(result != null) searcher.setDirectory(result);
    }
}
```

The QuitAction acts as both an ActionListener for the Quit menu item and a window listener for the main program window. When the user closes the window or selects the Quit item, this action closes the window and exits the program. Because we subclassed AbstractAction to create QuitAction, there are several unused WindowListener methods. These unused methods are required by the interface, but they are not necessary for our program so we implement them with empty methods.

```
import java.awt.*;
import java.io.*;
import java.util.*;
import com.sun.java.swing.*;
import com.sun.java.swing.border.*;
import com.sun.java.swing.tree.*;
import com.sun.java.swing.table.*;
import com.sun.java.swing.event.*;
import java.awt.event.*;
import java.awt.*;

public class QuitAction extends AbstractAction
implements WindowListener
{
    JFrame frame;

    public QuitAction(JFrame f)
```

```
        {
            frame = f;
            setText(Action.DEFAULT,"Quit");
        }

        public void actionPerformed(ActionEvent evt)
        {
            doQuit();
        }

        public void doQuit()
        {
            frame.setVisible(false);
            frame.dispose();
            System.exit(0);
        }

        public void windowOpened(WindowEvent e){}

        public void windowClosing(WindowEvent e)
        {
            doQuit();
        }

        public void windowClosed(WindowEvent e){}

        public void windowIconified(WindowEvent e){}

        public void windowDeiconified(WindowEvent e){}

        public void windowActivated(WindowEvent e){}

        public void windowDeactivated(WindowEvent e){}
}
```

Remember that when used in a menu the actions not only handle ActionEvents, but also provide the text for the menu items with which they are associated. Our actions have their text value initialized in their constructor.

Loaders

One of the issues with Swing event handling that we discussed in Chapters 2 and 10 is that all events are processed in a single thread. This is convenient, but it requires us to use threads ourselves wherever we want to overlap event handling and input/output. In the DocSearch program, these overlaps happen in two places: loading the index and displaying the current file. To encapsulate these two situations we created loader classes to handle each function. These loader classes implement the Runnable interface and are used to define the code for our background threads.

IndexLoader

IndexLoader loads the index for the DocSearch object. If you look at the entire program you may notice that we are not overly careful with thread synchronization around the index. This is acceptable for our application because the loader sets the index, and the DocSearch object reads it only if it's not null. A production application may need more careful planning of the thread safety issues.

The IndexLoader also sets the DocSearch window's cursor to the wait cursor during loading to provide some user feedback. The user sees a message in the status bar indicating that the index is loading, and a system beep is played when the index is loaded. HTMLIndex supports a logging feature that writes out its progress to the console while it creates an index. We have turned this feature on for our example, so the user sees a message in the console about the index built.

```
import java.io.*;
import java.util.*;
import com.sun.java.swing.*;
import com.sun.java.swing.border.*;
import com.sun.java.swing.tree.*;
import com.sun.java.swing.text.*;
import com.sun.java.swing.table.*;
import com.sun.java.swing.event.*;
import java.awt.event.*;
import java.awt.*;
import java.net.*;

public class IndexLoader implements Runnable
{
    DocSearch searcher;
    String dir;

    IndexLoader(DocSearch ds,String d)
    {
        searcher = ds;
        dir = d;
    }

    public void run()
    {
        HTMLIndex index;
        Cursor c = searcher.getCursor();
```

```
            Cursor waitCursor
                = Cursor.getPredefinedCursor(Cursor.WAIT_CURSOR);

            searcher.setCursor(waitCursor);

            index=new HTMLIndex(new File(dir),true);

            searcher.setIndex(index);
            searcher.setCursor(c);
        }
}
```

For directories that are already indexed, the process for loading the index is relatively quick, depending on the index size. We loaded the 400kb index in about 510 seconds on a 32MB Windows 95 PC. Building the index can take longer.

PageLoader

The second loader, PageLoader, is responsible for loading pages into the JEditorPane. This can be a slow process, depending on the HTML file and your computer configuration, so we decided to use this loader technique rather than include the code directly in the DocSearch object. PageLoader performs three tasks.

1. Sets the cursor for the editor pane.
2. Tries to load the provided URL.
3. Reloads the original document if the URL can't load correctly.

When the URL is loaded we scroll to the top of the document using a simple trick displayed in bold in the following code. Remember that all JComponents support scrolling. We tell the editor pane to scroll a rectangle to visible. Because this rectangle has an origin at (0,0) and is small (10 × 10), this resets the scroll pane to the upper-left corner of the editor pane.

```
import java.io.*;
import java.util.*;
import com.sun.java.swing.*;
import com.sun.java.swing.border.*;
import com.sun.java.swing.tree.*;
import com.sun.java.swing.text.*;
import com.sun.java.swing.table.*;
import com.sun.java.swing.event.*;
import java.awt.event.*;
import java.awt.*;
import java.net.*;

public class PageLoader implements Runnable
{
```

```
    URL url;
    Cursor cursor;
    JEditorPane pane;
    JLabel status;

    PageLoader(JEditorPane p,URL u, Cursor c,JLabel s)
    {
        pane = p;
        url = u;
        cursor = c;
        status = s;
    }

    public void run()
    {
        if (url == null)
        {
            // restore the original cursor
            pane.setCursor(cursor);

            if(status != null) status.setText("Load Failed.");
        }
        else
        {
            Document doc = pane.getDocument();
            try
            {
                pane.setPage(url);
                pane.scrollRectToVisible(new Rectangle(0,0,10,10));
            }
            catch(Exception exp)
            {
                pane.setDocument(doc);
            }
            finally
            {
                status.setText(url.getFile());
                url = null;
                status = null;
                SwingUtilities.invokeLater(this);
            }
        }
    }
}
```

Notice the use of the SwingUtilities class method invokeLater. This method causes the page loader's run method to be called from the event-processing thread, where it updates the editor pane's cursor.

Main Class: DocSearch

The remainder of the DocSearch example is implemented in the DocSearch class. This class creates the user interface, handles events, manages the index, and stores the current directory and file.

> **NOTE**
>
> Because the DocSearch class is rather large, we have broken our discussion up into sections. To see the complete code for this class, open it from the CD-ROM.

The DocSearch objects instance variables store the information they need to keep track of the index and user interface. The header for the file, including the import statements and class declaration, is shown in the following code:

```
import java.io.*;
import java.util.*;
import com.sun.java.swing.*;
import com.sun.java.swing.border.*;
import com.sun.java.swing.tree.*;
import com.sun.java.swing.table.*;
import com.sun.java.swing.event.*;
import java.awt.event.*;
import java.awt.*;
import java.net.*;

public class DocSearch extends JFrame
implements ActionListener, ListSelectionListener, HyperlinkListener
{
    protected JList results;
    protected JPanel top;
    protected JTextField searchField;
    protected JLabel dirLabel;
    protected JLabel statusBar;
    protected JEditorPane display;
    protected HTMLIndex index;
    protected String curFileName;
    protected Thread pageThread;
    protected boolean watchAnchor;

    public final static String SEARCH="search";
```

We use the static variable SEARCH as an action command. By defining the action command in a static variable, we don't have to memorize its value.

Creating the User Interface

The user interface for the DocSearch example is pictured in Figure 19.3. The content pane for the main window has a status bar in its south location and a split pane in the center. The split pane displays a scroll pane with an editor pane at the bottom. At the top of the split pane is a list in a scroll pane, a text area for entering the search, and a label that displays the current directory. This frame also has a menu with two items that represent the actions discussed earlier.

DocSearch is a subclass of JFrame, so we implemented the code to create the user interface in the constructor. We did, however, separate the code for creating the menu from the constructor, simply to reduce the size. The constructor is called from main, as we discuss later in this section. The main method also displays the frame on the screen. In the process for creating the user interface, the DocSearch object is assigned as a selection listener for the list, an action listener for the search text field, and a hyperlink listener for the editor pane. At the bottom of the constructor we initialize the current directory to null. The constructor looks like this:

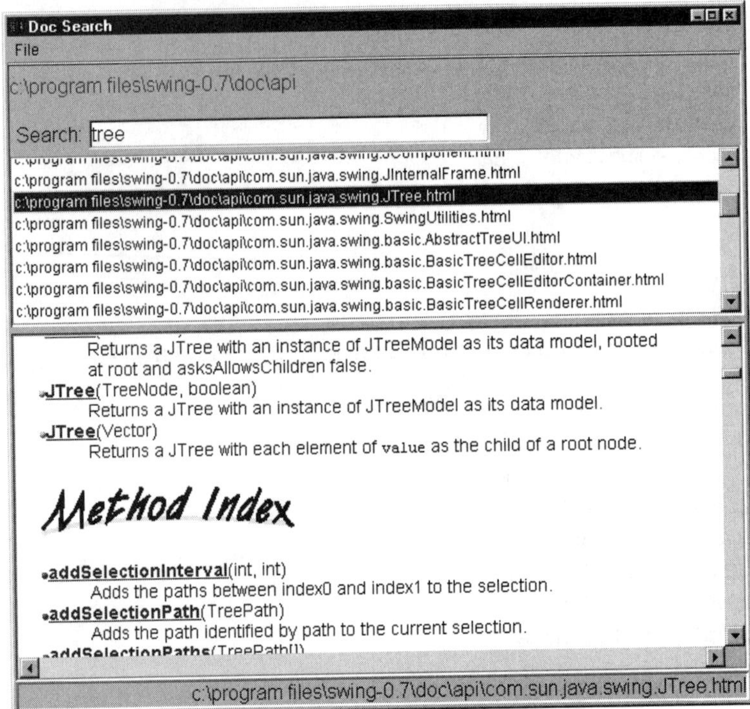

Figure 19.3 DocSearch user interface.

```
public DocSearch()
{
    JSplitPane split;
    JPanel tmp,tmp2;
    Font font = new Font("SanSerif",Font.PLAIN,16);

    setTitle("Doc Search");

    top = new JPanel();
    top.setLayout(new BorderLayout());

    results = new JList();
    results.addListSelectionListener(this);
    results.setSelectionMode(ListSelectionModel.SINGLE_SELECTION);
    top.add(new JScrollPane(results),"Center");

    tmp = new JPanel();
    tmp.setLayout(new GridLayout(2,1,5,5));

    dirLabel = new JLabel("No Directory Selected");
    dirLabel.setForeground(Color.darkGray);
    dirLabel.setFont(font);

    tmp.add(dirLabel);

    tmp2 =new JPanel();
    tmp2.setLayout(new FlowLayout(FlowLayout.LEFT,5,5));

    JLabel tmpLabel =new JLabel("Search:");
    tmpLabel.setFont(font);

    tmp2.add(tmpLabel);

    searchField = new JTextField(25);
    searchField.setActionCommand(SEARCH);
    searchField.addActionListener(this);
    searchField.setFont(font);

    tmp2.add(searchField);

    tmp.add(tmp2);

    top.add(tmp,"North");
```

```
    display = new JEditorPane();
    display.setEditable(false);
    display.setContentType("text/html");
    display.addHyperlinkListener(this);

    split = new JSplitPane(JSplitPane.VERTICAL_SPLIT
                            ,top
                            ,new JScrollPane(display));

    statusBar = new JLabel("Loaded",JLabel.RIGHT);
    statusBar.setFont(font);

    statusBar.setBorder(new BevelBorder(BevelBorder.LOWERED));

    getContentPane().setLayout(new BorderLayout());
    getContentPane().add(split,"Center");
    getContentPane().add(statusBar,"South");

    buildMenu();

    setDirectory(null);
}
```

The code to create the menu and assign the WindowListener is as follows:

```
protected void buildMenu()
{
    Action action;
    JMenuBar bar;
    JMenu menu;

    bar = new JMenuBar();
    menu = new JMenu("File");

    action = new SetDirAction(this);
    menu.add(action);
    menu.addSeparator();

    action = new QuitAction(this);
    this.addWindowListener((QuitAction)action);
    menu.add(action);

    bar.add(menu);

    setJMenuBar(bar);
}
```

Once the interface is created the user needs to select the directory to search.

Handling the Index

The DocSearch object assumes that setting the current directory includes requesting that the index be loaded. Two methods take care of this function. The first method is used by the IndexLoader to set the index. The second is called by the SetDirAction to set the directory. When the index is set, the DocSource updates the status bar and initiates the system beep. The following method provides the required feedback so the user knows the process is complete:

```
public void setIndex(HTMLIndex i)
{
    index = i;
    statusBar.setText("Index Loaded.");
    getToolkit().beep();
}
```

When the directory is set, the DocSearch makes sure the directory is valid, confirms that the user really wants to index that directory, and initiates the IndexLoader. We added the confirmation panel after accidentally indexing our entire hard drive! It just goes to show that it's always useful to confirm a lengthy operation with the user before performing it. This method displays an error if the user tries to select a directory that doesn't exist:

```
public void setDirectory(String dirName)
{
    if(dirName == null)
    {
        index = null;
        dirLabel.setText("No Directory Selected.");
        statusBar.setText("Loaded.");
        setFile(null);
    }
    else
    {
        File dir = new File(dirName);

        if(!dir.exists())
        {
            index = null;
            dirLabel.setText("No Directory Selected.");
            statusBar.setText("");
            setFile(null);

            String msg[] = new String[2];
```

```
            msg[0] = "No such directory:";
            msg[1] = dirName;

            JOptionPane.showMessageDialog(this
                                        ,msg
                                        ,"Error"
                                        ,JOptionPane.ERROR_MESSAGE);
        }
        else
        {
            int result;
            String msg[] = new String[2];

            msg[0] = "Are you sure you want to index:";
            msg[1] = dirName;

            result = JOptionPane.showConfirmDialog(this
                                        ,msg
                                        ,"Confirm Selection"
                                        ,JOptionPane.YES_NO_OPTION);

            if(result == JOptionPane.YES_OPTION)
            {
                statusBar.setText("Loading Index...");
                dirLabel.setText(dirName);

                Thread kicker = new Thread(new IndexLoader(this,dirName));
                kicker.start();
            }
        }
    }

    results.setListData(new Object[0]);
}
```

Now that the directory is set and the index loaded, let's look at how the DocSearch sets the current file to display.

Setting the Current File

As we developed this application we realized that there are a number of ways that we may want to set the current file. For example, some of the sources of information we use provide File objects, others file names, and still others URLs. To make life easy, we decided to build the main code around loading a URL and provide some convenient methods for retrieving this URL from a file or file name. The method setFile takes a File and resolves it to a URL. The method setFileByName takes a string and resolves it to a URL.

The convenience methods are as follows:

```
public void setFile(File file)
{
    URL url = null;

    if(file != null)
    {
        try
        {
            url = new URL("file",null,file.getAbsolutePath());
        }
        catch(Exception exp)
        {
            fileError(file.getAbsolutePath());
        }
    }

    setURL(url);
}

public void setFileByName(String file)
{
    URL url = null;

    if(file != null)
    {
        try
        {
            url = new URL("file",null,file);
        }
        catch(Exception exp)
        {
            fileError(file);
        }
    }

    setURL(url);
}
```

Both of these methods use another convenience method that displays an error dialog. This method is called fileError and uses the JOptionPane class to display the error to the user.

```
protected void fileError(String file)
{
    String msg[] = new String[2];

    msg[0] = "Error loading file:";
    msg[1] = file;

    JOptionPane.showMessageDialog(this
                                ,msg
                                ,"Error"
                                ,JOptionPane.ERROR_MESSAGE);
}
```

To improve efficiency, we keep track of the current file name. If the user tries to load the same file twice, we do nothing unless the user selected a link with a marker for the same file. If we want to display the new URL, we set the editor pane's cursor to the wait cursor and trigger a PageLoader in a new thread.

```
public void setURL(URL url)
{
    try
    {
        if(pageThread != null)
        {
            pageThread.stop();
            pageThread = null;
        }

        if(url==null)
        {
            curFileName = null;
            display.setContentType("text/plain");
            display.setText("");
        }
        else if(!url.getFile().equals(curFileName)
                ||((url.getRef() != null)&&watchAnchor))
        {
            curFileName = url.getFile();

            statusBar.setText("Loading page...");

            Cursor c = display.getCursor();
            Cursor waitCursor
                = Cursor.getPredefinedCursor(Cursor.WAIT_CURSOR);

            display.setCursor(waitCursor);
```

```
            if(!curFileName.equals(results.getSelectedValue()))
            {
                results.clearSelection();
                results.setSelectedValue(curFileName,true);
            }

            Thread pageThread =
                    new Thread(new PageLoader(display,url, c,statusBar));
            pageThread.start();

            watchAnchor=false;
        }
    }
    catch(Exception exp)
    {
        if(url != null) fileError(url.getFile());
        else fileError("No File Available");
    }
}
```

In case the user tries to load one page while another is already loading, we keep track of the page loader's thread and stop it before loading another page. We also clear the editor pane if no URL is provided. To make this easier, we set the editor pane to plain/text before clearing it.

Handling Events

The DocSearch object acts as three kinds of listeners: action, list selection, and hyperlink. Let's look at the methods for each of these in turn.

First, if the user presses a link in the editor pane, the DocSearch object is notified. The DocSearch object triggers a page load based on the URL selected in the link. We also select the search field, so that the user can make another selection. The watchAnchor instance variable is used to notify the setURL method that a link was pressed. We reload the current page if a link was pressed that stores a marker to the same page. This allows the editor pane to handle the marker.

```
public void hyperlinkUpdate(HyperlinkEvent evt)
{
    watchAnchor = true;
    setURL(evt.getURL());
    searchField.selectAll();
    searchField.requestFocus();
}
```

Second, if the user selects an item in the list, we load that file into the editor pane.

```
public void valueChanged(ListSelectionEvent evt)
{
    setFileByName((String) results.getSelectedValue());
}
```

Third, we handle the action generated by the search text field. Handling this event involves performing the search. First, we check that the text field is activated using its Action command. If we added a search button to the user interface, we could use the same action command for it and trigger the same code.

Next, we set our cursor to the wait cursor to provide user feedback.

Finally, we perform the search, update the list of results, reselect the text field, and validate the list's parent to make sure that it displays its scroll bars correctly. When the search is complete we reset the cursor. In most cases, the search is almost instantaneous, so the cursor change may be overkill, but it's better to be safe than sorry.

```
public void actionPerformed(ActionEvent evt)
{
    String cmd = evt.getActionCommand();

    if(SEARCH.equals(cmd))
    {
        Vector files;
        Cursor c = getCursor();
        Cursor waitCursor
                = Cursor.getPredefinedCursor(Cursor.WAIT_CURSOR);

        if(index != null)
        {
            setCursor(waitCursor);

            setURL(null);

            files = index.filesForWord(searchField.getText());

            results.setListData(files);
            results.ensureIndexIsVisible(0);

            searchField.selectAll();
            searchField.requestFocus();

            top.validate();

            setCursor(c);
        }
```

```
    }
}
```

Showing the Interface and Main

The last two methods for DocSearch are show and main. We override setVisible to center the frame when it's displayed. The method setVisible also calls pack to organize the interface.

```
public void setVisible(boolean tf)
{
    if(tf)
    {
        Dimension screenSize =
            getToolkit().getScreenSize();
        Dimension curSize;
        int x,y;

        this.pack();

        curSize = getSize();

        curSize.height = Math.max(550,curSize.height);
        curSize.width = Math.max(600,curSize.width);

        x = (screenSize.width-curSize.width)/2;
        y = (screenSize.height-curSize.height)/2;

        setBounds(x,y,curSize.width,curSize.height);
    }
    super.setVisible(tf);
}
```

The main method creates a DocSearch object and shows it. The DocSearch object does the rest.

```
public static void main(String s[])
{
    DocSearch frame = new DocSearch();

    frame.setForeground(Color.black);
    frame.setBackground(Color.lightGray);

    frame.show();
}
```

And of course, there is a bracket to close the class definition:

```
}
```

The entire code for this example is available on the CD-ROM.

Summary

Swing provides several useful features for creating this type of application. First, there are useful components like the split pane, list, and editor pane. Second, there are also borders to augment the interface. Third, actions provide a useful encapsulation of program functionality. Finally, the event queue organizes all of the Swing and event code into one place. This event queue allows programmers to use threads only where necessary and only for the work that doesn't require user interaction. In our case, we were able to push file input into the background threads without interrupting the user experience.

The Accessibility Framework

A

One of the more aggressive efforts JavaSoft presents in JFC 1.1 is the Accessibility framework. This framework is designed to provide a common structure for supporting assistive technologies within your applications. Assistive technologies are computer software and hardware devices that help people use the computer more effectively. In particular, assistive technologies are designed to help people with impairments such as blindness, lack of use of their hands, and other physical challenges. By providing a framework that all software developers can rely on, JavaSoft enables the millions of disabled workers around the world to use software applications more effectively.

The framework defines a relationship between user-interface elements, applications, and assistive software and technologies. The core API is provided with JFC 1.1 but doesn't include the final technologies for assisting users. These will be created later by JavaSoft and other companies. JavaSoft is providing a standard accessibility framework to insure that all assistive technologies can work with any Java program, without having to know about the program itself. All of the Swing components participate in the framework, so a Swing-based program automatically works with new assistive technologies as they become available, including Braille readers, text readers, and other technologies. This means that the software you write with Swing is useful to an even larger group of users (there are more than 40 million disabled people in the United States alone).

The Core API

The accessibility framework uses the interface Accessible as a typing mechanism for components or objects that want to and can participate in the accessibility framework. An Accessible object must define the method getAccessibleContext(). This method returns an AccessibleContext object that manages relationships with the information required by an assistive technology to interact with the component.

AccessibleContext

An AccessibleContext is a central data store for an Accessible object's information. This information is listed in Table A.1 along with classes in the core API that are used to store the information.

The goal of this AccessibleContext and its contents is to provide a very generic, component-independent mechanism for retrieving information from a Component or object. Instead of demanding that the object implement the JTextField's methods, it can implement the AccessibleText interface. This makes it easier for assistive technologies to work with all user interfaces.

The framework also provides objects that manage resources in a localized fashion for an accessible object or technology. An interface called AccessibleLayout can be implemented; a component or an object can provide a generic mechanism for searching the component hierarchy. This interface is actually designed around accessing Accessible objects, so the hierarchy addressed may not include any components at all.

Other Elements in the Framework

JavaSoft is also planning to provide several other components to the accessibility solution. There are a set of utility classes, an interface to native code, and the Swing framework itself.

Utility Classes

The Accessibility utility classes provide objects that can track events and find components. These classes work with or implement the Accessibility core API to provide easier implementations for assistive software solutions.

Table A.1 AccessibleContext Information

Information	Class	Description
Name	String	The localized name of the object.
Description	String	A description for the object.
Role	AccessibleRole	The Accessible's role, like table or tree.
State set	AccessibleStateSet	A collection of AccessibleState objects. These objects store the Accessible object's state. For example, is a button pressed, or is a text field focused?
Parent	Accessible	The parent Accessible that contains this object.
Children	Accessible	Any Accessible children for this object.
Component	AccessibleComponent	An object that provides a generic interface for Component style activities, like setting the font or background color.
Selection	AccessibleSelection	Manages a list of selected Accessible children.
Text	AccessibleText	An object that provides a generic interface to textual data, like the string at a position or the selection's position.
Action	AccessibleAction	A collection of Action objects.
Value	AccessibleValue	An object that provides a generic interface for retrieving information about the numeric value of an Accessible.

Native Interface

Some operating systems like Macintosh and Windows already provide access to assistive technologies. The Accessibility native interface provides a standard, Virtual Machine-based access mechanism to these platform-dependent technologies. This means that access to platform-specific resources is efficient. JavaSoft has said that it will provide this interface for some platforms and is working with other vendors to support all of the systems on which Java runs.

Swing and Accessibility

All of the Swing components implement the Accessible interface. The components also participate in the pluggable look-and-feel architecture. By leveraging custom look and feels, an assistive technology might provide a very different UI object than you see on standard Windows. For example, a Braille look and feel provides a tactile interface for each component. This means that as one user sees a window on the computer screen full of buttons and text fields, another user "feels" the interface on a specially designed Braille reader. Users may even choose to use several look and feels at the same time by leveraging the Swing multiple look and feel. This look and feel multiplexes requests to more than one look and feel. For example, a network monitoring application can provide a visual graph of the network, while another look and feel can be used to provide audio queues for the same UI. The programmer doesn't have to rewrite the application to take advantage of this audio UI. This shows that the accessibility framework has benefits for all applications.

Your application can easily extend to provide a UI for other devices with little or no modification to your existing application. For instance, imagine an order entry system that a user sees on his or her terminal. Normally a customer calls and the user enters the order by pressing buttons and filling in text fields on the screen. The user can move between fields, undo mistakes, and perform all of the typical application processes. Another look and feel can be designed that interacts with an assistive technology we are all familiar with—the telephone. This look and feel maps the behavior of buttons, text fields, and sliders to a telephone interface so that now customers can call and enter their order themselves over the phone. The software developer doesn't need to reimplement any of its business rules or even the UI behavior to do this. It simply tells the program to use this new look and feel. Can you imagine how you could take advantage of this?

Summary

Overall, the Accessibility framework is designed to work seamlessly with the Swing libraries. As a Swing programmer, you should know about this framework, but it is not necessary that you work directly with it. If, however, you are planning to write assistive technologies, this framework provides a generic, platform-neutral method for accessing information about the program run and the user's interaction with it.

B WHAT'S ON THE CD-ROM?

The CD-ROM included with this book contains all of the source code demonstrated in this book, as well as several other example programs and resources. To make the CD-ROM easier to use, it's indexed via an HTML file. This file appears in the root directory and is named index.html. Simply open this file in a browser, and follow the links to find examples, resources, and last-minute news or information.

The example programs are available directly from the CD-ROM in the directory jfc_examples and in the zip file jfc_ex.zip. We have provided the zip file for developers on operating systems that won't copy the long file names correctly from the CD-ROM. Inside the jfc_examples directory are a set of subdirectories named for the chapters in the book. These chapter directories contain directories for each example in that chapter. For example, the following directory contains the example on using JDBC with Swing tables.

```
jfc_examples/chapter_12/jdbc_model
```

Inside the jfc_examples directory there is also an index.html file that contains a list of links to the HTML descriptions for each chapter's examples.

What Is Freeware/Shareware?

Freeware is software that is distributed by disk, through BBS systems, and on the Internet for free. There is no charge for using it, and it can be distributed freely as long as it's used according to the license agreement included with it.

Shareware (also known as user-supported software) is a revolutionary means of distributing software created by individuals or companies too small to make inroads into the more conventional retail distribution networks. The authors of shareware retain all rights to the software under the copyright laws while still allowing free distribution. This gives the user the chance to freely obtain and try out software to see if it fits his or her needs. Shareware should not be confused with public domain software even though they are often obtained from the same sources.

If you continue to use shareware after trying it out, you are expected to register your use with the author and pay a registration fee. What you get in return depends on the author, but may include a printed manual, free updates, or telephone support.

The CD-ROM for *Programming with JFC* contains the shareware requiring the following license:

> *The Gif Construction Set software included with this publication is provided as shareware for your evaluation. If you try this software and find it useful, you are requested to register it as discussed in its documentation and in the About screen of the application. The publisher of this book has not paid the registration fee for this shareware.*

Hardware Requirements

Of course, the primary requirement for using the CD-ROM is a CD-ROM drive. To use the JDK and JFC you also need to meet their installation requirements. They include the following:

- 50 MB of available disk space. This includes the source code, documentation, and JavaSoft examples.
- 16 MB of RAM minimum, although more is always better.

The examples from the book are under 2MB including source and compiled files. You can run these from the CD-ROM or copy them to your hard disk so that you can change them to try out the various techniques.

Other resources on the CD-ROM include specific information regarding their requirements.

Installing the Software

You can either use the examples from this book directly from the CD-ROM or copy the examples to your hard disk. To copy the examples:

1. Start Windows on your computer.
2. Place the CD-ROM into your CD-ROM drive.
3. Copy the jfc_examples directory from the CD-ROM to your hard disk or open the jfc_ex.zip file and extract it to your hard disk.

Use the zip file to unpack the examples if you are on a computer that does not recognize the long file names on the CD-ROM. To test whether your system supports these file names, open several of the jfc_examples subdirectories and inspect the file names. All source code files end in ".java" and compiled files end in ".class."

Using the Software

To use the example programs, open a command-line prompt or shell and change your current directory to the directory for the example. For instance, to run the example on pop-up menus, go to the following directory:

```
/jfc_examples/chapter_08/popup_menu
```

View the source code in a text editor, or use the browser. Run the program with the interpreter on the main ".class" file. For example, the following source code runs the example for pop-up menus.

```
>java Popup
```

Use links on the index.html page to browse the example code, but you need to use the shell/command prompt to run the examples.

User Assistance and Information

If you find any problems in the examples included on the CD-ROM, please contact the authors using the links provided on the index.html page to access the Web site for errata and other issues.

The software accompanying this book is provided as is without warranty or support of any kind. Should you require basic installation assistance, or if your media is defective, please call our product support number at (212) 850-6194 weekdays between 9 A.M. and 4 P.M. Eastern Standard Time. Or, we can be reached via e-mail at: **wprtusw@wiley.com.**

To place additional orders or to request information about other Wiley products, please call (800) 879-4539.

INDEX

C

D

G

H

I

J

K

L

M

N

U

V

W

Z

Java^{TM} Development Kit
Version 1.1.x
Binary Code License

6. **Limitation of Liability.** SUN AND ITS LICENSORS SHALL NOT BE LIABLE FOR ANY DAMAGES SUFFERED BY LICENSEE OR ANY THIRD PARTY AS A RESULT OF USING OR DISTRIBUTING SOFTWARE. IN NO EVENT WILL SUN OR ITS LICENSORS BE LIABLE FOR ANY LOST REVENUE, PROFIT OR DATA, OR FOR DIRECT, INDIRECT, SPECIAL, CONSEQUENTIAL, INCIDENTAL OR PUNITIVE DAMAGES, HOWEVER CAUSED AND REGARDLESS OF THE THEORY OF LIABILITY, ARISING OUT OF THE USE OF OR INABILITY TO USE SOFTWARE, EVEN IF SUN HAS BEEN ADVISED OF THE POSSIBILITY OF SUCH DAMAGES.
7. **Termination.** Licensee may terminate this License at any time by destroying all copies of Software. This License will terminate immediately without notice from Sun if Licensee fails to comply with any provision of this License. Upon such termination, Licensee must destroy all copies of Software.
8. **Export Regulations.** Software, including technical data, is subject to U.S. export control laws, including the U.S. Export Administration Act and its associated regulations, and may be subject to export or import regulations in other countries. Licensee agrees to comply strictly with all such regulations and acknowledges that it has the responsibility to obtain licenses to export, re-export, or import Software. Software may not be downloaded, or otherwise exported or re-exported (i) into, or to a national or resident of, Cuba, Iraq, Iran, North Korea, Libya, Sudan, Syria or any country to which the U.S. has embargoed goods; or (ii) to anyone on the U.S. Treasury Department's list of Specially Designated Nations or the U.S. Commerce Department's Table of Denial Orders.
9. **Restricted Rights.** Use, duplication or disclosure by the United States government is subject to the restrictions as set forth in the Rights in Technical Data and Computer Software Clauses in DFARS 252.227-7013(c) (1) (ii) and FAR 52.227-19(c) (2) as applicable.
10. **Governing Law.** Any action related to this License will be governed by California law and controlling U.S. federal law. No choice of law rules of any jurisdiction will apply.
11. **Severability.** If any of the above provisions are held to be in violation of applicable law, void, or unenforceable in any jurisdiction, then such provisions are herewith waived to the extent necessary for the License to be otherwise enforceable in such jurisdiction.However, if in Sun's opinion deletion of any provisions of the License by operation of this paragraph unreasonably compromises the rights or increase the liabilities of Sun or its licensors, Sun reserves the right to terminate the License and refund the fee paid by Licensee, if any, as Licensee's sole and exclusive remedy.

Java^{TM} Foundation Classes
Version 1.1
Binary Code License Agreement

SUN MICROSYSTEMS, INC., THROUGH ITS JAVASOFT BUSINESS ("SUN"), IS WILLING TO LICENSE THE ACCOMPANYING JAVA FOUNDATION CLASSES VERSION 1.1 SOFTWARE AND ASSOCIATED DOCUMENTATION INCLUDING AUTHORIZED COPIES OF EACH (THE "SOFTWARE") TO YOU ("LICENSEE") ONLY ON THE CONDITION THAT LICENSEE ACCEPTS ALL OF THE TERMS IN THIS AGREEMENT

PLEASE READ THE TERMS CAREFULLY BEFORE INSTALLING THE SOFTWARE. BY INSTALLING THE SOFTWARE, LICENSEE ACKNOWLEDGES THAT LICENSEE HAS READ AND UNDERSTANDS THIS AGREEMENT AND AGREES TO BE BOUND BY ITS TERMS AND CONDITIONS.

IF LICENSEE DOES NOT ACCEPT THESE LICENSE TERMS, THEN SUN DOES NOT GRANT ANY LICENSE TO THE SOFTWARE, AND LICENSEE MUST NOT INSTALL THE SOFTWARE.

1. **License to Distribute.** Licensee is granted a royalty-free right to reproduce and distribute the Software provided that Licensee: (i) distributes the Software, in whole or in part, only when incorporated into Licensee's value-added applet or application ("Program"); (ii) does not distribute additional software intended to replace any component(s) of the Software; (iii) does not remove or alter any proprietary legends or notices contained in the Software; (iv) includes the provisions of Sections 2, 3, 4, 5, 7 and 8 in or in addition to Licensee's license agreement for the Program; (v) to the extent Programs are developed which utilize the Windows95 style graphical user interface or components contained therein, such applets or applications may only be developed to run on a Windows95 or Windows NT platform; and (vi) agrees to indemnify, hold harmless, and defend Sun and its licensors from and against any claims or lawsuits, including attorneys' fees, that arise or result from the use or distribution of the Program.
2. **Restrictions.** Software is confidential copyrighted information of Sun and title to all copies is retained by Sun and/or its licensors. Licensee shall not decompile, disassemble, decrypt, extract, or otherwise reverse engineer Software. Software may not be leased, assigned, or sublicensed, in whole or in part. Software is not designed or intended for use in on-line control of aircraft, air traffic, aircraft navigation or aircraft communications; or in the design, construction, operation or maintenance of any nuclear facility. Licensee warrants that it will not use or redistribute the Software for such purposes.
3. **Trademarks and Logos.** This Agreement does not authorize Licensee to use any Sun name, trademark or logo. Licensee acknowledges that Sun owns the Java trademark and all Java-related trademarks, logos and icons including the Coffee Cup and Duke ("Java Marks") and agrees to: (i) comply with the Java Trademark Guidelines at http://java.sun.com/trademarks.html; (ii) not do anything harmful to or inconsistent with Sun's rights in the Java Marks; and (iii) assist Sun in protecting those rights, including assigning to Sun any rights acquired by Licensee in any Java Mark.
4. **Disclaimer of Warranty.** Software is provided "AS IS," without a warranty of any kind. ALL EXPRESS OR IMPLIED REPRESENTATIONS AND WARRANTIES, INCLUDING ANY IMPLIED WARRANTY OF MERCHANTABILITY, FITNESS FOR A PARTICULAR PURPOSE OR NON-INFRINGEMENT, ARE HEREBY EXCLUDED.

5. **Limitation of Liability.** SUN AND ITS LICENSORS SHALL NOT BE LIABLE FOR ANY DAMAGES SUFFERED BY LICENSEE OR ANY THIRD PARTY AS A RESULT OF USING OR DISTRIBUTING SOFTWARE. IN NO EVENT WILL SUN OR ITS LICENSORS BE LIABLE FOR ANY LOST REVENUE, PROFIT OR DATA, OR FOR DIRECT, INDIRECT, SPECIAL, CONSEQUENTIAL, INCIDENTAL OR PUNITIVE DAMAGES, HOWEVER CAUSED AND REGARDLESS OF THE THEORY OF LIABILITY, ARISING OUT OF THE USE OF OR INABILITY TO USE SOFTWARE, EVEN IF SUN HAS BEEN ADVISED OF THE POSSIBILITY OF SUCH DAMAGES.
6. **Termination.** Licensee may terminate this Agreement at any time by destroying all copies of Software. This Agreement will terminate immediately without notice from Sun if Licensee fails to comply with any provision of this Agreement. Upon such termination, Licensee must destroy all copies of Software in its possession.
7. **Export Regulations.** Software, including technical data, is subject to U.S. export control laws, including the U.S. Export Administration Act and its associated regulations, and may be subject to export or import regulations in other countries. Licensee agrees to comply strictly with all such regulations and acknowledges that it has the responsibility to obtain licenses to export, re-export, or import Software. Software may not be downloaded, or otherwise exported or re-exported (i) into, or to a national or resident of, Cuba, Iraq, Iran, North Korea, Libya, Sudan, Syria or any country to which the U.S. has embargoed goods; or (ii) to anyone on the U.S. Treasury Department's list of Specially Designated Nations or the U.S. Commerce Department's Table of Denial Orders.
8. **Restricted Rights.** Use, duplication or disclosure by the United States government is subject to the restrictions as set forth in the Rights in Technical Data and Computer Software Clauses in DFARS 252.227-7013(c) (1) (ii) and FAR 52.227-19(c) (2) as applicable.
9. **Governing Law.** Any action related to this Agreement will be governed by California law and controlling U.S. federal law. No choice of law rules of any jurisdiction will apply.
10. **Severability.** If any of the above provisions are held to be in violation of applicable law, void, or unenforceable in any jurisdiction, then such provisions are herewith waived or amended to the extent necessary for the Agreement to be otherwise enforceable in such jurisdiction.However, if in Sun's opinion deletion or amendment of any provisions of the Agreement by operation of this paragraph unreasonably compromises the rights or increase the liabilities of Sun or its licensors, Sun reserves the right to terminate the Agreement.
11. **Entire Agreement.** This Agreement is the parties' entire agreement relating to the Software. It supersedes all prior or contemporaneous oral or written communications, proposals, warranties, and representations with respect to its subject matter, and following Licensee's acceptance of this license by clicking on the "Accept" Button, will prevail over any conflicting or additional terms of any quote, order, acknowledgment, or any other communications by or between the parties. No modification to this Agreement will be binding, unless in writing and signed by an authorized representative of each party.

To use this CD-ROM, your system must meet the following requirements:

Platform/Processor/Operating System: The Java Development Kit will run on Windows, Macintosh, and Unix-based machines.

Disk Space: The JDK and Swing applications require 30 MB disk space.

Peripherals: CD-ROM drive and Java-capable browser installed.

NOTICE

The Gif Construction Set software included with this publication is provided as shareware for your evaluation. If you try this software and find it useful, you are requested to register it as discussed in its documentation and in the About screen of the application. The publisher of this book has not paid the registration fee for this shareware.